The Compleat Angler

1653–1967

A New Bibliography

The Pittsburgh Bibliophiles
expresses its gratitude
to
Mr. and Mrs. James F. Hillman
for their generous support
in behalf of the publication
of this book

Izaak Walton (1593-1683)
By Jacob Huysmans

THE COMPLEAT ANGLER
1653-1967

A New Bibliography
by
Bernard S. Horne

The Pittsburgh Bibliophiles
Distributed by the
University of Pittsburgh Press
Pittsburgh, Pa.
1970

ISBN 0-8229-4036-1
Library of Congress Catalog Card Number 73-118263
Copyright © 1970, The Pittsburgh Bibliophiles
Manufactured in the United States of America

Contents

Illustrations

Preface

The Compleat Angler is one of the most popular books ever published in the English language. Yet, at the time of its author's death, his biographical works undoubtedly would have been considered the more lasting. Walton himself thought of it as ". . . a recreation of a recreation . . .," as he wrote in the introductory essay "The Epistle to the Reader," and although he signed "The Epistle . . ." and "To the Reader . . ." with his well known "Iz. Wa." in the first edition, it was not until the fifth edition appeared, 23 years later, that he deigned to include his name on the title-page.

Why, then, would a little fishing book, whose first edition (1653) fits comfortably into one's pocket, be represented more than three centuries later by nearly 400 editions or separate reissues? *The Compleat Angler* lives today, and may well do so more vibrantly tomorrow, because in its 17th-century English prose and verse it reports in idyllic form the quiet pastoral life of serene contentment toward which all those persons of goodwill aspire; a life that even then was becoming alien to England's city-dwellers. It was written, clearly, as more than a "how to do it" manual, and throughout its pages Walton — a staunch Anglican — interspersed his philosophy on the virtues of life and on moderate living, with homilies on the attributes of fishing as a recreation that not only effectively banishes idleness but at the same time engenders serious and pious contemplation. Students of Walton may find Sir Harris Nicolas' biography, prefixed to the first Nicolas edition (1836, No. 43) to be among the better of the early ones.

This anonymously published little fishing book first came to the attention of its readers with a modest advertisement in May 1653, and with it the key to its author's identity. At Trinity College, Hartford, Conn., there is an original issue of *The Perfect Diurnall* dated "From Munday. May 9. to Munday May 16. 1652"

ix

[1653]. On page 16, at the end, among a list of books published, appears the following:

> The Compleat Angler, or the Contemplative mans rec eation [sic], being a discourse of Fish and Fishing, not unworthy the perusal of most Anglers, of 18 pence price, Written by Iz. Wa. Also the known Play of the Spanish Gipsie, never till now Published; Both printed for Richard Marriot, to be sold at his shop in Saint Dunstans Churchyard, Fleetstreet.

From this modest birth there have followed four centuries of continuous republication of this work. Some are abridgements, some are reissues, and some are facsimiles, but all are one version or another of Walton. Douglas Bush, in his *English Literature in the Earlier 17th Century* (1945), referred to the *Angler* as ". . . a book which has been second only to the Bible in popular fame. . . ." The unsigned account of Walton in the 11th edition of *Encyclopedia Britannica* (1911) notes, ". . . There is hardly a name in English literature, even of first rank, whose immortality is more secure, or whose personality is the subject of a more devoted cult. . . ." And such favorable comment has continued through the years to the most recent critique, that by John R. Cooper; in his *The Art of the Compleat Angler* (1968), where he observed that ". . . *The Compleat Angler* gained a place in the canon of English literature that it has never lost."

The joy of happy contentment pervades the entire book. For those seeking something of the wholesome flavor of its prose, a few quotations from the fifth edition express this spirit, where Piscator tells Venator and Auceps,

> You are well overtaken, Gentlemen, A good morning to you both; . . .

and soon Venator replies,

> Sir, we are all so happy as to have a fine, fresh, cool morning; and I hope we shall be happier in each other's company. . . .

and here is Auceps speaking,

> . . . How do the blackbird and thrassel with their melodious voices bid welcome to the cheerful spring, as in their fixed mouths warble forth such ditties as no art or instrument can reach to? . . .

and saying further,

> . . . Lord, what music hast Thou provided for the saints in heaven, when Thou affordest bad men such music on earth? . . .

and Piscator says later,

... Indeed, my friend, you will find angling to be like the virtue of humility, which has a calmness of spirit, and a world of other blessings attending upon it. . . .

But perhaps the very essence of the book is expressed by Piscator in his conversation with his scholar Venator as they walk toward home after their fishing is finished,

... and we having still a mile to Tottenham-High-Cross, I will, as we walk toward it in the cool shade of this sweet honeysuckle hedge, mention to you some of the thoughts and joys that have possessed my soul since we two met together. And these thoughts shall be told you, that you also may join with me in thankfulness to the giver of every good and perfect gift, for our happiness. . . . there be many that have forty times our estates, that would give the greatest part of it to be healthful and cheerful like us, who, with the expense of a little money, have eat and drunk, and laughed and angled, and sung, and slept securely; and rose next day, and cast away care, and sung, and laughed and angled again; which are blessings rich men cannot purchase with all their money. . . . Let us therefore, be thankful for health and a competence, and above all, for a quiet conscience. . . .

and the Scholar replies,

... so when I would beget content, and increase confidence in the power and wisdom, and providence of Almighty God, I will walk the meadows, by some gliding stream, and there contemplate the lilies that take no care, and those very many other various little living creatures that are not only created, but fed, man knows not how, by the goodness of the God of Nature, and therefore trust in Him. . . .

John Buchan, 1st. Baron Tweedsmuir, in his Introduction to the edition published by Methuen & Co., London, 1901, (No. 199) gives one of the best summations of the literary quality and the fundamental reasons for the long-lasting popularity of this book:

... Walton, indeed, marks the beginning of true angling literature, for he was the first to give the sport a halo of letters which it has never lost. With all his modest intentions he is a past master of the little country idyl. Cotton can sketch you a fine scene, and tell of the cooking of the trout with gusto, but it is Walton who draws the unforgetable pictures of riverside inns, of gipsy singing and milkmaids' choruses. The pastoral drama, really a lost art since Theocritus, in spite of Roman, Italian, and Elizabethan revivals, is here restored to all its fresh and courtly grace. It is this which has made the book immortal, for while Maudlin and Coridon sing their catches in the meadow the world will always have ears for their singing. . . .

The *Angler* has been admired and edited by distinguished men of letters, illustrated by some of the most prominent of artists, designed by some of the best of typographers, printed by the finest pressmen and presses, bound by the best-known binders, and goes on and on, spreading its spirit of contemplative contentment to all who would seek peace, ". . . and love quietness, and vertue, and Angling."

Public interest in the *Angler* waned for nearly a century after its fifth edition (1676) and Walton's death (1683), but every decade from 1750 onward witnessed new issues of the book, together with studies and commentaries of its import—often as introductions to successive editions. It has been postulated with good reason by Margaret Bottrall (1962, see No. 370) that the revival of interest in the *Angler* "suggests that it touches some nostalgic nerve in Englishmen bred in an industrialized environment." For many present-day readers it evokes warm childhood memories or alternatively offers an intellectual escape from the madding crowd.

The appeal of the *Angler,* even of editions with modern spelling, has until recent decades been primarily to the English language reader. Understandably, more editions have come from Britain than from America. Surprisingly, it is only in relatively recent time that the work has been translated, or been published in other language areas. The first German translation (titled *Der Vollkommene Angler*) appeared in 1859 with nearly a century passing before three subsequent editions were issued, all in 1958. Four editions have appeared in Japan since 1926. An abridged edition was published in French in 1942 with another one twenty years later, followed by an unabridged translation in 1964. Three editions of a Danish translation appeared in 1943 with others following. The first Swedish translation came out in 1945 and the fifth Swedish edition in 1965. The first Finnish edition (in Swedish) appeared in 1947.

The refinement of publishing techniques through photo-reproduction made possible some early facsimiles of the first edition of Walton; that by Stock appeared in 1876 and was sufficiently successful as to warrant a reissue the next year, and a third in 1880. The market situation encouraged Griggs to bring out his facsimile in 1882 and others followed in each decade. The publication of the Black facsimile in 1928 provided a superior work of its kind, as yet unsurpassed.

In its 17th-century editions the *Angler* was neither auspicious nor attractive for typography or illustrations. But the 18th-century revival of the work soon attracted the attention of important illustrators, editors, and leading typographers in England and America.

Notable among the former are Abraham Cooper and Thomas Stothand in the 18th century and more recently E. J. Sullivan, James Thorpe, Eric Daglish, Robert Ball, Frank Adams, and Arthur Rackham. The early important editors such as Moses Browne (the first), Sir John Hawkins, James Rennie and Sir Harris Nicolas, were followed by the Rev. Dr. George Washington Bethune (the first American editor and one of the best), James Russell Lowell, Andrew Lang, Richard Le Gallienne, Austin Dobson, John Buchan, Sir Geoffrey Keynes, and Bliss Perry. Some of the well-known printers of the *Angler* include, Charles Whittingham, William Pickering, Caradoc Press, Riverside Press (Cambridge, Mass.), Clarendon Press, De La More, Nonesuch, and Peter Pauper. Surprisingly, it did not appear among the works from either the Kelmscott or the Doves press.

Any work whose popularity has witnessed the production of several hundred publisher's editions also enjoys a coterie of serious collectors and this in turn leads to scholarly studies of the author and his writing. To assist one to know better of the scope and nature of the many editions and printings, several bibliographies and bibliographical studies of the *Angler* have been published (see Appendix A). The best, largely because of their completeness when published, are three: Westwood and Satchell's *The Chronicle of The Compleat Angler* (London, 1883, reprinted in the first Marston edition of the *Angler,* 1888), Arnold Wood's *A Bibliography of "The Compleat Angler" of Izaak Walton and Charles Cotton . . .* (New York, 1900), and Peter Oliver's *A New Chronicle of The Compleat Angler* (New York and London, 1936). The Westwood and Satchell *Chronicle* (1888), included 102 editions and reissues. Wood's work (published in a limited edition of 120 copies) was the first to provide collations of any large number (140) of editions and issues. That by Oliver, published three and a half decades later, recognized and treated 284 editions and issues. For the period covered by Wood, Oliver reported 179 editions and issues. Although both of these works were based on collections available in America, Oliver recorded some data obtained in England. Oliver is at his best as a bibliographer in his meticulous and detailed treatment of the first five editions, those published during Walton's lifetime. For subsequent ones his work is, as he intended it to be, a chronicle of the *Angler* and not, as was Wood's, an analytical bibliography. While Wood enumerated each illustration in the editions treated, Oliver contributed useful recitations on the publishers and illustrators of most of the editions he covered. Oliver provided also a rather complete list of literature sources. His notes and annotations, which accompany most of his bibliographical entries, are useful to all serious students and collectors of the *Angler*.

This present bibliography is the consequence of some twenty years of interest in Walton and collecting *Anglers*. Initially it was my plan to compile in essence a supplement to Oliver's work of 1936, but as editions or issues not heretofore recorded were located, it became apparent that a new bibliography and chronicle was justified. This present study does not supplant Oliver completely, for I have made no attempt to supplement his excellent background material on printers, publishers, and illustrators.

On the other hand researches of Walton's five editions have yielded new material (*e.g.*, concerning the misquoted biblical quotation in his first edition, corrected in the second; that relative to the dating of the laudatory verses by the Rev. Edward Powel and the Rev. Thomas Weaver in the second edition), new facts concerning the illustrating, printing, and format of certain editions (such as the Bagster publications of 1808 and 1810), and the laying to rest or properly identifying certain ghost editions reported in the literature.

Thus the *Angler* goes on and on, spreading its spirit of contemplative contentment to all who would seek peace, ". . . and love quietness, and vertue, and Angling."

Bernard S. Horne

Hyannis Port, Mass.
July 9, 1969

Introduction

This bibliography is an endeavor to provide a description of each edition of *The Compleat Angler,* commensurate with the importance of the edition. Thus the degree of bibliographic detail varies from one that is all-inclusive to a condensed listing of title, publisher's imprint, and date. Guidelines for the determination of degree of importance have included scarcity, influence on later editions, format, editing, illustrations, and typography.

It was decided initially that every edition of the *Angler,* beginning with the first, should be examined and that bibliographic data be derived as much as possible from copies in hand. This requirement became the more obvious when it was realized that some of the great angling collections are of relatively recent formation, and that they provide resources not available thirty years ago when Peter Oliver published the most recent bibliography of the *Angler* (1936). These American collections, plus copies studied in England and Ireland, revealed the existence of editions unknown either to Arnold Wood (1900) or Peter Oliver, and also have made possible the correction of previous listings, have permitted verification or establishment of publication dates heretofore unavailable, and have proved that a few editions thought and reported to have been published, have never existed. Thus the canon has been further authenticated, and some relatively ancient ghosts laid to rest. But for all this researching, perhaps some new ghosts now have been conjured up that similarly may annoy, irritate, and otherwise disturb future bibliographers of the *Angler.*

Every effort has been made to provide a description sufficient to identify each edition. In a few instances this has not been possible. The inclusion of editions not seen is based, as individually noted, on treatments in previous bibliographies, library and angling catalogues, trade journals, publishing and publisher's records, and personal interviews. Some of these sources have provided very complete information while others, due to the passage of time or, in some instances — in Britain — to loss of records by war damage, proved to be no more than a report of publication.

The entries in this work are numbered sequentially to provide a handle for ready reference. Such an entry may be an edition, or it may be a state or an issue of that edition. I have treated as an *edition* every printing from a new typesetting, with or without any textual change. Reproductions of an original typesetting (facsimiles) with or without the addition of new material are treated as new editions. Copies of an edition differing from others of the same edition (*e.g.,* by the presence of corrected leaves, or by different title-pages) are treated as *states*. Here are included works with substituted textual leaves. Likewise, copies of simultaneous publication that are variants in leaf size, such as large paper and small paper "editions" are properly treated as variant states of the one edition, as are those published in quarto and octavo, but without change of textual typesetting (exclusive of running heads, folio numbers, or chapter titles). A work republished at a later date (perhaps only a month or less later) after the appearance of the first printing of given typesetting, with or without textual changes but with a new or different title-page, is treated as an *issue* of the earlier edition. In this bibliography, in the interest of nomenclatural uniformity with earlier listings of the *Angler*, I have retained the general term reprint for items that technically are treated as issues.

One or more copies of each important edition has been examined by me. Those copies not seen consist almost entirely of reissues of the long runs in an inexpensive edition or issue such as were published successively by Burt, Cassell, Crowell, and the Modern Library.

The entries are listed by year of publication as given on the title-page or as has been determined from internal or external evidence, as reported individually in the notes. When possible, the listing sequence within a year-date is by related editions, states, or issues.

The basic account for each entry includes: title; author(s) [*i.e.,* Walton, Walton and Cotton, or Walton, Cotton, and Venables]; publisher's imprint and related data; location of copies examined and, to the extent available from literature sources, of other copies; size of copy or of pages, and number of pages. This account in some instances, especially for the earlier editions, is often expanded to include title-page transcription, collation, and a report of contents. Pertinent notes and annotations are provided on, or supplement, these data and on the illustrations. For entries not seen, only such data as are available from the literature are given. An innovation in this bibliography is the inclusion of descriptions of the publisher's bindings. This is believed particularly contributory for editions of the early 19th century and later when gilt decorated cloth publisher's bindings became commonplace. Because of its history of long continuous and frequent publication, the *Angler* is especially well suited to illustrate the history of the cloth binding from examples of stark simplicity to those gilt and enamel productions that are garishly ornate.

The title, to the extent given, is verbatim from the title-page for all entries for which copies have been seen. Italics or black-letter type-faces are used for those words cited where the same face is in title-page text. The key title words THE COMPLEAT ANGLER are set in roman caps without regard for title-page typography. The first eight words of the title-page of entry numbers one through five and of Part I of entry number six, which are framed by the piscatorial cartouche, are in script (see Fig. nos. 1-5 and 10). The balance of the title given is in Roman caps and lower case. Vertical bars, when used, designate title-page line breaks; the latter not otherwise designated except by a new line(s) following the author(s) name giving the facts of publication.

Date of publication is that of the publisher's imprint on the title-page. In the absence of this record the inferred date is given in square brackets, based on internal evidence (such as copyright or preface dates), or from external evidence as identified in the notes.

The facts of publication (place of publication and name of publisher and/or printer) are taken from the title-page imprint, or, for copies not seen from available literature. Bracketed information is supplied from internal or external evidence as is done for publication dates.

The location of copies is given both for those examined by me (and which served as the primary source of bibliographical data sup-plied), and as reported in the card catalogue of the Library of Congress *National Union Catalog*. When, in some instances, the information supplied by the latter was insufficient to positively identify the work as a particular edition or state, the reported record of location is omitted. Additional records of copy location are supplied from personal correspondence or other sources.

NOTE: Names of private or institutional holders of copies examined are cited by name. The identity of location of other copies are by the abbre-viation adopted in *Symbols used in the National Union Catalog of the Library of Congress*, ed. 9 (Washington, D.C., 1965), given in full, with location address, in Appendix E of this bibliography.

Size of copy, with few exceptions, is cited by leaf size (height×width) in inches of the largest copy examined. Where a range in size is noted, the extremes may be given. Likewise, the dimensions of large and small paper states are reported (except as otherwise noted) from copies seen, and under the one entry for that edition. The size designations of quarto and octavo, for example, have not been applied consistently nor with intent of bibliographic pre-cision (*i.e.*, they are not based on signature foldings regardless of leaf size dimensions). When used, and more often so for works not seen and for which no leaf dimension was available, the desig-nation has been taken from the literature.

Pagination is reported with completeness, or in summary form, depending on the bibliographic importance of the entry. Missing folio (pagination) numbers from the preliminary, or from the last, portions of a book are given inferentially in square brackets. Parentheses enclose folio numbers when the printed parentheses enclose the folio number in the work itself (*e.g.*, page (1) of text, first edition).

Illustrations have played an important role in the success of many editions of the *Angler*. While the notes of an entry may identify the artists and media used, and may list the number of illustra-tions, no evaluation has been given of their artistic quality.

Publisher's bindings, not treated in earlier bibliographies, are re-ported when available. For clothbound editions of the 19th and 20th centuries they have an identifying importance deserving notation in the record. Bindings of most earlier editions, of course, vary from copy to copy. The absence of a binding description in this account infers that the copy seen has been rebound or, if an early edition, presented no evidence to substantiate it as a binding of the publisher. There are a few references to so-called original bindings, such as for the binding of the first edition, and some copies have been reported as rebound. When the back cover of a cloth binding is not mentioned in this work, it is to be assumed to be without decoration. Colors of binding cloths are given in untechnical general terms, solely to provide a degree of visualization sufficient for recognition. When various cloth colors are reported for different copies of an entry, no attempt is made to determine if a color priority existed at time of publication. Publisher's dust jackets have been described as available.

The presence of uncut (unopened) or untrimmed leaves is reported for some copies examined. Copies in which the signature folds have not been opened are designated uncut, those whose leaves have not been guillotined are designated untrimmed. Some copies have the top edges gilt (guillotined and gilded) with fore and bottom edges untrimmed.

The personal assistance and advice of many kind friends are gratefully acknowledged. From the beginning, George H. M. Lawrence, Director of the Rachel McMasters Miller Hunt Botanical Library, at Carnegie-Mellon University, Pittsburgh, has given counsel and encouragement beyond price, has made valuable suggestions after reading the typescript, and has provided the index. Thomas C. Pears, III, Chairman of the Pittsburgh Bibliophiles, with Frederick A. Hetzel, Director of the University of Pittsburgh Press, have given expert advice on typographical and publishing details. Very special assistance has been given by W. H. Bond, Librarian, and Miss Carolyn Jakeman and her staff, the Houghton Library, Harvard University; by Earle E. Coleman and Paul R. Wagner, Princeton University Library; Donald B. Engley, Librarian, Trinity College Library, Hartford; William H. Runge, Alderman Library, University of Virginia, Charlottesville; Frederick R. Goff, Chief, Rare Book Division, Library of Congress, Washington, D.C.; and Herbert Cahoon, Pierpont Morgan Library, New York City. The privilege of unlimited study of the angling collections assembled by Daniel B. Fearing now at Harvard University, of the Sherman C. Parker collection at

Trinity, and the Kenneth H. Rockey collection in memory of Isabelle A. Rockey at Princeton, has been exceedingly helpful. Permission granted by C. O. v. Kienbusch to quote from manuscript material in The Kienbusch Library on Fresh Water Angling in the Firestone Library at Princeton University, is gratefully acknowledged. In addition, and without exception, everyone concerned has been most helpful with advice and assistance on the occasion of visits to the Bodleian Library, Oxford University; Boston Public Library; British Museum, London; Cathedral Library, Washington, D.C.; The Fly Fishers' Club, London; Hunt Library, Carnegie-Mellon University, Pittsburgh; New York Public Library; Beinecke Rare Book and Manuscript Library and the Sterling Library, Yale University; Trinity College, Dublin; University Library, Cambridge University; and the Widner Library, Harvard University.

There are persons, recognized in the text, whose particular knowledge has clarified a number of bibliographical difficulties; problems have been solved through the kind assistance of publishers and booksellers, not only in the United States, but also in Denmark, England, France, Japan, and Sweden. These problems have related in particular to establishment of actual existence of elusive editions and obtaining copies of them, to determination of dates of publication, to the location of variant publisher's bindings and reprints, and to affording access to publisher's records. The very gracious cooperation given by all concerned is greatly appreciated.

A bibliography is out of date by the time it is published, and it is realized that, despite every effort to the contrary, misprints and errors in transcription will occur, but it is hoped that this bibliography will be helpful to everyone interested in *The Compleat Angler*.

The Compleat Angler

1653–1967

A New Bibliography

Catalogue

1653

1. The First Edition

The | *Compleat Angler* | *or the* | *Contemplative Man's* | *Recreation.* | Being a
Diſcourſe of | FISH and FISHING, | Not unworthy the peruſal of
moſt *Anglers.* | ——— | Simon Peter *ſaid, I go a fiſhing: and they ſaid,*
We | *alſo wil go with thee.* John 21.3 | ——— | *London,* Printed by *T. Maxey*
for RICH. MARRIOT, in | *S. Dunſtans* Church-yard Fleetſtreet, 1653.

Copies examined: Bodleian, British Museum (3+1)*, Carnegie-Mellon,
Harvard (3), Horne, Morgan. Others: CSmH, CtY (2), CU, DLC, InU,
MWiW-C, NN, NNC, NjP (2), ViU, WU**.

Sizes: 5$\frac{9}{16}$″×3$\frac{3}{8}$″ to 5$\frac{11}{16}$″×3$\frac{5}{8}$″.

Collation: A–Q^8, R^4=132. Leaf G4 is incorrectly keyed F4.

Contents: recto [A], title, with first eight words within engraved piscatorial
cartouche (Figure 1); verso [A], blank; recto A2–verso A4, "The Epistle
Dedicatory;" recto [A5]-verso [A7], "To the Reader;" recto and verso [A8],
"The Table" [of contents]; recto B–verso [R3] (pages (1)–246), Text; [R4] is
blank. Page 70 is misnumbered 80; 71 is 81; 73 is 37; 74 is 84; 75 is 85; 78 is 88;
and 79 is 89.

The illustrations consist of the title-page cartouche, and six small engravings of fish in the text; Trout p. 71 (misnumbered 81); Pike, p. 148; Carp,
p. 168; Tench, p. 177; Pearch, p. 182; Barbel, p. 198; and "The Anglers Song,"
words and music for two "Voyces" by Henry Lawes on pages 216 and 217,
the latter page printed upside down. Neither the artist nor the engraver of
the well-known title-page cartouche has been identified.

Sir John Hawkins, in his Life of Walton in the 4th Hawkins edition of 1784
(No. 13), wrote of the engravings, ". . . there is great reason to suppose they
are the work of *Lombart,* . . . and also that the plates were of *steel.*" The Grolier

---

*In 1933 the British Museum produced a photostatic reproduction of its "Jos. Banks"
copy of the "contention" issue.
**For full names, and addresses, see pp. 321-324.

Club's *Chronological Hand-List . . . of The Complete Angler*, 1893, referred to the fish engravings as follows,

> the cuts of fish, six in all, have been ascribed to Peter Lombart, with the possible alternative of Faithorne or Vaughn. Supposed at one time to be engravings on silver, and again (by Sir John Hawkins, 1784) steel engravings; the cuts were probably engraved on copper, retouched at intervals . . .

More recent references to these engravings, The Grolier Club exhibit, December 7, 1911 to January 6, 1912 and Oliver, refer to them as copperplates. Sparrow, in his *Angling in British Art*, London, 1923, writes of the engravings, "Pierre Lombart has been named as the engraver but this conjecture has remained unconfirmed." The engraving of the trout on page 71 (misnumbered 81) occurs either in the middle or at the foot of the page. In the latter position it is captioned, "*The Description of a* Trout." Of the ten copies examined, the trout engraving was in the middle of the page in nine, and at the foot, with the caption, in one (the Carnegie-Mellon copy). In Marston's reprint of Westwood and Satchell's *Chronicle* (1888), it is stated in the first note to the first edition, ". . . the trout was first placed in the middle of the page and afterward removed to the foot, for the greater convenience we may suppose, of printing from the copper plate. . . ."

A tabular checklist of 48 misprints and variations that occur in five first editions and eight different facsimiles of the first edition, is given in Appendix B. While most of the errors undoubtedly appear in all first editions, I have not found all of them in any one copy.

A cursory examination of any copy of this first edition reveals most of the errors, with the variations in the C of "Complete" in the running-head (spelled "Compleat" on the title-page), and the misnumbering of seven of the pages between 70 and 79 being the most noticeable. The best known of the misprints is undoubtedly the last one in the checklist of Appendix B, "contention" for "contentment," which occurs on page 245, line 17. Of the ten copies examined in detail, six are "contention" copies, and four are "contentment" copies. Since it would seem more than likely that such an obvious misprint certainly would have been noticed and corrected during printing, it is probably logical to assume that the "contention" copies are the earlier.

But what appears to be the most improbable variation, which apparently has not been pointed out heretofore, occurs on the title-page. The quotation from *John* 21.3, which is printed just below the subtitle on the first edition title page, reads as follows,

> Simon Peter ſaid, I go a fiſhing: *and they ſaid, We | alſo wil go with thee.* John 21.3

Appendix C is a compilation of ten versions of the quotation from John 21.3 as it appeared in the English translations of the Bible prior to 1653. The version printed on the title-page of the first edition of the *Angler* does not agree with any of them, most notably in the fact that the *Angler* version omits entirely the words "to them" or "unto them," and "to him" or "unto

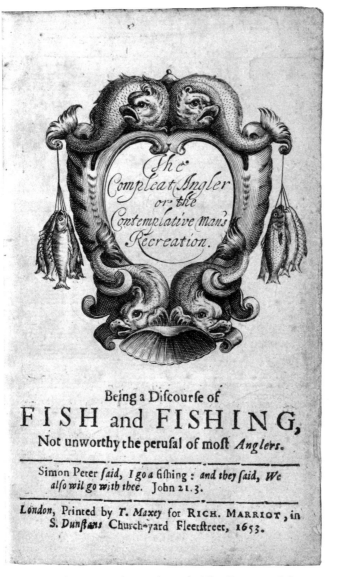

The
Compleat Angler
or the
Contemplative man's
Recreation.

Being a Discourse of
FISH and FISHING,
Not unworthy the perusal of most *Anglers*.

Simon Peter *said, I go a* fishing *: and they said, We
also wil go with thee.* John 21.3.

London, Printed by *T. Maxey* for RICH. MARRIOT, in
S. Dunstans Church-yard Fleetstreet, 1653.

Figure 1 The First Edition (No. 1). The Pierpont Morgan
Library

him" which occur in all the biblical versions seen. It would seem that someone took a little liberty with the biblical text when it is remembered that
the version printed on the title-page of the second edition follows exactly
the King James version, and reads, "John 21.3. *Simon Peter faith unto them, I go a
fifhing, they fay unto him, We alfo go with thee.*"

Of course it is possible that a reissue of one of the Bibles examined, or an
unchecked version, could have contained the quotation as printed on the
first edition title-page, but the very fact of the change in the second edition
seems in itself to indicate an irregularity in the first edition which must
have been most annoying to Walton, the ardent Anglican and onetime
vestryman of St. Dunstan's in the West, in London. The biblical quotation
did not appear on the title-page of the third, fourth, or fifth edition.

The first known public notice of the *Compleat Angler* appeared in an advertisement in *The Perfect Diurnall* . . . dated From Munday. 9. to Munday May 16.
1652 [1653], which was printed as follows (from the copy at Trinity College
Library, Hartford):

> The *Compleat Angler,* or the *Contemplative mans* Rec eaton, [*sic*] being a
> discourse of Fish and Fishing, not unworthy the perusal of most
> Anglers, of 18 pence price, Wirtten [*sic*] by Iz. Wa. . . . printed for
> Richard Marriot, to be sold at his shop in Saint Dunstans Church-
> yard, Fleetstreet.

Three days later a similar advertisement appeared in the *Mercurius Politicus.*

Westwood (*Chronicle* . . . 1864) described the first edition as, "A small square
duo-decimo, clad in a modest overcoat of brown calf—such was the form
and fashion of the book as it first appeared." The Pierpont Morgan Library
copy is the only one seen that apparently is in an original binding of undecorated sheepskin, the edges speckled red and blue. The Black facsimile,
1928 (No. 287) has a similar type of binding.

There seem to have been three previous comments on the date of the
actual writing of the *Compleat Angler.*

Moses Browne, in his first edition, 1750 (No. 7), at the foot of page 55, has
a blunt note which reads, without additional elaboration, "Mr. *Walton* wrote
his *Compleat Angler* about the Year 1650."

Sir Harris Nicolas, in his "Life of Izaak Walton," prefixed to his 1836 edition
of the *Angler* (No. 43), made some interesting comments on the dates of the
laudatory verses of the Rev. Edward ("Edw.") Powel and the Rev. Thomas
("Tho.") Weaver. Powel's verses addressed, "To the Reader of my most
ingenuous Friend's Book, *The Complete Angler,*" first appeared, undated, as
are the other compliments, in the second edition of 1655 (No. 2). However,
in the third edition, 1661 (No. 3), Powel's verses are dated April 3, 1650, the
only ones to have a dateline. Commenting on the date, Nicolas observed,
". . . it may be inferred that the work [*i.e.,* the *Angler*] was written and prepared for the press nearly three years before it was published. This circum-
stance may perhaps be attributed to the unsettled state of the times. . . ."
[*i.e.,* the Puritan Revolution].

The laudatory verses, by Thomas Weaver addressed, "To my deer Friend, Mr. Iz. Walton, in praife of *Angling*: which we both love," had also appeared, undated, in the second edition. It was not until the fifth edition of 1676 (No. 6), that the dateline 1649 appeared. Nicolas commented on these verses as follows, ". . . as they were addressed not to the readers of the book, but 'to my dear friend Mr. Iz. Walton, in praise of Angling, which we both love,' it admits of no inference as to the time when the treatise [the *Angler*] was written."

R. B. Marston, in his Lea and Dove edition, 1888 (No. 136), was skeptical of both dates, and raised the question of typographical error.

I also question the dates, and believe further that there is possible evidence in both sets of verses which could lead one to conclude that both Powel and Weaver wrote their verses in 1653, following the publication of the first edition.

The last four and a half lines of Powel's verses read as follows,

> . . . *and* Fisherman *begile.*
> *Thus whilst some vex they from their lands are thrown,*
> *He joys to think the waters are his own;*
> *And, like the* Dutch, *he gladly can agree*
> *To live at peace now, and have* fishing *free.*

It seems entirely possible that the last two lines, especially the word "now," could well refer to the defeat of the Dutch by the British on July 31, 1653, which ended the first Dutch War.

The last eight lines of Weaver's verses read as follows,

> *Then on these banks let me sit down,*
> *Free from the toilsome* Sword *and* Gown,
> *And pity those that do affect*
> *To conquer* Nations *and protect.*
> *My Reed affords such true content,*
> *Delights so sweet and innocent,*
> *As seldom fall unto the lot*
> *Of Sceptors, though they'r* justly *got.*

The line, "To conquer Nations and protect," undoubtedly could refer to Cromwell's Protectorate, which was established in 1653.

It would seem that Powel and Weaver, as the other laudatory versifiers, were inspired by the first edition when it appeared in 1653, to write their verses, which then appeared with the second edition in 1655, and that they should have been undated, as were those of the other contributors.

Laudatory verse and prose have continued to be written for over 300 years.

[5]

1655

2. The Second Edition

The | *Compleat Angler* | *or the* | *Contemplative Man's* | *Recreation.* | Being a difcourfe of RIVERS, and | FISH-PONDS, and FISH, | and FISHING. | Not unworthy the perufal of moft Anglers. | —— | *The fecond Edition much enlarged.* | —— | John 21.3. *Simon Peter faith unto them, I go a fifhing,* | *they fay unto him, We alfo go with thee.* | —— | *London,* Printed by *T.M.* for *Rich, Marriot,* and are | to be fold at his Shop in St. *Dunstans* | Church-yard Fleetftreet, 1655.

Copies examined: Harvard, Horne. Others: CSmH, CtHT, CtY, DLC, InU, MWiW-C, NIC, NN, NjP, ViU, WU. IU has a microfilm of a Yale copy.

Size: $5\frac{11}{16}'' \times 3\frac{1}{16}''$.

Collation: A–Q^{12}=192. Leaf C4 is incorrectly keyed B4; D4 and E4 lack signature marks.

Contents: Recto [A] (see Fig. 2), with first eight words within engraved piscatorial cartouche; verso [A], blank; recto A2–verso A4, "The Epistle Dedicatory;" recto A5–recto [A8], "To the Reader;" verso [A8], blank; recto [A9]–verso [A12], laudatory verses; recto B–recto [Q10], (pages [1]–355), Text; verso [Q10], blank; recto [Q11]–recto [Q12], "The Contents;" verso [Q12], blank.

The pages of text have been increased in number from 246 in the first edition to 355 in the second, and all the pages are numbered correctly. Chapter XVII, however, is incorrectly headed XVI, but the arabic numbering in the "Contents" is correct.

The illustrations consist of the title-page cartouche and ten small copperplate reproductions of fish in the text, four more than in the first edition. These are Trout, at the foot of page 113; Pike, 203; Carp, 225; Bream, 234; Tench, 248; Pearch, 253; Eele, 268; Barbel, 276; Loach, 321; Bullhead, 323; and, the "Anglers Song," on pages 298 and 299, the latter printed upside down. This should not be confused with Piscator's song which begins on page 209 in the first edition, and 290 in the second, in which the first line has been changed from, "*Oh the brave Fifhers life,*" in the first edition, to "*Oh the gallant Fifhers life,*" in the second.

Of the 48 misprints and variations in the first edition five were not corrected in the second edition (see Appendix B); the C still varies in *Complete* in the running-head; on page 96, second indention, "Topfel of" instead of "Topfel on;" on page 107, line 6, "that" is repeated; and on page 257, line 17, "use" is still printed "Use." This reduction of errors in the second edition, however, is offset by new irregularities not in the first edition. For example, on the recto of A4, line 4, and on page 3, line 5, "mee" for "me;" page 3, lines 9 and 11, "bee" for "be;" page 12, lines 5-6, "carere" for "career;" page 13, line 7, "dyes" for "die;" page 16, line 2, "forrain" for "foreign;" page 74,

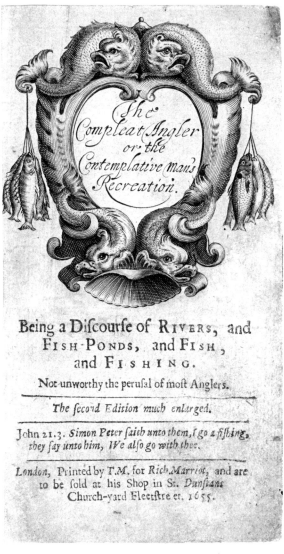

Figure 2   The Second Edition (No. 2)

line 2, "Divel" for "Devil;" page 186, last line, "uſuall" for "uſually;" in the "Contents," page [357], Chap. 6, line 3, "them" for "him," which also occurs in the heading for Chapter VI, and there are many more such as these.

Although Walton revised his text as the political situation changed from Protectorate to Kingdom (see comment under the third edition of 1661, No. 3) he seems to have overlooked what might have caused political eyebrow raising at the time when he wrote, in describing the life of the bees, page 224, that ". . . they have obeyed their King and governed their Common-wealth. . . ." But so it appeared thus in the following four editions.

Walton made a number of important changes in the second edition. Seven chapters were added, making twenty-one, and there are 109 additional pages. As mentioned previously, this edition is the first to contain the laudatory verses written by seven of Walton's friends. The interlocutors in the first edition, Piscator and Viator, were changed to Piscator, Venator, and Auceps, and much descriptive dialogue and practical fishing instruction were added to the text.

These are the major revisions leading toward the final form of Walton's part of *The Compleat Angler* in the fifth edition of 1676 (No. 6), the last published during his lifetime.

1661

3. The Third Edition of 1661

The | Compleat Angler | or the | Contemplative Man's | Recreation. | BEING | A DISCOURSE | of | Rivers, Fiſh-ponds, Fiſh and Fiſhing. | *To which is added* | The Laws of Angling: with a new Table | of the Particulars in this Book. | ———— | *The third Edition much enlarged.* | ———— | *London,* Printed by *J.G.* for *Rich, Marriot,* at his Shop | in St. *Dunſtans* Church yard, Fleetſtreet, 1661.

Copies examined: Harvard, Horne. Others: CSmH, CtHT, CtY, DLC, InU, MWiW-C, NIC, NjP, ViU, WU.

Size: 5⅝″×3⁹⁄₁₆″.

Collation: A–S⁸=144. Signature mark lacking on P4.

Contents: Recto [A], title (Figure 3), first eight words within engraved piscatorial cartouche, in Horne copy, the hyphen omitted in Church yard, present in Harvard copy; verso [A], blank; recto A2–verso A3, "The Epiſtle Dedicatory;" recto A4–verso [A5], "To the Reader;" recto [A6]–verso [A8], laudatory verses, those by Alex. Brome omitted; recto B–recto [R8], or pages 1–255, Text; verso [R8], blank; recto S–recto S4, "Lawes of Angling;" verso S4,

Figure 3   The Third Edition of 1661 (No. 3). The Harvard
Copy in the Fearing Angling Collection, the Houghton
Library, Harvard University

blank; recto-verso [S5], "The Contents;" recto [S6]–middle of verso [S8], "The Table;" lower part verso [S8], "Errata" and "Finis." Page 87 is incorrectly numbered 78, and 223 is 233. The six and one-half pages of the "Lawes of Angling" are printed in black letter with the first three leaves signed in black letter, the fourth in roman. Chapter XVII (p. 217) remains titled XVI as it was in the second edition, and the title of the correct Chapter XVI, page 206, has been changed to "Is of nothing, or that which is nothing worth," from "Merriments, Songs and Muſick."

The illustrations are the same as the second edition and consist of ten small copperplates of fish in the text. These are Trout, on page 82; Pike, 150; Carp, 165; Bream, 171; Tench, 180; Pearch, 184; Eel, 194; Barbel, 199; Loach, 231; Bullhead, 233; and, the "Anglers Song" on pages 214 and 215, the latter page printed upside down.

Eight of the irregularities and variations noted in the second edition have been corrected, notably the C in *Complete* in the running head is now the same throughout. However, six of the second edition errors are repeated: on page 9, line 2, "carere" for "career;" page 11, line 21, "forrain for "foreign;" page 69, second indentation, "Topſel of" for "Topſel on;" page 187, line 13, "Uſe" for "uſe;" the "Contents," recto [S5], Chap. 6, line 2, and the title for Chapter VI, "them" for "him."

The "Errata" at the end lists of the volume consists of two errors (p. 19, line 8 [plane for] *plant;* and *are* for *have* p. 147), the second not present in the Horne copy but in addition other errors appeared which were not in the second edition. For example:

Verso [A4], line 30, "i" missing in "is"
Recto [A5], lines 18-19, "expements" for "experiments"
Page 7, line 3, "dye" for "die"
Page 48, line 17, "him" for "her"
Page 69, line 28, "un ike" for "unlike"
Page 78, line 2, "yeelds" for "yields"
Page 158, line 6, "note quall" for "not equal"

On page 3, line 26, the text has been changed from, "penſions from the Commonwealth," which appeared in the first and second editions, to "penſions from the King," in this third edition, the first to appear after the Restoration of Charles II.

In the last paragraph of "To the Reader," when Walton wrote, verso [A5], ". . . in this third Impreſſion there are many enlargements, . . ." he was undoubtedly referring to the addition of "The Lawes of Angling," as well as to the text.

4. The Third Edition of 1664

The | Compleat Angler | or the | Contemplative Man's | Recreation. | BEING | A DISCOURSE | of | Rivers, Fiſh-ponds, Fiſh & Fiſhing. | To which is added, | The Laws of Angling: With a new Table | of the Particulars in this Book. | ———— | *The third Edition much enlarged.* | ———— | *London,* Printed for *R. Marriot,* and are to be ſold by *Simon* | *Gape* neer the Inner Temple-gate in Fleetſtreet, 1664.

Copies examined: Harvard, Yale. Others: NN, ViU.

Size: $5\frac{7}{16}'' \times 3\frac{1}{2}''$.

Collation: A–S^8=144. Signature mark lacking on P4 (music).

Contents: Recto [A], title, with first eight words within engraved piscatorial cartouche (Figure 4); verso [A], blank; recto A2–verso A3, "The Epistle Dedicatory;" recto A4–verso [A5], "To the Reader;" recto [A6]–verso [A8], laudatory verses, those by Alex. Brome omitted; recto B–recto [R8], or pages 1–255, Text; verso [R8], blank; recto S–recto S4, "Lawes of Angling;" verso S4, blank; recto–verso [S5], "The Contents;" recto [S6]–middle of verso [S8], "The Table;" lower part verso [S8], "Errata" and "Finis."

Page 87 is incorrectly numbered 78, and 223 is 233. The six and one-half pages of the "Lawes of Angling" are printed in black letter, with the first three leaves signed in black letter, the fourth in roman. Chapter XVII is misnumbered XVI (as in third ed. of 1661), and the title of the correct Chapter XVI, page 206, has been changed to, *Is of nothing or that which is nothing worth,* from *Merriments, Songs and Muſick.*

The illustrations are the same, and on the same pages as in the third edition of 1661 (No. 3), consisting of the title-page cartouche and ten small copperplate reproductions of fish in the text. These are Trout, on page 82; Pike, 150; Carp, 165; Bream, 171; Tench, 180; Pearch, 184; Eel 194; Barbel, 199; Loach, 231; Bullhead, 233; and the "Anglers Song" on pages 214 and 215, the latter page printed upside down.

All the irregularities and errors listed for the third edition of 1661 (No. 3) also present in the third edition of 1664 (No. 4).

The only title-page changes are the new date (1664), elimination of *J.G.* (the printer's initials), the transfer from Marriot's Shop to Simon Gape, "neer the Inner Temple-Gate," and the change of "to which is added" from italic to roman type with the addition of a comma.

With the same collation, contents, and illustrations, and with a new title-page, this edition is a reissue of the 1661 edition.

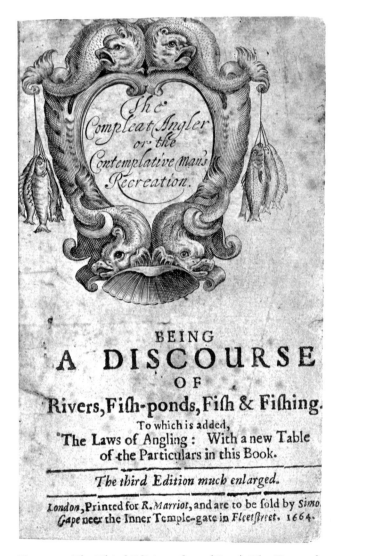

The Compleat Angler or the Contemplative Mans Recreation.

BEING

A DISCOURSE

OF

Rivers, Fiſh-ponds, Fiſh & Fiſhing.

To which is added,

The Laws of Angling : With a new Table
of the Particulars in this Book.

The third Edition much enlarged.

London, Printed for *R. Marriot*, and are to be ſold by *Simo.
Gape* neer the Inner Temple-gate in *Fleetſtreet*, 1664.

Figure 4   The Third Edition of 1664 (No. 4). The Harvard
copy in the Fearing Angling Collection, the Houghton
Library, Harvard University

5. The Fourth Edition

The | Compleat Angler | or the | Contemplative Man's | Recreation. | BEING | A DISCOURSE | of | Rivers, Fiſh-ponds, Fiſh, & Fiſhing. | To which is added, | The Laws of Angling: With a new Table | of the Particulars in this Book. | —— | *The fourth Edition, much corrected and enlarged.* | —— | *London,* Printed for *R. Marriot,* and are to be ſold by | *Charles Harper* at his Shop, the next door to the | *Crown* near *Sergeants-Inn* in *Chancery-lane,* 1668.

Copies examined: Harvard, Horne. Others: CSmH, CtHT, DFo, DLC, InU, MWiW-C, NIC, NjP, NN, ViU, WU.

Size: $5^{13}\!/_{16}'' \times 3^{11}\!/_{16}''$.

Collation: A–S^8=144. Signature marks lacking on A3 and P4; E3 is incorrectly keyed B3.

Contents: Recto [A], title, with first eight words within piscatorial cartouche (Figure 5); verso [A], blank; recto A2–verso [A3], "The Epiſtle Dedicatory;" recto A4–verso [A5], "To the Reader;" recto = [A6]–verso [A8], laudatory verses; recto B–recto [R8], or pages 1-255, Text; verso [R8], blank; recto S-recto S4, "Lawes of Angling;" verso S4, blank; recto–verso [S5], "The Contents;" recto [S6]–middle of verso [S8], "The Table;" lower part verso [S8], "Finis."

The pages are numbered correctly in the copies checked, but as for the second and third editions, Chapter XVII continues to be misnumbered XVI. The six and one-half pages of the "Lawes of Angling" are printed in black letter, with the first three leaves signed in black letter, the fourth in roman.

The title-page cartouche (Figure 5) and ten small copperplate reproductions of fish are the same, and on the same pages, as in the third edition (No. 3). The "Anglers Song" also is on the same pages (214 and 215), the latter printed upside down. However, on page 214, the lower line of the musical accompaniment printed under the lyric in the first, second, and third editions was not included.

The six irregularities of the second edition, uncorrected in the third edition of 1661 (No. 3), persist here, the only change being that "foreign," spelled "forrain" in the second and third editions, has been changed to "forraign" on page 11, line 21. On the other hand, all the errors listed as new in the third edition were corrected except "him" instead of "her" on page 48, line 17; "note quall" for "not equal" on page 158, line 6, now reads "not equall." A list of these irregularities is given for the third edition of 1661 (No. 3).

While the title-page reads ". . . much corrected . . ." and probably many of the errors made in the third were corrected, as indicated by the sample, a whole new batch of irregularities appear in the fourth edition.

BEING
A DISCOURSE
OF
Rivers, Fiſh-ponds, Fiſh, & Fiſhing.
To which is added,
The Laws of Angling : With a new Table
of the Particulars in this Book.

The fourth Edition, much correĉted and enlarged.

London, Printed for *R. Marriot,* and are to be ſold by
Charles Harper at his Shop, the next door to the
Crown near *Sergeants-Inn* in *Chancery-lane,* 1668.

Figure 5　The Fourth Edition (No. 5). The Harvard copy in
the Fearing Angling Collection, the Houghton Library,
Harvard University

For example:

    Page 48, line 11, "Huntſ-ma" for "Huntſman"
    Page 66, line 4, "Trous" for "Trout"
    Page 83, line 17, "bope" for "hope"
    Page 103, line 24, "ano her" for "another"
    Page 194, line 4, "of" for "off"
    Page 195, line 18, "at" repeated
    Page 196, line 4, "Sholar" for "Scholar"
    Page 206, line 2, "S" in "Summers" inverted and set incorrectly
    Page 206, last line, "yon" for "you"
    Page 238, line 15, "beeu" for "been"

This edition differs from the third in some typographic particulars, such as a change in the type ornaments and initial letters and, in some instances, in the use of different roman and italic capital letters.

However, with a new title-page, and other minor changes such as those mentioned above, this is a corrected paginal reprint of the third edition (No. 3).

1676

6. The Fifth Edition

The | Universal | ANGLER, | Made ſo, by | Three Books | of | FISHING. | The *Firſt* | Written by Mr. Izaak Walton; | The *Second* | By Charles Cotton, Eſq; | The *Third* | By Col. Robert Venables. | ———— | All which may be bound together, or sold | each of them ſeverally. |———— | London, | Printed for *Richard Marriott,* and ſold by | moſt Bookſellers. MDCLXXVI.

Copies examined: Harvard (5), Horne, Princeton. Others: CSmH, CtHT, CtY, DLC, ViU.

Size: 5¾" × 3⁹⁄₁₆".

Collation: First two leaves without signatures; A–T⁸, V⁴; A⁴, B–H⁸; A–G⁸, H⁴=278. Signature marks lacking on A4 in Parts I and II; in Part II, F3 is incorrectly keyed B2; the verso of T8 is incorrectly numbered 276.

Contents: Recto of first leaf, blank; verso of first leaf, Part I title, with first eight words within piscatorial cartouche (Figure 6), as follows: The | Compleat Angler | or the | Contemplative Man's | Recreation. | *The first part* | Part I. | Being A | Discourse | of | *Rivers, Fiſh-ponds, Fiſh* and *Fiſhing.* | ———— | Written by Izaak Walton. | ———— | *The Fifth Edition much corrected and enlarged.* | ———— | London, | Printed for *Richard Marriott,* 1676. | ; recto of second leaf, general

THE
UNIVERSAL
ANGLER,
Made so, by
Three BOOKS
OF
FISHING.

The First
Written by Mr. IZAAK WALTON;
The Second
By CHARLES COTTON Esq;
The Third
By Col. ROBERT VENABLES.

All which may be bound together, or sold
each of them severally.

LONDON,
Printed for Richard Marriott, and sold by
most Booksellers. MDCLXXVI.

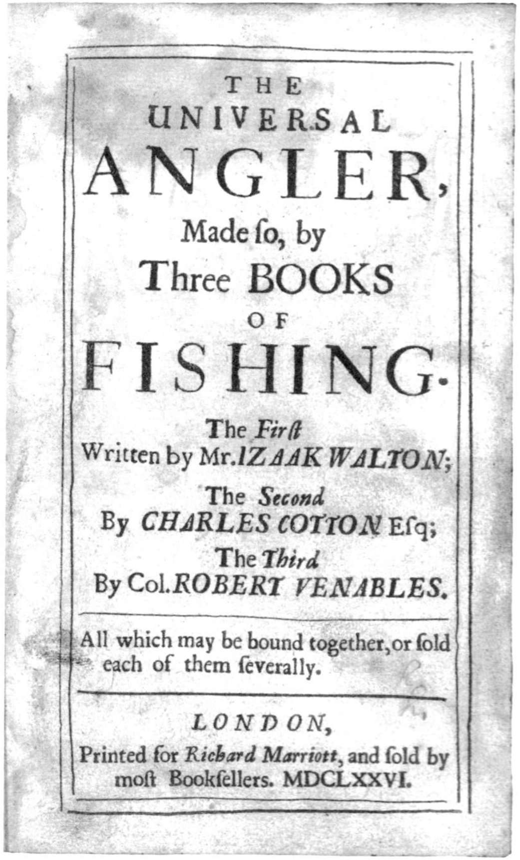

Figure 7 The Universal Angler (No. 6).
The general title-page

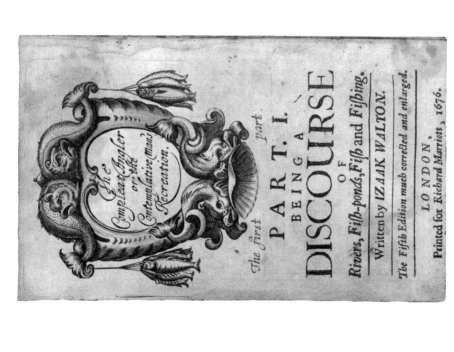

Figure 6 The Universal Angler (No. 6). The
first title-page to Part I; it precedes and faces
the general title-page (Figure 7)

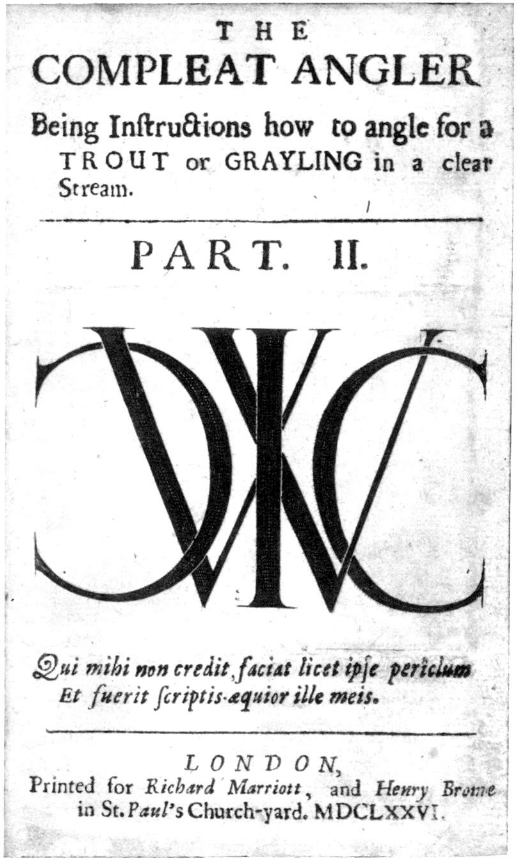

THE
COMPLEAT ANGLER

Being Instructions how to angle for a
TROUT or GRAYLING in a clear
Stream.

PART. II.

OXO

Qui mihi non credit faciat licet ipse periculum
Et fuerit scriptis æquior ille meis.

LONDON,
Printed for *Richard Marriott*, and *Henry Brome*
in St. *Paul's* Church-yard. MDCLXXVI.

Figure 9   The Universal Angler (No. 6).
The title-page to Part II

P A R T. I.
BEING A
DISCOURSE
OF
Rivers, Fish-ponds, Fish & Fishing.

Written by IZAAK WALTON.

The Fifth Edition, much corrected and enlarged.

London, Printed for *R. Marriot*, and are to be fold by
Charles Harper at his Shop, the next door to the
Crown near *Serjeants-Inn* in *Chancery Lane*, 1676.

Figure 8   The Universal Angler (No. 6). The
second title-page (upper part blank) to Part I;
it follows the general title-page (Figure 7)

THE
EXPERIENC'D
ANGLER:
OR,
ANGLING IMPROV'D.

BEING
A General Discourse
OF
ANGLING.

Imparting the Aptest ways and
Choicest Experiments for the ta-
king of most sorts of FISH in
Pond or River.

By Col. ROBERT VENABLES.

The Fourth Edition much Enlarged.

LONDON,

Printed for Richard Marriot, 1676.

Figure 11   The Universal Angler (No. 6).
The title-page to Part III

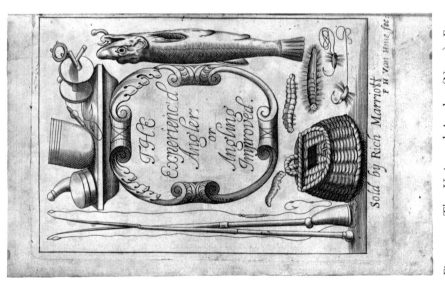

THE
Experienc'd
Angler;
or
Angling
Improved.

Sold by Rich Marriott

F H Van Houe fec.

Figure 10   The Universal Angler (No. 6). Engraved frontispiece to Part III

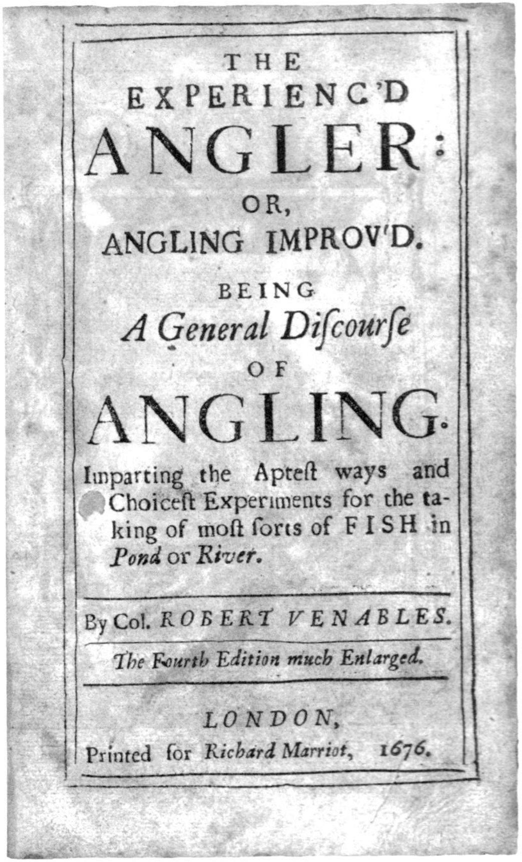

title, *The Universal Angler,* within a parallel rule, as given above (see Fig. 7); verso second leaf, blank; recto [A], second title to Part I, upper half of page (Figure 8). Part I. | Being A | DISCOURSE | of Rivers, Fiſh-ponds, Fiſh, & Fiſhing. | —— | Written by Isaak Walton. | —— | *The Fifth Edition, much corrected and enlarged.* | —— | *London,* Printed for *R. Marriot,* and are to be ſold by | *Charles Harper* at his Shop, the next door to the | *Crown* near *Sergeants-Inn* in *Chancery Lane,* 1676. | , verso of [A], blank; recto A2–recto [A4], "The Epistle Dedicatory;" verso [A4]–verso [A6], "To the Reader;" recto [A7]–recto B4, laudatory verses; verso B4, blank; recto [B5]–recto [T6], or pages 1-275, text; verso [T6], blank; recto [T7]–recto V2, "Lawes of Angling;" verso V2, blank; recto and verso [V3], "The Contents;" [V4], blank leaf.

Recto [A], blank; verso [A], license leaf; recto [A2], Part II title (Figure 9): The | COMPLEAT ANGLER | Being inſtructions how to angle for a | Trout or Grayling in a clear | Stream. | —— | Part. II. | large Walton-Cotton cipher | *Qui mihi non credit faciat licet ipſe periclum* | *Et fuerit ſcriptis aequior ille meis.* | —— | London, | Printed for *Richard Marriott,* and Henry Brome | in St. *Paul's* Church-yard. MDCLXXVI. | verso [A2], blank; recto A3-verso A4, "The Epistle Dedicatory;" recto B-verso H4, or pages 1-104, text; recto and verso [H5], *To my moſt Honoured Friend* | Charles Cotton, Eſq; | recto [H6]-recto [H8], The | Retirement | ; verso [H8], *Courteous* Reader. | , [advertisement of John Margrave.]

One blank leaf; recto [A], blank; verso [A], engraved frontispiece to Part III (Figure 10). *The Experienc'd Ang'ler . . .,* by F. H. Van Hove; recto [A2], Part III title within a parallel rule (Figure 11), as follows: The | Experienc'd | ANGLER: | or, | Angling Improv'd. | Being | *A General Diſcourſe* | of | ANGLING. | Imparting the Apteſt ways and | Choiceſt Experiments for the ta- | king of moſt ſorts of FISH in | *Pond* or *River.* | —— | By Col. Robert Venables. | —— | *The Fourth Edition much Enlarged.* | —— | London, | Printed for *Richard Marriot,* 1676. | , recto [A2]; verso [A2], blank; recto A3-verso [A6], *To the Reader;* recto and verso [A7], *To His Ingenious Friend . . .;* recto [A8], *To the Author . . .;* verso [A8], *The Contents;* recto B-verso [G8], or pages 1-96, text; recto H-verso [H3], *The Table;* [H4], blank leaf.

The pages are numbered correctly in the copies examined, but Chapter XVII continues to be misnumbered XVI. As before, the "Lawes of Angling" are printed in black letter with the signature V^2 in roman and, in this edition, the running head reads, *The Compleat Angler,* instead of *The Complete Angler,* and is also printed in black letter. The publisher's name is spelled either "Marriott" or "Mariot," as for example, the former on the general title, and the latter on the second title to Part I. The Harrison manuscript in The Kienbusch Library on Fresh Water Angling in the Firestone Library at Princeton University, *An Analytical Catalogue* states in reference to the Walton-Cotton cipher printed on the title-page of Part II, "The cipher was by Mr. Cotton's desire, placed in the title-page of his portion of the book . . ."

The illustrations in Part I consist of the same title-page cartouche and small copperplates of the same fish portrayed in former editions, but the fish are re-engraved in reverse. They are on pages 86, 156, 172, 179, 189, 193, 203, 209, 244, and 245. The music on pages 225 and 226, has the second page printed right side up, whereas it is upside down in the previous editions. The musical accompaniment follows the pattern of the fourth edition. There are no illustrations in Part II, but in Part III, in addition to the frontispiece referred to above, the same small copperplate reproductions of fish as in Part I appear in the text on pages 50, 51, 52, 53, 54, 55, 57, and 59 (2).

It would seem that even Walton's sweet temper would have been tried by the errors that continued to appear in the *Angler*. Just as fast as those in a previous edition would be corrected (seven out of the nine listed for the fourth edition), a new crop would show up in the next, and one, "Topfel of frogs" for "Topfel on frogs," persisted through all the first five editions. A list of twenty-eight irregularities, including seven carried over from previous editions to the fifth, and twenty-one appearing for the first time in the fifth edition, is given in Appendix D and, as Walton would have said, "doubtless there are many more." Some examples are "Simber-falts" for "Summer-falts," "Fifhers" for "Flies," "North" for "month," and "Flie" for "File." Perhaps the printer didn't think accuracy was necessary in what he undoubtedly considered a relatively unimportant book on fishing, but it would seem that Marriot, the publisher, could have insisted on more printing accuracy in what must have been a very popular book.

The fifth edition, the last to appear in Walton's lifetime, and the first to have his name on the title-page, was issued as Part I of *The Universal Angler* which included the first printing of Charles Cotton's, *The Compleat Angler Being Inftructions how to angle for a Trout or Grayling in a clear Stream* as Part II, and the fourth edition of Col. Robert Venables', *The Experienced Angler*, as Part III. This is the only time that this improbable trio of Walton, retired businessman and friend of bishops; Cotton, onetime captain in the King's army, financially irresponsible estate owner, and poetaster; and Venables, commander in Cromwell's army and veteran of a West Indies campaign, ever appeared together in print. The general title-page states of the three parts, "All which may be bound together or sold each of them severally." The parts by Walton and Cotton have appeared together and separately; the part by Venables separately but never with either Walton or Cotton, only with both Walton and Cotton.

The fact that the fifth edition has been much more popular than any other may in part be due to Walton's addition of Piscator's observations on happiness, thankfulness, and contentment which summarizes the spirit, feeling, and charm of a little book which has now been republished some three hundred and eighty-five times.

1750

7. The First Moses Browne Edition

THE COMPLEAT ANGLER : . . . by Mr. Isaac Walton. . . .
(and) . . . by Charles Cotton, Eſq ; . . .
London: Printed and sold by Henry Kent, at the Printing-
Office in *Finch-Lane,* near the *Royal Exchange.* MDCCL.

Copies examined: Harvard, Horne, Princeton. Others: CLU-C, CSmH, CtHT, CtY, GEU, IU, MB, MdBP, NN, OU, ViU, WU.

Size: 6¾₆″ × 3⁹⁄₁₆″.

Collation: a⁸, A–I¹², K–N¹², O⁴=168. There is no signature mark on B³ or I⁵, the latter being the title-page to Part II; and D⁵ is miskeyed D⁴.

Pagination: [i-iii], iv-ix, [x-xi], xii-xiv, [xv-xvi], [1]–312, [8].

Following the text are the "Laws of Angling," pp. [279]-284; "An Appendix" and "Short Rules" (on rivers, baits and fishing) pp. [285]-312; and an eight-page Index. A list of errata appears on the final page, but omits the misprint "Tackle" for "Hackle," on page 80, line 15.

The illustrations consist of six copperplates engraved and signed by H. Burgh; one page of music, printed right side up; one fishing scene head-piece, and 15 woodcuts of fish. Many of these illustrations were copied or adopted in later editions.

This edition, the first to be published since the *Universal Angler* of 1676 (last to appear in Walton's lifetime), was edited by Moses Browne, author of *Piscatory Eclogues,* to whom the idea was suggested by the famous Dr. Samuel Johnson. In his six and one-half page "Editor's Preface," Browne's lavish commendation of Walton, and his recognition of the merit of Cotton's part of the *Angler* is tempered by his statement that ". . . some few Inaccuracies and Redundancies have insinuated themselves, which I should be injurious to him as his Editor, not to retrench and prune away. . . ." This objective is probably reflected in his choice of the fourth, rather than the fifth edition of Part I to which Walton added substantial material. A comparative reading of only the first page or two indicates Browne's editorial approach which, unfortunately, "prunes away" vigor and charm from Walton's prose. Even the opening sentence is changed from "You are well overtaken, Gentlemen, . . . " to "Well overtaken, Gentlemen, . . ." Although Browne's editing may not be appreciated now, and his misstatement that Cotton married Walton's daughter should be ignored, he rescued the *Angler* from apparent oblivion, and this first Moses Browne edition (Figure 12), the first reissue of the work in 83 years, marks a revival of interest in Walton, and initiated the long continuing popularity of *The Compleat Angler.*

Part I is a reissue from the fourth edition of 1668 (No. 5), and Part II of the second part of the fifth edition of 1676 (No. 6).

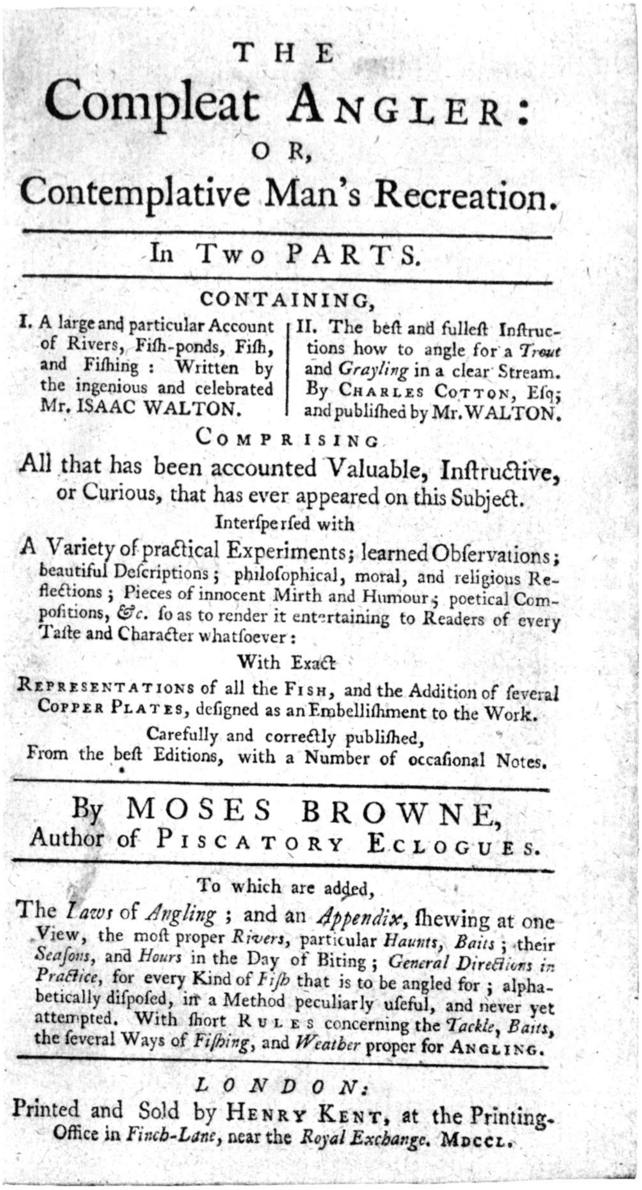

THE
Compleat ANGLER:
OR,
Contemplative Man's Recreation.

In Two PARTS.

CONTAINING,

I. A large and particular Account of Rivers, Fish-ponds, Fish, and Fishing : Written by the ingenious and celebrated Mr. ISAAC WALTON.

II. The best and fullest Instructions how to angle for a *Trout* and *Grayling* in a clear Stream. By CHARLES COTTON, Esq; and published by Mr. WALTON.

COMPRISING

All that has been accounted Valuable, Instructive, or Curious, that has ever appeared on this Subject.

Interspersed with

A Variety of practical Experiments; learned Observations; beautiful Descriptions; philosophical, moral, and religious Reflections ; Pieces of innocent Mirth and Humour; poetical Compositions, &c. so as to render it entertaining to Readers of every Taste and Character whatsoever :

With Exact

REPRESENTATIONS of all the FISH, and the Addition of several COPPER PLATES, designed as an Embellishment to the Work.

Carefully and correctly published,
From the best Editions, with a Number of occasional Notes.

By MOSES BROWNE,
Author of PISCATORY ECLOGUES.

To which are added,

The *Laws* of *Angling* ; and an *Appendix*, shewing at one View, the most proper *Rivers*, particular *Haunts*, *Baits* ; their *Seasons*, and *Hours* in the Day of Biting ; *General Directions in Practice*, for every Kind of *Fish* that is to be angled for ; alphabetically disposed, in a Method peculiarly useful, and never yet attempted. With short RULES concerning the *Tackle*, *Baits*, the several Ways of *Fishing*, and *Weather* proper for ANGLING.

LONDON:
Printed and Sold by HENRY KENT, at the Printing-Office in *Finch-Lane*, near the *Royal Exchange*. MDCCL.

Figure 12   The First Moses Browne Edition (No. 7).
Revived interest in the *Angler*

8. The Second Moses Browne Edition

THE COMPLEAT ANGLER: . . . by . . . Mr. Isaac Walton and
Charles Cotton, Esq; . . .
London: Printed and Sold by Henry Kent, at the Printing-
Office in *Finch-Lane,* near the *Royal Exchange.* MDCCLIX.

Copies checked: Harvard, Horne. Others: CtHT, CSmH, CtY, DLC, NN, NjP, WU.

Size: 6$\frac{3}{16}$″ × 3$\frac{9}{16}$″.

Collation: a^{12}, A–O^{12}, P^6=186. Leaf N^4 has no signature mark, and N^5 is keyed N^4.

Pagination: [i-iii], iv, [v], vi-xiv, [xv], xvi-xviii, [xix], xx-xvii [*sic* for xxii], [xxiii], xxiv, [1]-216, [217-221], 222-303, [304-305], 306-310, [311], 312-334, [335], 336-340, [8]. Page xxii is misnumbered xvii, and the misprint, "Tackle" for "Hackle," (page 84, line 19), overlooked in the "errata" of the first Moses Browne, is recorded on the last page.

H. Burgh engraved the ten copperplates of which six, also used and signed in the 1750 edition, are unsigned in this printing. Of the four new Burgh plates in this edition, one is unsigned and three are signed. A page of music, a headpiece of a fishing scene, and 15 woodcuts of fish are from the first Moses Browne edition (No. 7).

The title-page identifies this as "The Seventh Edition, Very much amended and improved," and the title-page to Part II reads, "The Third Edition, improved with Notes, etc." It is, in reality, little more than a reprint of the fifth edition of 1676, since Part I, which in the first Moses Browne, was a reprint of the 1668 edition, has been extended by the addition of most of the changes that Walton made for the edition of 1676, and Part II is a reprint from the fifth edition. In both Parts I and II, the notes have been enlarged. The Harrison manuscript in The Kienbusch Library on Fresh Water Angling in the Firestone Library at Princeton University, *An Analytical Catalogue,* comments in reference to this edition, "This edition caused a controversy with Sir John Hawkins who was at the same time bringing out his first edition of the Angler." See further comments on this in connection with the first Hawkins edition of 1760 (No. 9).

9. The First Hawkins Edition

THE COMPLETE ANGLER: . . . by Mr. Izaak Walton, . . . By Charles Cotton, Efq; . . . London: Printed *only* for Thomas Hope, at the *Bible* and *Anchor,* oppofite the North Gate of the *Royal-Exchange, Threadneedle-Street;* and fold by him and Sackville Parker, at *Oxford;* Richard Matthews, at *Cambridge;* and Samuel Trimmer, at *Derby.* 1760.

Copies examined: Harvard, Horne, Yale. Others: CSmH, CtHT, DLC, NjP, NN.

Size: $7'' \times 4\frac{1}{2}''$.

Collation: A^8, a–b^8, c^4, B^8–$2K^8$, $2L^4$=288.

Pagination: [i-iii], iv-x, [xi], xii-lvi, [i]-xxii, [1]-303, [304]. [i-iii], iv-xlviii, [i], ii-iv, [i], ii, [i]-iv, [1]-128, [8].

In the Life of Walton the quotations from *The Treatyfe of Fyfshynge Wyth an Angle* are in black letter. On the verso of a leaf at the front of the Yale copy is a full page advertisement addressed "To all Lovers of Angling" of the fishing tackle maker JOHN HERRO who, with Onesimus Ustonson later (see nos. 13 & 14) might well have been substantial subscribers toward the publication of the Hawkins' *Anglers.* There are 11 engravings by William W. Ryland, of which nine are after S. Wale, one after T. Smith and one after P. Lely; one engraved and two woodcut headpieces; two plates of music and three of fishing gear, plus 17 woodcuts of fish. On page 28, Part I, "he" on line 23 is repeated on the next line; on page 40, in line 2 of the first note, "beginning" is "begiuning." On page 121 Part II, the "2" is inverted. The Life of Walton is by John Hawkins and the biography of Cotton is by William Oldys.

Like the Moses Browne edition of 1750, this first Hawkins edition may also have been inspired by Samuel Johnson, since the editor, Sir John Hawkins, was a member of the famous Literary Club organized by the great critic and conversationalist (see Figure 13).

With further reference to the controversy between editors Browne and Hawkins regarding their editions of the *Angler,* the Harrison manuscript in The Kienbusch Library on Fresh Water Angling, in the Firestone Library at Princeton University, *An Analytical Catalogue,* comments as follows on the first Hawkins edition: "Advertised 27 Sep. 1759 as in the press and speedily will be published, in opposition to Moses Browne's edition published in that year. On the 1st July 1760 it appeared announced as the only correct and complete edition. . . ." Browne answered with an advertisement which stated that in Hawkins' edition, "the boasted plates 'copied from the designs in his, and the Life of Walton in chief part borrowed from the one printed by him'."

This edition is a reprint from the fifth edition of 1676 (No. 6).

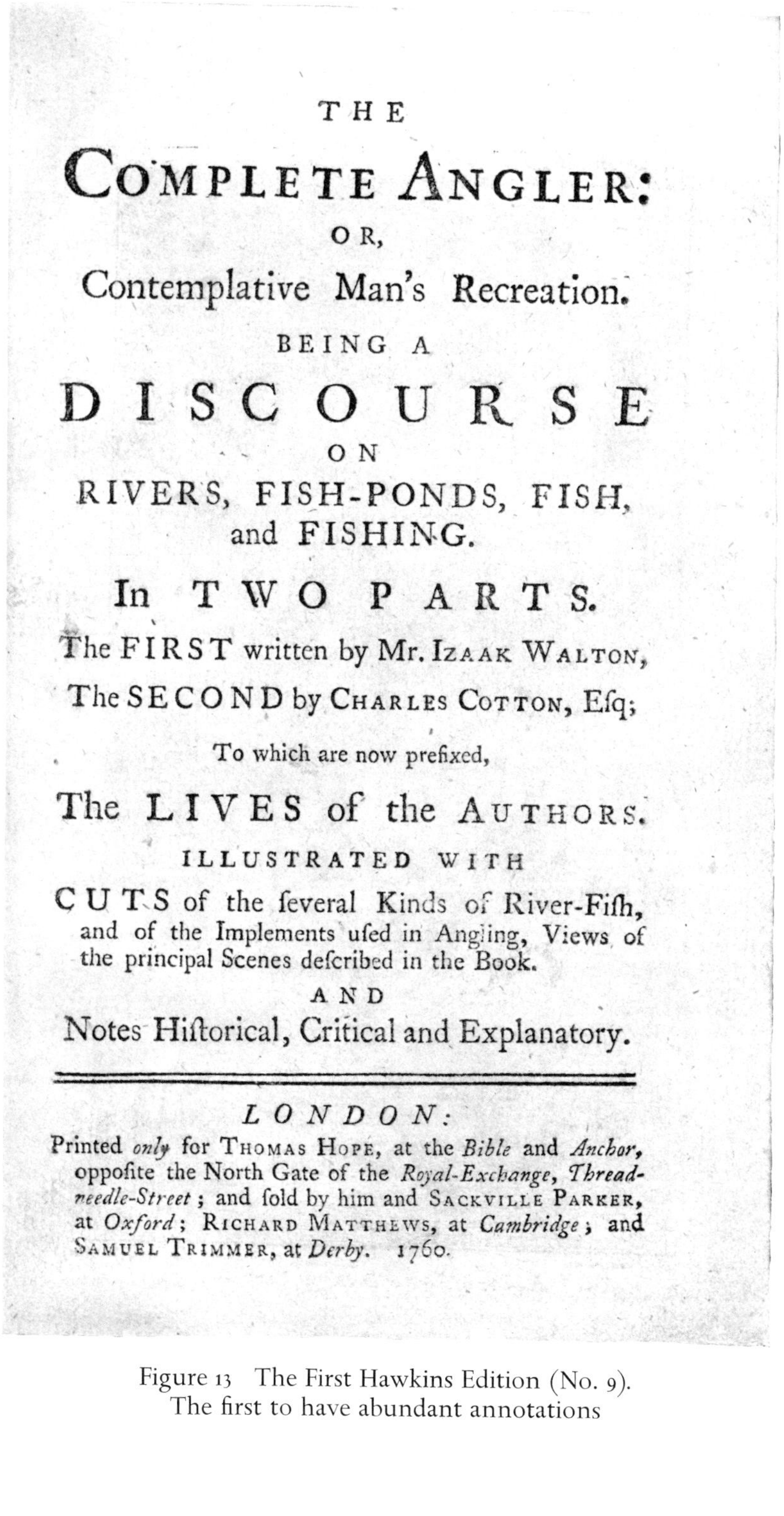

THE
COMPLETE ANGLER:
OR,

Contemplative Man's Recreation.

BEING A

DISCOURSE
ON

RIVERS, FISH-PONDS, FISH,
and FISHING.

In TWO PARTS.

The FIRST written by Mr. IZAAK WALTON,

The SECOND by CHARLES COTTON, Efq;

To which are now prefixed,

The LIVES of the AUTHORS.

ILLUSTRATED WITH

CUTS of the feveral Kinds of River-Fifh,
and of the Implements ufed in Angling, Views of
the principal Scenes defcribed in the Book.

AND

Notes Hiftorical, Critical and Explanatory.

LONDON:

Printed *only* for THOMAS HOPE, at the *Bible* and *Anchor*,
oppofite the North Gate of the *Royal-Exchange*, *Threadneedle-Street*; and fold by him and SACKVILLE PARKER,
at *Oxford*; RICHARD MATTHEWS, at *Cambridge*; and
SAMUEL TRIMMER, at *Derby*. 1760.

Figure 13   The First Hawkins Edition (No. 9).
The first to have abundant annotations

10. The Second Hawkins Reprint

THE COMPLETE ANGLER : . . . by Mr. Izaak Walton, . . .
by Charles Cotton, Esq. . . .
London: Printed For J. Rivington, At The *Bible* And *Crown,* in
St. Paul's Church-Yard; T. Caslon, in *Stationers Court;* And R. Withy,
in *Cornhill.* MDCCLXVI.

Copies examined: Harvard (2), Horne. Others: CSmH, CtHT, CtY, MdBJ,
NN.

Size: 6⅞″×4½″.

Except for the addition of two pages of advertising at the front for "Books
Printed for R. Withy, in Cornhill," the collation and pagination are the same
as the Hawkins edition of 1760, of which this is a reissue with the same illustrations. In the two copies examined at Harvard, and the Horne copy, the same
errors of 1760 have been repeated.

While the title-page, imprinted "The Second Edition" has been reset and
dated as noted, the title-page to Part II remains dated M.DCC.LX [1760], as
in the first Hawkins edition.

11. The Third Moses Browne Edition

THE COMPLEAT ANGLER : . . . By . . . *Mr.* Isaac Walton
and Charles Cotton, *Esq;* . . .
London: Printed and sold by Richard and Henry Causton (Suc-
ceffors to the late Mr. Henry Kent) at the Printing Office, No. 21,
Finch-Lane, near the *Royal Exchange.* MDCCLXXII.

Copies examined: Harvard, Horne. Others: CLSU, CSmH, CtHT, CtY, MB,
NjP, NN.

Size: 6 1/16″×3½″.

Collation: a^{12}, A–P^{12}, Q^6=198. a^3, a^4, C^4, C^5, F^5, O^3 and O^5 lack signature
marks; K^6 is miskeyed as K^5, L^6 as L^5, N^4 as N^5, O^4 as O^3.

Pagination: [i-iii], iv, [v], vi-viii, [ix], x-xix, [xx-xxi], xxii, [xxiii], xxiv. [1]-237,
[238-243], 244-325, [326-327], 328-332, [333], 334-357, [358], 359-363, [364], [8].

The illustrations consist of ten copperplates engraved by H. Burgh, of which three are signed, music for nine different songs, an angling scene headpiece, and 15 woodcuts of fish.

The title-page is imprinted, "The Eighth Edition, with the Addition of all the Songs ſet to muſic" and, the title-page to Part II, "The Fourth Edition improved, with Notes, etc." Actually, because of the Hawkins edition of 1760 and reprint of 1766, this is the tenth reprinting of Part I, and the sixth reprinting of Part II. It is the last to have been edited by Moses Browne.

1775

12. The Third Hawkins Reprint

THE COMPLETE ANGLER: . . . by Mr. Isaac Walton, . . . by Charles Cotton, Esq; . . .
London: Printed for John and Francis Rivington (No. 62) at the *Bible* and *Crown*, in *St. Paul's Church-Yard*; and T. Caslon, in *Stationer's-Court*. MDCCLXXV.

Copies examined: Harvard, Horne. Others: CSmH, CtHT, CtY, NjP, NN.

Size: 6⅝″ × 4¾₁₆″.

Collation: A⁸, a–c⁸, d⁷, B–Ii⁸, Kk¹=288.

Pagination: [i-iii], iv-vii, [viii], ix-x, [xi], xii-lvi, [lvii], lviii-lxxviii. [1], 2-303, [304]; [i-iii], iv-xlviii, [xlix], l-lii, [liii], liv-lviii, [1], 2-128, [8].

There are nine copperplates after Wale, two after T. Smith, and the portrait of Cotton after Lely, all engraved by Ryland; 17 fish woodcuts; one engraved headpiece; two pages of music; and three copperplate reproductions of fishing tackle and flies at the end of Part I.

The typographical and page numbering errors in the previous Hawkins editions have been corrected. The title-page, imprinted, "The Third Edition," is dated 1775; the title-page to Part II is dated 1774.

This is a reprint of the first Hawkins edition.

1784

13. The Fourth Hawkins Edition

THE COMPLETE ANGLER, . . . by Mr. Isaac Walton, . . . by Charles Cotton, Esq; . . .
London: Printed for John, Francis, and Charles Rivington (No. 62) at the Bible and Crown, St. Paul's Church-Yard. M.DCC.LXXXIV.

Copies examined: Harvard, Horne. Others: CSmH, CtHT, CtY, DLC, NN, OU, NjP.

Size: 7¾₁₆″ × 4½″.

Signatures: A⁸, a–d⁸, e¹, B–Dd⁸, Ee⁴=253.

Pagination: 31. [i-ii], iii-vi, [vii], viii-lxii, [lxiii], lxiv-lxxxii. [1], 2-267, (1); [i-ii], iii-xxiii, [xxiv-xxv], xxvi-xxviii, [xxix], xxx-xxxiv, [1], 2-77, [78], 79-90, [91], 92-111, [112], (10).

Page 242 is numbered 42. Imprinted on the verso of the third leaf of one copy examined is a full-page advertisement addressed "To all Lovers of Angling," of the fishing tackle makers ONESIMUS USTONSON and Son, who might well have been substantial subscribers toward the publication of this and the fifth Hawkins.

The illustrations from previous Hawkins reprints are the same, except for the changes required in the page numbers on the plates, and include nine copperplates after Wale, two after T. Smith, and the portrait of Cotton after Lely all engraved by Ryland; 17 fish woodcuts; two pages of music; three plates of fishing tackle and flies at the end of Part I. In addition, there are three woodcut text illustrations not in the previous Hawkins reprints. Hawkins provided a biography of Cotton, replacing the earlier life by William Oldys.

In this Hawkins edition, the title-pages to both parts are dated 1784.

1791

14. The Fifth Hawkins Reprint

THE COMPLETE ANGLER, . . . By Mr. Isaac
Walton, . . . by Charles Cotton, Esq; . . .
London, Printed for J. F. and C. Rivington,
(No. 62) St. Paul's Church-yard. M.DCC.XCI.

Copies examined: Harvard, Horne. Others: CU, CtHT, CtY, DLC, NjP, NN.

Size: 7⅛″ × 4⅝″.

Collation: A⁸, a–d⁸, e¹, B–Dd⁸, Ee⁴=253. I⁴ lacks signature and catchword.

Pagination: 2l. [i-ii], iii-vi, [vii], viii-lxii, [lxiii], lxiv-lxxxii; Part I. [1]-267, (1); Part II, [i-ii], iii-xxiii, [xxiv-xxv], xxvi-xxviii, [xxix], xxx-xxiv [sic for xxxiv] [1]-77, [78], 79-90, [91], 92-111, [112], (10).

The ONESIMUS USTONSON advertisement mentioned in my notes to the fourth Hawkins (No. 13) is imprinted on the recto of the second leaf (1st blank) in the Horne copy. In both editions this leaf has been seen only in copies in contemporary bindings.

There are five copperplates after Wale, two after T. Smith, and the portrait of Cotton is after Lely, all engraved by Ryland; 17 fish woodcuts; two pages of music; three plates of fishing tackle and flies at the end of Part I; and three large woodcut illustrations. Four of the Wale plates from the fourth Hawkins were not included but the remaining illustrations are the same except for the changes required in the page numbers on the plates.

The title-page of this and the sixth Hawkins (No. 15) are both imprinted, "The Fifth Edition, with Additions." The title-page of Part II is dated 1791 in both the 1791 and the 1792 editions.

The additions, mentioned in the "Advertisment . . ." on page vi, are the notes added by Sir John's son, John Sidney Hawkins, who states also that the changes in the plates were required because they had ". . . become so worn as to be no longer any ornament to the work . . ."

This is a reissue of the fourth Hawkins of 1784 (No. 13).

1792

15. The Sixth (titled Fifth) Hawkins Reprint

THE COMPLETE ANGLER, . . . By Mr. Isaac Walton, . . . By Charles Cotton, Esq; . . . London, Printed for F. and C. Rivington, G. G. J. and J. Robinson, W. Goldsmith, J. and J. Taylor, R. Faulder, Scatcherd and Whitaker, and E. Jefferey. MDCCXCII.

Copies examined: Harvard, Horne. Others: CSmH, CtHT, CtY, NN, PP.

Size: $6^{13}\!/_{16}''\times4^{3}\!/_{16}''$.

Collation: A⁸, a–d⁸, e¹, B–Dd⁸, Ee⁴=253. I⁴ lacks both signature mark and catchword.

Pagination: [i-ii], iii-vi, [vii], viii-lxii, [lxiii], lxiv-lxxxii; Part I, [1], 2-267, [1]; Part II, [i-ii], iii-xxiii, [xxiv-xxv], xxvi-xxviii, [xxix], xxx-xxiv [sic for xxxiv], [1]-77, [78], 79-90, [91], 92-111, [112], [10].

The illustrations are as in the previous Hawkins edition with the necessary changes in the page numbers on the plates. They include five copperplates after Wale, two after T. Smith, and the portrait of Cotton after Lely, all engraved by Ryland; 17 fish woodcuts; two plates of music; three plates of fishing tackle and flies at the end of Part I; and three large woodcut illustrations. In the Horne copy the music to face page 208 is bound in at page 108.

Since this is a reissue of the 1791 edition except for a new title-page to Part I, it has been designated as the sixth reprint to avoid the confusion caused by the fact that the title-pages of both the 1791 and 1792 issues are imprinted "The Fifth Edition, with Additions." However, the title-page to Part II in the 1792 edition is dated 1791.

[29]

16. The Seventh (Titled Sixth) Hawkins Reprint

THE COMPLETE ANGLER; . . . by Mr. Isaac Walton, . . . by Charles Cotton, Esq. . . . London: Printed for F. and C. Rivington, G. G. and J. Robinson, J. and J. Taylor, R. Faulder, W. Bent, J. Scatchera, E. Jefferey, and T. N. Longman. 1797.

Copies examined: Harvard, Horne. Others: CSmH, CtHT, CtY, NjP, NN.

Size: $6\frac{11}{16}'' \times 4\frac{1}{8}''$.

Collation: $-^4$, a–c^{12}, d^2, B–S^{12}, T^5=251. K^5 has no signature mark. C^3 appears in Part I on pages 21 and 29.

Pagination: [i-v], vi, [vii], viii; [i]-lvi, [lvii], lviii-lix, [lx], lxi-lxxvi, [1]-262, 1l., [i-ii], iii-xxiii, [xxiv-xxv], xxvi, [xxvii], xxviii-xxxii, [1]-77, [78], 79-90, [91], 92-111, [112], [10]. In Part I, page 198 is numbered 168.

The illustrations in the Horne copy consist only of three large woodcuts in the text. The copy at Harvard has the same three woodcuts plus two plates of music, and three plates of tackle of which two are signed, H. Roberts, Sc. and the other is not signed.

The change in the illustrations of this reprint was explained in the "Advertisement to the Sixth Edition" (page vii), written by John Sidney Hawkins, Son of Sir John,

> As the plates have, in consequence of the number of impressions furnished from them for the preceding editions, become so worn as to be no longer any ornament to the work, it has been found necessary to omit them. Such of them, however, as represent the materials for fishing (and which fortunately had sustained less injury) have been retained . . .

The anonymous manuscript in The Kienbusch Library on Fresh Water Angling, in the Firestone Library at Princeton, *Catalogue of Books on Angling,* states in reference to this edition, "Twenty-five copies were printed on large and fine paper." A copy in a contemporary binding has also been examined which comprised only Part II, followed by the Laws of Angling, Appendix I through VII, and the general Index.

This is a reprint of the fourth Hawkins edition.

17, 18, and 19. The First Bagster Edition
(Also so-called Eighth, half-titled seventh, Hawkins Reprint)

THE COMPLETE ANGLER: . . . by Mr. Isaac Walton; . . . by Charles Cotton, Esq. . . . London: Printed for Samuel Bagster, in the Strand. 1808.

Note: Bibliographers seem not be have recorded the differences in the *Angler* printed for Bagster in 1808, other than mentioning the sizes. Westwood reports that Bagster's first edition of 1808 was ". . . in the shape of a handsome octavo . . ." and ". . . was also printed in royal octavo and quarto . . ." Westwood and Satchell's *Bibliotheca Piscatoria* notes, "The edition was printed in three sizes: demy octavo, royal octavo and quarto," the last priced at five guineas. Wood (1900) collated an octavo, and in a note states, "Published also in large octavo and quarto." Oliver (1936) designates an octavo, and does not mention the other two sizes. The Harrison manuscript, in The Kienbusch Library on Fresh Water Angling in the Firestone Library, at Princeton, . . . *An Analytical Catalogue* . . . states that this edition was published at 15 shillings in boards and in three sizes, demy octavo, royal octavo and quarto. No one described the quarto, and no one apparently realized that two printing firms were involved with the production of the octavo. Although Mercier was involved with both, two different imprints occur.

The two states and the quarto edition are described as follows:

17. Mercier and Co. Octavo

Copies examined: Harvard, Horne (2), N.Y. Public. Others reporting an octavo: CU, CSmH, CtHT, CtY, NjP.

Sizes (Octavo): $8\frac{3}{16}'' \times 5\frac{1}{16}''$ and $9\frac{3}{8}'' \times 5\frac{3}{4}''$.

Collation: $\pi 2$, a^8, B–E^8, *E^2, F–G^8, H^8(H7+1), I^8, K^8(K1+1), L^8, M^8(M8+1), N^8(N3+1, N8+1), O^8(O6+1, O8+1), P^8(P2+1, P3+1, P6+1, P8+1), Q^8(Q2+1), R^8(R3+1+1), S^8(S2+1+1), T–Z^8, 2A–2F^8, 2G^4, H^2(–2H[lacking]).
    Note: The collation is similar to that of No. 21, which see for details. R2 is miskeyed R.

Engravings of fish appear on all the inserts, which are on heavier paper than other leaves.

Pagination summary: [iv], [i]-vi, 7-61, [lxii]-lxvi, 67-344, [347]-512 (*i.e.*, 510), [lf].

Page 344 is followed by page [347]. Two of the four copies examined lack folio numbers on page 488. At the foot of the page numbered 512 is the catchword

This, followed by two pages of advertising for Bagster's publications (lacking in Horne copies). On the half-title verso is imprinted, "Printed by C. Mercier and Co., St. Paul's Church-yard" and, at the foot of page 512, "Printed by C. Mercier and Co. King's Head Passage, St. Paul's Church-yard." There is no title-page to Part II other than a heading on the first page of text.

There are eight full-page plates after Wale (the plate opposite page 415 is misprinted 413); two after George Samuel; the frontispiece of Walton-Cotton-Hawkins; a plate of Walton's five Biographees; three plates of fishing tackle; and 17 engravings of fish; all 32 engraved by Philip Audinet. In addition there are two engraved pages of music; two large woodcuts; and the half-title vignette by Berryman after Craig.

As described in the "Advertisement to the Seventh Edition" (pp. v, vi), Bagster incorporated additional material from notes by Hawkins, corrected errors and added his own notes, and inserted others ". . . from esteemed Writers on Angling . . ."

This is a state of the first Bagster edition, from the fifth edition of 1676 (No. 6).

18. Mercier and Chervet Octavo

Copy examined: Harvard.

Size: Octavo, $9\frac{3}{8}'' \times 5\frac{3}{4}''$.

Collation: The same as No. 17 except R^2 is keyed correctly.

Pagination: The same as No. 17 except that page 252 is misnumbered 52, page 488 is paginated, and the two-page publisher's advertisement at the end is wanting. However, since the catchword *This* does not appear at the foot of the page numbered 512 as in 17A, it is presumed that the advertisment was not planned for inclusion in this state as it was for No. 17.

The illustrations are the same as in No. 17.

On the half-title verso the publisher's imprint reads "Printed by Mercier and Chervet, 32 Little Bartholomew Close," which, except for the street number, is repeated at the foot of page 512.

19. C. Mercier and Co. Quarto Edition

Copies examined: Harvard, Horne (2), N.Y. Public. Other: ViU.

Sizes (Quarto): $10\frac{7}{8}'' \times 8\frac{3}{8}''$ to $11\frac{1}{2}'' \times 9''$.

Collation: π^2, 1-10^4, 11^2, 12-16^4, 17^4(17^{3+1}), 18-19^4, 20^4(20^{+1}), 21-24^4, 25^4(25^{4+1}), 26^4(26^{3+1}), 27^4(27^{4+1}), 28^4, 29^4(29^{2+1}, 29^{4+1}), 30^4(30^{2+1}, 30^{3+1}), 31^4(31^{2+1}, 31^{4+1}), 32^4(32^{2+1}), 33^4, 34^4(34^{3+1+1}), 35^4, 36^4(36^{2+1+1}), 37-60^4, 61^2. Signature 6 is not keyed. Engravings of fish appear on all the inserts which are on the same paper as the text.

Pagination summary: [i-v], vi-x, 11-(66), [lxvii]-lxx, 71-348, [351]-516 [517-518]. Page 348 is followed by page [351], so [518] should be [516].

The folio number on page 44 is imprinted on the gutter side of the page, and 502 is misnumbered 602.

The printer's imprints on the half-title verso and on page 516, are the same as in No. 17. The last two lines on the half-title recto, in roman and italic small capitals respectively, have been reset from one line of italics in Nos. 17 and 18.

At the foot of the page numbered 516 is the catchword *This*, followed by two pages of advertising for Bagster's publications.

The title-page (Figure 14), unlike that of the octavos, has an unusual combination of *italic CAPITALS* and lower case letter *s* in the word *MAN's*. There is no title-page to Part II other than a heading on the first page of text as in No. 17. However, one of the rebound copies checked, in addition to an extra plate of the 1653 cartouche and two plates depicting the six fish woodcuts in the first edition of 1653 (No. 1), has a Part II title-page which was obviously inserted and, although dated MDCCCXV, bears no resemblance to the title-page to Part II in the 1815 Bagster edition (No. 21) which, in both the regular and large paper copies examined, are reproduced from the title-page to Part II of the fifth edition of 1676 (No. 6), and are so dated.

The inserted title-page to Part II is imprinted at the foot of the verso with a woodcut printer's device which depicts a church and graveyard set amidst trees. Below the device appears, "Printed by R. Watts at Broxbourne on the River Lea. MDCCCXV." On the recto is a large woodcut (engraved by Clennel) of one of the mantlepieces in a bedroom used by Walton when visiting Cotton at Beresford Hall. The woodcut is the same as that on page 407 in the Bagster edition of 1815 (No. 21), where it is described at the foot of the page in note (2). The Walton-Cotton cipher is imprinted near the foot of the title-page.

The inserted title-page to Part II has been described in some detail since it was printed by R. Watts, who printed the 1815 Bagster edition (No. 21). It is wholly unlike the Part II title-page in the copies of the 1815 Bagster edition examined by me and may have been prepared for a proposed large paper state or may be from a large paper state not yet located.

The largest copy checked is in the original boards, covered with mottled

[33]

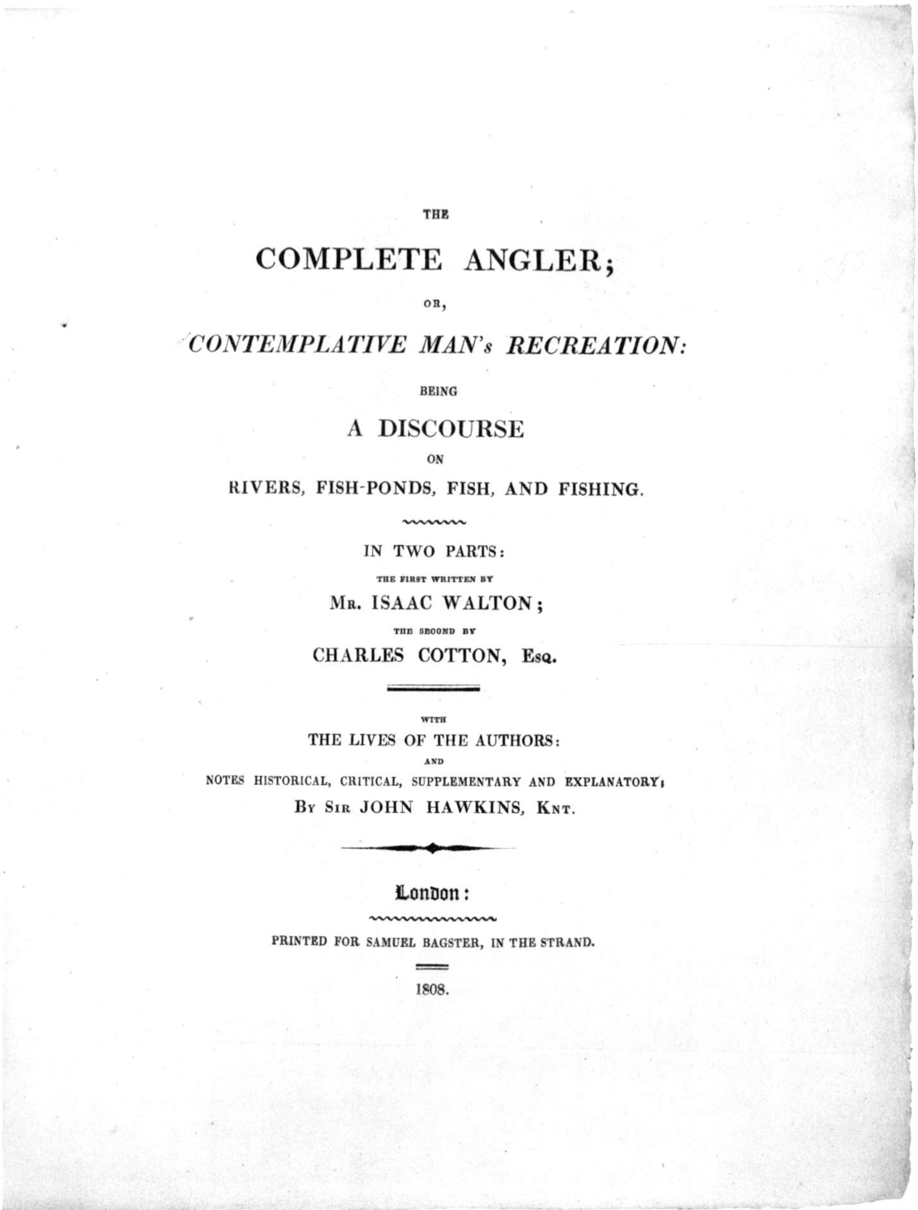

THE

COMPLETE ANGLER;

OR,

CONTEMPLATIVE MAN's RECREATION:

BEING

A DISCOURSE

ON

RIVERS, FISH-PONDS, FISH, AND FISHING.

~~~~~~

IN TWO PARTS:

THE FIRST WRITTEN BY

Mr. ISAAC WALTON;

THE SECOND BY

CHARLES COTTON, Esq.

WITH

THE LIVES OF THE AUTHORS:

AND

NOTES HISTORICAL, CRITICAL, SUPPLEMENTARY AND EXPLANATORY;

By Sir JOHN HAWKINS, Knt.

London:

~~~~~~~~~~

PRINTED FOR SAMUEL BAGSTER, IN THE STRAND.

1808.

Figure 14   The First Bagster (Quarto) Edition (No. 19).
The first sumptuous edition

brown paper as issued, with a printed paper label on the spine printed thus, | ——— | The | Complete Angler. | ——— | *Seventh Edition,* | with Additions, | both of | Matter and Plates. | ——— |. All edges are untrimmed. Inside both the front and the back cover is a single white leaf, both apparently from the same stock. The leaf at the back is watermarked 1809, suggesting that the year the signatures, on paper watermarked 1807, were bound up. Pasted inside the front cover of this copy is a printed index list of the illustrations, as for the other two printings. The list has the same ruled lines at top and bottom, and appears to be on the same paper as the spine label.

While the Bagster quarto is, like the octavo, a reprint of the 1676 edition (No. 6), bibliographers have heretofore apparently considered it merely a large paper issue of the octavo (No. 17). But it is evident that it is quite a different book, not only in the points mentioned above, but also in that the type is set differently, with fewer lines per page, and more words per line than in the octavo issues.

The sequence of the three printings has yet to be established, perhaps from comparative study of contemporary reviews and announcements in the British press.

1810

20. Bagster's Reprint

THE COMPLEAT ANGLER, by Isaac Walton.
London: MDCCCX. Printed for S. Bagster, in the Strand.

Copies examined: Harvard, Horne (3), Princeton. Others: CSmH, CtHT, CtY, DLC, NN, TxU.

Size: $5\frac{3}{4}'' \times 4\frac{1}{2}''$.

Pagination: [18], [1]-215, [216-217], 218-246, [2].

On the title-page verso and, at the foot of page 246 is imprinted, "Printed by Mercier and Chervet, Bartholomew-Close, London." A reprint of the 1653 title-page precedes the text. Two pages of advertisements of Bagster's publications follow page 246, where *The Complete Angler* (the 1808 Bagster, Nos. 17, 18, 19) is listed as number one, "being a splendid edition" and selling at "15s. or, on royal paper, 1l 7s."

The illustrations consist of six engravings of fish and two pages of music (the second of which is printed upside down) from the first edition of 1653 (No. 1). Some copies of this edition are extra illustrated with as many as 16 or 17 full-page engravings of fish, sometimes contemporarily hand colored, (one of the Horne copies contains all 17 of the engravings, hand colored). These additional engravings are identical with the 17 by Philip Audinet that are in Bagster's first edition of 1808 (Nos. 17, 18, 19).

[35]

The Scott engraving of the Huysman portrait of Walton, although inserted in some copies, was not made for this edition, as stated in previous bibliographies. In its untrimmed state, the following appears below the foot of the plate's impression, "Published August 31st, 1811, By J. Weble, 18, Warwick Square, London." It was used originally to illustrate an article, "Memoirs of Isaac Walton" in the August, 1811, issue of the *Sporting Magazine,* vol. 38, No. 227. The ascription error arose from the publisher's dateline having been trimmed before the frontispiece was tipped in by the binder.

This reprint was published in paper covered boards, untrimmed. A typesetting of the first edition title-page, without the cartouche, is printed on the front cover, with an announcement of Bagster's 1808 *Angler* on the back cover. In addition to the usual titling, the spine is imprinted, "Engravings | (illegible word) | from | Silver Plates." John A. Simpson, well-known London bookseller, has called attention to the section in *Gentleman's Magazine* for April, 1810, "Literary Intelligence," page 336, which, in referring to this edition states, *inter alia,* "The Lovers of Walton and of Angling will soon be gratified with an exact reprint of the first edition of the Complete Angler; the Plates will be exquisitely engraved on silver . . ." and ". . . The number printed will be limited . . ." The use of silver plates was in the tradition of the first edition fish engravings which many thought were engraved on silver (see notes to the first edition). The article makes no reference to a portrait. According to *Westwood's Chronicle* (1864), stocks of both this edition, and that of 1808, were partly consumed by a fire at Bagster's.

While not to be considered a facsimile, this is the first attempt at an exact reprint of the first edition of 1653 (No. 1).

1815

21. The Second Bagster Edition
(Also called Ninth, half-titled eighth, Hawkins)

THE COMPLEAT ANGLER, . . . by Mr. Izaak Walton, . . . by Charles Cotton, Esq. . . . London: Printed for Samuel Bagster, in the Strand, By R. Watts, at Broxbourne, on the River Lea, Herts. MDCCCXV.

Copies examined: Harvard, Horne (2). Others: CSmH, CtHT, CtY, DLC, NjP, NN, PPA, ViU, WU.

Size: 8vo. $9\frac{1}{8}'' \times 5\frac{7}{8}''$, and in a large paper, extra illustrated "edition," $11'' \times 8\frac{5}{8}''$, with special title-page.

Collation: 8^0: π^2, A^4, $B^8(B_1+_1)$, C^8, $D^8(D_5+_1, D_6+_1)$, $E^8(E_8+_1)$, $F^8(F_8+_1)$, G^8, $H^8(H_5+_1+_1, H_7+_1)$, I^8, $K^8(K_3+_1)$, $L-M^8$, $N^8(N_5+_1, N_7+_1)$, $O^8(O_5+_1)$,

$P^8(P4+1, P6+1)$, $Q^8(Q1+1, Q2+1, Q6+1)$, $R^8(R1+1, R3+1)$, $S^8(S4+1+1)$, $T^8(T3+1, T4+1)$, U^8, $X^8(X4+1)$, $Y^8(-Y6$ or $Y7)$, $Z^8(Z4+1)$, $2A^8(2A3+1+1, 2A5+1)$, $2B^8(2B6+1+1+1)$, $2C^8(2C8+1)$, $2D^8-2G^8$.

Note: This complicated collation, kindly prepared for me by Dr. A. G. F. Buchheim, of the Hunt Botanical Library, reports the location of inserted leaves (here identified by the "+1") bearing the appropriate text with continuous pagination and reproducing the engraved figures. These leaves on a thicker paper with harder finish, chosen presumably to ensure figure reproductions of maximum crispness, are very skillfully tipped in (sometimes two together, as in H5). This very unusual situation was planned prior to imposition of any of the formes for the book, for at that time their page numbers had to be determined and omitted from paginations assigned the signatures. The properly numbered 29 inserted leaves were printed separately, as were the engraved plates, and added at time of binding.

Pagination summary: [1-11], 12-514, followed by 20-page index.

At the foot of the last page of the index is imprinted, "Printed by R. Watts at Broxbourne, on the River Lea." The title-page to Part II, imprinted with the Walton-Cotton cipher, and dated 1676, is from the fifth edition (No. 6).

There are 50 illustrations consisting of eight full-page copperplates after Wale, 17 engravings of fish, two plates each of fishing tackle and music from previous Hawkins editions, all engraved by Philip Audinet, who reproduced for this edition the cartouche from the first edition (No. 1) on the half-title, and ten small text engravings. In addition, there are six plates by George M. Greig after John Linnell, who also engraved the Peter Lely portrait of Cotton. The Huysman frontispiece portrait of Walton was engraved by Charles Hayter. There are also two woodcuts from previous Hawkins editions.

The anonymous manuscript in The Kienbusch Library on Fresh Water Angling, in the Firestone Library at Princeton, *Catalogue of Books on Angling,* states that this edition was "Published at [*sic*] Demi octavo, one pound, four shillings. Royal octavo, two pounds, two shillings." The Harrison manuscript in the same library states on page 535, in reference to this edition, "The advertisement is dated May, 29, 1815 ... published at 24 shillings. Boards." This is probably the same advertisement which, without the selling price, appeared at the front of this edition.

This Bagster edition, one of the most handsome of the early *Anglers,* is from the fifth edition of 1676 (No. 6), edited with notes by Sir Henry Ellis (1777-1869), who became chief librarian of the British Museum.

1822

22. The Tenth (so-called Ninth) Hawkins Edition

THE COMPLETE ANGLER, . . . By Mr. Izaak Walton. . . . By Charles Cotton, Esq. . . . London: Printed for James Smith, 163, Strand. 1822.

Copies examined: Harvard, Horne (3), Princeton. Others: CSmH, CU, CtHT, CtY, NBu, ViU.

Size: 7¹⁵⁄₁₆″ × 5⅛″.

Pagination: [i-iii], iv-vi, [vii-ix], x-xliii, [xliv-xlv], xlvi, [xlvii], xlviii-l, [li], lii-lx. [1]-241, [242-243], 244, [245-247], 248-257, [258-259], 260-262, [263], 264, [265], 266, [267], 268, [269-271], 272-361, [362], 363-377, [378], 379-383, [384]-388.

On the woodcut vignette verso of the title-page there is imprinted "London: Printed by W. Lewis, Finch-Lane." At the foot of page 388 this reads "Printed by W. Lewis, 21, Finch-Lane, London." At the foot of page 383 appears "Directions to the Binder" showing the suggested placement of the illustrations. "A List of New and Popular Works, published and sold by James Smith, 163, Strand, opposite the new church," is on pages [384]-388. (see no. 15 re sequence designation of Hawkins eds.)

This edition is illustrated with 15 plates: portraits of Walton and Cotton by Jacob Huysman and Sir Peter Lely respectively, both engraved by George Maile; a group of fish by Stephen Elmer; a view of St. Albans by Patrick Nasmyth; Prior Silksteed's Chapel (Winchester) engraved by Wilson Lowry after H. C. Shenton; and ten engravings of Walton association and fishing scenes which, according to Arnold Wood's *Bibliography* . . . (p. 41), were "re-engraved after drawings by S. Wale," and he adds that, "Some copies were issued with the portraits only."

These 15 illustrations, some in this edition with a Gosden imprint, are listed in Thomas Gosden's Catalogue (London 1825), as having been published by him. All appear in Thomas Zouch's *The Life of Isaac Walton; including notices of his Contemporaries,* London, Septimus Prowett, London, 1823, 14 with Gosden's name, and one, "Fly Fishing," unsigned, which, however, does carry Gosden's name in the Zouch *Life* . . . of 1826.

The copy at Princeton is in the original gray paper over boards with a paper label on the spine which, in addition to the usual titling, reads, "with 15 plates 18s." A Horne copy, in blue paper, has paper spine-label reading in addition "portraits only, 12s." All edges are untrimmed in both copies.

This reissue of the previous Hawkins editions is one of the earliest of the *Anglers* to be of interest primarily because of the illustrations. In the series of Hawkins editions and reissues, this tenth Hawkins follows the seventh Hawkins (No. 16). The eighth Hawkins is treated as the first Bagster edition (Nos. 17-19), and the ninth Hawkins is treated as the second Bagster edition (No. 21).

[38]

1823

23. The First Major Edition

THE COMPLETE ANGLER of Izaak Walton and Charles Cotton:
... London: John Major, Fleet-Street, Adjoining Serjeant's-Inn.
MDCCCXXIII.

Copies examined: Harvard (2), Horne (2), Others: CSmH, CtHT, CtY, ICN, ICU, MB, MdBP, NjP, NN, OC, OCU.

Size: 6⁹⁄₁₆″ × 3¹⁵⁄₁₆″; large paper 7⁹⁄₁₆″ × 4⁹⁄₁₆″.

Collation: a⁴, b-g⁴, h², B-I⁴, K-U⁴, X-Z⁴, 2A-2II⁴, 2K-2U⁴, 2X-2Y⁴, 2Z⁸, 3B-3F⁴, 3G²=236.

Pagination: [i-iii], iv-xx, [xxi], xxii-lx, [1]-262, [263-265], 266-361, [362], 363-367, [368], 369-403, [404], 405-411, [412].

On the title-page verso, and on the last page, is printed, "Printed at the *Shakspeare Press,* by W. Nicol, Cleveland Row, St. James's." A device of the publisher, John Major, appears on the title-page (see Fig. 11) and on the last page.

The illustrations consist of 14 copperplates engraved or etched by R. Ashby, H. Cook, Charles Pye, E. Smith, J. T. Smith, after drawings or paintings by Huysman, Peter Lely, Frederick Nash, and Wale. In addition there are 77 woodcuts drawn by D. Blaine, W. Blake, G. W. Bonner, W. H. Brooke, John Capes, Francis Chantry, A. Cooper, J. Linnell, J. Meadows, T. Mosses, Robertson, Shepherd, W. Smith, J. Thompson, R. Thomson, J. Thurston, and H. White, engraved by G. W. Bonner, R. Branston, W. Hughes, T. Mosses, J. Thompson, and H. White. Among the woodcuts is the familiar headpiece to the Introductory Essay (p. xxi), drawn by W. H. Brooke and engraved by G. W. Bonner. This woodcut, depicting Walton's five biographies, was altered by J. W. Archer for the fourth Major edition of 1844 (No. 55), and used repeatedly thereafter. Little is known of the W. Blake mentioned above, but he was not *the* famous William Blake. In the "Descriptive List of the Embellishments," at the top of page xvi, number 70, the page number for the "Exterior View of Theobald's Palace" is given incorrectly as 382 (instead of p. 384), and woodcut 77 (p. 411) indexed as "Copied and Engraved by H. White," is signed "Thompson." The plates in some of the large paper copies are mounted on India paper.

In 1834 Francis Douce gave his large library to Oxford University. In the Douce Collection at Oxford's Bodleian Library there is a set of proofs on India paper of the 18 woodcuts of fish in this edition. The set was given to Douce by T. F. Dibdin the bibliographer, whose presentation, in Dibdin's handwriting reads:

Francis Douce Esq.
from his attached and obliged Friend T. F. Dibdin, June 24, 1828.

[39]

"There were *very few* copies of these cuts (from Mr. Major's beautiful edition of Walton's Angler) separately printed on India paper. They are preserved to exhibit the perfection of the Art of wood engraving." T.F.D.
Titling on the spine reads:
PISCES WALTONIANA. EDIT MAJOR MDCCCXXIV

However, all the cuts apparently are from the 1823 edition since the only cut which is not identical in the 1823 and 1824 editions, the grayling, is present with its 1823 background of a village with church steeples. Since this background was eliminated in the 1824 edition, the entire set of plates is probably from the 1823 edition.

The anonymous manuscript, *Catalogue of Books on Angling,* in The Kienbusch Library on Fresh Water Angling, in the Firestone Library at Princeton, states that this edition was "Published at 12 mo. 18 shillings — Crown octavo one pound sixteen shillings, called large paper." Based on the fifth edition of 1676, this is the first of some 60 Major editions and reprints. Although the introduction was by John Major, the publisher, the actual editor who prepared the notes was the antiquary, Richard Thompson.

1824

24. The Second Major Edition

THE COMPLETE ANGLER of Izaak Walton and Charles Cotton: ... London: John Major, Fleet-Street, Adjoining Serjeant's-Inn. MDCCCXXIV.

Copies examined: Harvard, Horne, Trinity, Others: CSmH, CU, CU-A, CU-I, CtY, FU, ICU, MA, MdBP, NN, NNC, NRU, RPB, ViU.

Size: $6\frac{3}{4}'' \times 4''$ regular; $8'' \times 5\frac{1}{16}''$ large paper.

Pagination summary: [i]-lviii, [1]-416 plus two leaves of the publisher's advertisements.

On the title-page verso appears, "Printed at the Shakspeare Press, by W. Nicol, Cleveland-Row, St. James's." The publisher's device is on the title-page only, and does not appear on the last page as in the first Major. The error in the first Major edition, ascribing woodcut 77 to H. White, has been corrected; likewise the error in indexing the "Exterior view of Theobald's Palace" has been rectified by having been moved to page 21. On page xxx "will be" is misprinted "willeb;" on page xlix, line 19, "been" is misprinted "bee;" and in the last word on line 20 on the same page, the "o" in "to" did not print completely.

The illustrations consist of 14 copperplates from the first Major edition of which nine have been re-engraved; one each by B. Gibbon, W. Raddon,

J. H. Robinson, and C. Rolls; and five by W. R. Smith. In addition there are the 77 woodcuts from the first Major edition of 1823 (No. 23).

The large paper copies of this edition, issued in very dark gray paper over boards, have a white paper titling label on the spine, which reads in addition to the titling, *Large Paper* Price £1. 16 *s.* The plates are printed on India paper and laid down. The anonymous manuscript in The Kienbusch Library on Fresh Water Angling, in the Firestone Library at Princeton, *Catalogue of Books on Angling,* gives the same sizes and prices for this edition as for the first Major edition of 1823 (No. 23), 12 mo. 18 shillings, crown octavo, called large paper, one pound sixteen shillings.

Although Oliver (p. 53), referring to the 77 woodcuts, states, "these also are re-engraved for the most part by W. R. Smith," there seems to be little, if any supporting evidence in the woodcuts for this statement, and Oliver does not elaborate on his observation.

The "Descriptive List of the Embellishments" gives evidence of careful editing as it was changed to show W. R. Smith as the engraver of five plates, as well as changes in the engravers of other plates and errors cited above for the woodcut listings were corrected. However, W. R. Smith is not cited as the engraver of any of the woodcuts—in fact the artists and engravers of the woodcuts (with the exception of the corrections noted above) are the same as the first Major edition. Each woodcut in the first and second Major edition has been compared with its counterpart and changes could be found only in two; the background in "The Grayling" (p. 32 each ed.) has been eliminated in the 1824 edition, and the description corrected in the index; the "Portrait of Thomas Coriate the Traveller" (p. 400, 1st Major; p. 402, 2nd Major) has an elaborate frame added in the second Major, but no change was made in the index. Westwood and Satchell's *Bibliotheca Pisca-toria* . . . , Westwood's *Chronicle* . . . , and Wood's *Bibliography* . . . , all refer to new or re-engraved plates, but do not mention any changes in the woodcuts.

Based on the cited details in the editions examined as set forth above, and the three opinions noted, I can find no indication that more than the two woodcuts mentioned above were re-engraved for this edition, and in neither case is W. R. Smith to be credited with the changes, as he was in the re-engravings he did for the plates.

This reissue of the first Major edition has some minor changes in Thompson's "Notes," and Major composed and added a four-page poem to his "Introductory Essay."

25. The First Tegg (11th Hawkins) Edition

THE COMPLETE ANGLER of Izaak Walton and Charles Cotton. Chiswick: Printed by C. Whittingham, College House. Sold by Thomas Tegg, 73, Cheapside; R. Jennings, Poultry, London: and Richard Griffin and Co. Glascow. 1824.

Copies examined: Fly Fishers' Club, Harvard, Horne (3). Others: CSmH, CtHT, CtY, IU, NjP, NN, OClRC.

Size: leaves vary from 5³⁄₁₆″ to 5⁷⁄₁₆″×3⅛″ to 3⁵⁄₁₆″ untrimmed.

Pagination summary: Vol. I, Part I, [i]-viii, [1]-64, lxv-lxxvi, [77]-267. Vol. II, Part I (continued), [1]-108. Part II, [109]-284, [4].

The four pages at the end advertise "Books printed by C. Whittingham, Chiswick." At the foot of the last page in Volume I, and at the foot of page 284 in Volume II the printer's imprint reads, "C. Whittingham, College House, Chiswick." The illustrations consist of two engraved, unsigned, portrait frontispieces, of Walton in Volume I, of Cotton in Volume II, and, in addition, a different woodcut vignette by Thompson on each of the two title-pages. In one of the Horne copies, the folio number is lacking on page 17, Volume I.

This edition was issued by the publisher in paper covered boards, in two separate volumes, untrimmed. "Whittingham's Cabinet Library" and full titling is imprinted within type ornament borders on the front covers. The page of advertising at the end of Volume II listing 38 previous titles, in 48 volumes in the Cabinet Library, is repeated on the back covers, also within type ornament borders which, however, are not those on the front; at the top right corner, just outside the border, Volume I is numbered 49; and Volume II, 50. In addition to the usual titling, the spines are imprinted "Cabinet Library" and "Price 8s."

This reissue of the Hawkins edition of 1797 (No. 16), is the first *Angler* to be published in two separate volumes.

[1824]

26. [The Maunder Edition]

Walton's [Isaac] Angler
[London?] Maunder [1824].

Copies examined: None seen.

Size reported: Foolscap 8vo.

The possibility of the existence of this edition is mentioned by Westwood and Satchell in both their *Bibliotheca Piscatoria . . . 1883*, and *The Chronicle of The Compleat Angler . . . 1888*; also by Oliver in *A New Chronicle of The Compleat Angler* (No. 22, 1936). In each case, reference is made to the *London Catalogue*, or *London Catalogue of Books*, where it is listed three times between 1810 and 1839, and described as,

"Walton's (Isaac) Angler   f'cap 8vo.   6 shillings — Maunder"

Diligent search on my part has been no more successful than that of others before me and, so far as is known, the publication of this edition by Samuel Maunder has yet to be established. It might well be a ghost.

1825

27. The Gosden (12th Hawkins) Edition

THE COMPLETE ANGLER; . . . By Isaac Walton, and Charles Cotton. Esq. . . . London: Thomas Gosden, Bedford Street, Covent Garden. MDCCCXXV.

Copies examined: Harvard (2), Horne, Virginia, Yale. Other: ViW.

Size: 7%6″ × 4¹³⁄₁₆″.

Pagination: [i-iii], iv-vi, [vii-ix], x-xliii, [xliv-xlv], xlvi, [xlvii], xlviii-l, (li), lii-lx, [1]-241, [242-243], 244, [245-247], 248-257, [258-259], 260-262, [263], 264, [265], 266, [267], 268, [269-271], 272-361, [362], 363-377, [378], 379-383.

The title-page is printed within three ruled lines on what appears to be a prebinding wrapper (see Figure 15). The title-page to Part II, unchanged for this edition, is dated 1822.

The illustrations comprise eight engraved portraits, 50 other plates, and 18 woodcuts. Two of the portraits and 12 plates are from the Hawkins edition published by James Smith in 1822 (No. 22); and 19 plates are from Thomas Zouch's *Life of Isaac Walton; . . .* published in 1823 by Septimus Prowett. Those illustrations which were printed separately and mounted in the text include woodcuts from Thomas P. Lathy's, *The Angler . . .* (published by Thomas Gosden in 1819), and engravings after Gosden's *Sportsman's Buttons.* The artists include Huysman, Lely, Nasmyth, Elmer, Stanfield, Wilson, Cooper, Shepherd, and Wale, while among the engravers are Maile, Giller, Kernot, Scott, Lowry, and Greig.

It seems likely that each copy produced may be unique, since there are 11 separately printed and mounted illustrations which vary to some extent in each of these copies. Three copies each have three such illustrations not

Figure 15   The Gosden (12th Hawkins) Edition (No. 27). One of 25 copies published and bound by Thomas Gosden, sportsman, bibliopole, and binder of angling books

THE

COMPLETE ANGLER;

OR

CONTEMPLATIVE MAN'S RECREATION:

BEING

A DISCOURSE

ON

RIVERS, FISH-PONDS, FISH,

AND

FISHING.

By ISAAC WALTON,

AND

CHARLES COTTON, Esq.

WITH

BIOGRAPHICAL AND ELUCIDATORY NOTES,

By SIR JOHN HAWKINS, Knt.

ILLUSTRATED BY SEVERAL FINELY ENGRAVED
PORTRAITS, VIEWS, FISH, &c.

LONDON:

THOMAS GOSDEN, BEDFORD STREET,
COVENT GARDEN.

MDCCCXXV.

in the others. One other copy has nine that are different from those in any of the other copies. Fishing motifs, most of them from Lathy's *The Angler* . . . , constitute the majority of such illustrations in these copies while all but one figure in the fourth copy depict field sports motifs in small circular engravings from Gosden's *Sportsman's Buttons*, and a fifth copy has four engravings not present in any of the other copies. These illustrations are on pages vi, xl, lix, 50, 262, 266, 278, 303, 335, 349, and 361.

The copies examined are all in the green morocco of the well-known Gosden binding, embellished with his bronze Walton and Cotton medals and fishing buttons, a binding that W. L. Andrews in his book on Gosden (1906), likens to the work of a blacksmith. The emblematic gold tooling is not identical in the copies seen, but all four copies have "Gosden's Illustrations" in gold at the foot of the spine.

This Gosden reissue of the Hawkins edition published by James Smith in 1822 (No. 22), was limited to 25 copies. There is a pencilled note to this effect in one of the Harvard copies. Oliver makes a similar statement regarding Dr. Samuel W. Lambert's copy. In the Horne copy there is a note in ink, signed and apparently written by Gosden, which reads, "Only 25 Copies Illustrated & Bound."

1825

28. The Dove (13th Hawkins) Edition

THE COMPLETE ANGLER: . . . by I. Walton and C. Cotton. . . . London: Printed for the Proprietors, by J. F. Dove. 1825.

Copies examined: Harvard, Horne (2), Trinity. Others: CSmH, CtY, DI, MA, NjP, NN.

Size: 5⅛″ × 2¹⁵⁄₁₆″.

Pagination summary: [1]-420.

At the foot of the last page is imprinted "Printed by J. F. Dove, St. John's Square."

The illustrations consist of a frontispiece portrait of Walton, framed by the cartouche of the 1653 edition and an engraved title-page with a vignette of Cotton, both engraved on copper by John Romney, son of *the* Romney. This is the only title-page known to me to bear Cotton's portrait, since he is usually portrayed in connection with Part II. Following the engraved title-page is the printed title-page from which the above heading is taken. Between pages 408 and 409 are four unsigned full-page woodcuts, two showing four fish and two with five fish.

This edition was issued in paper covered boards. On the front cover, within double rule borders, is a title-page dated 1825 which, while similar to the printed one mentioned above, has been embellished by a circular device surmounted by a crown, with the motto of the Order of the Garter on the perimeter. The spine has the usual titling and, near the foot, "Price 5s." On the back cover, headed "The English Classics," is a long list of titles including this edition which is listed as "Walton's and Cotton's Angler," priced 5 shillings. The leaves are untrimmed.

This is a new printing of the Hawkins edition of 1797 (No. 16).

1825

29. The First Pickering Edition

THE COMPLETE ANGLER; . . . by Izaak Walton, . . . by Charles Cotton. . . . London: William Pickering. MDCCCXXV.

Copies examined: Harvard, Horne (2), Princeton (2). Others: CSmH, CU, CtHT, CtY, IaU, NN.

Size: $3^{11}\!/_{16}''\times2\frac{1}{8}''$.

Collation: 8π, 1-19⁸, 20⁷(−8, −20)=167. Signature 15 miskeyed 5.

Pagination summary: [2], [i-v], vi-xvi, 1-314, [4].

On the printed title-page verso appears "Thomas White, Printer, Johnson's Court," and, at the foot of the last page, "Printed by Thomas White." The illustrations consist of a frontispiece (The Greeting), and an engraved title-page, both dated 1825 and engraved by Augustus Fox after Stothard; 15 woodcuts of fish, and one page of music. The two pages at the front were used by Pickering to announce and request subscribers for a new edition of the Angler," . . . with Designs by T. Stothard, Esq. R. A. . . . notes original and selected . . . and, in an appendix, will be reprinted entire, the celebrated Treatyse of Fysshynge with an Angle . . . by Dame Julians [sic for Juliana] Barnes. . . ." So far as is now known this proposed edition did not materialize.

Pages [v]-ix are devoted to "Biographical Notices of Walton and Cotton," and the only editorial comment consists of one page at the end containing notes A and B, that elaborate on the textual descriptions of the Walton-Cotton cipher over the door of Cotton's fishing house, and in the figure of the famous Pike Pool on pages 257 and 275.

This edition was issued in cloth in at least three colors, red, very dark green, and mustard yellow, with a paper label on the spine reading "Walton's Angler 6s bds." The leaves are uncut. It was published as part of Pickering's Diamond Classics series, and is a reprint from the fifth edition of 1676 (No. 6).

1826

30. The Second Pickering Edition

THE COMPLETE ANGLER; . . . by Izaak Walton, . . . by Charles Cotton. . . . London: William Pickering. MDCCCXXVI.

Copies examined: Harvard, Horne, Princeton. Others: CSmH, CtHT, ViU.

Size: $4\frac{15}{16}'' \times 2\frac{11}{16}''$.

Collation: 1π, [a⁸], b⁴(b4+1), 1-4⁸, 5⁸(2nd 5+1, 4th 5+1), 6⁸(4th 6+1), 7⁸(7th 7+1, 9th 7+1), 8⁸(4th 8+1), 9-19⁸, 20⁴, 21⁴(−4th 21)=179.

Pagination summary: [2], [i-iii], iv-xxv, [xxvi], [1]-325, [326], [4].

The printer's imprint appears four times; on the half-title verso and the verso of page 325 as "Thomas White Printer Crane Court" and, above the 1826 date on the title-page to Part II, and at the foot of the last index page at the end as, "Printed by Thomas White." A four-page index is at the end.

The illustrations, all woodcuts, consist of the title-page vignette (repeated on page [1]), and seven additional woodcuts, all recut from scenes in the first Hawkins edition (No. 9); a page of music; and 20 woodcuts of fish. All illustrations appear to be by C. Nesbit, who signed the fish woodcut on page 180. The initials C.N. are on seven additional illustrations—the rest are unsigned.

Sixteen of the preliminary pages at the front contain a "Biographical Notice of Walton," which also includes some material on Cotton, including his poem, "The Retirement: . . ." (repeated after Walton's letter to Cotton in Part II). Following Walton's "To All Readers . . . ," is a paragraph (p. xxv) which reads:

> It has not been thought necessary or desirable to introduce notes in this edition of the "Complete Angler," which is got up rather in relation to its literary and poetical than its technical character. To most readers they are necessary or readily supplied by the common books of reference, while on the other hand, they have often only the effect of disturbing the tone of the more agreeable thoughts excited by the text.

Nevertheless, notes A and B from the first Pickering edition (No. 29) are included (p. 325).

The publisher's binding examined is in green cloth with yellow end papers. Both covers and the spine are blind stamped with decorative designs. Gilt stamped near the top of the spine is "Walton's Angler" and, at the foot, also in gilt, "Pickering." All edges are untrimmed.

This edition, as issued in the publisher's binding, certainly could not be confused with the 1827 edition, and undoubtedly was issued by Pickering in 1826 (see Oliver p. 69, who agrees). Its *Angling* text is a reissue from the fifth edition of 1676 (No. 6).

31. The Prowett (3rd Pickering) Reprint

The | COMPLETE ANGLER; | or the | Contemplative Man's | Recreation. | —— | Two Parts. | The First | By Izaak Walton, | The Second | By Charles Cotton. | —— | London: | Septimus Prowett. | 1826.

Copies examined: Harvard, Trinity. Other: CSmH.

Size: 4⅞″×2¹¹⁄₁₆″.

Collation: (Trinity copy) [a⁸], b⁴(b4+1), 1-4⁸, 5⁸(2nd 5+1, 4th 5+1), 6⁸(4th 6+1), 7⁸(7th 7+1, 9th 7+1), 8⁸(4th 8+1), 9-19⁸, 20⁴, 21⁴(−2nd, 3rd, 4th 21)=176. Harvard copy is the same except b² instead of b⁴(−b3 and b4)=173.

Pagination summary (Trinity copy) [i-iii], iv-xxv, [xxvi], [1]-325, [326]. Harvard copy: [i-iii], iv-xx, [1]-325, [326].

The pagination of the copies examined is the same except that the Harvard copy lacks pages [xxi], xxii-xxv, "To all readers of this discourse...," and [xvi], a blank. Both lack the half-title and the four-page index at the end, present in the second Pickering of 1826 (No. 30). With these exceptions, and a different title-page which is within single ruled lines with a type ornament at each corner (Figure 16), the sheets are the same as (No. 30). On the printed title-page verso, and at the foot of page (326) is imprinted, "Thomas White, Printer, Crane Court," and, above the 1826 date on the title-page to Part II, "Printed by Thomas White." Notes A and B from the first Pickering edition (No. 29) are included on page 325 in both copies examined. The note on page xxv which appears in both the Trinity copy of this edition and the second Pickering (No. 30) has been excised and pasted at the foot of page xx in the Harvard copy which, as noted, lacks page xxv.

The woodcut illustrations are those of the second Pickering, except that the title-page lacks the vignette. However, the Walton and Cotton portraits and the engraved title-page, all from the fourth Pickering edition (No. 33), and all dated 1827, have been inserted before the printed title-page at the front of the Trinity copy. In the Harvard copy, an oversize, engraved, but undated title-page, trimmed to fit the book, has been inserted at the front.

The Trinity copy is in blue-green watered silk over boards, with tan leather lettering piece on which is imprinted "Walton's Angler," between double rules all in gilt. The end papers are very pale green. The leaf edges are untrimmed. The Harvard copy is in unlettered and undecorated violet cloth with white end papers. Both copies are printed on thin paper.

In Wright's *Sporting Books in the Huntington Library* (1937), this reprint is number 191, and is listed thus, "No. 190 with a new title-page; pp. [xxi]-xxv and index omitted" (No. 190 is the 2nd Pickering). These are the same pages lacking in the Harvard copy.

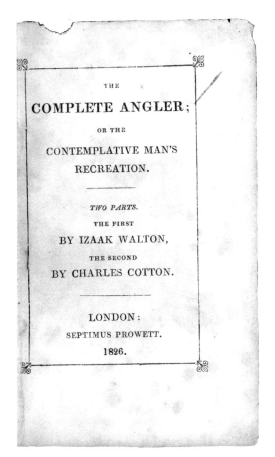

THE

COMPLETE ANGLER;

OR THE

CONTEMPLATIVE MAN'S
RECREATION.

TWO PARTS.

THE FIRST

BY IZAAK WALTON,

THE SECOND

BY CHARLES COTTON.

LONDON:

SEPTIMUS PROWETT.

1826.

Figure 16   The Prowett (3rd Pickering) Reprint (No. 31). The Sherman C. Parker Angling Collection copy in The Izaak Walton Room at Trinity College, Hartford, Connecticut. One of three known copies

Although Oliver stated in 1936 (p. 64) that Harvard's Fearing copy of this edition "... is the only copy of this edition known to exist, ..." the Huntington Library copy was probably then at San Marino, California, since it is included in its checklist of 1937. The third known copy appeared in 1965, and is now part of the Parker Angling collection at Trinity College, Hartford, Connecticut.

It is believed that these three copies, made up from sheets of the second Pickering edition of 1826 (No. 30), were probably put together in slightly different formats by Prowett, a good and reputable publisher (see Zouch, *The Life of Isaac Walton*... London, 1823), as sample copies for a proposed edition of the *Angler*, which apparently was never published.

1826

32. The Second Tegg (14th Hawkins) Edition

THE COMPLETE ANGLER of Izaak Walton and Charles Cotton.
... Chiswick: Printed by C. and C. Whittingham.
Sold by Thomas Tegg, 73, Cheapside; N. Hailes, Piccadilly;
Bowdery and Kirby, Oxford Street, London; and Richard
Griffin and Co. Glasgow. 1826.

Copies examined: Harvard, Horne (2), Princeton. Others: CSmH, CU, CtHT, CtY, NBu, NN.

Size: 5⅜″ × 3¼″.

Pagination summary: Vol. I, Part I, [i]-lxxiv, [75]-291, [292]. Vol. II, [4], Part I (continued), [1]-92, Part II, [93]-264.

The printer's imprint appears as "C. & C. Whittingham, College House, Chiswick" (foot of p. 291, in Vol. I), and as "C and C Whittingham, Chiswick" (foot of p. 264, Vol. II). The "Commendatory Verses," although included in the first Tegg, were omitted in this edition.

The illustrations consist of the frontispiece and title-page vignette from each volume of the first Tegg edition (No. 25) plus 21 woodcuts of fish and nine other woodcut illustrations (five by S. Williams, six by S. Thompson), of which 19 are unsigned, but apparently by the same engravers. The only woodcut with two signatures is the headpiece for Part II, signed by Thompson and Harvey who, according to Westwood and Satchell's *Bibliotheca Piscatoria* (1883), provided the designs for "... neat woodcuts on title-pages and in text ..."

This edition was issued by the publisher in paper covered boards, in two separate volumes, uncut, in a format very similar to the first Tegg. "Whittinghams Cabinet Library," and full titling, including ". . . with Portraits and 32 Engravings on Wood, . . ." is imprinted within type ornament borders on the front covers. Similar borders on the back covers enclose a list of 58 volumes in the Cabinet Library, where this *Angler* is listed as "49 & 50, Walton and Cotton's Angler, 9s;" at the top right hand corner, just outside the border, Volume I is numbered 49., and Volume II, 50. In addition to the usual titling, the spines are imprinted "Cabinet Library" and "Price 9s."

The copy at Princeton, issued as two volumes in one, is apparently in the publisher's cloth binding which was probably originally green, but has now faded to tan. A black leather lettering piece on the spine is gilt stamped, "Walton and Cotton's Complete Angler — with Engravings — nine shillings."

This is a new typesetting of the Tegg edition of 1824 (No. 25), in Whittingham's "Cabinet Library" series.

1827

33. The Fourth Pickering Reprint

THE COMPLETE ANGLER by Izaak Walton and Charles Cotton. London: William Pickering, Chancery Lane. MDCCCXXVII.

Copies examined: Fly Fishers', Harvard, Horne. Others: CSmH, CtY, IU, NjP, NN, ViU.

Size: 4³⁄₁₆″ × 2³⁄₄″.

The signatures, pagination, and the four printers' imprints are the same as the second Pickering edition of 1826 (No. 30).

The illustrations consist of a frontispiece portrait of Walton and a portrait of Cotton, both dated 1827, and both engraved by Mitchell after Huysman and Lely; the 1827 vignette title-page engraved by Worthington after Stothard; the 1826 title-page vignette, the music, and 27 woodcuts of the 1826 Second Pickering edition (No. 30).

The Fly Fishers' Club of London copy is in the publisher's binding of green boards with a paper spine label reading, "The Complete Angler. Walton and Cotton 7s bds."

Except for the addition of the three engravings, this reprint is a reissue of the 1826 edition (No. 30). It seems obvious that Pickering, having added the engraved title and the two plates, all dated 1827 and all bearing his name, intended this as a different edition to be issued in 1827 (see Oliver, p. 69, who agrees).

The *Angling* text is a reissue from the fifth edition of 1676 (No. 6).

1828

34. The Cole Reprint

THE COMPLEAT ANGLER ; . . . by Isaac Walton and
Charles Cotton . . .
London: Printed for William Cole, 10, Newgate Street. [1828].

Copies examined: Harvard, Horne. Others: CtHT, CtY, NN, NjP, PU.

Size: 6⅝″ × 4″.

Pagination: [i-v], vi-xx, [1]-234, [235], 236-314, (2.)

The illustrations, none of which is signed, consist of a plate of Walton and
one of Cotton plus 18 woodcuts of fish. The last two pages advertise "New
Books" published by Cole.

Page xiii has the misprint "Watkins" for "Hawkins" and in the "Contents"
the page listing for Part II, Chapter I, is misprinted 285 for 235.

The date 1828 is assigned to this undated reissue. The early bibliographers
identified it as N.D. [no date] or *circa* 1828; later ones have reported 1828,
without citation of information source. The Horne copy has the inscription
inside the front cover, "William Mathews-July 8-1828," which is accepted as
adequate evidence for the date 1828.

This edition was issued by the publisher in pinkish boards. Although
Walton's given name is spelled "Isaac" on the title-page, it was printed
"Izaac" on the paper label that gives the price as "Six Shillings."

This is a reissue of the fifth edition of 1676.

1833

35. The First Rennie Edition

THE COMPLETE ANGLER ; . . . by Izaak Walton and
Charles Cotton . . .
Edinburgh: Published, for the proprietors,
by W. & R. Chambers, Edinburgh;
W. Orr, London, and W. Curry, Jun. & Co. Dublin.
MDCCCXXXIII.

Copies examined: Harvard, Horne. Others: CU-A, CtHT, CtY, NN, NjP.

Size: 6⅝″ × 4³⁄₁₆″.

Pagination: [6], [1]-30, [31], 32-34, [35], 36-40, [41], 42-218, [219-223], 224-236, [237-239],
240, [241], 242-298, [299], 300-305, [306-309], 310-320, [321], 322-328.

On the title-page verso and at the foot of page 328 is imprinted, "Edinburgh: Printed by Andrew Shortrede, Thistle Lane."

There are two copperplates by W. H. Lizars, consisting of a frontispiece of Walton and a page of music; four woodcuts by H. Y. Sears that show Walton's house on Fleet street, Amwell Hill, punt fishing at Bowerbanks, Tottenham, and Alstonfield Church; unsigned are 21 woodcuts of fish and one of a large insect. The title-page is imprinted with the device of an owl over an arrangement of printer's flowers, which has not been noted in the reprints. The publisher's binding is in self-color boards, with a green cloth back and paper label. The leaves are untrimmed.

This Rennie edition is the first of some 20 editions or reissues published through 1857, all believed to be textually the same except for such slight title-page variations as "Izaac" for "Izaak" and, of course, the different imprint dates. While the same illustrations are used over and over for all the editions, the engraved plate of music and the full-page woodcuts of Walton's House and Amwell Hill are placed differently in almost every edition; the position of the frontispiece of Walton and the text cuts is, of course, constant. No two bindings seen are exactly the same. These reprint variations are set forth in the notes under the listing for each item examined.

This edition is a reissue from the fifth edition of 1676 (No. 6).

1834

36. The Second Rennie Reprint

THE COMPLETE ANGLER; . . . by Izaak Walton and
Charles Cotton . . .
London: Allan Bell & Co; Fraser & Co; Dublin,
W. Curry, Jr. & Co. 1834.

Copies examined: None seen.

Size reported: 16mo.

Pagination summary: [8], [1]-328.

The data given for this edition are taken from Oliver (his No. 34), who reports the illustrations to be the same as those of the 1833 Rennie edition (No. 35) of which this is a reprint.

This reprint is also listed in Wood, and Westwood and Satchell's *Bibliotheca Piscatoria*, both stating that it contains a "list of illustrations" and the last that it "forms a volume of the *British Library*."

37. The Third Rennie Reprint

THE COMPLETE ANGLER; . . . by Izaak Walton
and Charles Cotton. . . . A New Edition . . .
London: Allan Bell & Co. and Simpkin & Marshall. 1834.

Copies examined: Harvard, Yale. Others: CtHT, NN.

Size: 6¾″ × 4³⁄₁₆″.

Pagination summary: [6], [1]-328.

At the foot of page 328 is imprinted, "Edinburgh: Printed by Andrew Short-rede, Thistle Lane."
　　The two copies examined are in publisher's bindings; the Harvard copy in green cloth, the Yale copy in purple moire, each with a black paper label titled in gilt between double gilt rules. The edges are untrimmed.
　　The illustrations are those of the first Rennie edition of 1833 (No. 35) of which this is a reissue.

38. The Fourth Rennie Reprint

THE COMPLETE ANGLER; or Contemplative Man's Recreation
. . . With lives and notes by Sir John Hawkins Knight,
Edited by James Rennie, A.M. A New Edition.
Lond.: Allan Bell & Co. and Simpkin & Marshall. 1834.

Copies examined: None seen.

Size reported: 16mo.

Pagination reported: "Port. adv't. 1., pp. 328."

This reprint is listed by Oliver (his No. 36), whose description is from item No. 2044 in the Heckscher *Catalogue* (1909), in which, he writes, "this edition is the same [referring to a preceding Rennie reprint] with a different title-page."

1834

39. The Fifth Rennie Reprint

THE COMPLETE ANGLER ... by Izaak Walton and
Charles Cotton. . . .
London: Simpkin & Marshall. 1834.

Copies examined: None seen.

Size reported: 16mo.

Pagination and illustrations: Presumed to be the same as previous Rennie
reprints.

The existence of this edition is questionable. Although Oliver (p. 75), who
examined no copy, stated that his listing was based on the entry in W. W.
Sabin's *1001 Books on Angling* (London, 1882) and Westwood's mention of this
edition in his *Chronicle of the Compleat Angler* (1864), writing "It should perhaps
be added that Sabin's list is in many cases inaccurate, and his mention of this
edition is hardly conclusive proof of its existence." My careful search revealed no reference to this edition in Westwood's *Chronicle* (1864) or in Westwood and Satchell's reprint of 1888. However, in Westwood and Satchell's
Bibliotheca Piscatoria, 1883 (p. 227), the following statement appears in reference
to the early Rennie editions and reprints, "There are probably copies bearing
the name of Simpkin and Marshall alone but we have not examined one."
  Perhaps the inclusion of this listing will stimulate further a search to
establish conclusive proof of the existence of this elusive "edition." In the
absence of evidence it is treated as a reprint.

1834

40. The Sixth Rennie Reprint

THE COMPLETE ANGLER; ... by Izaak Walton and
Charles Cotton. . . .
Edinburgh: Published by Fraser & Co.
Smith, Elder, & Co. Cornhill,
London; W. Curry, Jun. & Co. Dublin. MDCCCXXXIV.

Copies examined: Horne, Princeton, Yale.

Size: $6\frac{11}{16}'' \times 4\frac{1}{8}''$.

Pagination summary: [4], [1]-328, [4].

At the foot of page 328 is imprinted, "Edinburgh: Printed by Andrew Short-rede, Thistle Lane."

In the rebound copy at Princeton, the list of illustrations, and the directions to the binder, are found in the four pages at the end, where this edition is referred to as part of the "British Library."

The Horne copy, which lacks the four pages at the end, is in the publisher's binding of rough reddish-brown cloth, with a paper label on the spine. The leaves are untrimmed.

This is a reprint of the first Rennie edition of 1833 (No. 35), with the same 28 illustrations.

1835

41. The Seventh Rennie Reprint

THE COMPLETE ANGLER; by Izaak Walton and
Charles Cotton. . . .
London: Thomas Tegg & Son, Cheapside;
R. Griffin & Co. Glasgow; Tegg, Wise & Co. Dublin. 1835.

Copies examined: Harvard, Horne, Yale. Others: CtHT, NN, NjP, ViU.

Size: $6\frac{3}{4}'' \times 4\frac{1}{8}''$.

Pagination summary: [8], [1]-328.

At the foot of page 328 is imprinted, "Edinburgh: Printed by Andrew Short-rede, Thistle Lane." The illustrations are those of the first Rennie edition of 1833 (No. 35) of which this is a reissue. The title-page identifies it "A New Edition."

Two publisher's bindings were seen; the Horne copy in self-color boards, with a dark blue cloth back and paper label, the Yale copy in purple cloth with paper label, each with the leaves untrimmed.

1835

42. The Third Major Reprint

THE COMPLETE ANGLER of Izaak Walton and
Charles Cotton: . . .
London: J. Major, Great Russell-Street, Bloomsbury.
Printed by W. Nicol, 51, Pall Mall. MDCCCXXXV.

Copies examined: Harvard, Horne, Yale (2). Others: CtHT, NjP.

Size: 6½″×4⅟₁₆″.

Pagination summary: [i]-lviii, [1]-416.

The illustrations consist of 15 plates and 77 woodcuts. These are the same, and by the same artists and engravers, as those in the 1824 Major edition, (No. 24), with the addition of a "portrait of Dr. Thomas Wharton, engraved by W. H. Worthington from a Picture in Royal College of Physicians," as noted on the title-page verso, and is number 10 in the list of copperplates.

One Yale copy is in a publisher's binding of rough dark blue-green cloth with three blind rules on the edges of the covers and decorations in blind at the corners. In the center of each cover is stamped a large vase, in gilt on the front and in blind on the back. Titling is in gilt within a gilt decoration on the spine.

This is a reprint of the Major edition of 1824, with the publishers' title-page device changed and the misprints corrected. The change in the "Introductory Essay" is the omission of the note in the second Major (p. xxiv), regarding the preparation of ". . . a distinct work, to be entitled *Waltoniana*. . . ." The rest of the "Essay," including Major's poetry, is the same.

The anonymous manuscript in The Kienbusch Library on Fresh Water Angling, in the Firestone Library at Princeton, *Catalogue of Books on Angling*, reports this issue as having been published to sell for one pound, one shilling.

1836

43. The First Nicolas Edition

THE COMPLETE ANGLER . . . by Izaak Walton and
. . . Charles Cotton . . .
London: William Pickering 1836.

Copies examined: Boston Public, Harvard (2), Horne (2), Princeton, Trinity, Yale (in parts). Others: CSmH, CtHT, DLC, ICU, MB, NN, PU, WU, ViU. In 12 separate parts at Yale. Set of separate illustrations on India paper at CtY and NN.

Size: Large paper, 10¹³⁄₁₆″×7⅜″; regular 10⁵⁄₁₆″×6⅞″; copy in parts 10⅞″× 7⁷⁄₁₆″.

Pagination summary: Vol. I, [14], [i]-ccxii, 1l., [1]-129, [130]. Vol. II 1l., [131]-436, [32].

The Pickering Anchor and Dolphin title-pages, printed in red and black, have no volume numbering, and are the same for both volumes. The

Figure 17   The First Nicolas Edition (No. 43). The Yale copy issued in 12 parts.
The Beinecke Rare Book and Manuscript Library, Yale University

printer's imprint, "C. Whittingham, Tooks Court, Chancery Lane," is on the title-page verso for each volume, and at the foot of the last page in the 32-page index in volume II. In addition, there is an engraved title-page (at "The Epistle Dedicatory"), originally used for the first Pickering edition of 1825 (No. 29), here enlarged, and dated MDCCCXXXII (1832, the year when the first three of the 12 parts in which this edition originally appeared were published). The fourth and fifth parts are dated 1833, the sixth, 1835, and seven through 12, 1836. The illustrations by some 27 artists, consist of 61 plates engraved by J. Adcock, J. G. Armytage, Byfield, W. J. Cooke, Augustus Fox, Freebairn, W. Humphrys, J. Richardson, H. Robinson, Roberts, Sparrow, J. Thompson, W. J. Wilkinson, and W. H. Worthington, after paintings and drawings by T. S. Cafe, Delamotte, Derby, Edward Hassall, W. Hixon, Huysman, Inskipp, Lely, Pine, T. Stothard, Sir Francis Sykes, Vinkenboom, Willement, and Worthington.

There are also two woodcuts of the seal given to Walton by Dr. Donne, and two pages of music.

This edition, issued in paper wrappers, to be bound as desired by the purchaser, was printed on regular and large paper, the latter having the plates on India paper and laid down. The Yale copy, in parts (Figure 17), is in brown paper wrappers, the title-pages on the front wrappers are dated as described above. The part number (*i.e.*, Part I), is printed in the upper right corner, and "*Proofs*" in the lower left hand corner of the front wrappers. "Conditions," printed on the outside of the back wrappers, describe this state as an "Imperial octavo . . . The Work will not exceed Twelve Parts. . . . The Price to Subscribers will be 9s. 6d. each Part, or with proof impressions on India paper, price 16s. each Part. . . . A few sets of the Engravings will be taken off on India paper, separately, price 16s. each Part." A slip titled "Directions to the Binder" is inserted at the front of Part XII. This Yale copy has six extra plates.

It was a favorite of the extra illustrator, and some productions have reached prodigious proportions. Probably the most elaborate is in the personal library of the Foyle family (well-known London booksellers) at Beeleigh Abbey, Maldon, Essex, England. The original two volumes have been extended to 12 folios (21″ × 15″), by the insertion of 1,438 extra illustrations listed in the bookseller's description. The relatively small leaves of the text are mounted over cutouts in the folio leaves so that both pages of a leaf may be read. The compiler was one A. A. Weston who had special title-pages printed on which appeared his initials, with the dates 1864-68 (the four years occupied in the compilation) but alas, in the title text, the editor's name, "Nicolas," is misspelled "Nicholas."

Edited by Sir Harris Nicolas, this edition was illustrated by the foremost contemporary artists, produced by an excellent printer and issued by an outstanding publisher. It has been acclaimed as the finest *Angler* ever published, although some have been critical of the plates and the editing. Although Westwood (1864), thought it "over-dressed," he called it, ". . . one of the handsomest publications of modern times, an ornament to the

Angler's Library, unique of its kind, and perhaps destined to remain so."

It was the first edition to be divided into days, contains many editor's notes and comments, and has new material on Walton and Cotton. It is a reprint from the fifth edition of 1676 (No. 6).

1836

44. The Eighth Rennie Reprint

THE COMPLETE ANGLER ; . . . by Izaak Walton and
Charles Cotton . . .
London: Allan Bell & Co. Warwick Square. 1836.

Copies examined: Harvard, Horne, Yale. Others: CSmH, DLC, MeB, NN, NjP, RPB.

Size: $6\frac{1}{2}'' \times 4\frac{1}{4}''$.

Pagination summary: [8], [1]-328.

At the foot of both the title-page verso and page 328 is imprinted, "Edinburgh: Printed by Andrew Shortrede Thistle Lane." The illustrations are the same as those of the 1833 Rennie edition (No. 35) of which this is a reprint.

Two publisher's bindings have been seen. The first is in full rough bluish-green cloth with tan end papers, the second in self-colored boards backed with dark green cloth and with white end papers. Each is titled in gilt on the spine, and has untrimmed leaves. The description in the *Hecksher Catalogue* (1909) reports marbled edges, not present in the copies examined.

1836

45. The Ninth Rennie Reprint

Walton and Cotton's COMPLETE ANGLER ; . . .
A New Edition . . .
London: Allan Bell and Co., Warwick Square; and
H. Washbourne, Salisbury Square. 1836.

Copies examined: Harvard.

Size: $6\frac{9}{16}'' \times 4\frac{1}{8}''$.

Pagination summary: [6], [1]-328.

At the foot of page 328 is imprinted "Edinburgh: Printed by Andrew Short-rede, Thistle Lane." This is a reprint of the Rennie edition of 1833 (No. 35), but the Harvard copy lacks the woodcuts of Walton's House and Amwell Hill, present in the first Rennie edition (No. 35). Note the absence of "THE" before "COMPLETE" on the title-page.

1836

46. The Tenth Rennie Reprint

THE COMPLETE ANGLER; . . . by Izaak Walton and
Charles Cotton. . . .
Edinburgh: Fraser & Co. 54, North Bridge;
H. Washbourne, London. 1836.

Copies examined: Harvard, Horne, Yale. Others: NN, NNU, NjP.

Size: $6\frac{5}{8}'' \times 4\frac{3}{16}''$.

Pagination summary: [4], [1]-328.

On the title-page verso and at the foot of page 328 is imprinted, "Edinburgh: Printed by Andrew Shortrede, Thistle Lane."
   This reprint was seen in two publisher's bindings. The first in brown cloth (faded in the copy described), with yellow end papers. Both covers are blind-stamped with a single rule on the edges, corner decorations, and a large decorative design in the middle. The spine is elaborately decorated in gilt with fish, devices related to fishing, and streamside foliage. "Walton's Angler" and "Professor Rennie" are separately gilt stamped between the decorations. The second binding is in self-colored boards backed in brown cloth (perhaps purple originally) with a paper label. The leaves are untrimmed in each copy.
   This is a reissue, with the same illustrations, of the Rennie edition of 1833 (No. 35).

1837

47. The Tilt (5th Pickering) Edition

THE COMPLETE ANGLER. by Izaak Walton and
Charles Cotton.
London: Charles Tilt, 86, Fleet-Street; J. Menzies, Edinburgh;
T. Wardle, Philadelphia. MDCCCXXXVII.

(The first edition with an American imprint)

Copies examined: Harvard, Horne (5), Princeton. Others: CtY, DLC, NN.

Size: 4″×2½″ to 4⅟₁₆″×2⅝″ uncut.

Pagination: Vol. I. [i-v], vi-[xii], [1]-152; Vol. II. [4], [1]-62; Part II, [63-65], 66, [67], 68, [69], 70-72, [73]-149, [150], [10].

"London: Bradbury and Evans, Printers, Whitefriars," is imprinted on the verso of the title-page of Vols. I and II, at the foot of page 152 of Vol. I, and in the center of page [150] of Vol. II. The illustrations consist of a frontispiece in each volume engraved on wood by Ebenezer Landells.

The half-title of each volume identifies this edition to be part of Tilts Miniature Classical Library. At the end are usually two, but as many as ten, pages of advertising for Tilt's publications, where this edition, in two volumes, is listed as available thus,

> Ornamented cloth gilt edges........1s. 6d
> Prettily bound in silk...............2   0
> Very handsome in morocco.........3   0

Four copies examined are in the least expensive group, which is further described in the advertising as "... elegantly bound in fancy embossed cloth, gilt edges, letter in gold (see Figure 18);" the fifth copy examined is in silk.

The *first* copy is in dark blue cloth, yellow end papers, all edges gilt, blind stamped borders on the covers. The gilt decoration includes a design of three small fish on the front cover and a lavish display of angling equipment and motifs, in addition to the titling on the spine. The *second*, also with all edges gilt and yellow end papers, is in green cloth with a blind embossed border on both covers, and simulated compartments and titling in gilt on the spine. The *third* in very dark green rough cloth, white end papers, gilt rules, date and titling on the spine, has the leaves uncut. All three were issued as two volumes in one. The *fourth*, in two volumes, is in brown cloth, with yellow end papers, all edges gilt, and the covers blind stamped in an overall design. The spines are titled and decorated in gilt with an elaborate display of angling equipment, similar to number one, but designed for the narrower spines of the two volume set. The *fifth*, also in two volumes, is in green moiré silk, yellow end papers, all edges gilt, the spine with gilt titling and overall gilt foliage decoration.

This edition lacks both preface and introduction, and the only editorial matter (the earlier Pickering editions), is the statement on page xi, Volume I, regarding the omission of notes and, in Volume II, part II (p. 149), Notes A and B, that elaborate on the textual descriptions of Cotton's fishing house, the Dove valley, and Pike Pool. In Volume II, reference to Note A is foot-noted on page 93 and to Note B on page 110.

This is a reissue, with the three Pickering notes, of the fifth edition of 1676 (No. 6).

The First Bethune Edition (No. 60)

The Lewis (4th Major) Edition (No. 48)

The Tilt (5th Pickering) Edition (No. 47)

Figure 18   Publishers' Bindings

1839

48. The Lewis (4th Major) Edition

THE COMPLETE ANGLER . . . by Izaak Walton and
Charles Cotton. . . .
London: L. A. Lewis, 125, Fleet-Street. MDCCCXXXIX.

Copies examined: British Museum, Harvard, Horne, Yale (2). Others: CSmH,
CtHT, DLC, NN, NjP, PU.

Size: $7^{15}\!/_{16}'' \times 5''$ (untrimmed).

Pagination summary: (26), [iv-v], vi-lxxii, [1]-396.

On the title-page verso is imprinted "London: Printed by Maurice, Clark
and Co., Howford-Buildings, Fenchurch Street."
    This edition contains 76 of the 77 woodcuts of the third Major reprint of
1835 (No. 42), the only one omitted being No. 5 in the "Descriptive List of
Embellishments," titled "Walton surrounded by the Graces." All the copperplates of the 1835 edition are repeated.
    The publisher's cloth binding, the British Museum copy in dark blue, the
Horne copy in light purple, and the Yale copies in the publisher's maroon
morocco (one light, the other very dark) all have an elaborate piscatorial
design stamped in gilt on both the front and back covers, and on the spine.
All edges are gilt. It has also been examined (in a private collection) in paper
over boards, untrimmed, without decoration except the paper label on the
spine, banded by double rules is printed, "The Complete Angler of Walton
and Cotton. Illustrated with 76 wood engravings and 15 Copper Plates
Price 15s" (see Figure 18).
    Although this is a reissue of the third Major reprint, his introductory
essay was omitted, and was replaced by the Hawkins biographies of Walton
and Cotton. It is an independent edition.

1841

49. The Chidley Reprint

THE COMPLETE ANGLER; . . . by Isaac Walton and
Charles Cotton . . .
London: I. J. Chidley, 123, Aldersgate Street. 1841.

Copies examined: Harvard, Horne (2), Princeton. Others: CtHT, CtY.

Size: $6\frac{1}{2}'' \times 4''$.

Pagination summary: [i-v], vi-xx, [1]-234, [235], 236-314, [2].

Except for two pages at the end advertising "New Books Published by W. Cole, 10, Newgate Street," the pagination and the illustrations are the same as the Cole edition of 1828 (No. 34), of which this is a reissue with a new title-page.

Misprints in the Cole edition have not been corrected: page xiii continues to read "Watkins" for "Hawkins" and, in the "Contents," the page number for Part II, Chapter I, remains 285 for 235.

Two publisher's bindings have been examined. The first (at Princeton) is in reddish-brown ribbed cloth, both covers blind stamped in the center with an arrangement of angling symbols, with a scroll type-design on the edges. The spine is elaborately decorated in gilt with angling emblems, fish, and waterside plants. The gilt titling reads "Walton's Angler | — | Many Plates." All edges are untrimmed. The second binding (Horne copy) is in similar cloth, both covers blind stamped in a simple, single line border design with ornamentation at the corners but no center decoration. All edges are untrimmed. The spine is decorated in gilt with an overall scroll-like design below gilt titling which is that of the first binding.

This is a reissue of the Cole edition of 1828, from the fifth edition of 1676 (No. 6).

1842

50. The Washbourne (5th Major) Reprint

THE COMPLETE ANGLER; . . . By Izaak Walton and
Charles Cotton. . . .
London: Henry Washbourne, Salisbury Square, Fleet Street.
MDCCCXLII.

Copies examined: Harvard, Horne, Princeton, Trinity, Yale. Others: NIC, NN, PPL, PPWI, PU.

Size: 8″×5″.

The pagination and illustrations are those of the Lewis edition of 1839 (No. 48) of which this is a reprint.

The publisher's bindings examined, one in dark green, the other in blue-green watered silk over boards, are backed with black morocco, top edges gilt. The spine is gilt stamped with the same piscatorial design used for the Lewis edition. The fore edge and lower edge of the leaves are untrimmed.

The Yale copy has eight pages of Washbourne advertisments at the end where this *Angler* is described as "Post 8vo. half morocco, gilt top, 12s., originally published at 21s." This is the earliest *Angler* known to me to have been advertised as a remainder.

51. The Sherwood and Bowyer Edition

Pocket English Classics
THE COMPLETE ANGLER. by Isaak Walton and
Charles Cotton . . .
London: Sherwood and Bowyer, 137, Strand. MDCCCXLIV.
J. Scott, Printer, 50 Hatfield-Street

Copies examined: Harvard, Horne (cloth, two volumes in one), Princeton.
Other: CtY.

Size: $4\frac{5}{16}'' \times 2\frac{5}{8}''$.

Pagination summary: Published in two paper covered volumes imprinted
Part I and Part II; the latter contains Cotton's portion of the *Angler,* which
is also designated Part II. Vol. I, Part I, [4], Text, [i]-vii, [viii], [9]-169, [170], [4];
Vol. II, Part I (continued), [171]-241, [242]; Part II, [243-244], Text, [245]-335, 246,
[247], 248, [249], 250-252, [253], 254-335.

The only illustration is a "Fac simile (*sic*) of The Original Frontispiece 1653."
Four pages of advertisments for Sherwood and Bowyer's publications are
at the end of Volume I.

 This is number 17 in the series of *Pocket English Classics,* the two paper
covered volumes sold for six pence each. A note printed inside the back
cover of Volume I reads, "Part II Will be published on the 15th of July,"
which appears to establish the priority of this edition over the three undated
issues to follow. The cover of Part I, which serves as a title-page, is dupli-
cated for Volume II, imprinted Part II. The title and imprint given above is
from the cover (within double and parallel rules) since the book actually
begins with a half-title, and has no title-page.

 This edition (of two volumes in one) was distributed also in a binding of
brown cloth, yellow end papers and, on the spine, a black leather lettering
piece with gilt titling. Only a half-title is present in this copy, which lacks
date, place of publication, publisher, printer, and advertisements (the paper
cover not retained at time of binding).

 This edition of the *Angler* is from the fifth edition of 1676 (No. 6). By con-
sensus of bibliographers, the three undated issues (Nos. 52, 53, 54) which
follow, are to be dated 1844.

52. The Lockwood Reprint

THE COMPLETE ANGLER ; . . . by Izaak Walton and
Charles Cotton . . .
London: Lockwood and Co. 7 Stationers-Hall Court [1844].

Copy examined: Harvard. Others: CtHT, CtY.

Size: 4⅛″ × 2⅝″.

Pagination summary: Vol. I, Part I, [8], [i]-vii, [viii], [9]-169, [170], [2]; Vol. II,
Part I (continued), [171]-241, [242]; Part II, [243-244], [245]-335.

The only illustration is the "Fac simile [*sic*] of The Original Frontispiece
1653." On the title-page versos of each volume and in the middle of the last
of volume II is the imprint, "London Printed by Spottiswoode and Co.
New-Street Square." Two pages of Lockwood's advertisments are at front
and back, where this reprint is listed as "Walton's Complete Angler. In Two
Parts, 6d. each; or one Vol., price 1s."
   The publisher's binding examined is dark green cloth, edges cut and
sprinkled with red dots. The front cover is blind stamped "Pocket English
Classics" at the top, and "London Lockwood & Co. Stationers Hall Court
one shilling," at the foot, with "Complete Angler" in gilt between. Both
covers have blind stamped ruled line edges with corner decorations. The
spine is titled in gilt.
   See comment regarding the publication date under the Sherwood and
Bowyer reprint (No. 51), of which this is a reissue from the same typesetting
(with new title-page).

53. The Piper Reprint

THE COMPLETE ANGLER ; . . . by Isaak Walton and
Charles Cotton. . . .
London: Piper Brothers & Co., 23, Paternoster Row. [1844].

Copies examined: Princeton, Yale.

Size: 4¹⁄₁₆″ × 2⅝″.

Pagination summary: Vol. I, Part I, [4], [i]-vii, [viii], [9]-169, [170]; Vol. II, Part I
(continued), [2], [171]-241, [242]; Part II, [243-244], [245]-335.

The only illustration is a "Fac simile [*sic*] of The Original Frontispiece 1653."
On the title-page verso of each volume is imprinted "London: Printed by
Rogerson and Tuxford, 246, Strand."

The publisher's binding examined is dark green cloth. The cover is blind
stamped "Pocket English Classics" and "London Lockwood & Co, Stationers,
Hall Court one shilling," which frames the gilt titling.

See comment regarding the publication date under the Sherwood and
Bowyer reprint (No. 51), of which this is a reissue.

[1844]

54. The First Lippincott Reprint

THE COMPLETE ANGLER; . . . by Izaak Walton and
Charles Cotton.
Philadelphia: J. B. Lippincott and Co. [1844].

(The second "edition" with an American imprint.)

Copies examined: Harvard, Princeton, Yale (2).

Size: $4\frac{3}{16}'' \times 2\frac{9}{16}''$.

Pagination summary: Vol. I. Part I, [6], [i]-vii, [viii], [9]-169, [170]: Vol. II. Part I
(continued), [2], [171]-[242]; Part II, [243-244], [245]-335. "London: Printed by
Spottiswoode and Co., New-Street Square and Parliament Street" is imprinted the title-page verso for each part, and on the verso of page 335, Part II.

The only illustration is a "Fac simile [*sic*.] of The original Frontispiece 1653."

The Yale copies (2 vols. in one) are in identical publisher's binding except
that the first copy is in dark purplish-blue cloth, the second in grayish-blue
cloth. The covers (front and back) are blind stamped "British Pocket
Classics" within a single rule panel; the spines are titled vertically in gilt
within gilt decorations. The end papers are chocolate-brown. All leaf edges
are gilt.

Although there remains uncertainty regarding the date of this reprint,
there is tentative agreement among bibliographers that it is 1844. The list
of editions in the Le Gallienne and Oxford *Anglers* (Nos. 177, 195) gives 1844
with a question mark, as does the 1888 reprint of Westwood and Satchell's
Chronicle. . . . Wood, in the fourth note under the Sherwood and Bowyer
edition of 1844 (No. 51), writes, "It is claimed that copies of this book appear
with the imprints of Lockwood & Co., Piper Brothers & Co., and Lippincott
of Philadelphia, all printed from the same plates." Oliver favors 1844 or possibly 1845 as the date for this edition; Princeton uses 1844.

It would appear that 1844 is the most probable publication date, which makes this the second *Angler* to be printed with an American imprint, the first is the Tilt edition of 1837 (No. 47). While Dr. Bethune's edition of 1847 (No. 60) was the first to be edited, printed, and published in America, it was the third edition with an American imprint.

This is a reissue of the Sherwood and Bowyer edition (No. 51) in the "Pocket English Classics" series, printed from the same plates (with new title-page). For the second Lippincott reprint (1881) which is a reissue of the 1866 Little Brown edition, see No. 87.

1844

55. The Sixth (Titled 4th) Major Edition

THE COMPLETE ANGLER, . . . of Izaak Walton and
Charles Cotton. . . .
London: D. Bogue, Fleet-Street; H. Wix, New Bridge-Street.
MDCCCXLIV.

Copies examined: Harvard, Horne (5), Princeton. Others: CSmH, CtHT, CtY, DLC, NN, NcD, OClCS, PP, PU.

Size: 6⅞″ × 4⁵⁄₁₆″; large paper, 7¹³⁄₁₆″ × 5¹⁄₁₆″.

Pagination summary: [i]-lx, [1]-418, [2], [1]-24.

The printer's imprint on the verso of the title-page reads, "Printed at the *Shakspeare Press,* by W. Nicol, 60, Pall Mall." On the page following 418 it reads: "Printed by William Nicol, Shakspeare Press, 60 Pall Mall." In the 24-page Bogue catalogue included at the end (Horne copy) dated January 1850, this edition is listed (p. 4) among the "Illustrated Works" as, "Edited by John Major, with Illustrations by Absolon. New Edition, fcp. 8vo. cloth, 12s.; morocco; 18s; large paper, boards, 24s.; morocco 31s. 6d." Since Bogue's previous style of business was "Tilt and Bogue," the miniature Tilt *Angler* of 1837, is also listed (p. 19). The title-page vignette, "View from Lea Bridge," from a drawing by T. Creswick, was used over and over in the many Major editions.

The illustrations consist of 12 engravings on steel, comprising portraits of Walton and Cotton by Huysman and Lely (copied by C. R. Bone) both engraved by Henry Robinson; a facsimile of the 1653 title-page engraved by W. Collard; and nine new renderings by John Absolon, engraved by J. T. Willmore of the familiar scenes in the earlier Major editions. There are also 74 wood engravings by John Jackson and his brother Mason Jackson from drawings or paintings by J. W. Archer, who re-engraved G. W. Bonner's head-piece of the Walton biographees for this edition. Other engravers include A. Cooper, T. Creswick, Alexander Fussell, Gompertz, George Lance, F. R.

Lee, Leitch, K. Meadows, and W. Smith. There are four errors in the "List of Embellishments;" woodcut number 7 is listed as on page lv instead of li; number 8 on page lx instead of lvi; number 9 on page lxiv instead of lx; and on page xiv the note following illustration 69 refers to a previous note on John L. Andernon as being on page viii instead of ix.

The illustrations, while similar to those in the previous Major editions, were newly drawn and engraved, and used in this form in the long succession of Major editions.

Four different publisher's bindings have been examined, each in a similar, but varying shade of brownish-purple cloth. The Princeton copy has blind stamped decorations on the covers, and the spine gilt stamped with the title, the Walton-Cotton cipher and the publication date. The covers of each of the other three have blind stamped borders, all different, but basically comprised of three rules in blind with varying decoration at midpoints and corners. In addition, the first of these, with white end papers, has the 1653 title-page cartouche in gilt on the front cover and in blind on the back cover; the spine is decorated in gilt with an angling motif which includes titling and the Walton-Cotton cipher; "Major's Illustrated Edition" is gilt stamped at the foot between gilt rules with single reversed barbs. The leaves are untrimmed.

The second copy, with cream end papers, has a conventional non-angling decoration blind stamped in the center of each cover; "Walton and Cotton" gilt stamped within a gilt ruled square at the head of the spine; and MDCCCXLIV in gilt at the foot. The leaves are untrimmed. The third, with yellow end papers, has the 1653 title-page cartouche enclosing an angling motif blind stamped on both covers; the gilt titling on the spine is within an oval of gilt foliage, from which is suspended a stringer of golden fish; at the foot in gilt is "Major's Illustrated Edition," between double barbed gilt rules. The leaves are untrimmed.

Because the publishers ignored both the Lewis and the Washbourne editions of 1839 and 1842, which are reissues of the third Major edition of 1835, this Major edition of 1844 is actually the sixth, instead of the fourth Major, as it is titled. All are from the fifth edition of 1676 (No. 6).

This edition undoubtedly was one of the prototypes for the many sumptuous editions which have appeared over the years.

1844

56. The Eleventh Rennie Reprint

THE COMPLETE ANGLER; . . . by Izaak Walton and Charles Cotton.
Manchester: Samuel Johnson and Son, No. 3, Oldham-Street; and, 48 Church-St, Liverpool. MDCCCXLIV.

Copies examined: Fly Fishers', Harvard, Horne, Yale. Other: NN.

Size: 6½″ × 4″.

Pagination summary: [4], [1]-328.

At the foot of both the title-page verso and page 328 is imprinted, "S. Johnson and Son, Printers, Livesey St., Manchester."

The publisher's cloth binding has been seen in both red and green with yellow end papers. In each both covers are decorated with blind stamping, and the spines are impressed with an overall design in gilt incorporating the titling and depicting in the center an angler under a tree, holding his rod and a small fish just caught, while above and below him are decorative devices related to fishing.

This is a reprint, with the same illustrations, of the Rennie edition of 1833 (No. 35).

1846

57. The Twelfth Rennie Reprint

THE COMPLETE ANGLER; . . . by Izaac Walton and
Charles Cotton. . . .
Manchester: Printed and Published by S. Johnson and Son,
Oldham Street. MDCCCXLVI.

Copies examined: Congress, Yale. Other: CtHT.

Size: 6⁷⁄₁₆″ × 4″.

Pagination summary: [6], [1]-328.

At the foot of page 328 is imprinted, "S. Johnson & Son, Printers, Livesey St., Manchester."

The Yale copy has a publisher's binding in light olive-green cloth, both covers decorated with a blind stamping within a broad rule panel. The gilt decoration of the eleventh Rennie reprint (No. 56) is on the spine. The leaves are untrimmed.

The illustrations are the same as the first Rennie edition of 1833 (No. 35), of which this is a reprint, but with "Izaak" changed to "Isaac" on the title-page.

1847

58. The Thirteenth Rennie Reprint

THE COMPLETE ANGLER . . . by Izaak Walton and
Charles Cotton . . .
Dublin: W. Curry, Jun., & Co. 1847.

Copies examined: None.

Size reported: 8vo.

Pagination and illustrations: Presumed to be the same as the previous
Rennie reprints.

This reprint is listed in *Bibliotheca Piscatoria* where the size is given as above,
and where it is designated "Another impression from the same plates." It
is also in Westwood and Satchell's . . . *Chronicle* . . . (1888 reprint). While
Wood assigns London as the place of imprint, Oliver (his No. 56) commented, "Though we have not seen a copy, we believe it to have been
published in Dublin, and so to state on the title page."
This listing is in accordance with three of the four bibliographies cited.

1847

59. The Fourteenth Rennie Reprint

THE COMPLETE ANGLER; . . . By Izaac Walton and
Charles Cotton. . . .
Manchester: Printed and Published by Thomas Johnson,
Livesey Street. MDCCCXLVII.

Copies examined: Princeton, Yale. Other: CtHT.

Size: $6\frac{11}{16}'' \times 4\frac{3}{16}''$.

Pagination summary: [6], [1]-328.

At the foot of page 328 is imprinted "T. Johnson, Printer, Livesey St., Manchester." The publisher's binding examined is in blind-stamped green cloth.
The illustrations are the same as those of the 1833 Rennie edition (No. 35)
of which this is a reprint.

60. The First Bethune Edition

THE COMPLETE ANGLER ; . . . by Isaac Walton and
. . . by Charles Cotton. . . .
New York and London : Wiley & Putnam, 161 Broadway. 1847.

(The third edition with an American imprint)

Copies examined : Harvard, Horne (5), Princeton, Trinity, Virginia. Others :
CSmH, CtY, CU-A, FU, InU, MB, MiU, NN, PPA, PPFn, PU.

Sizes: 7¼″×4⅞″ Regular "edition" (two parts in single volume)
7½″×4⅞″ Paper cover state (two separate volumes)
10½″×7⅞″ Large paper state (two parts in single volume)

Pagination summary : Part I, [8], [i], ii-lxxxiv, [lxxxv-lxxxvii], lxxxviii, [lxxxix],
xc-xciii, [xciv-xcv], xcvi, [xcvii], xcviii-xcix, [c], ci, [cii-civ], cv, [cvi], cvii,
[cviii-cx], cxi, [xcii], [1], 2-249, [250]; Part II, [i-v], vi-xxix, [xxx], (text of Part II
starts with unnumbered page 31), 32-114; Appendix : verses and songs [115]-128 ;
Arrangement of the American Species of Fish (by James E. De Kay), 129-133 ;
Extracts from the Journal of the Lake Piseco Trout Club, 134-138 ; Trout Fishing on Long Island (by Frank Forester), 139-149, [150]; A Waltonian Library,
[151-153], 154-191 ; Works referred to in The Complete Angler, [192]-195 ; Books in
the Cathedral Library, Salisbury, formerly belonging to Izaak Walton, [196]-
197 ; Works by and ascribed to Izaak Walton [198]-202 ; Works of Charles Cotton,
[203] ; blank [204] ; General Index [205]-210 ; Wiley & Putnam's Advertisement, [6].

The three states have identical pagination except that the six pages of Wiley
and Putnam advertisements at the end of the regular and paper covered
states are not present in the large paper state. Each state is imprinted on the
title-page verso, "Robert Craighead, Printer, 112 Fulton Street. T. B. Smith,
Stereotyper, 216 William Street." Part II has a special title-page, lacking the
London imprint.

The illustrations in the regular "edition" consist of engraved plates of
both Walton and Cotton, two engraved scenes, a facsimile of the 1653 title-
page, five pages of music (that on page 203, Part I upside down), four pictorial
woodcuts of which the fishing house and Walton's residence are marked
J. W. ORR SC., and nineteen woodcuts of fish of which 12 are signed J. W.
ORR Sc., one, J. W. ORR, three J. W. ORR, S., and three are not signed. The
large paper state has the same illustrations with the addition of the woodcuts
in duplicate, which were proofs before letters. In the state in two separate
volumes with paper covers, the four engraved plates are omitted.

An interesting error in the preface was reported by C. E. Goodspeed in his
Angling in America. . . . (1939, p. 176). Referring to the illustrations, Bethune
stated, in the Biographical Preface (p. lxxxi), that "Bagster, in 1808, published
a revised edition of Hawkins, in a most liberal manner. The engravings of the

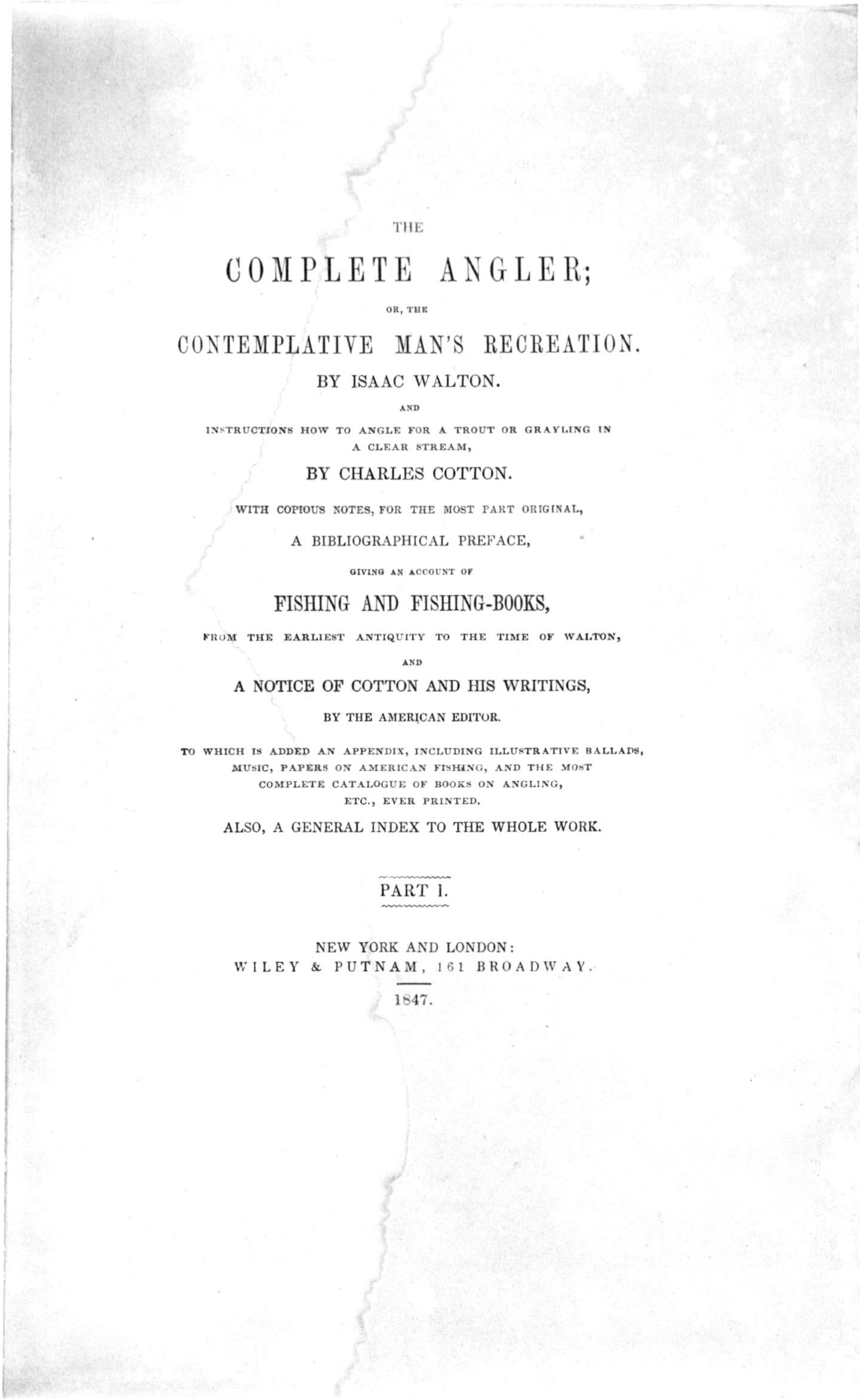

THE

COMPLETE ANGLER;

OR, THE

CONTEMPLATIVE MAN'S RECREATION.

BY ISAAC WALTON.

AND

INSTRUCTIONS HOW TO ANGLE FOR A TROUT OR GRAYLING IN
A CLEAR STREAM,

BY CHARLES COTTON.

WITH COPIOUS NOTES, FOR THE MOST PART ORIGINAL,

A BIBLIOGRAPHICAL PREFACE,

GIVING AN ACCOUNT OF

FISHING AND FISHING-BOOKS,

FROM THE EARLIEST ANTIQUITY TO THE TIME OF WALTON,

AND

A NOTICE OF COTTON AND HIS WRITINGS,

BY THE AMERICAN EDITOR.

TO WHICH IS ADDED AN APPENDIX, INCLUDING ILLUSTRATIVE BALLADS,
MUSIC, PAPERS ON AMERICAN FISHING, AND THE MOST
COMPLETE CATALOGUE OF BOOKS ON ANGLING,
ETC., EVER PRINTED.

ALSO, A GENERAL INDEX TO THE WHOLE WORK.

PART I.

NEW YORK AND LONDON:
WILEY & PUTNAM, 161 BROADWAY.

1847.

Figure 19   The First Bethune Edition (No. 60). The first *Angler* to be edited, printed, and published in the United States. Large paper state, in The Kienbusch Library on Fresh Water Angling at Princeton University

scenes by Audinet, from Wale, and the fish, from fresh taken specimens, are very excellent; . . . It is from them the cuts in this edition are copied." The plates and woodcuts (except that from the *Treatyse of Fysshynge Wyth An Angle* and the Music) are from the so-called 4th Major edition of 1844 (No. 55). This error is mentioned on a paste-down in the Horne copy of the second Bethune edition 1848 (No. 61), at the top of the first page of the Bibliographical Preface, and reads: "After the stereotype plates of the Bibliographical Preface were cast, the Publishers determined to copy the cuts of fish, &c., from Major's edition, instead of Baxter's [*sic*], as stated in the Preface." It is obvious that the correction slip should have read "Bagster" instead of "Baxter."

The regular "edition" was issued in at least four colors of binding. *First* the Trinity copy is in dark green cloth with gilt decorations; *second*, Bradley, in *The New Gold in Your Attic* (1958), refers to a binding in light tan cloth with red stripes; *third*, one Horne copy, leaves untrimmed, is in dark blue cloth, a large fish and titling in gilt on the spine, and a blind stamped panel on both covers containing a group of fish in gilt on the front and in blind on the back; *fourth*, the second Horne copy is in bright red cloth, light yellow end papers, all edges gilt, the spine with gilt fish and titling, and extra gilt decorations not present on the blue cloth copy at top, center, and heel; the covers are paneled with three gilt rules, with extra gilt decorations within the panels, and each have the groups of fish gilt stamped in the center. All the fish decorations are impressions repeated from the woodcut illustrations (see Figure 18).

Each volume of the paper cover state is covered in brown paper and, as part of Wiley and Putnam's "Library of Choice Reading," marked CI and CII (101 & 102). The title, by "The American Editor," and the publisher's name, are also imprinted on the covers. Other titles are listed on the back and the inside of the covers.

The large paper state of this edition was limited to 50 copies issued in uncut sheets.

This edition, edited by the Rev. George Washington Bethune, although the third with an American imprint, was the first to be edited, printed, and published in the United States (see Figure 19).

It is a reprint of the fifth edition of 1676 (No. 6), and the "Advertisement to the American Edition" on the recto of the fourth leaf at the front is dated July, 1847.

1848

61. The Second Bethune Reprint

THE COMPLETE ANGLER; . . . by Isaac Walton.
. . . by Charles Cotton. . . .
New York: John Wiley (Old Stand of "Wiley and Putnam"),
161 Broadway: and Paternoster Row, London, 1848.

Copies examined: Harvard, Horne, Princeton, Virginia. Others: CtY, DLC, MeB, NN.

Size: 7⅟₁₆″ × 5⅟₁₆″.

The pagination, illustrations, and title-page verso are the same as the regular "edition" of 1847 (No. 60). The Horne copy contains the paste-down referred to and quoted in the description of the 1847 states, and the Bibliographical Preface repeats the error on page lxxxi.

The binding, in plum-colored cloth, with light yellow end papers, has the same impressions of fish from the illustrations as the first Bethune, stamped in gilt on the spine and front cover, and in blind on the back cover. Both covers are paneled with three rules and decorations in each corner, all in blind.

This is a later issue of the regular "edition" (two parts in one volume) of the first Bethune edition (No. 60).

1848

62. The Fifteenth Rennie Reprint

THE COMPLETE ANGLER . . . by Izaak Walton and Charles Cotton . . .
Liverpool: Thomas Johnson. 1848.

Copies examined: none seen.

Size reported: 8vo.

Pagination and illustrations: Presumed to be the same as the Rennie edition of 1833.

The size is derived from *Bibliotheca Piscatoria* where this edition is identified as "A stereotype-reprint of the Manchester issue of 1844 [No. 56], with the same illustrations." (The Manchester edition is described therein as "A paginary reprint of the Edinburgh edition of 1833 with the same illustrations.")

This edition is also listed by Oliver, Wood and in Westwood's *The Chronicle of The Compleat Angler* (1864) where the statement is made with reference to the

[76]

numerous Rennie editions (p. 50), ". . . they were all identical with the first, . . ." with which I agree, except for the "Izaac" spelling on the title-pages of seven of the Rennie editions (Nos. 57, 59, 63, 64, 65, 71, and 72), and in the ninth edition (No. 45) where "The" is omitted before "Complete" on the title-page. The bindings also differ as noted.

1849

63. The Sixteenth Rennie Reprint

THE COMPLETE ANGLER; . . . by Izaac Walton and
Charles Cotton. . . .
London: John Johnson, 30, High Holborn;
Thomas Johnson, 22, Livesey St., Manchester. MDCCCXLIX.

Copies examined: British Museum, Horne, Yale. Others: MH, NN, NjP.

Size: $6\frac{11}{16}'' \times 4\frac{1}{8}''$.

Pagination summary: [6], [1]-328.

At the foot of page 328 is imprinted, "T. Johnson, Printer, Livesey St., Manchester." The illustrations are the same as those of the 1833 Rennie edition (No. 35) of which this is a reprint.

There are 12 errors in page numbering; the numeral 1 is missing on pages 126, 150, 152, 154, 160, and 192; 149 is printed as 14, 203 as 20, 216 as 16, 255 as 2, and the numbers are omitted entirely from pages 276 and 326. Some of the numerals on other pages are from broken fonts.

The publisher's binding seen is in blue cloth, with yellow end papers, the front and back covers blind stamped in a frame design and the spine impressed with a design in gilt identical to that used for the eleventh Rennie edition of 1844 (No. 56). The leaves are untrimmed.

[1849]

64. The Seventeenth Rennie Reprint

THE COMPLETE ANGLER . . . by Izaac Walton and
Charles Cotton . . .
Manchester: Printed and Published by Thomas Johnson,
Livesey Street. [1849].

Copies examined: British Museum, Harvard, Princeton. Other: CtY.

Size 6 9/16" × 4 1/8".

Pagination summary: [6], [1]-328.

At the foot of page 328 is imprinted, "T. Johnson, Printer, Livesey St., Manchester."
    The illustrations are those of the 1833 Rennie edition (No. 35) of which this is a reprint. Westwood and Satchell's *Bibliotheca Piscatoria* and Westwood's *Chronicle* list this edition but question the date; Wood assigns 1849 without question and is Oliver's authority for acceptance of the same date; and the British Museum's *General Catalogue* dates this edition 1849, which is followed here.
    The Princeton copy, dated 1849 in pencil, is in a publisher's binding of blue cloth, blind stamped covers and gilt decorated spine, which is the same as the binding of the eleventh Rennie edition of 1844 (No. 56).

1851

65. The Eighteenth Rennie Reprint

THE COMPLETE ANGLER; . . . by Izaac Walton and
Charles Cotton. . . .
Manchester: Printed and Published by Thomas Johnson,
Livesey Street. 1851.

Copies examined: Horne, Princeton. Others: CtHT, CtY, NN, ViU.

Size: 6 13/16" × 4 3/16".

Pagination summary: (6), [1]-328

At the foot of page 328 is imprinted, "T. Johnson, Printer, Livesry (misprint for Livesey) St., Manchester."
    The illustrations are the same as those of the 1833 Rennie edition (No. 35) of which this is a reprint.
    At least 14 printing errors occur in page numbering; the one is missing from the numerals on pages 126, 146, 150, 152, 160, and 192; 141 and 149 are both numbered 14; 121 as 12; 203 and 207 are both numbered as 20; 216 as 16; 255 as 2; and the numerals have been omitted entirely from page 276.
    The publisher's binding examined is in very dark blue cloth with yellow end papers, the front and back covers each have a blind stamped border, and the spine is impressed with a design in gilt identical to that used for the eleventh (No. 56) and sixteenth (No. 63) Rennie editions of 1844 and 1849. The leaves are untrimmed.

[78]

1851

66. The Causton (4th Moses Browne) Edition

THE COMPLETE ANGLER ; . . . by Izaak Walton and
Charles Cotton: . . .
London: Henry Kent Causton. MDCCCLI.

Copies examined: Cambridge, Harvard, Horne, Princeton, Yale. Others:
CSmH, CtHT, NN, ViU.

Size: 6⅝" × 4³⁄₁₆".

Pagination summary: [i-iii], iv-lxviii, 33-418.

On the vignette title-page verso is imprinted, "Printed by Henry Kent
Causton, Nag's Head Court, Gracechurch Street" and, at the foot of page
418, "H. K. Causton, Printer, Nag's Head Court, Gracechurch Street."
   The illustrations, including a page of music, consist of thirteen plates
engraved by J. T. Smith, W. R. Smith, and "Cook et Pye," after Huysman,
Lely, and "Wale et Nash," and 72 unsigned wood engravings, including 20
fish cuts. The woodcut initial Y appears on pages 33 and 317. Many of the
illustrations are from earlier Major editions, and the fishing wood engravings appear to have been derived from Bewick.
   The publisher's binding seen is in light blue cloth with a decorative edge
panel blind stamped on the front and back covers. The spine is divided into
five compartments, four blind stamped in the center with a decorative
circular design; the one second from the top is without decoration and
gilt stamped "Walton's Angler." The end papers are yellow and the leaves
are untrimmed.
   This edition, edited by Henry Kent Causton, was issued from the same
press used for the first Moses Browne edition of 1750 (No. 7), printed by
Henry Kent, who was succeeded by Causton's forebears. It is a reprint from
the fifth edition of 1676 (No. 6).

1852

67. The Third Bethune Edition

THE COMPLETE ANGLER ; . . . by Isaac Walton.
. . . by Charles Cotton. . . .
New York: John Wiley, 167 Broadway. 1852.

Copies examined: Harvard, Horne (2), Virginia, Yale. Other: NN.

Size: 7⅝" × 4⅛".

Pagination summary: [8], [i]-[cxii], [1]-[250]; [i]-[xxx], [31]-210.

This is the same as the 1847 Bethune edition, except that in this edition the pages following 195, Part II, have been rearranged, so that the blank page 204 in the 1847 edition provides a list of "Addenda" to Bethune's Waltonian Library as page 196. The six pages of advertising are lacking at the end. In Part I, page 111 is misnumbered 11; in Part II, page 51 is numbered as 5. On the title-page verso is imprinted "R. Craighead, Printer, 53 Vesey Street, N.Y."

The illustrations are the same as the 1847 edition except that the music on page 203, Part I, is right side up. The error on page lxxxi of the Bibliographical Preface (see Nos. 60 and 61) has been corrected.

There are minor variations in the two publisher's bindings of the two Horne copies. While both are gilt stamped on the spine and front cover with the same fish decoration used on the first Bethune edition of 1847, the shade of the brown cloth differs and different decorative bands are blind stamped on the cover edges. The gilt titling on the spine also varies slightly, with the word "Illustrated" added on one copy. The end papers are yellow in both copies. The Yale copy is in a similar shade of purplish-brown cloth with a decorative band blind stamped on the cover edges. The fish decoration (an impression of the woodcut on page 220, Part I) of the Horne copies is in gilt on the front cover and in blind on the back cover. The gilt titling at the upper part of the spine is within a blind stamped oval design and near the foot is a piscatorial decoration depicting a basket with fishing tackle and fish. The end papers are yellow.

This edition is from the Bethune edition of 1847 (No. 60).

1853

68. The First Ephemera Edition

THE COMPLETE ANGLER. By Izaak Walton, and Charles Cotton. . . .
London: Ingram, Cooke and Co. M.DCCC.LIII.

Copies examined: Bodleian, Harvard, Horne (2), Virginia, Yale (2). Others: CtHT, MB, NN, NjP, TU.

Size: 7⅜″ × 5″.

Collation: [A]², G⁵, B-X⁸, Y², Z¹ = 170.

Pagination summary: [i]-xiv, [1]-326. Page 268 is numbered as 862.

The title-page verso is imprinted, "Wertheimer and Co, typp, Circus Place, Finsbury Circus" and, at the foot of page 324, "J. Wertheimer and Co., Printers, Finsbury Circus."

The illustrations consist of an idealized portrait of Walton as a frontis-piece; an engraved title-page; four portraits, including Walton on the vignette title-page; a facsimile of the 1653 title-page; the Walton-Cotton cipher on the title-page to Part II; 11 woodcuts of places and fishing stations; 19 of fish; and 6 of tackle. Twenty of the illustrations are signed by Cornelius Pearson, the rest are unsigned.

The publisher's binding examined is in light green cloth, often faded to brown, blind stamped with a lightly embossed overall design that incorporates an imprint of "National Illustrated Library," on the front and back covers. The spine is decorated in an overall gilt floral design with the usual titling also in gilt. The end papers are white. The Yale copies are in the same binding with yellow end papers.

This "New Edition" as it is identified on the title-page, was edited by Edward Fitzgibbon who wrote under the pen name of "Ephemera." Author of a number of books on angling, he provided notes of his own and used some from the Hawkins editions.

This edition is from the fifth edition of 1676 (No. 6), and according to *The English Catalogue of Books,* was published to sell for two shillings six pence. It was one of the volumes in "The Illustrated National Library" series, published by Ingram Cook & Co.

1854

69. The Second Ephemera Edition

THE COMPLETE ANGLER. By Izaak Walton and
Charles Cotton.
London: Nathaniel Cooke, Milford House, Strand. MDCCCLIV.

Copies examined: Harvard, Horne, Princeton, Trinity, Yale (2). Other: ViU.

Size: regular $7\frac{7}{16}'' \times 4\frac{7}{8}''$; large paper, $7\frac{11}{16}'' \times 5''$.

Collation: [-]², a⁴, b¹, B-U⁸, X⁵=164.

Pagination summary: [i]-xiv, [1]-309, [310], [4].

The vignette title-page identifies this as the "Second Edition," but there is no printer's imprint on the verso as in the first Ephemera. Through the use of smaller type for the notes, and shortened margins, this edition was produced on 12 fewer pages than the first printing. The numbering error of page 268 is corrected.

The illustrations are the same as those of the first Ephemera (No. 68), but with an additional woodcut on the last of the four pages at the end not added to the "List of Illustrations." There are also floral decorations on pages 102 and 173 which are not present in the first Ephemera edition.

The publisher's binding of the Horne copy is the same as the first Ephemera except that the end papers are yellow. The regular size Yale copy is in rough green cloth. The covers are edged with a double rule enclosing a band of scroll decoration, all in blind; the spine is titled and decorated in gilt with a full floral design; the end papers are yellow. The large paper Yale copy (not mentioned in previous bibliographies) is in very dark green rough cloth. The covers are edged with a double rule enclosing a decorative design all in blind; the spine is titled in gilt above blind stamped decorations.

In his Note (a) to the third Ephemera edition of 1859 (No. 74), Wood states, "The plates from which the edition of 1854 was printed were purchased by Routledge from Ingram, Cooke & Co., the original publishers of Ephemera's edition—and all subsequent editions are printed from these plates."

This edition, one of the "National Illustrated Library" series, is a reissue of the first Ephemera edition of 1853 (No. 68), which is from the fifth edition of 1676 (No. 6).

1856

70. The First Jesse Edition

THE COMPLETE ANGLER, . . . of Izaak Walton and Charles Cotton. . . .
London: Henry G. Bohn, York Street, Covent Garden.
MDCCCLVI.

Copies examined: Harvard, Horne, Princeton, Yale. Others: CSmH, CtHT, CU, KyBgW, MB, NN, OCl, OClW, ODW, PPGi, PU.

Size: 7⅛″ × 4½″.

Pagination summary: [7], [i]-xix, [xx], 1 l., [1]-320; Appendix on Fishing Tackle [321]-338; Part II [339]-[448]; Henry G. Bohn's "Where to Fish" [449]-483; Index [484]-496; Fishing Tackle Makers [497]; Printer's Imprint [498]; [7].

On the title-page verso and on the last page is imprinted, "London: Bradbury and Evans, Printers, Whitefriars." Walton's given name is spelled Izaak on the title-page and Isaac in the title of the biography. At both the front and the back are seven pages of advertising for Bohn's publications.

While the list of "Engravings on Wood" comprises 203 illustrations, there are actually 206 engravings, since one was omitted, and four present were not included in the list. Number six, "Seal-ring, a bequest from Sir H. Davy to W. H. Pepys," was the one omitted. It is indexed for on page xli, which is not present in this edition, but the listing was probably taken from the sixth Major edition of 1844 (No. 55), in which this cut is on page xli. Two headpieces, the engravings for the half-title, and the dedication (pages [i], v, [xv], and [484]) are not included in the list. The cut of Madeley Manor is listed as on page xxi, which should be xix, and the five plates of "Angling Apparatus," which are on pages 334-338, are indexed for pages 33-48. In the copies with extra plates, there is a list of the 26 steel engravings. In this plethora of illustrations, 59 artists are represented, including Huysman, Archer, Absolon, Lely, Bewick, Hofland, Cruikshank, Linton, and Lizars.

Both the dedication page (to the Thames Angling Preservation Society), and the half-title page, have sporting motif borders. The title-page vignette woodcut, "View from Lea Bridge," is from the Major edition of 1844 (No. 55).

The publisher bound the extra plate issue in red cloth, with the front and back covers blind stamped in an overall design which has "Henry Bohn's Illustrated Library" impressed in the form of a circle in the center. The spine, with blind stamped decoration, is titled in gilt at the top and, near the foot, the words "Bohn's Illustrated Library | Extra Plates 7/6″ are stamped in gilt. Green cloth, with the same decorations, was used for the regular edition, with "Extra Plates 7/6″ omitted from the spine. *The English Catalogue of Books* for 1856 priced the regular edition at 5s.

This edition, which was edited, and provided with a Preface and notes by Edward Jesse, a writer on natural history, is from the fifth edition of 1676 (No. 6).

[1857]

71. The Nineteenth Rennie Reprint

THE COMPLETE ANGLER ; . . . by Izaac Walton and
Charles Cotton. . . .
Manchester: Printed and Published by Thomas Johnson,
Livesey Street. [1857].

Copy examined: Horne.

Size: 6⅝″ × 4³⁄₁₆″.

Pagination summary: [4], [1]-328.

At the foot of page 328 is imprinted, "T. Johnson, Printer, Livesey St., Manchester."

The illustrations are the same as those of the 1833 Rennie edition (No. 35), of which this is a reissue.

There are 16 page numbering errors; the numeral 1 is missing from page numbers 126, 146, 150, 152, 154, 160, and 192; 121 is numbered as 12, 141 as 14, 149 as 14, 203 as 20, 207 as 20, 216 as 16, 255 as 2, and all page numerals are lacking from pages 276 and 326. Some of the numerals on other pages are broken.

The publisher's binding seen is in dark blue cloth with the blind stamped design on the covers and the gilt design on the spine used for the sixteenth Rennie edition of 1849 (No. 63). The end papers are yellow and the leaves are untrimmed.

Westwood and Satchell, Wood, and Oliver (who saw a copy) all date this reprint 1857 without brackets. The copy which I examined is not dated.

1857

72. The Twentieth Rennie Reprint

THE COMPLETE ANGLER ; . . . By Izaac Walton and
Charles Cotton. . . .
Halifax: Milner and Sowerby. 1857.

Copies examined: Harvard, Horne, Princeton, Yale. Others: NN, ViU.

Size: $6\frac{7}{16}'' \times 4\frac{3}{16}''$.

Pagination summary: [6], [1]-328.

At the foot of page 328 is imprinted, "Milner and Sowerby, Printers, Halifax."

The illustrations are the same as those of the 1833 Rennie edition (No. 35) of which this is a reissue.

This reprint was issued in both green and brown pebbled cloth, with light yellow end papers. A panel enclosing a decorative design in blind is embossed on both the front and back covers, and the spine is impressed in gilt with the angling motif design used for the eleventh and sixteenth Rennie editions of 1844 (No. 56), and 1849 (No. 61). The leaves are untrimmed.

1858

73. The Groombridge (6th Pickering) Edition

THE COMPLETE ANGLER. By Izaak Walton and
Charles Cotton. . . .
London: Groombridge and Sons, Paternoster Row. 1858.

Copies examined: Harvard (2), Horne, Yale. Other: NN.

Size: $4\frac{5}{8}'' \times 3\frac{1}{4}''$.

Pagination summary: Vol. I, [i-v], vi-xi, [xii]; Part I, [1]-152. Vol. II, [i-iv], [1]-62; Part II, [63]-149, [150].

In volume I the page numbers are lacking on page 42; in volume II they are lacking on pages 17, 71, 72, 120, and the numeral 1 is lacking on page 128. The title-pages, text, and the three notes are printed within a frame of single rules. The publisher's device is imprinted on the title-page of each volume. "London: Printed by Groombridge Brothers" appears at the foot of page 152, volume I, and 149, volume II.

The illustrations, as in the Tilt edition of 1837 (No. 47), consist of a frontispiece in each volume, engraved on wood by Ebenezer Landells.

The two volumes in one seen in publisher's binding were issued in dark green cloth, end papers light chocolate, all edges stained light red. The beveled edge covers are bordered with single blind stamped rule. A fisherman is portrayed in gilt within a panel formed by parallel rules blind stamped on the front cover; an identical panel on the back cover is without decoration. Three rules at the head and foot of the spine, the usual titling, and a small three leaf ornament are gilt stamped on the spine. Bushell, in his *Private Angling Library* (1953) reports two volumes as original cloth binding with gilt edges. Both Harvard copies (one in two volumes) have been rebound.

This edition lacks both preface and introduction and, like the Tilt, the editorial matter is from the earlier Pickering editions, which consists only of the statement on page xi regarding the omission of notes, and Notes A and B on page 149 in volume II, Part II.

This is a reissue of the Tilt edition of 1837 (No. 47), and is listed in *The English Catalogue of Books* as having been published in 1858 to sell for three shillings.

1859

74. The Third Ephemera Reprint

THE COMPLETE ANGLER. By Izaak Walton &
Charles Cotton.
London: Routledge, Warnes, and Routledge, Farringdon Street.
New York: 56, Walker Street. 1859.

Copies examined: Harvard, Horne, Princeton. Others: CtHT, CtY, DI, ICRL, IU, KyU, NIC, NNC, PP, ViU.

Size: 7⁵⁄₁₆″ × 4⅛″.

Pagination summary: [i]-xii, [13]-313, [4], 1 l.

On the last leaf (verso of the fishing catch register) is imprinted, "London: Savill and Edwards, Printers, Chandos Street, Covent Garden."

The illustrations are those of the first Ephemera edition, except that the woodcuts of the Salmon, Pike, and Pearch are on appropriate text pages, instead of all three imprinted on one page without text. The fishing catch register, referred to above, is on the recto of the last leaf, arranged in columns headed Date, Number of fish, Description, Weight, etc., where details of the angler's catch may be recorded.

The publisher's binding examined, with white end papers, is the same as the first Ephemera edition (No. 68).

In his Note (b) to this edition, Wood states, "The sheets of this edition were first imported to the United States in 1862, were bound here and sold by Routledge's New York house, but without date on the title-page," and undoubtedly used for numbers 79 and 80.

This reprint, one of the "National Illustrated Library" series, is a reissue of the second Ephemera edition of 1854 (No. 69), which is from the fifth edition of 1676 (No. 6).

1859

75. The First German (Fourth Ephemera) Edition

DER VOLLKOMMENE ANGLER von Isaac Walton und Charles Cotton. . . .
Hamburg: P. Salomon & Co. 1859.

Copies examined: Harvard, Horne. Others: CtY, DLC, NN, ViU.

Size: 8½″ × 5¹¹⁄₁₆″.

Pagination summary: [i-v], vi-xii, [1]-240, [241-245], 246-308, 11l.

On page (ii) is imprinted "Druck von W. Gente, Kniesch Nachf." (Printed by W. Gente, successor to Kniesch.)

The illustrations consist of 17 engravings of fish, two of hooks, a salmon fly, six natural flies, six artificial flies, and six steps in artificial fly construction. These are printed on the rectos (versos blank) of the leaves at the end, numbered 1-7 on the rectos; [8] is blank; and the last three are designated "Platte" No. 1, No. 2, No. 3.

This edition was issued in light brown paper wrappers. The title-page is repeated on the front wrapper within a frame of single rules with type ornament decorations at the corners. P. Salomon publications are advertised on the back wrapper. The leaves are untrimmed.

This Ephemera edition (translated by I. Schumacher from the first Ephemera edition of 1853, No. 68) is the first published in a foreign language, and is one of the most difficult to obtain, since a fire is reported to have destroyed most of the copies before distribution. In some 20 years, I have seen only one copy offered for sale.

1859

76. The Fourth Bethune Reprint

THE COMPLETE ANGLER . . . by Isaac Walton.
and . . . Charles Cotton. . . .
New York: John Wiley, No. 56 Walker-Street. 1859.

Copies examined: Harvard, Princeton. Other: ViU.

Size: 7½″ × 4¹⁵⁄₁₆″.

Pagination summary: [8], [i]-[cxii], [1]-[250]; [i]-[xxx], [31]-210, [4], which is the same as the 1852 Bethune edition, except there are four pages of advertising at the end.

In Part I, page 111 is misnumbered 11; in Part II, page 51 is misnumbered as 5; 142 as 42; 160 as 60; and 162 as 62. The printer's imprint is lacking on the title-page verso.
   The illustrations are identical with the 1852 Bethune edition (No. 67). The error on page lxxxi of the Bibliographical Preface has been corrected. (See comments under the 1847 edition, No. 60.)
   The binding is brown cloth similar to the 1852 edition (No. 67), of which this is a reissue.

1860

77. The Second Nicolas Reprint

THE COMPLETE ANGLER . . . by Izaak Walton and
. . . Charles Cotton . . .
London: Nattali and Bond. 1860.

Copies examined: Harvard, Horne, Yale. Others: CLU-C, CtHT, DLC, MB, McBP, NN, NjNbS, NjP, OU, PP, ViU.

Size: 9½″ × 6⅜″.

Pagination summary: Vol. I, [14], [i]-ccxii, [4], [1]-129; Vol. II, [2], [131]-436, [32].

At the foot of the last page of the 32-page index in volume II is imprinted, "G Norman, Printer, Maiden Lane, Covent Garden, London."
   This is a reissue of the first Nicolas edition of 1836 (No. 43), with the same illustrations, except that following the account of Cotton's life, two pages have been added to show the pedigrees of Ken and Chalkhill. The Pickering Anchor and Dolphin title-pages for each volume, printed in red and black, identify this as the "Second Edition." The engraved title-page (at "The

Epistle Dedicatory"), dated 1832, is here enlarged from the first Pickering (No. 29) as in the first Nicolas (No. 43). Wood states that, ". . . large paper copies have all of the plates and illustrations printed on India paper and laid down."

Since the title-page of this *Angler* is explicit as to edition, date, and publisher, there is complete agreement with Oliver's observation (see his page 116) that references describing this reprint as herein, but dating it 1869 and 1873 (the latter as published by Routledge), and an additional reference found in *The English Catalogue of Books* dating it 1870, are erroneous, and actually refer to this 1860 reprint.

This reissue of the first Nicolas edition is from the fifth edition of 1676 (No. 6).

1861

78. The Second Jesse Reprint

THE COMPLETE ANGLER, . . . of Izaak Walton and Charles Cotton. . . .
London: Henry G. Bohn, New York, Covent Garden.
MDCCCLXI.

Copies examined: Harvard, Princeton, Virginia. Others: CtHT, CtY, DI, DLC, PHC, PV.

Size: $6\frac{15}{16}'' \times 4\frac{1}{2}''$.

Pagination summary: [7], [i]-xix, [3], [1]-496, [497-498], [7].

On the title-page verso, and that of page [498], is imprinted, "London: Bradbury and Evans, Printers, Whitefriars."

Except for a new title-page, this reprint is the same as the first Jesse edition of 1856, with the same 206 woodcuts and, in both copies examined, 26 steel-engraved plates. The errors in the index of "Engravings on Wood" have not been corrected (see notes under the first Jesse edition of 1856, No. 70).

This reprint was issued in the same red cloth with the decorations of the extra plate issue of the first Jesse edition.

[1862]

79. The Fifth Ephemera Reprint

THE COMPLETE ANGLER by Izaak Walton and
Charles Cotton.
George Routledge & Sons, Broadway, Ludgate Hill
New York: 416 Broome Street [1862].

Copy examined: Harvard.

Size: 7⅝″ × 4¹³⁄₁₆″.

Pagination summary: [i-iii], iv-xii, [13]-313, [314]-[320].

On page 320 is imprinted, "London: Savill and Edwards, Printers, Chandos Street, Covent Garden."
    This edition lacks the printed title-page with the vignette of Walton which is found in the first three Ephemeras (the fourth is the first German edition), but does have the engraved title-page of the earlier editions. With this exception, the illustrations and their pagination are those in the third Ephemera reprint (No. 74), and are the same, but not on the same pages, as those in the first and second Ephemeras. These illustrations are an idealized portrait of Walton (frontispiece); an engraved title-page; three portraits; a facsimile of the 1653 title-page; the Walton-Cotton cipher on the title-page to Part II; 11 woodcuts of places and fishing stations; 19 woodcuts of fish, and six of tackle. Twenty of the illustrations are signed by Cornelius Pearson, the rest are unsigned. The fishing catch register from the third Ephemera is included at the end.
    The publisher's binding examined is in green cloth with chocolate-brown end papers and top edges gilt. The front cover is bordered with three black rules, the outer one is plain, the two inner ones with decorative designs at each corner and centered on each side. This design is repeated in blind on the back cover. The spine is elaborately embellished. *Complete | Angler,* slanting upward from left to right, is printed in black on gilt, and "Walton" and "Cotton" are in gilt, with their given names in black. Below the titling the spine is decorated with silver fish swimming in a golden river, with fishing gear on the bank in gilt.
    In his Note (b) to the third Ephemera reprint of 1859 (No. 74), Wood states, "The sheets of this edition were first imported to the United States in 1862, were bound here and sold by Routledge's New York house, but without date on the title-page," and now, with identical printer's imprint, undoubtedly used here.
    This reprint, with identical printer's imprint and with illustrations on the same pages as the third Ephemera, was undoubtedly made up from the imported sheets referred to by Wood and, since it was probably issued shortly after their importation in 1862, it is so dated.

[89]

This is a reissue of the 1859 Ephemera reprint (No. 74), printed from the same plates.

[1862]

80. The Sixth Ephemera Reprint

THE COMPLETE ANGLER by Izaak Walton and
Charles Cotton. . . .
London and New York: George Routledge & Sons. [1862]

Copies examined: Harvard, Horne, Yale.

Size: 7⅝₁₆″ × 4¹³⁄₁₆″.

Pagination summary: [i-iii], iv-xii, [13]-313, [314]-[320]. (The Horne copy has three pages of advertising at both front and back for Routledge publications.) Page 150 is misnumbered 50.

On page [320] is imprinted, "London: Savill, Edwards and Co., Printers, Chandos Street, Covent Garden."

This reprint has the engraved title-page of the earlier Ephemeras but lacks the printed title-page with the vignette of Walton, which is found in the first three. With this exception, the illustrations are the same, and on the same pages, as those in the third and fifth Ephemeras (Nos. 72 & 79), and are the same, but not on the same pages, as those in the first and second Ephemeras. The fishing catch register from the third Ephemera is included at the end.

This reprint has been seen in two publisher's bindings. The first is the same as the fifth Ephemera (No. 79), except that the end papers are cream, all edges gilt. The second is in bright yellow paper over boards. Three pages of Routledge advertising, consisting of a paste-down and one leaf, were used for end papers at front and back. The engraved title-page is imprinted on the front cover within a frame of double rules; "Two Shillings" is added at the top; "London and New York" is dropped at the foot leaving "George Routledge & Sons." On the back cover, also within a frame of double rules, is a list of 41 Routledge "Books for the Country." The spine, within a single rule frame, is decorated with a large cut of sporting equipment, titled at the head and, at the foot, priced "Two Shillings."

This reprint is very similar to the fifth Ephemera (No. 79); the size, pagination, illustrations, and catch register are identical. One binding examined is the same except for the slight differences noted. However, there are some differences: the title-page imprint is not the same, page 150 is misnumbered 50, and the printer's imprint shows that Savill and Edwards, printers of the fifth Ephemera, had become Savill Edwards and Co. when this edition was printed. Since the normal development of a business enterprise is from partnership to company, it has been assumed that the printing of this reprint was by the latter of the two. However, since both impressions could well have been issued the same year, both are dated 1862.

This is a reissue of the third Ephemera reprint of 1859 (No. 74), printed from the same plates.

1863

81. The First Bell-Daldy and Low Edition

THE COMPLETE ANGLER by Izaak Walton and
Charles Cotton.
London: Bell and Daldy, 186, Fleet Street; and
Sampson Low, Son, and Co., 47, Ludgate Hill. 1863.

Copies examined: Harvard, Horne (2), Princeton, Yale. Others: CtHT, PU.

Size: 5¼"×3¼".

Collation: A-U⁸=160.

Pagination summary: [i-vii], viii-xvi, [1]-304, [2].

Two pages of advertising are at the end. The Bell-Daldy device of an Aldine anchor and dolphin combined with a carillon bell is imprinted on the title-page, which is followed by a typeset reproduction of the 1653 edition title-page, lacking the cartouche. At the foot of page 304 is imprinted "Chiswick Press: -Whittingham and Wilkins, Tooks Court, Chancery Lane." There are a few short footnotes from previous editions but no introduction.

The illustrations consist of a plate of Walton and one of Cotton, each engraved by Mitchell after Huysman and Lely, 13 woodcuts of fish, and on the last page, the Walton-Cotton cipher. One Horne copy lacks the plates.

The Yale copy seen is in dark purple cloth with beveled covers framed by three blind rules. The spine has three gilt rules at top and foot and is titled in gilt. The end papers are chocolate-brown and the top edges are gilt.

This edition is listed in *Bibliotheca Piscatoria* as having been published in 1863, and in the publisher's advertisements at the front of the fifth Jesse edition of 1882, as one of Bell's "Pocket Volumes," the latter giving the selling price as 3s.

This edition is a reprint from the fifth edition of 1676 (No. 6).

1864

82. The Bell-Daldy Reprint

THE COMPLETE ANGLER by Izaak Walton and
Charles Cotton.
London: Bell and Daldy, 186, Fleet Street. 1864.

Copies examined: Harvard, Horne (3), Princeton. Others: CtHT, CtY, NN.

Size: $6\frac{3}{8}'' \times 4\frac{1}{8}''$.

Collation: A-U^8=160.

Pagination summary: [i-vii], viii-xvi, [1]-304.

The Bell-Daldy device of the Aldine anchor and dolphin combined with a
carillon bell, is imprinted on the title-page. Following it is a typeset reproduction of the 1653 edition title-page lacking the cartouche. At the foot of
page 304 is imprinted, "Chiswick Press: -Whittingham and Wilkins, Tooks
Court, Chancery Lane."
    The illustrations are a frontispiece, "Landing the Trout," by Willmore
after Absolon, 13 woodcuts of fish, and the Walton-Cotton cipher on the
last page.
    Two publisher's bindings have been seen. The first is in bright red cloth
with beveled edge covers framed by three gilt rules on the front, and in
blind on the back. The title-page device is gilt stamped on the front cover.
Titling and a small decoration are gilt stamped on the spine, as is a narrow
band between single rules at the top and foot. The end papers are very
dark blue, top edges gilt. The fore and bottom edges of the leaves are untrimmed. The second, in dark green cloth, is otherwise identical except for
chocolate-brown end papers and lacking the front cover title-page device.
    According to *The English Catalogue of Books,* this is one of the "Elzivir" series.
It is a reprint of the Bell-Daldy and Low edition of 1863 (No. 81).

1865

83. The Second Bell-Daldy and Low Reprint

THE COMPLETE ANGLER by Izaak Walton and
Charles Cotton.
London: Bell and Daldy, 186, Fleet Street; and
Sampson Low, Son, and Co., 59 Ludgate Hill. 1865.

Copies examined: Harvard, Princeton, Yale. Other: CtHT.

Size: $5\frac{1}{8}'' \times 3\frac{1}{4}''$.

Pagination summary: [i]-xvi, [1]-304.

At the foot of page 304 is imprinted "Chiswick Press: -Whittingham and Wilkins, Tooks Court, Chancery Lane."

The Bell-Daldy title-page device, the typeset reproduction of the 1653 edition title-page lacking the cartouche, and the illustrations, are the same as those in the first Bell-Daldy and Low edition (No. 81), except that the plate of Walton has been changed to an oval shape.

This reprint was published in both dark green and dark red cloth, with chocolate colored end papers. The edges of the front cover are ruled in gilt enclosing a circular gilt device in the center. The back cover is plain. The spine is gilt titled, and banded in gilt at head and foot. The top edges are gilt, the others untrimmed.

According to *The English Catalogue of Books,* this reprint of the first Bell-Daldy and Low edition (No. 81) is one of the "Elzivir" series.

1866

84. The First Ticknor and Fields Reprint

THE COMPLETE ANGLER by Izaak Walton and Charles Cotton.
Boston: Ticknor and Fields. 1866.

Copies examined: Harvard, Horne.

Size: $5\frac{1}{4}''\times3\frac{1}{4}''$.

Collation: A-U^8=160.

Pagination summary: [i-vii], viii, [ix], x-xiii, [xiv-xv], xvi, [1]-304.

At the foot of the last page is imprinted, "Chiswick Press: -Whittingham and Wilkins, Tooks Court, Chancery Lane."

Bibliographers have not noted heretofore that Ticknor and Fields imported the sheets, for not one, but two different reprints of the *Complete Angler,* and published both in 1866 under their own imprint.

This reprint, not reported in previous bibliographies, is from the same small sheets used for the first Bell-Daldy and Low reprint of 1863 (No. 81). It has the same illustrations as the English reprint, which consist of the Mitchell engravings of the Huysman portrait of Walton and the Lely portrait of Cotton, as frontispieces for Part I and Part II; 13 woodcuts of fish and, on the last page, the Walton-Cotton cipher. Following the title-page is the same typeset reproduction of the 1653 title-page without the cartouche. The only change in the illustrations is that the frontispiece portrait of

Walton is oval in shape, instead of the usual rectangular form in the 1863 edition.

Both copies seen are in a dark blue cloth publisher's binding. The front and back covers are blind stamped with an oval decoration reaching almost to the edges. The spine is gilt-stamped with a decorative pattern, the usual titling and, at the foot, also in gilt, is imprinted, "James R. Osgood & Co." All edges are gilt.

Ticknor and Fields also published Walton's *Lives,* Shakespeare's Plays in six volumes, and works by Dibdin, Basil Hall, George Herbert, Lamb, Southey, and White's *Selbourne.* These also were all of imported sheets, all dated 1866, and all bound in the same blue cloth with gilt stamping. The Southey *Life of Nelson* occurs with either Osgood or Ticknor's name at the foot of the spine, which could possibly occur also on the *Angler* binding. James R. Osgood and Co. were successors to Ticknor and Fields, and to Fields, Osgood and Co. I am indebted to George T. Goodspeed, of Boston, for these supplementary data on Ticknor and Fields' publishing activities.

This is a reprint, without notes or introduction, from the 1676 edition (No. 6).

1866

85. The Second Ticknor and Fields Reprint

THE COMPLETE ANGLER by Izaak Walton and Charles Cotton.
Boston: Ticknor and Fields. 1866.

Copies examined: Harvard, Yale. Other: NjP.

Size: 6¼″ × 4⅛″.

Collation and pagination identical with No. 82.

At the foot of the last page is imprinted, "Chiswick Press: -Whittingham and Wilkins, Tooks Court, Chancery Lane."

This reprint is from the sheets used for the Bell-Daldy reprint of 1864 (No. 82), which were larger than the sheets used for the 1863 reprint (No. 81). It has the same illustrations as No. 82, which consist of a frontispiece fishing scene, "Landing the Trout," engraved by J. T. Willmore after John Absolon, 13 woodcuts of fish and, on the last page, the Walton-Cotton cipher. Following the title-page is the typeset reproduction of the 1653 title-page without the cartouche.

The publisher's binding, seen at Yale, is in purple cloth with dark chocolate end papers, and with the top leaf edges gilt. Both covers are double ruled in blind on the edges and, in the center, stamped in gilt on the front and in blind on the back. The titling within a clover-like decoration is "Izaak Walton's Angler 1866." The spine also is titled in gilt. The fore edge and lower edge of the leaves are untrimmed.

This is a reprint, without notes or introduction, from the 1676 edition (No. 6).

1866

86. The Fifth Bethune Reprint

THE COMPLETE ANGLER; . . . by Isaac Walton.
and . . . Charles Cotton. . . .
New York: John Wiley & Son, 535 Broadway. 1866.

Copies examined: Harvard, Princeton, Yale. Others: NN, OClW.

Size: 7⁹⁄₁₆″ × 4⅞″.

Pagination summary: [10], [i]-[cxii], [1]-250; [i]-[xxx], [31]-210.

This is the same as the 1859 Bethune reprint (No. 76) except that there is one more sheet at the front, no advertising pages at the end. The page numbering errors of that reprint are repeated and, in addition, in Part II, page 119 is misnumbered as 19. The printer's imprint is lacking on the title-page verso.

The illustrations are those of the 1852 edition (No. 67), and the error on page lxxxi of the Bibliographical Preface in the 1847 edition (No. 60) has been corrected.

The Princeton copy is in the publisher's binding of brown cloth, plain covers with beveled edges, and elaborate gilt decorations on the spine, which consist of bands and rules at head and foot; a loop, formed by a curved line extending from a flexed fishing rod, encircles the titling, which is printed diagonally, reading up from the left; and the unlikely combination of a float and a fly are near the end of the line, which dangles below the rod. The Yale copy, in green cloth, is otherwise the same.

With a new title-page, this is a reprint of the third Bethune edition of 1852 (No. 67).

87. The First Little, Brown (7th Major) Edition

THE COMPLETE ANGLER, . . . of Izaak Walton and
Charles Cotton. . . .
Boston: Little, Brown, and Company. 1866.

Copies examined: Harvard, Horne, Princeton. Others: CSmH, CtHT, CtY, DLC, NN.

Size: 8¾″×5⅞″.

Pagination summary: [i]-xiv, [1]-445.

On the title-page verso is imprinted, "One Hundred Copies printed. University Press: Welch, Bigelow, & Co., Cambridge." At the foot of page 445 is, "Cambridge: Printed by Welch, Bigelow, & Co." The title-page, printed in red and black, has the vignette from the 1844 Major edition (No. 55).

The illustrations consist of the 12 engravings on steel and the 74 engravings on wood, found in the Major edition of 1844. Westwood and Satchell's *Bibliotheca Piscatoria* states on page 234, "...the woodcuts have been re-engraved and are held to be finer than those used in the English edition [*i.e.,* No. 55]. The steel engravings are from the original plates." The four paging errors noted in the "List of Embellishments" have been corrected.

The Horne copy is in pebbled light blue cloth, with a red leather lettering piece gilt titled on the spine, has the blue binder's ticket of McNamee, Cambridge, Mass., on a corner of the front paste-down. The leaves are untrimmed.

A pencilled note on the front paste-down is "A note on the fly-leaf to another copy of this book states that nearly one-half of the edition (of 100 copies) was destroyed by fire in the bindery."

This edition is from the Major edition of 1844 (No. 55), which was based on the 1676 edition. It was reissued from the same plates in 1881 as the second Lippincott reprint (No. 110).

88. The Second Little, Brown (8th Major) Edition

THE COMPLETE ANGLER, . . . of Izaak Walton and
Charles Cotton. . . .
Boston: Little, Brown, and Company. 1867.

Copies examined: Harvard, Horne (2), Princeton, Yale. Others: CtHT, NcU.

Size: $6\frac{11}{16}'' \times 4\frac{5}{16}''$.

Pagination summary: [i]-xiv, [1]-445.

On the title-page verso is imprinted "University Press: Welch, Bigelow, & Co., Cambridge" and, at the foot of page 445, "Cambridge: Printed by Welch, Bigelow, & Co." Unlike the first Little, Brown edition (No. 87) the title-page is printed in black only, but has the same vignette of the "View from Lea Bridge."

The illustrations are the 12 steel engravings and 74 wood engravings from the first Little, Brown edition, of which this is a reissue in a smaller format, on less expensive paper.

The publisher's binding occurs in both brown and green cloth with beveled edge covers, top edges gilt, light chocolate-brown end papers. "Waltons Angler" in gilt within the cartouche from the first edition (1653) title-page reproduced in gilt, is on the front cover, and the usual titling is in gilt on the spine.

1869

89. The First Murray Edition

THE COMPLEAT ANGLER; . . . by Izaak Walton . . . London: Alex. Murray and Son, 30, Queen's Square, W.C. 1869.

Copies examined: Fly Fishers' Club, Harvard, Horne, Princeton, Yale. Others: CtHT, DLC, NN, NcD, OO.

Size: $7\frac{1}{8}'' \times 4\frac{1}{8}''$.

Pagination summary: [1-3], 4-7, [8]-106, (1 l.).

At the foot of page 106 is imprinted "Billing Printer, Guildford." On the title-page verso in a notice dated May 20th, 1869, referring to *Murray's Reprints, The Compleat Angler* "Forms the second of this series; . . ." On the advertising leaf at the end (printed on the recto only), the *Angler* is listed as having "112 [*sic*] pages. Cloth limp, 1s. Reprinted from the First Edition." At the top of page 52 is the misprint "preach it" instead of "precht it" as in the 1653 edition. There are no illustrations.

The author's name, the title, and "Edit. 1653," are stamped in gilt on the front cover, and "Murray's Reprint" within a decorative device is blind stamped on the back cover. The publisher's cloth binding, seen in both amethyst and royal blue, with yellow end papers, edges speckled red, and both covers framed by a single blind rule along the edges.

In the "Bibliography of this Work" (p. 106), imprinted "Lowndes" at the end (apparently from the sale Catalogue of the H. L. Lowndes angling

[97]

collection sold by Sotheby on November 7, 8 & 9, 1843), this reprint is listed as "35. [London,] 1869, crown 8vo. [*this edition*," (*sic*) the last *Angler* included in the bibliographical list.

Although advertised as a reprint by the publisher this is a resetting of type and should be considered as a new edition of the first edition of 1653 (No. 1). *The English Catalogue of Books* lists it as published in 1869 to sell for one shilling.

1870

90. The Third Jesse Reprint

THE COMPLETE ANGLER, . . . of Izaak Walton and Charles Cotton. . . .
London: Bell and Daldy, York Street, Covent Garden. 1870.

Copies examined: Harvard, Horne, N.Y. Public, Princeton. Others: CtY, DLC, KAS, TU.

Size: 7⅛" × 4⅝".

Pagination summary: [7], [i]-xix, [3], [1]-496, [497-498], [7].

On page 490, "Index" is misprinted "indix," in the running head. On the vignette title-page verso, and on the verso of page [498], is imprinted, "London: Printed by William Clowes and Sons, Stamford Street and Charing Cross." Except for a new title-page, this is a reissue of the first Jesse edition of 1856 (No. 70) with the same 206 woodcuts and, in the Harvard copy, the additional 26 steel plates. The errors in the index of "Engravings on Wood," (same as No. 70) have not been corrected. Of the 26 steel plates in the Harvard copy, the Horne copy contains only the portraits of Walton and Cotton.

Seven pages (page one pasted to the inside of the front cover) at the front, and seven at the end (last page pasted to the inside of the back cover), comprise "A Catalogue of Bohn's Various Libraries." This reprint is listed under section X, "Bohn's Illustrated Library," priced at 5s per volume; "or with 26 additional page Illustrations on Steel, 7s.6d."

The publisher's binding seen is in light green cloth, has an overall decoration in blind, with the words "Henry Bohn's Illustrated Library" in the form of a circle in the center of the front and back covers. In gilt at the head of the spine is the usual titling and, at the foot, "Bohn's Illustrated Library," each enclosed in a separate gilt garland. The remainder of the spine is decorated in blind. The leaf edges are untrimmed.

This is a reissue of the first Jesse edition of 1856 (No. 70).

[98]

91. The Third Little, Brown (9th Major) Reprint

THE COMPLETE ANGLER, . . . of Izaak Walton and
Charles Cotton.
Boston: Little, Brown, and Company. 1870.

Copies examined: Harvard, Princeton, Yale. Other: PP.

Size: 6⅝″×4⁵⁄₁₆″.

Pagination summary: [i]-xiv, [1]-445.

On the title-page verso is imprinted, "Cambridge: Presswork by John Wilson
and Son." This has the same vignette title-page present in the first Little
Brown edition of 1866 (No. 84).

Although the "List of Embellishments" calls for the 12 steel engravings
and the 74 wood engravings of the 1866 edition, the engravings on steel are
not present in the Harvard copy, which is as published.

All copies examined are in publisher's bindings. The Harvard copy is in
dark reddish-brown cloth with beveled edges and dark brown end papers.
The cartouche from the first edition of 1653, enclosing the words "Walton's
Angler," is stamped in gilt on the front cover. The usual gilt titling is on
the spine and the top edges are gilt. The Yale copy is the same except that
it is in light green moiré cloth and the covers are not beveled.

This is a reissue of the first Little, Brown edition of 1866 (No. 87).

92. The Second Murray Reprint

THE COMPLEAT ANGLER; by Izaak Walton. . . .
London: Alex. Murray and Co., 30, Queen Square, W.C. 1872.

Copies examined: Harvard, Horne, Princeton, Yale. Others: CtHT, NN.

Size: 7³⁄₁₆″×4¾″.

Pagination summary: [1-3], 4-7, [8]-106, 1 l.

At the foot of page 106 is the imprint, "Bradbury Evans, and Co., Printers,
Whitefriars." On the title-page verso is a notice dated May 20th 1869, referring
to *Murray's Reprints,* the *Compleat Angler* being the second of the series. The
end leaf contains notices of Walton and *The Compleat Angler* by Hallam, Lamb,
Mitford, Hawkins, Bowles, Nicolas, Bethune and Allibone. There are no
pages of advertising. At the top of page 52, "Preach it," from the first Murray

becomes "Preach't it," as compared to "precht it" in the 1653 edition. The "Bibliography of this Work" is reprinted on page 106.

This reprint was issued in dark purplish-brown cloth with yellow end papers. Both covers are edged with a double rule in blind, and both are blind stamped "Murray's Reprint" within the same decorative device used for the first Murray. The titling is stamped lengthwise on the spine in gilt.

This reprint, which later appeared in *The Fishing Gazette* during 1879 (see No. 106), is a reissue of the first Murray edition of 1869 (No. 89).

[1872]
93. The Anonymous Murray Reprint

THE COMPLEAT ANGLER; . . . by Izaak Walton. . . . [1872]

Copy examined: Horne.

Size: $7^{15}\!/_{16}'' \times 5^{3}\!/_{4}''$.

Pagination summary: [1-3], 4-7, [8]-106.

This apparently unrecorded issue has no identification as to printer, publisher, or place of publication. It appears, however, to be an anonymous printing, on large paper, of the 2nd Murray Reprint of 1872 (No. 92). Except for the leaf of notices present at the end of the 2nd Murray Reprint, the pagination, title-page, and typography are identical, even including the printing error of "Preach't it" at the top of page 52, as noted in the description of the 2nd Murray Reprint, and therefore its date, 1872, has been assigned to this printing. This might perhaps be a pirated issue or one intended for presentation.

It is covered in light blue paper over boards, with the spine (now missing except for the sides) in parchment paper. The leaves are untrimmed.

1875
94. The Third Nicolas Edition

THE COMPLETE ANGLER . . . by Izaak Walton and
. . . Charles Cotton . . .
London: Chatto and Windus, Piccadilly. 1875.

Copies examined: Harvard, Horne (2), Princeton, Virginia. Others: CtHT, CtY, CU, DLC, MB, NN, OO, OU.

Size: 7$\frac{9}{16}$″ × 5$\frac{1}{8}$″.

Pagination summary: [i-v], vi-cxxxi, 132-135, [cxxxvi]-cci, 202-205, [3], [1]-320, [1]-40.

On the title-page verso and at the foot of page 320 is imprinted, "Printed by Ballantyne and Company Edinburgh and London." The engraved title-page, from previous Pickering and Nicolas editions, is undated in this edition, and the printed title-page is decorated with a circular device of the publisher. Although the latter claims, "And Sixty Illustrations from designs by Stothard and Inskipp," 16 of the 61 illustrations enumerated in the "List of Embellishments" were produced by others.

The illustrations are the same as for the previous Nicolas editions except that, other than the preface and chapter headings, they are printed on full pages separately from the text, including many that formerly appeared as vignettes.

The 40 pages at the end consist of a list of books published by Chatto & Windus, which is dated November, 1874, in the Harvard and one Horne copy (lacking in the second). This edition is described on page 38 as, "With the whole 61 Illustrations, precisely as in the royal 8vo. two volume Edition issued by Pickering. A New Edition, complete in One Volume, large crown 8vo. . . . price 7s.6d." Oliver states (his number 89), that the advertisements in a copy in his possession are dated October, 1876.

This edition was issued in reddish-brown cloth, with light chocolate end papers. The cartouche enclosing the titling of the 1653 edition, is gilt stamped on the front cover within a panel bordered by black parallel rules. The back cover is ruled in blind. There are five compartments on the spine; of the four gilt panelled, two contain titling and two are blank; the fifth (second from the top) is a black leather lettering piece gilt stamped with the title. The publisher's names are in gilt at the foot. The leaf edges are untrimmed. The copies seen are on ordinary paper. The Heckscher Catalogue copy (lot 2089) is described as "Thin paper."

This is a one-volume edition reset from the two-volume second Nicolas edition of 1860 (No. 77).

1875

95. The First George Bell Reprint

THE COMPLETE ANGLER. by Izaak Walton and Charles Cotton.
London: George Bell and Sons, York Street, Covent Garden. 1875.

Copies examined: Harvard, Horne, Princeton, Yale. Other: DLC.

Size: $6\frac{1}{4}" \times 4\frac{1}{8}"$.

Pagination summary: [i-vii], viii-xvi, [1]-304.

On the title-page verso is imprinted, "Chiswick Press: -Printed by Whittingham and Wilkins Tooks Court, Chancery Lane," and at the foot of page 304, "Chiswick Press: -Whittingham and Wilkins, Tooks Court, Chancery Lane." The title-page is followed by a typeset reproduction of the 1653 edition title-page without the cartouche.

The illustrations are a frontispiece by Willmore after Absolon, "Landing the Trout," 13 woodcuts of fish and the Walton-Cotton cipher from the earlier Bell-Daldy and Low edition (No. 81), and Bell-Daldy reprint (No. 82).

The publisher's binding is in dark green cloth. The covers, with beveled edges, are banded by three lines, in gilt on the front, and in blind on the back. Titling, a small decoration, and three lines at the top and foot, are gilt stamped on the spine. The end papers are dark brown, the top edges gilt, the others untrimmed.

In the front of the Harvard copy of the fourth Jesse edition of 1876 (No. 97), there are 15 pages of "Standard Works" published by Bell, dated 1880, where this Bell reprint is listed as one of the ELZEVIR Series at four shillings six pence.

This is a reissue of the Bell-Daldy and Low edition of 1863 (No. 81).

[1876]

96. The Seventh Ephemera Reprint

THE COMPLETE ANGLER by Izaak Walton & Charles Cotton . . .
London: George Routledge and Sons. Limited Broadway, Ludgate Hill Manchester and New York [1876].

Copy examined: Princeton.

Size: $7\frac{1}{4}" \times 4\frac{3}{4}"$.

Pagination summary: [i]-xii, [13]-313, [314], [6].

On page [314] is the imprint, "Printed by Ballantyne, Hanson and Co. London and Edinburgh."

In the "List of Illustrations" on page x are four portraits (including the title-page vignette of Walton by Pearson), 11 vignettes, three cuts of tackle, and 19 cuts of fish.

The Princeton copy, although rebound, has the original binding preserved at the end. It was in green cloth, with gilt titling on the front cover;

back cover plain; gilt titling at the top of the spine and, in a circular device at its foot in gilt, "Routledge's Books for the People."

This copy has six pages of advertisements at the end, two for Morley's Universal Library, and four showing Routledge publications, the latter listing, among "Books for the People," an *Angler,* Crown 8vo, Cloth 2/-, and in Paper Covers, 1/6.

The American Catalogue lists an illustrated Ephemera edition in print as of July 1, 1876, described as crown octavo, selling at $1.25, and published by Routledge. The size and price indicate that it could well be this edition, and it has been so dated.

This is a reissue of the third Ephemera reprint of 1859 (No. 74), printed from the same plates.

1876

97. The Fourth Jesse Reprint

THE COMPLETE ANGLER, . . . of Izaak Walton and
Charles Cotton. . . .
London: George Bell and Sons, York Street, Covent Garden. 1876.

Copies examined: Harvard, Horne, Yale. Other: CtHT.

Size: $7\frac{1}{8}'' \times 4\frac{5}{8}''$.

Pagination summary: [15], [i]-xix, [xx], [1]-496, [15].

The title-page verso is imprinted, "London: Printed by William Clowes and Sons, Stamford Street and Charing Cross." Except for a new title-page, this reprint is the same as the third Jesse reprint of 1870 (No. 90), with the same 206 woodcuts. The errors in the index of "Engravings on Wood" continue. See notes to No. 70.

The Harvard and Horne copies were issued without the 26 extra steel plates in some Jesse editions (present in the Yale copy), but have the portraits of Walton and Cotton engraved by H. Robinson after Huysman (copied by C. R. Bone), and Lely.

At the front are 15 pages of "Standard Works" dated 1880 (page one pasted to the inside of the front cover), and at the end 15 pages of "Bohns Libraries," dated 1881 (last page pasted to the inside of the back cover), published by Bell. The first lists an "Angler" in the "Pocket Volume" series at 3s, and in the "Elzevir" series at 4s.6d; the second lists this edition in the "Illustrated Library" section priced at 5s, "or with 26 additional page illustrations on Steel, 7s.6d."

The publisher's binding of the Harvard copy is in light green cloth, has an overall pattern embossed in blind, with the words, "Bohn's Illustrated

Library" in a circle on the front and back covers. The spine has the usual gilt titling, and, at the foot, "Bohn's Illustrated Library." The Horne copy, with later leather rebacking, has plain, purplish-blue cloth covers. The Yale copy is in the red cloth and decorations of the previous extra plate issues.

This is a reissue of the first Jesse edition of 1856 (No. 70).

1876

98. The First Stock Facsimile

THE COMPLETE ANGLER ; . . . By Izaak Walton. . . . London: Elliot Stock, 62, Paternoster Row, E.C. 1876.

Copies examined: Harvard, Horne, Princeton, Trinity, Yale. Others: DI, KU, NN, PPL, PSC, ViU.

Size: regular state $7\frac{1}{16}'' \times 4\frac{3}{4}''$; large paper state $8\frac{1}{2}'' \times 6\frac{3}{4}''$.

Pagination summary: [i-v], vi-x, [16], (1)-246.

There are six engravings of fish and two pages of music, the second of which is printed upside down.

Although the unsigned Preface states (p. ix), "to save all risk of departure from the exact form these, [the original types], as well as the sharp, vigorous little cuts of fish and the very tasteful title-page, have been reproduced by a photographic process which is simply infallible; . . ." this statement must be taken with reservations.

Because of the many misprints and variations which occur in different copies of Walton's first edition (No. 1), a checklist of 48 of these irregularities has been devised, which shows to what extent the facsimiles follow the originals in these 48 examples (see Appendix B).

This first Stock facsimile contains 36 of the 48 errors or irregularities which is probably reasonable, considering the character and variance in errors which occur in first editions. However, the major variance in setting up this facsimile was in not reproducing the "C" in "Complete," in the running head, from different fonts on some pages, as probably happened on the pages of all first editions. On page 67, line 10, there are two unusual apparently deliberately printed black marks which do not occur as such in the first editions seen.

The publisher's binding of the regular state (Harvard copy) is in light tan cloth with titling in dark brown. A reproduction of "The Breakfast," an engraving on copper by Ryland after Wale, which appeared initially in the first Hawkins edition of 1760 (No. 9), is printed in dark brown on the front cover. The large paper state (Yale copy) was issued of the publisher in dark-blue cloth, backed with a brown morocco spine titled and ruled in gilt. The top edges are gilt, the others untrimmed.

This is the first attempt to produce a true facsimile of the first edition. It is listed in *The English Catalogue of Books* for the year 1876 as a 12 mo. priced at six shillings.

1877

99. The Second Stock Facsimile

THE COMPLETE ANGLER; . . . By Izaak Walton.
London: Elliot Stock, 62, Paternoster Row, E.C. 1877.

Copies examined: Harvard, Horne, Princeton, Trinity, Yale. Others: ICRL, MdBP, OU.

Size: $7\frac{1}{16}'' \times 4\frac{3}{4}''$.

Pagination summary: [i-v], vi-x, [16], (1)-246. See comments on the first Stock, and Appendix B for listing of 36 irregularities, which are the same as the first Stock of 1876.

The publisher's binding of the Yale copy is in dark brown cloth with parallel rules on both covers and the spine which is titled in gilt.

This is a reissue, with a new title-page, from the plates of the first Stock facsimile of 1876 (No. 98). The Preface is included.

[1878]

100. The Eighth Ephemera Reprint

THE COMPLETE ANGLER by Izaak Walton and
Charles Cotton . . .
London and New York: George Routledge & Sons. [1878]

Copies examined: None.

Size reported: 8vo.

This listing is based on Westwood and Satchell's *Bibliotheca Piscatoria* . . . 1883 (p. 235), where such a reprint is described as follows:

> Collation: frontispiece; pp. 313 and three leaves with explanation of plates and register; 2 plates. The publishers have issued other undated reprints of this edition with no alteration save in the illustrations. They are unable to furnish any information respecting them and we have failed to obtain copies.

It would seem from the above that while no information was forthcoming about other Ephemera editions, the publisher acknowledged an 1878 issue which, if as described with two, instead of the usual three plates at the end, is different in this respect from all other Ephemera issues examined.

[1878]

101. The First Davies Edition

"Chandos Library."
THE COMPLETE ANGLER. by Izaac Walton and
Charles Cotton. . . .
London: Frederick Warne & Co., Bedford Street, Strand. [1878].

Copies examined: Bodleian, British Museum, Harvard, Horne, Princeton, Publisher's.

Size: $7'' \times 4\frac{3}{4}''$.

Collation: π^2, [a^4], 1-29^8, 30^2.

Contents: p. [i], half-title, "The Complete Angler;" p. [ii], blank; p. [iii], title (see Fig. 15); p. [iv], printer's imprint; pp. [v]-vii, preface; p. [viii], blank; pp. [ix]-xii, "Contents;" pp. [1]-7, "Life of Izaac Walton;" pp. 8-12, "Walton's Will;" pp. 13-14, "The Subsequent History of The Complete Angler;" p. [15], facsimile of original title-page; pp. 16-17, "The Epistle Dedicatory;" pp. 18-21, "To The Reader;" p. 22, reproduction of the Seal given to Walton by Donne; pp. 23-32, "Commendatory Verses;" pp. 33-[360], text, "Part the First," etc.; p. [361], half-title, Part II; p. [362], blank; pp. 363-373, "The Life of Charles Cotton;" p. [374], woodcut; p. [375], title, "Part the Second;" p. [376], woodcut; p. 377, "To My Most Worthy Father;" p. 378, "To My Most Honoured Friend;" pp. 379-460, text, etc., "Part the Second;" p. [461], half-title, "Appendix the Last;" pp. [462]-467, appendix p. [468], advertisements.

"Chandos Library" appears at the top of the title-page (see Figure 20), as does a Warne device below, the black shield with the cipher F. W. crossed, in the manner of a fess, by a ribbon with "&" and "Co" on it. On the title-page verso is the printer's imprint which reads, "Dalziel Brothers Engravers & Printers Camden Press."

The illustrations consist of a frontispiece of Walton; 65 woodcuts (including one repeat on pages v and 87) from the first Major edition of 1823; the headpiece on page 33 from the second Major edition of 1824; a facsimile of the title-page of the first edition of 1653; and 23 additional woodcuts. There are also 20 pages with text illustrations of various kinds and types of fishing tackle, and 25 decorative chapter headings.

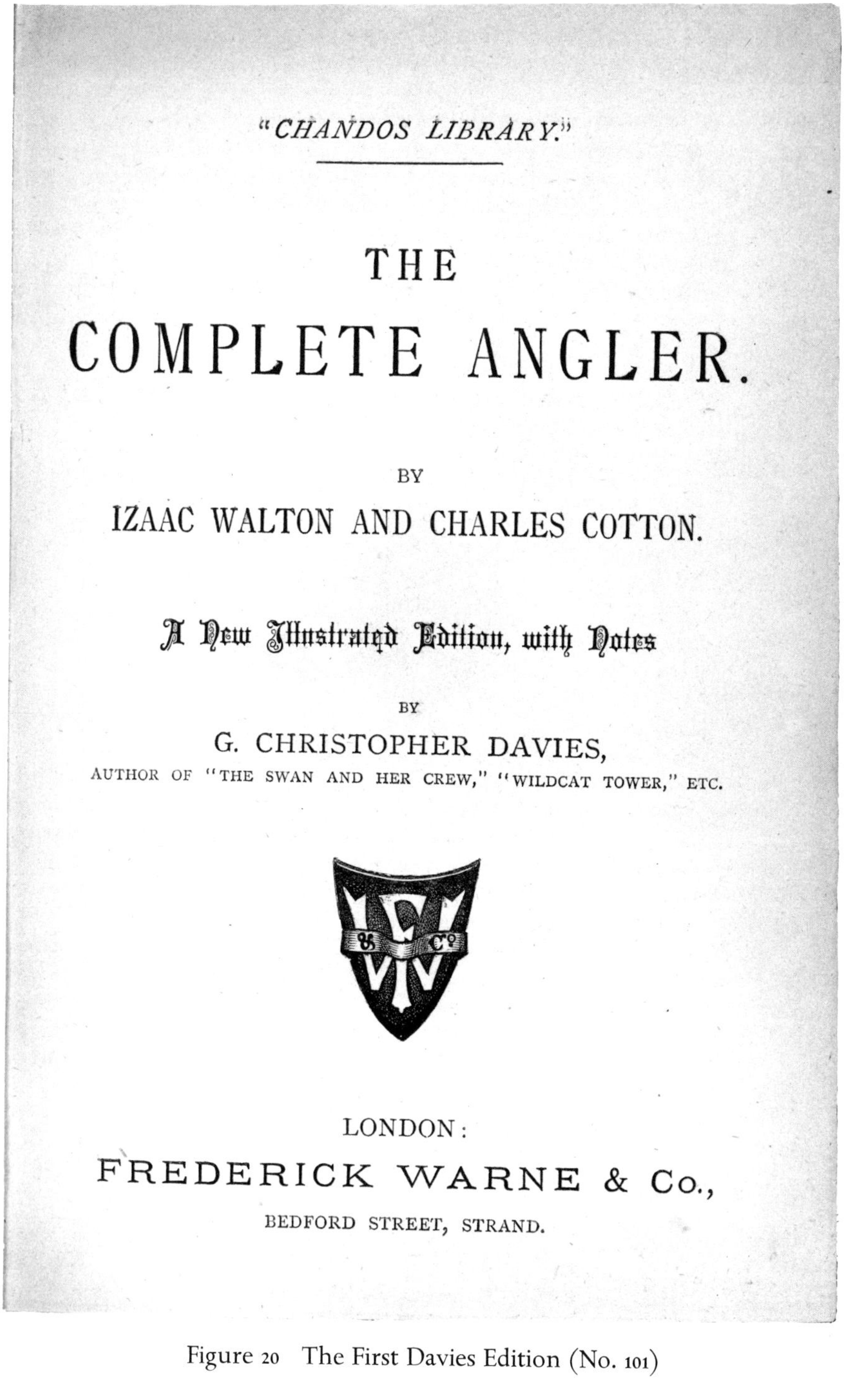

"*CHANDOS LIBRARY.*"

THE
COMPLETE ANGLER.

BY

IZAAC WALTON AND CHARLES COTTON.

A New Illustrated Edition, with Notes

BY

G. CHRISTOPHER DAVIES,

AUTHOR OF "THE SWAN AND HER CREW," "WILDCAT TOWER," ETC.

LONDON:

FREDERICK WARNE & Co.,

BEDFORD STREET, STRAND.

Figure 20   The First Davies Edition (No. 101)

The copy in the British Museum is bound in dark brown cloth blind stamped on the front cover with "The Chandos Library" and a landscape, with the latter forming a background for a gilt stamping depicting an angler and his helper about to net a fish. The title, names of the authors, "with illustrations," "notes by G. C. Davies," and an angler with his rod looped, playing a fish, are gilt stamped on the spine; in addition, "F. Warne & Co" in blind on a gilt shield is at the foot of the spine.

The binding of the Bodleian copy is in dark green cloth, with the same design and gilt stamping as the British Museum copy.

The copy seen in the publisher's office is in tan cloth. On the front cover are two fish, a reel, the title, and editor's name, all in gilt with a background design in black and dark brown. The title, authors' names, editors, and publisher are in gilt on the spine with a fill-in design in dark brown. On the back cover is stamped in blind the publisher's imprint of a shaded circle which encloses F. W. in cipher between "&" and "Co," all within a larger circle which is marked on the perimeter with four equidistant fleur-de-lis.

The Horne copy is bound in greenish-blue cloth with the same decorations as the copy seen in the publisher's office (see Figure 22).

The Princeton copy was issued in dark green cloth with an overall pattern of embossed squares, each containing a circular device having 16 radiants. "The Chandos Library" is blind stamped on both the front and back covers. The usual titling is gilt stamped on the spine.

According to the publisher, this first Davies edition was the only one published by Warne with a frontispiece of Walton, and only 1,500 copies were produced, with no other *Anglers* labeled "Chandos Library." The publisher further advises that it was produced in 1878, at the same time as an edition of 6,000 copies in the "Chandos Classics Series," which is listed as the second Davies reprint (No. 102). The smaller issue, with the portrait of Walton, is designated as the first Davies edition because it is the only one published by Warne as part of the "Chandos Library," because of the smaller printing, the better quality of paper, and because it would seem that a first printing would be the one most likely to have the portrait of Walton.

According to *The English Catalogue of Books*, Davies *Anglers* were published by Warne in 1878 to sell for 3s.6d., 2s., and 1s.6d. Since the second Davies was priced 1s.6d. and 2s. according to binding (see No. 101), the higher price undoubtedly refers to this edition. This listing is in accord with conversations with the publisher on the issuance of two Davies editions in 1878. *Bibliotheca Piscatoria* and the libraries listed date this edition 1878.

Oliver reproduced the title-page of the "Chandos Library" printing (see his No. 96), with the shield device on the title-page, as being the first edition, which is in agreement with this listing; but his description of it is headed "The Chandos Classics" and is for the issue of the larger printing, with the circular device. Wood (1900) illustrated and collated the edition described by Oliver, and apparently considered it the first edition (see notes to No. 102).

Aided by the availability of Warne editions apparently not thoroughly studied heretofore, through correspondence with Frederick Warne & Co.,

Ltd, and a personal interview with Director R. A. V. Priddle, who has completed his fiftieth year with the firm, accurate dates and data for all the "Anglers" published by Warne are believed to have been established herein despite the loss of records destroyed in the World War II bombing of London. This has resulted in verification, elimination and changes from previous listings, and the inclusion of five editions not listed in previous bibliographies.

This edition is from the fifth edition of 1676 (No. 6).

[1878]

102. The Second Davies Reprint

"The Chandos Classics."
THE COMPLETE ANGLER. by Izaac Walton and
Charles Cotton. . . .
London: Frederick Warne & Co., Bedford Street, Strand. [1878].

Copies examined: Harvard, Horne. Others: CU, CtY, NN, OU, NjP, ViU, WU.

Size: 7¼₆″ × 4¾″.

Collation, contents, and illustrations are the same as the first Davies edition (No. 101), lacking the frontispiece of Walton.

"The Chandos Classics" appears at the top of the title-page, with the circular Warne device below, which, in this reissue, is a shaded circle with F. W. in cipher between "&" and "Co." The printer's imprint on the title-page verso is the same as for the first Davies edition.

The Horne copy is in the publisher's binding of elaborately decorated mustard-yellow cloth, with blue paste-down and end papers at front and back listing Warne publications where this edition appears as number 58 in *The Chandos Classics* series priced "1/6 each, Stiff Wrapper. 2/- each, Cloth Gilt." The front cover is edged and bordered with ruled lines and type ornament borders in black enclosing two panels with black titling, and a central panel, stamped with an overall pattern of green foliage, which is bisected by a gilt strip stamped "The Complete Angler" in black capitals. A similar but much less elaborate pattern is stamped in blind on the back cover, with most of the type ornament omitted and the central panel blank, except for the titling strip. All titling is in blind, as is the number 58 stamped in the lower right corner. The spine is titled with raised letters on gilt strips and is decorated in black with rules, type ornaments, and a panel enclosing a shield marked "Chandos Classics" amongst the same foliage pattern in black used in green on the front cover.

The facts of printing and publication are in accordance with information supplied by the publisher that this printing was at the same time, from the same plates, as the first edition, and with the same illustrations, except the portrait of Walton. Harvard also dates this edition 1878, as does Wood. (See notes to the first Davies regarding priority, and *The English Catalogue* listing.)

This is a reissue in the "Chandos Classics" of the first Davies from the fifth edition of 1676 (No. 6).

[1878]

103. The Ward Lock Reprint

THE COMPLEAT ANGLER; . . . by Izaak Walton. . . .
London: Ward, Lock, & Co., Warwick House,
Salisbury Square, E.C. [1878].

Copies examined: Bodleian, Fly Fishers', Harvard, Princeton, Yale. Other: CtHT.

Size: regular state, 7¾"×5"; large paper state, 7⅛"×5⅝".

Pagination summary: [1-3], 4-7, [8], 9-106, [22].

At the foot of page 106 is imprinted, "Bradbury, Agnew, & Co., Printers, Whitefriars." As issued there were no illustrations; the copy at the Flyfishers however is extra illustrated with 11 plates. The 22 pages at the end are for Ward, Lock & Co. publications.

The publisher's binding of the regular state is in light blue paper over boards, with a paper label on the spine. The large paper copy seen is in light blue paper over boards backed with white parchment. A leather lettering piece, titled in gilt, is on the spine which is dated 1878 in black type at the foot.

This reprint of the first Murray edition (No. 89) is listed in *The English Catalogue* as having been published in August 1878, priced at five shillings.

1879

104. The Second George Bell Reprint

THE COMPLETE ANGLER. by Izaak Walton and
Charles Cotton.
London: George Bell and Sons, York Street, Covent Garden. 1879.

Copies examined: Harvard, Horne, Virginia, Yale. Other: NjP.

Size: 6¼"×4¼".

Pagination summary: [i-vii], viii-xvi, [1]-304.

On the title-page verso, and at the foot of page 304 is imprinted, "Chiswick Press: -C. Whittingham, Tooks Court, Chancery Lane." In the Horne copy, on page 281, only the very foot of the 1 is imprinted.

The illustrations and the binding are those of the 1875 Bell reprint (No. 95), of which this is a reissue.

[1879]

105. The Third Davies (First Scribner & Welford) Reprint

THE COMPLETE ANGLER. By Izaac Walton and
Charles Cotton. . . .
New York: Scribner and Welford, 743 and 745 Broadway. [1879].

Copies examined: Harvard, Horne.

Size: $6\frac{13}{16}'' \times 4\frac{1}{4}''$.

Collation: The same as the first Davies except π^1 instead of π^2, since there is no half-title.

Pagination summary: [i] & [ii], half-title leaf lacking; otherwise as for the first Davies, i.e., [iii]-xii, [1]-467, [468].

There is no printer's mark or device except on the title-page. The illustrations are the same as the second Davies edition of 1878, and there is the same advertising on page [468].

The circular title-page device of Frederick Warne, with F. W. in cipher on a shaded background in its center, encircled by the words, "F. WARNE & Co. BEDFORD St. COVENT GARN." differs from those seen on the other Warne *Angler* title-pages.

The Harvard copy is bound in brown cloth, blind stamped on the front cover with an overall pattern, which is impressed with gilt in the form of a large H, across the bar of which appears, "Walton & Cotton's Complete Angler." Below the bar, in a gilt design incorporating a lyre, is "Illustrated." The back cover is blind stamped in an overall decorative design. On the spine is "Illustrated" as part of an overall design in blind, with gilt decorations at the top, center, and foot; appearing on gilt bands are "Walton & Cotton's Complete Angler" and "Scribner & Co." The end papers are dark brown, and the leaves are gilt edged.

The Horne copy binding is identical with the Harvard copy except it is in dark purplish-blue cloth.

This reprint, not known to have been listed in previous bibliographies, is herein dated from the Horne copy, a Christmas present to a John Sprague, and inscribed on the front end paper, "Xmas 1879."

[111]

It is a reprint of the first Davies edition of 1878 (No. 101).

Although Oliver records a Scribner and Welford *Angler* which is included herein under his date of 1885, it is obviously different from this issue not only in the date, which he obtained from *The American Catalogue*, but also in the title-page which, from his own copy, he describes as bearing the black shield device of Warne, as contrasted with the circular device described above.

The sheets of this reissue are those of the first Davies (No. 101), but lacking the half-title, and with a new title-page, were distributed by Scribner & Welford in the United States.

1879

106. The Fishing Gazette Edition

THE COMPLEAT ANGLER, by Izaak Walton. Reprinted in
The Fishing Gazette; . . . Vol. III. 1879. . . .
London: Published by Charles William Bradley & Co
Offices: 12, 13 & 14, Fetter Lane, London, E.C. (All Rights Reserved).

Copy checked: Harvard.

The edition begins on page 60, (January 31, 1879) with a note from the editor (R. B. Marston).

"TO OUR READERS"

As promised, we commence this week to give our reprint of "The Compleat Angler," by Izaak Walton. We shall give a page to the work every other week, and the whole will be included in the Volume of the *Fishing Gazette* for 1879. We shall closely follow the original Edition, a copy of the Title-page of which is given below.-Ed.

There follows a typeset reproduction (lacking the cartouche), of the first edition title-page of 1653.

This issue, from the second Murray reprint of 1872 (No. 92), appeared in *The Fishing Gazette* during 1879 in 27 installments beginning on the pages listed below (Oliver, who listed only 16 installments, must have been working from an incomplete file; Wood listed 26, omitting that for December 6):

Date	Page	Date	Page	Date	Page
January 31	60	May 2	216	June 6	276
February 21	96	May 9	228	June 20	300
March 7	120	May 16	240	June 27	312
March 28	156	May 23	252	July 4	324
April 18	192	May 30	264	July 11	336

Date	Page	Date	Page	Date	Page
July 25	360	August 22	408	October 11	500
August 1	372	September 5	432	November 1	536
August 8	384	September 12	444	December 6	595
August 15	396	September 20	456	December 27	635

Following the December installment a note reads, "Mr. A. Murray from whose reprint of the first (1653) edition we have copied Walton's work, gives the following notes to his edition." These are notices of Walton and *The Compleat Angler* by Hallarn, Lamb, Mitford, Hawkins, Bowles, Nicolas, Bethune, and Allibone, repeated from two unnumbered pages at the end of the second Murray reprint of 1872 (No. 92). Since these notices were not included with the first Murray edition of 1869 (No. 89), it is certain that Marston "copied Walton's work" from the 1872 Murray reprint.

Marston ended his notes with the statement that, "The work has also been translated into German and French." He is of course referring to the first German edition of 1859 (No. 75), but his reference to the French translation must refer to a rendering of five pages printed in Part III, "Varieties, Études, Recits," added to the second edition of *Le Pecheur a la Mouche Artificielle et Le Pecheur a Toutes Lignes*, by Charles de Massas (Paris, 1859).

The French translation, on pages 256-261, was by Alfred d'Angleville, undoubtedly a pseudonym, and is in the form of a dialogue between Piscator and Piscator Junior. It covers part of Walton's description of chub fishing, and touches on trout fishing. It is preceded by a note to the author of *Le Pecheur* from d'Angleville, in which he says he is fulfilling his promise of furnishing ". . . la traduction d'un dialogue d'Isaac Warton [sic] . . ." There is a short note at the end, apparently by de Massas, thanking d'Angleville for "la fragment" and saying he will follow the advice of "Warton" in fishing for chub. *Le Pecheur* continued with "Warton" in the note at the front in the third edition, but finally corrected to "Walton" in the note at the end. "Walton" was used in both instances in the fourth and fifth editions of *Le Pecheur*.

Bibliotheca Piscatoria (1883) lists four editions of *Le Pecheur* by de Massas (p. 149), but does not mention this translation of a fragment of the *Angler* which has not been pointed out in previous bibliographies.

The first French edition is believed to be the abridged edition of 1942 (No. 322).

Appended to Marston's notes is a "Bibliography of Walton's Compleat Angler," which lists 39 editions, starting with the first of 1653 (1), "of which the *Fishing Gazette* copy is a reprint," the last in the list.

1880

107. The Sixth Bethune Edition

THE COMPLETE ANGLER, . . . by Izaak Walton, and
. . . by Charles Cotton. . . .
New York: John Wiley & Sons. 1880.

Copies examined: Harvard, Horne (3), Princeton. Others: CSmH, CU, CU-A, CtHT, CtY, DLC, MB, NNC, OCl, ViU.

Size: regular, 9½″×6¼″; large paper limited, issued in sheets, 10½″×7½″.

Pagination summary: Two Vols. Vol. I, [2], [i-iv], v-cxxi, [cxxii], [1]-294; Vol. II, [2], [i-iv], v-xxxii, [1]-215.

Except for the addition of a portrait of Bethune, issued with the sheets of the limited edition, and apparently intended as a frontispiece for Volume II, the illustrations are those of the 1847 edition (No. 60). The title-page verso has the imprint "Press of J. J. Little & Co., Nos. 10 to 20 Astor Place, New York." The title-page reads, ". . . By the American Editor (Geo. W. Bethune, D.D.) . . ." and the Bibliographical Preface is signed, "The American Editor, G.B.D."

An addition to the imprint on the title-page verso for both volumes of the large paper state reads as follows: "We certify that we have made for and delivered to the Publishers only 100 copies of this edition of Walton and Cotton's Angler. J. J. Little & Co. Oct. 20, 1880." The copyright reads the same in both printings "Copyright, 1880, by John Wiley & Sons."

Despite the note at the front "From the Publisher to the Reader" concerning corrections in the text, the error about the source of the illustrations, rectified in the third edition, appears once again on page lxxxix. (See notes to the 1847 Bethune edition, No. 60.)

The regular "edition" was issued by the publisher in dark green cloth with blind horizontal ruling spaced on the covers and with small angling motifs and the titling in gilt on the spine. The top leaf edges are gilt, the others untrimmed. The limited "edition" was issued in loose sheets uncut. The board covers, with ties, are backed and cornered with parchment. The Walton-Cotton cipher from the title-page to Part II is imprinted in red on the light green paper sides of the covers, with the titling, and the same small angling motifs used for the regular "edition," printed in red on the parchment spine.

This *Angler*, described on the title-page as a "New Edition, with some additions and corrections from the Editor's Own Copy," is a revised edition of the earlier Bethune editions.

[1880]

108. The Third Stock Facsimile

THE COMPLETE ANGLER ; . . . By Izaak Walton. . . .
London: Elliot Stock, 62, Paternoster Row, E.C. [1880].

Copies examined: Harvard, Horne (5), Princeton. Others: CtY, IU, ViW.

Size: 6¼″×4 uncut; 5¾″×3¹³⁄₁₆″ cut.

Pagination summary: [i-v], vi-x, [16], (1)-246.

See comments on the first Stock, and Appendix B for the 36 irregularities,
which are identical with those of the first Stock of 1876 (No. 98). Six copies
were printed on vellum, one of which is the Harvard copy.

The publisher distributed this issue of the facsimile in at least four different
bindings and in a paper cover, all of which have been seen. The *first* is in dark
greenish-blue cloth, leaves uncut. The only decoration is "Walton's | Com-
plete | Angler" between horizontal lines in parallel rule, all in gilt on the
spine. The *second* is in very dark green cloth, backed in parchment paper, top
edges stained yellow, others uncut. The only decoration is "Walton's Complete Angler" lengthwise on the spine, which has horizontal lines in parallel
rule at foot and head, all in gilt. The *third* is in brown paper over boards, top
edges stained brown, others yellow. A tan frame is set in from the edges of
each cover forming a rectangular brown panel; a fleur-de-lis is blind stamped
at each outer corner of the frame. The spine has two bands in the color of
the tan frame each with gilt titling, and four bands in the brown of the cover,
each gilt stamped with a fleur-de-lis. "Elliot Stock" is in gilt at the foot of the
spine. The *fourth* is in full parchment paper, uncut. A rectangular panel is
ruled on each cover by double red lines extended to the cover edge to form
corner squares, which are bisected by single oblique red lines extending from
each outer corner of the panel to the corner of the cover. A red decoration
is in the middle of each panel. The spine is banded with six sets of double red
lines, the middle four extending and joining at the base of a fleur-de-lis on
the inner rules of each cover panel. Titling, 1653, and fleur-de-lis are gilt
stamped on the spine. The *fifth* copy in light gray paper is untrimmed. At the
top of the front cover is imprinted in black *"Walton's Angler as it was originally
published;"* titling is in the center and, below this, *"Price One Shilling."* Other
Stock facsimiles of first editions are advertised on the back cover. On the
spine is imprinted lengthwise in black, "The Compleat Angler, 1653."

This is the only facsimile published by Stock lacking a title-page date;
Wood, Oliver, Harvard, and Princeton all assign 1880, which is followed here.

This issue is from the plates of the first Stock facsimile of 1876 (No. 98).

109. The Ninth Ephemera Reprint

THE COMPLETE ANGLER by Izaak Walton &
Charles Cotton . . .
London George Routledge and Sons Broadway, Ludgate Hill.
New York: 416 Broome Street. 1881.

Copies examined: Horne (2), Princeton, Yale. Others: MH, CtHT.

Size: 7⅛" × 4¾".

Pagination summary: [2], [i]-xii, (13)-313, [314], [8].

On page [314] is imprinted, "Printed by Ballantyne and Hanson London and Edinburgh." The title-page vignette, signed by Pearson, is that of the first Ephemera of 1853 (No. 68). There are two pages of Routledge advertising at the front where this edition is listed as number 59 in the Excelsior Series in cloth at 2s., and in the eight pages at the back it is listed as number 54 among new volumes in the series also in cloth at 2s. Six new Excelsior volumes are listed on the title-page verso.

The illustrations consist of four portraits including the vignette title-page; 11 chapter headings, tailpieces and text cuts; 19 cuts of fish and three of tackle.

This issue was seen in three publisher's bindings. The *first* (see Figure 22) is in red cloth with paste-downs and end papers of Routledge advertising. The front cover is edged by a black rule enclosing gilt titling, green floral decorations and "Excelsior Series" in black on a green background in the center. The back cover is blind stamped with a similar but less elaborate pattern with "Excelsior Series" in blind in the center. The same and similar decorations in green and black are on the spine with titling in red on gilt bands and "Excelsior Series" in red on a black scroll. The *second* binding is in green cloth, also with paste-downs and end papers of Routledge advertising. Both covers are ruled in black on the edges enclosing "Excelsior Series," titling, strip decorations and a central device of two sprigs of laurel entwined in a lyre, all in black. The same and similar decorations are in black on the spine, with titling in green on gilt bands and "Excelsior Series" printed in gilt at the top. The *third* binding is the same as the second, except that the cloth is mustard-yellow.

This is a reissue of the third Ephemera reprint of 1859 (No. 74), printed from the same plates.

110. The Second Lippincott (10th Major) Reprint

THE COMPLETE ANGLER ; . . . of Izaak Walton and
Charles Cotton. . . .
Philadelphia J. B. Lippincott & Co. [1881].

Copies examined: Harvard, Horne, Yale. Others: CtHT, NjP, ViU.

Size: 8¾″×5⅛″.

Pagination summary: [i]-xv, [xvi], [1]-445.

The half-title verso is imprinted, "Edition De Luxe. 250 Copies Printed — 150
for America, 100 for England."* The title-page is printed in red and black
with the vignette from the 1844 Major edition on India paper, laid down. The
"List of Embellishments," reprinted from the 1844 edition (No. 55), enumerates only the same (12) steel engravings and the 74 wood engravings found in
the 1844 Major and first Little, Brown edition of 1866 (No. 87). However, there
are 14 additional steel engravings (12 reported in *Bibliotheca Piscatoria* and by
Wood; none by Oliver) of which 12 are by J. W. Archer, S. T. Davis, J. Godden,
Griffiths, W. Henshall, Radclyffe, W. R. Smith and A. Willmore, after
G. Balmer, C. Bently, A. Cooper, T. Creswick, W. Linton, and L. J. Wood.
The portraits of Sir Henry Wotton and Nicholas Laneare are not signed. All
the illustrations are on India paper, with the wood engravings laid down in
the text, and the full-page steel engravings mounted.

The publisher's binding is in dark green cloth. The spine has a paper label
printed in red and black. The end papers are dark gray. The leaf edges are
untrimmed.

Although undated, seven lists and bibliographies consulted agree on 1881
as the year when this sumptuous reprint was published.

This reissue of the Major edition of 1844 and the Strahan reprint were
printed at the same time from the same plates as the Little, Brown editions
of 1866 (No. 87) and 1867 (No. 88), and consisted of the 150 copies printed for
sale in America, from a total printing of 250 copies.

111. The Strahan (11th Major) Reprint

THE COMPLETE ANGLER ; . . . of Izaak Walton and
Charles Cotton. . . .
London Strahan & Co. (Limited), 34 Paternoster Row. [1881].

*For description of ". . . 100 for England" see No. 111.

[117]

Copies examined: Cambridge, Harvard, Horne, Trinity Dublin. Others: CtY, ICN, NN.

Size: 8⅝" × 5⅞".

Pagination summary: [i]-xv, [xvi], [1]-445.

On the half-title verso is imprinted, "Edition De Luxe. 250 Copies printed — 150 for America, 100 for England." This is the latter issue.

The publisher's binding is in tan vellum sides, cornered and backed with parchment ruled with parallel gilt lines on its edges which meet the vellum. The spine ruled in gilt with a single line at the top and two at the foot, is gilt titled within two large superimposed gilt squares positioned between single gilt lines above and below the squares. Top edges gilt, others untrimmed, which accounts for the slightly taller leaves of the Lippincott edition.

With the change of the publisher on the title-page, this state consists of the 100 copies of the second Lippincott edition (No. 110) printed for sale in England. Each was printed simultaneously from the same plates but with its own title-page. It also has the same illustrations (see No. 110 for details).

1882

112. The Fifth Jesse Reprint

THE COMPLETE ANGLER, . . . of Izaak Walton and Charles Cotton. . . .
London: George Bell and Sons, York Street, Covent Garden. 1882.

Copy examined: Horne.

Size: 7⅛" × 4⅝".

Pagination summary: 2-14, 1, [1], [i]-xix, [xx], [1]-496, [1], 18-31. The 15 pages front and back are publisher's advertising. Pages 23* and 24* at the front are inserted after page 24. On page 490, "Index" is printed "indix" in the running title.

The title-page verso is imprinted, "London: Printed by William Clowes and Sons Limited, Stamford Street and Charing Cross."

The illustrations in the Horne copy consist of steel engravings of Walton and Cotton as frontispieces to Parts I and II respectively and the same 206 woodcuts of the prior Jesse editions. An attempt was made to correct the errors in the list of engravings on wood, but even so it continues to enumerate only 203 of the 206 engravings present. In prior editions, cut number six, "Seal-ring, a bequest from Sir H. Davy . . .," indexed for page xli, but never printed, has now been eliminated from the list, and the "Engraved Dedication" page, not listed in prior editions, substituted as number two. However, the half-title engravings and the two headpieces (pp. [i], [xv], and 484) are omitted as heretofore. The page index entry for the cut of Madeley Manor has been corrected from xxi to xix, but the five plates of "Angling Apparatus," on pages 334-338, continue to be indexed for pages 33-48. Walton's given name is spelled "Izaak" on the title-page, and "Isaac" in the title of the biography, Page [1].

Thirty pages of the publisher's advertising are in the copy checked, 15 at the front and 15 at the back. Those at the front (page one pasted to the front end paper) constitute a list of "Standard Works Published by George Bell & Sons," in which the *Angler* appears twice. The first, priced three shillings in the "Pocket Volumes" series, which were issued in "Imperial 32 mo. cloth;" the second, priced four shillings six pence in cloth, is in the "Elzevir Series," issued in "Small fcap. 8 vo." These are the Bell-Daldy and Low reprint, first issued in 1863 (No. 81), and the George Bell reprint, first issued in 1875 (No. 95). The pages at the end, a "Complete Catalogue of Bohn's Libraries," dated 1882, includes this edition of the *Angler* as part of the "Illustrated Library" series with "Upwards of 203 Engravings," at five shillings or, "with 26 additional page Illustrations on Steel, 7s.6d."

The publisher's binding is that of the third Jesse of 1870 (No. 90) lacking the gilt garlands on the spine.

With the changes noted, this is a reprint of the first Jesse edition of 1856 (No. 70).

[1882]

113. The Griggs Facsimile

THE COMPLEAT ANGLER . . .

London. Printed by *T. Maxey* for Rich. Marriot . . . 1653. [1882].

Copies examined: Harvard, Horne, Princeton. Others: CtY, ICN.

Size: 5⅝″ × 3⅞″.

Collation: The same as the 1653 edition.

Pagination summary: [16], (1)-246.

This facsimile of the first edition contains 40 of the 48 misprints and variations cited in Appendix B. In this printing the "C" in "Complete" on some running heads is from different fonts as it should be, and on page 245, line 17, "contention" is printed for "contentment."

Wood states that this is, "A photographic reproduction of the first edition without date or place, but by William Griggs, Photo-Lithographer to the Queen and to the Science and Arts Department, South Kensington." Oliver agrees that "this is actually a photographically exact reproduction." The best evidence to support this conclusion would seem to be line 8, on page 245; a line so long that in many copies of the first edition it has been cut by the binder to read "lov" (for loves) as in this facsimile. However, Appendix B shows that in two cases, "grov" for "grow" (page 133, line 18), and "sigh" for "sight" (page 181, last line), it does not agree with any one of the five first editions.

It is apparently the only facsimile with "contention" for "contentment" (page 245, line 17), which provides quick identification.

The publisher's binding is tan cloth with dark chocolate brown end papers, all edges untrimmed. The edges of the covers and the top and foot of the spine are ruled in dark brown. "Walton's Compleat Angler 1653," is stamped in gilt on the spine.

Library cataloguers and bibliographers generally agree that the publication date of this undated facsimile is 1882.

1883
114. The Nimmo and Bain (12th Major) Reprint

THE COMPLEAT ANGLER . . . of Isaak Walton and
Charles Cotton . . .
London J. C. Nimmo and Bain
14, King William Street, Strand, W.C. 1883

Copies examined: Harvard, Horne, Princeton. Others: CtHT, CtY, NN, PP.

Size: $8\frac{9}{16}'' \times 5\frac{7}{8}''$.

Pagination summary: [i]-xv, [xvi], [1]-445.

The half-title verso is imprinted, "Ballantyne Press, Ballantyne, Hanson and Co. Edinburgh and London" and at the foot of page 445 appears "Printed by Ballantyne, Hanson and Co. Edinburgh and London."

The illustrations consist of eight etchings with two impressions of each on different paper by Ben Damman after A. H. Tourrier, plus 74 text woodcuts from the Major edition of 1844 (No. 55) printed on India paper and laid down. The etchings, described on the title-page as "original," are probably better termed new interpretations. The title-page, printed in red and black, has the vignette, "View from Lea Bridge," which first appeared in the 1844 Major edition.

The binding is in dark bluish-green cloth stamped in gilt on the front cover with the 1653 edition cartouche (lacking the center titling). The spine is decorated with three gilt fish, and in addition to the usual titling, "London, 1883," is in gilt at the foot of the spine which is gilt ruled top and foot. Top edges are gilt, others are untrimmed. The small purple paper binding ticket of Leighton, Son and Hodge is attached to the back pastedown of the Horne copy in the binding described.

Both Wood and Oliver report this reprint of the Major edition of 1844 to have been printed from plates purchased by Nimmo from Little, Brown & Co. *The English Catalogue of Books* lists its price as 31s 6d.

1884

115. The Sixth Jesse Reprint

THE COMPLETE ANGLER, . . . of Izaak Walton and Charles Cotton. . . .
London: George Bell and Sons, York Street, Covent Garden. 1884.

Copies examined: Congress, Harvard.

Size: 7⅛″ × 4⅝″.

Pagination summary: [i]-xix, [xx], 1l., [1]-496, [24]. Pages 23* and 24* at the front are inserted after page 24.

The title-page verso is imprinted, "London: Printed by William Clowes and Sons, Limited, Stamford Street and Charing Cross." The illustrations are the same 206 woodcuts and 26 steel engravings of the first Jesse edition of 1856 (No. 70). The index errors of "Engravings on Wood" have not been corrected. See notes to (No. 70).

The 24 pages at the end are a "Catalogue of Bohn's Libraries," dated February 1888, which lists this edition in the "Illustrated Library" section (with the 26 steel plates) at 7s.6d.

The publisher's binding, in red cloth, has an overall pattern embossed in blind, with the words, "Bohn's Illustrated Library" in a circle in the middle of the front and back covers. The spine has the usual titling and, at the foot, "Bohn's Illustrated Library Extra Plates 7/6," both in gilt.

This is a reissue of the first Jesse edition of 1856 (No. 70).

[1884]

116. The First Crowell (13th Major) Edition

THE COMPLETE ANGLER, . . . of Izaak Walton and Charles Cotton. . . .
New York: Thomas Y. Crowell & Co., No. 13 Astor Place. [1884].

Copies examined: Horne, Princeton, Yale. Others: CtHT, GU.

Size: 7 1/16" × 4 7/8".

Pagination summary: [i-iv], v-li, [lii], liii-lx, 1-262, [263-264], 265-361, [362-363], 364-367, [368], 369-418.

There are 12 steel engravings, including portraits of Walton and Cotton, and 74 woodcuts, all from the Major edition of 1844 (No. 55). The woodcut of Archbishop Sheldon, indexed for page 203, is on page 202.

    The title-page reads "Edited by John Major" and "From the Fourth London Edition." These confusing statements should have simply said "From the 1844 Major Edition." The title-page has the same vignette as in that edition and, on the verso, a three line quotation from Act II, Scene 1 of Shakespeare's *As You Like It*.

    The publisher's binding of the Horne copy is in olive-green cloth, with end papers in an overall tan floral pattern, upside down in the back. The front cover and the spine are gilt titled, with a gilt stamped fish emblem in a sunburst.

    Although undated, the 1901 supplement to *Bibliotheca Piscatoria* lists this edition as having been published in 1884 in 12 mo. to sell for $2.00.

    This edition has been reset from the Major edition of 1844 (No. 55) which was from the fifth edition of 1676 (No. 6).

1884

117. The Fourth Davies Reprint

"THE CHANDOS CLASSICS."
THE COMPLETE ANGLER by Izaac Walton and
Charles Cotton. . . .
London: Frederick Warne & Co., Bedford Street, Strand. [1884]

Size: 7 1/2" × 4 11/16".

Pagination summary: [i]-xii, [1]-467.

The half-title verso is imprinted, "Dalziel Brothers, Camden Press, London N.W." and, on the verso of page 467, the same Camden Press mark that appears on the title-page verso in the first and second Davies, but in this case the following numbers are printed below it: 938.3***.6384.939. In the Warne device of the Wings and Horseshoe on the title-page, the spread between the tips of the wings measures 2.1 centimeters, as compared to 1.8 cm. for this device in other Davies editions. During an interview in London with R. A. V. Priddle, Director of Warne, he stated that this device had been used by the firm since at least 1881.

The pagination and illustrations are the same as for the second and third Davies except that the page of advertising at the end, and the woodcut on page [374] are lacking.

The publisher's bindings of the copies seen are in smooth dark blue cloth, with dark chocolate end papers. There are no decorations except a red ruled paper label on the spine.

According to information supplied by the publisher, this appears to be the second printing in the *Chandos Classics* series, and was published in March, 1884. With the exceptions mentioned above, it is a reissue of the second Davies (No. 102) which was the first printing in the *Chandos Classics*.

[1884-1886]

118. The Angler's Journal Edition

THE COMPLETE ANGLER | Part the First
[By Izaak Walton and Charles Cotton]
[The Angler's Journal, 20 Moorgate Street E. C. London 1884-1886]

Copy examined: Harvard.

Chronology:

> October 18, 1884: *Angler's Journal* announcement of plan to publish "Walton's Complete Angler . . . at intervals . . ." in its columns.

> October 25, 1884 through July 18, 1885: Walton's Part I in installments 1-39.

> July 25, 1885 through November 14, 1885: Cotton's Part II in installments 40-55.

> November 21, 1885 through August 21, 1886: Appendix, including Berners' *Treatyse of Fysshynge* . . ., Dennys' *Secrets of Angling* . . ., and additional text notes, in installments 55-91, apparently the concluding one, as none appear later.

The illustrations in Walton's Part I consist of 64 of the 66 woodcuts (including the frontispiece portrait of Walton and the music) in the edition in book form, plus two not in the book (an untitled view of a river house and Walton's house). The two book woodcuts not used here are titled "Otter and Trout" and "View on the River Ash." In Cotton's Part II there is one large woodcut of various caddis worms and flies; and in the Appendix there are five woodcuts (four repeated from Part I).

The Angler's Journal announcement, October 18, 1884, titled this the Bi-Centenary Edition of the Complete Angler, and included the names of the editor, Captain H. Jervis Alfred, and 13 others who contributed notes and comments. It is dedicated (by permission) to the then Duke of Edinburgh, Alfred, second son of Queen Victoria.

In the September 19, 1885 issue, the *Journal* had announced (Part I was finished July 18, 1885, and eight installments of Part II published), "We need scarcely remind our readers . . . that six monthly parts have been issued. . . . we propose to issue Part VII in a few days, together with the first volume – which will include all that portion of the work written by Izaak Walton. . . . The second and concluding volume will be a worthy pendant to the first."

The seven parts and the first volume were issued in 1885 (see No. 124). Part II and the Appendix were completed by the *Journal*, but neither the second volume nor more than seven parts have been recorded.

Wood (1900, p. 137) erroneously reported, "This reprint . . . was started in the Angler's Journal during the years 1883-'4 . . . Six parts are all that were issued and the work was never completed," and, in his Note (*b*), ". . . the title-page, Vol. I, was issued with the sixth part . . ." (The title-page appeared in Part I.) Oliver (1936, p. 149) reported Wood's observations given above, and wrote further, "This we have not been able to confirm." (See his No. 116.) He did not report further on *The Angler's Journal* issue.

This serial edition, of which Cotton's Part II and the Appendix have not been reported in previous bibliographies, is from Parts I and II of the fifth edition of 1676 (No. 6).

[1885]

119. The Fifth Davies (2nd Scribner & Welford) Edition

THE COMPLETE ANGLER by Izaac Walton and
Charles Cotton . . .
New York: Scribner and Welford, 743-745 Broadway. [1885].

Copies examined: None.

Size reported: 12mo.

Pagination reported: [1]-467, [1].

The above are as recorded by Oliver, his No. 112, which reads in part: "The colophon of Frederick Warne, a black shield with the cipher F. W. crossed fessways by a ribbon with '&' and 'Co.' on it, is on the title-page. The illustrations are the same as in the other Davies editions." His date is from *The American Catalogue*.

This edition with its black shield, of which Oliver states he owned a copy, is obviously different from the edition with the circular device on the title-page which is listed herein with detailed notes, as the third Davies edition (No. 105).

120. The First Baker & Taylor (4th Stock) Facsimile

Walton's Angler as it was originally published.
𝕿𝖍𝖊 𝕮𝖔𝖒𝖕𝖑𝖊𝖆𝖙 𝕬𝖓𝖌𝖑𝖊𝖗; . . . Being a facſimile
Reprint of the Firſt Edition . . . 1653
Baker & Taylor, Publishers, 9 Bond Street, New York. [1885].

Copy examined: Yale. Others: NIC, NN, NNC, NjP.

Size: 5⅞"-5⁵⁄₁₆"×3⅝"-4", leaves vary.

Contents: (cover-title as above); title-page (facsimile of 1st ed. 1653), [i];
blank, [ii]; author's dedication, [iii]-[viii]; To the reader, [ix]-[xiv]; Table,
[xv]-[xvi]; text, (1)-246.

Baker and Taylor advertisements appear on the back of the publisher's gray
paper wrappers, preserved in the bound copy examined. It was issued with
wrapper-title as above and facsimile title-page only. In this copy the half-
title, Baker and Taylor's title-page, and the Preface are lacking. The top
edges are gilt, the others untrimmed.

Wood's reproduction of the wrapper-title is as given here. He writes,
Note (*b*) on page 145: "A reissue of the reprint published by Elliot Stock of
London and imported to this country bound and complete, ready for sale,
with the imprint of Baker & Taylor on paper cover, as per reproduction.
The preface which originally appeared in Stock's 1876 edition is omitted."
Wood's date of (1885) is followed herein.

It has the 36 typographical errors and irregularities of the first Stock
facsimile of 1876 (No. 98). See Appendix B.

121. The Second Baker and Taylor (5th Stock) Facsimile

THE COMPLETE ANGLER; . . . By Izaak Walton
Being a *Fac-simile reprint of the first edition* . . . 1653
New York: Baker & Taylor, 9, Bond Street, [1885].

Copies examined: Harvard, Oliver, Yale. Other: CU.

Size: 5⅞"-5¹⁵⁄₁₆"×3⅝"-4", leaves vary.

Contents: half-title, "The Complete Angler," [i]; blank, [ii]; title-page (as
above), [iii]; blank, [iv]; Preface, [v]-x; facs. 1st ed. title-page, [xi]; blank, [xii];
author's dedication, [xiii]-[xviii]; To the reader, [xix]-[xxiv]; Table, [xxv]-
[xxvi]; text, (1)-246.

This facsimile is believed to have been issued in various publisher's bindings other than paper *with* half-title, title-page as above, Preface, and facsimile title-page.

The Oliver and Yale copies are both in the publisher's binding of dark brown heavy paper embossed with an overall tan pattern of cupids, angels and unusual animals, apparently derived from early manuscript decoration. The coated end papers are deep yellow; the top edges are gilt, the others are untrimmed.

Westwood and Satchell's supplement to *Bibliotheca Piscatoria* (1901), has the following entry (p. 19): "Compleat Angler. Facsimile reprint of the first edition, 1653. Illus. 16mo. in various bindings, $1.25, $2.50. Baker &Taylor, 85." The Oliver copy is inscribed, ". . . Dec. 25/'85."

This facsimile is dated [1885] herein. It has the 36 typographical errors and irregularities of the first Stock facsimile of 1876 (No. 98). See Appendix B.

1885

122. The Crawhall Abridged Edition

Izaak Walton: His WALLET BOOKE CIƆ.IƆ.CCC.LXXXV. London: Field & Tuer, The Leadenhall Press. Sampson Low, Marston, Searle, & Rivington.

Copies examined: Harvard, Horne.

Size: regular, $7\frac{1}{2}'' \times 4\frac{7}{8}$; large paper, $8\frac{3}{4}'' \times 6\frac{1}{2}''$.

Pagination summary: [1-6], 7-119], [120].

A handcolored woodcut is on the title-page recto and on the verso is "Imprynted by Field & Tuer, London, t 4,232," which is below a handcolored printer's mark reading "F&T" on a shield hanging from a tree branch. On page [117] is "Imprynted at Ye Leadenhalle Preſſe, 50 Leadenhall Street, London, E.C.;" on the following page, "ffield & Tuer London," and on page [119], a final handcolored printer's mark reading "Ye Leadenhalle Preſſe" and "F & T" in cipher.

The illustrations, "Sculptures curiously engraven by Joseph Crawhall," are, as stated on page [115], 174 handcolored woodcuts. The first is the title-page vignette, 122 are text decorations, 17 are on otherwise blank pages, and 34 are decorative initials. Signature renderings of "Izaak" and "Walton" appear at the top of facing pages [108-109]. Only 14 of the 119 pages are without some decoration. The last page [120] advertises Field and Tuer publications.

The large paper state, limited to 100 copies signed by the publishers, was issued in full vellum with ties, gilt stamped, with the usual titling on the front cover and spine. In addition, a small gilt decoration is on the front cover and at the foot of the spine, while the back cover is gilt stamped with the large woodcut on page 5. This state also has 48 blank pages at the end for "Fysshe Stories," and humorously labelled pockets attached inside each cover.

This abridged edition of 36 songs and posies from the fifth edition of 1676 (No. 6) is listed in the *British Museum Catalogue* under abridgements (Walton, Izaak — *The Compleat Angler*), and has not been included in previous bibliographies of the *Angler*.

1885

123. The First Nimmo (14th Major) Reprint

THE COMPLETE ANGLER . . . of Izaak Walton and
Charles Cotton . . .
London John C. Nimmo, 14, King William Street,
Strand, W.C. 1885

Copies examined: Harvard (2), Horne, Princeton. Others: CtHT, CtY, NN.

Size: $10\frac{9}{16}'' \times 7\frac{5}{16}''$.

Pagination summary: [i]-xv, [xvi], [1]-445, [1], [18].

The title-page is printed in red and black, and has the vignette from the 1844 Major edition. The verso is imprinted, "Ballantyne Press Ballantyne, Hanson and Co. Edinburgh and London," and at the foot of page 445, "Printed by Ballantyne, Hanson and Co. Edinburgh and London." In the Horne copy the numeral "8" is broken on page 48.

On the half-title verso the first paragraph of a "Publisher's Note" reads, "This extra illustrated edition of 'The Complete Angler' is specially designed for collectors of this famous work; and in order to enable them to take from or add to the illustrations, it will simply be issued unbound, but folded and collated." According to Oliver, "It was sold in a cardboard box, on the cover of which was a plate by Fox after Stothard."

The illustrations, as stated in the "Note" and on the title-page, consist of 50 steel engravings, which are by G. Adcock, J. C. Armytage, W. J. Cooke, Derby, Augustus Fox, Freebairn, W. Humphreys, Roberts, J. Richardson, H. Robinson and Wilkinson, after De La Motte, W. Gliscon, G. Hassell, J. Inskipp, Peter Lely, Huysman, Thomas Stothard, E. Sykes, and Vinkenboone; the 74 engravings on wood from the Major and first Little, Brown editions of 1844 and 1866; and "Six Original Etchings and Two Portraits," probably better described as new interpretations than as original. Although mentioned in the "Publisher's Note," the 50 steel engravings are not included in the "List of Embellishments."

At the end is John Jackson's *Treatise on Flies and Fly-Hooks*, consisting of a title-page with two engravings, 16 pages of text, and ten full-page handcolored plates of natural flies with their imitations. According to Wood, the plates for those illustrations are purchased from John Stark.

Although the "Publisher's Note" states in part, "One Hundred and twenty copies only are printed, each of which is numbered," Westwood and Satchell's supplement to *Bibliotheca Piscatoria* (1901) has an additional listing of 80 copies for America, and gives Scribner & Welford, New York, as the publisher (distributor), as does R. B. Marston in the "List of Editions of the Compleat Angler" in his third edition of the *Angler*, 1915 (No. 255). The selling price was $25.00.

This is a reprint from the same plates as the Nimmo and Bain reprint of 1883 (No. 114).

1885

124. The Alfred Edition

THE COMPLETE ANGLER . . . by Izaak Walton, . . .
by Charles Cotton. . . .
London: W. H. Allen & Co., 13 Waterloo Place. 1885.

Copies examined: Bound – Harvard, Horne; Copy in seven parts – Horne. Others: CtHT, CtY.

Size: Bound – $8\frac{5}{16}'' \times 5\frac{5}{16}''$; In parts – $8\frac{7}{16}''$-$8\frac{9}{16}'' \times 5\frac{1}{2}''$.

Collation: Bound – [A]-Y^8, Z=177, (G$_2$ is miskeyed F$_2$). In parts – Part 1, [A]^4, B-D^8; Part 2, E-G^8; Part 3, H-K^8; Part 4, L-N^8; Part 5, O-Q^8; Part 6, R-T^8; Part 7, [A]^4, U-Y^8, Z=177, (G$_2$ is miskeyed F$_2$).

Pagination summary: Bound – [16], [1]-338, [14]; In Parts – Part 1, [8], [1]-48, [8]; Part 2, [7], 49-96, [8]; Part 3, [8], 97-144, [8]; Part 4, [8], 145-192, [8]; Part 5, [8], 193-240, [8]; Part 6, [8], 241-288, [8]; Part 7, 289-338, [6].

Fourteen pages at the end of the bound copy advertise such diverse items as fishing tackle, insurance, a bank, stationery, liniment, whiskey, gold fish (live), and a small piano for a yacht. Each separate part has much the same type of advertising, which appears on the front and back of the paper wrappers, on eight pages front and back in Parts 1, 3, 4, 5, and 6, on seven pages in the front and eight pages in the back of Part 2, and in Part 7, on six pages in the back only.

On the title-page verso is imprinted, "Darling and Son, Minerva Steam Printing Office, 35, Eastcheap, E.C." At the foot of the outside front wrapper of Part 1, this appears as, "Darling & Son, Minerva Steam Printing Office,

FEBRUARY, 1885.]   [Part 2.
PRICE SIXPENCE.

JANUARY, 1885.]   [Part 1.
PRICE, SIXPENCE.

To be completed in about Twelve Monthly Parts.

THE

Complete Angler

BY

IZAAK WALTON

AND

CHARLES COTTON

BI-CENTENARY EDITION

WITH

ENTIRELY NEW NOTES AND NUMEROUS
ILLUSTRATIONS.

DEDICATED

BY SPECIAL PERMISSION

TO

H.R.H. THE DUKE OF EDINBURGH, K.G.,

ETC., ETC.

London:
W. H. ALLEN & CO., 13, WATERLOO PLACE,
1885.

DARLING & SON,
Minerva Steam Printing Office, 35, Eastcheap, E.C.

CHEAP BOOKS.—GILBERT & FIELD allow Threepence discount in the Shilling from the published prices of all New Books, School Books, School Prizes, and Magazines. Country and Export orders promptly executed. Catalogues gratis and post-free. All orders to the amount of £5 sent carriage-free to any part of the United Kingdom.
GILBERT & FIELD, 67, Moorgate Street, and 18, Gracechurch Street, London, E.C.

Est. 1823.] GRAVELL & SON, 21 to 24, WHITECROSS STREET, LONDON, E.C., [Est. 1823.

Carvers, Gilders, Restorers of Fine Arts, etc., etc.

CHEAP BOOKS.—GILBERT & FIELD allow Threepence discount in the Shilling

CHEAP BOOKS.—GILBERT & FIELD allow Threepence discount in the Shilling

PRICE, SIXPENCE.
MARCH, 1885.]   [Part 3.

APRIL, 1885.]   [Part 4.

PRICE, SIXPENCE.
Part 5.

Part 6.

Part 7.

Figure 21   The Alfred Edition (No. 124), in all seven
separately issued parts

35 Eastcheap, E.C." In the same place on Part 2 the street address number is changed to 31. The remaining parts lack a printer's imprint on the front wrapper.

The list of illustrations is for 66 woodcuts, including six pages of music, mostly by W. H. J. Alfred. There are also an unsigned tailpiece of a grasshopper on page 94 and 21 ornamental head and tailpieces of which one is used four times, one three times, and one twice. The frontispiece of Walton is in Part 2.

Since this is apparently the first time that all seven separately issued parts of this edition have been recorded, they have been described in detail. Previous bibliographies have reported only six parts to have been issued separately, with the seventh part present and bound with the other six when the edition was published in book form. Although on the front cover of each part is printed, "To be completed in about Twelve Monthly Parts," Part 7, which completed Part I of the *Angler*, was the last to be issued. Inserted in Part 7 of the complete set of parts examined is a postcard from the publisher, apparently in response to an inquiry, dated and postmarked April 16, 1887, addressed to Messrs. Cornish & Bros, Booksellers, Birmingham, and reads, "Complete Angler — part 7 is the last part & very unlikely if any more will be pub." Since no additional parts are known, the inclusion of Cotton's name and his part of the *Angler* on the title-page is incorrect.

In book form, the publisher's binding is in dark green cloth with beveled edges and yellow end papers. The front cover is stamped in black with three ruled edges and a decorative design at the top and foot. Gilt stamped in the center is a device of an Aldus anchor and a large A, entwined with a rope, surmounted by a gilt crown. (The same device is at the top of the dedication page.) The edges of the back cover are blind stamped with two ruled lines and the center with a circle surrounded by flowers. In addition to the usual titling in gilt on the spine, "Bi-Centenary Edition" is stamped at the foot.

The seven parts were issued in greenish-gray paper (Figure 21). The titling on the front cover of each part is framed by a printed border of fish cuts and decorations from the illustrations. Advertising is printed vertically (and on some also along the top) outside the frame on the front wrapper and conventionally on the entire back. All wrappers are blank inside.

The front wrappers are all dated 1885 in the titling. In addition, Parts 1 and 2 at the top, and 3 and 4 at the foot, are dated respectively January, February, March, and April, 1885.

The one-page introduction, signed "H. J. A.," was by the editor Captain H. Jervis Alfred who, with 13 other gentlemen, "well-known in the piscatorial world," collaborated in the notes and comments, many of which are concerned with the technical mechanics of angling.

This edition, dedicated by permission "To his Royal Highness The Duke of Edinburgh, K.G. etc," (*i.e.*, Alfred, second son of Queen Victoria) is called the "Bi-Centenary Edition" on the title-page, and is based on Walton's Part I of the 1676 edition (No. 6).

1886

125. The First Cassell Edition

CASSELL'S NATIONAL LIBRARY
THE COMPLETE ANGLER : . . . by Isaac Walton.
Cassell & Company, Limited : London, Paris, New York &
Melbourne. 1886.

Copies examined : Harvard, Horne, Princeton. Others : CtY, NN, PSC, TxU.

Size : 5⅝″×3¾″.

Collation : [A]¹⁶, B¹⁶, C-5¹⁶, D-5¹⁶, E-5¹⁶, F-5¹⁶=96.

Pagination summary : [1-3], 4-192, [4].

At the foot of page 192 is imprinted, "Printed by Cassell & Company, Limited, La Belle Sauvage, London, E.C." The circular device of Cassell & Company appears on the title-page. The device derived from their place of address, La Belle Sauvage Yard, portrays an idealized young Amazon, kneeling in the center, with the words "La Belle" and "Sauvage," draped left and right respectively. In various interpretations, Cassell used this device for many years. Walton's dedication to John Offley is omitted from the text.

The edition described here is not identical with the edition listed by Wood, who gives the signatures as one of 12 leaves, five of 16, and one of four, while shown above are six of 16; Wood's reproduction of the title-page does not show the colons after "Angler" and "Limited," and omits the periods after "Walton," "Melbourne," and "1886."

Four pages of Cassell advertising are at the end, where this edition is priced at three pence in paper covers, and six pence in cloth. It was part of "Cassell's National Library" and is the fifth title listed. Advertisements by British merchants for such items as health products, table linen, bicycles, and mattresses appear on the pastedowns and the back cover.

The publisher's binding is in grayish-tan cloth. In the middle of the front cover "Cassell's National Library" is imprinted in the center of a large circular floral type decoration. Above this, on a black background, the title and author's name are gilt stamped. Although Henry Morley provided only a two-page introduction, he is designated on the foot of the front cover as the editor. The spine is titled lengthwise in black and the numeral 5 is in black at the foot.

This is a new edition, without notes, of Walton's part of the fifth edition of 1676 (No. 6), lacking the dedication, and is listed on the title-page verso of the eleventh Cassell edition of 1898 (No. 179) as, "First published in this series, January, 1886."

1886

126. The Second Cassell Reprint

CASSELL'S NATIONAL LIBRARY
THE COMPLETE ANGLER: . . . by Isaac Walton.
Cassell & Company, Limited: London, Paris, New York &
Melbourne. 1886.

Copy examined: Horne. Others: CSmH, CtY, MH, NjP.

Size: 5⅝″×3¹⁵⁄₁₆″.

Collation: [A-5]¹⁶, B-5¹⁶, C-5¹⁶, D-5¹⁶, E-5¹⁶, F-5¹⁶=96.

Pagination summary: [1-3], 4-192.

At the foot of page 192 is imprinted, "Printed by Cassell & Company, Limited, La Belle Sauvage, London, E.C." Cassell's circular Belle Sauvage device, appearing a little worn, is printed on the title-page, as in No. 124. Walton's dedication to John Offley is omitted.

The binding examined (with the Samuel W. Lambert book plate in the front pastedown), in marbled boards with a red leather spine, top edges gilt, others untrimmed, is apparently contemporary, which may have been provided for a special purpose, such as a school prize, as almost the entire back pastedown is scarred by the removal of a plate of the size often used in such books. The leaves are about ³⁄₁₆ of an inch wider than those of the preceding edition.

The same plates were used for the first Cassell (No. 125) and this reissue, but the clear impressions secured in the first printing were not obtained in the second. This may be noted in the title-page device, the poor impressions of some running titles, page numbers and words in the text.

This is apparently the reprint listed on the title-page verso of the eleventh Cassell reprint of 1898 (No. 179), as "Reprinted February 1886." It is also listed in *The English Catalogue of Books* as published by Cassell in February 1886 priced at 3 pence and six pence.

This is a reissue of the first Cassell edition of 1886 (No. 125).

[1886]

127. The Third Cassell Reprint

THE COMPLETE ANGLER: . . . by Izaac Walton.
Cassell & Company, Limited: 739 & 741 Broadway
New York. [1886].

Copies examined: Oliver (2).

Size: 5½″×3⅞″ (one in paper wrappers, one in cloth).

Pagination summary: [1-3], 4-192, [16].

The title-page bears the publisher's circular device of La Belle Sauvage. The printer's imprint is lacking on page 192. The 16 terminal pages are publisher's advertising; this reprint is the fourth listed in Cassell's National Library, priced 10 cents in paper; the cloth bound copy, priced 25 cents, is not mentioned.

The 10-cent version was issued in gray paper wrappers, imprinted in the center of the front one with a large circular decoration in which appears, in white on a black background, "Cassell's National Library edited by Professor Henry Morley." Titling is above the decoration and, at the upper edge is "Vol. I., No. 4. Subscription price per year. $5.00. Feb. 20, 1886. Issued Weekly." Below the decoration is "Ten Cents," with the publisher's name and the address, "739-741 Broadway." The outside of the back wrapper advertises The Chicago and Northwestern Railway; the inside of both covers, druggist's wares. The front cover of the copy in gray cloth is as described for that in paper, but lacks the printing on the upper edge. It is priced "Twenty five cents." Its covers have no advertising. Both copies are titled vertically on the spine.

This reissue, with a new title-page, of the first Cassell edition of 1886 (No. 125), is No. 4 in Cassell's National Library. *The Annual American Catalogue* reports its publication on February 27, 1886.

[1886]

128. The Fourth Cassell (Leipzig) Reprint

THE COMPLETE ANGLER: . . . by Isaac Walton.
Leipzig Gressner & Schramm [1886].

Copy examined: Yale.

Size: 5⁹⁄₁₆″×3¾″.

Pagination summary: [1-3], 4-192.

At the foot of page 192 is imprinted, "Printed by Cassell & Company, Limited, La Belle Sauvage, London, E. C."

The publisher's binding is in red cloth with a Grolieresque design on the front cover in black. The spine is titled vertically in black. The end papers are white and the page edges are trimmed.

This reprint is reported by Marston, Oliver, and in the supplement to

Westwood and Satchell's *Bibliotheca Piscatoria* as having been published in 1886, which is followed by Yale and is used herein.

This is a reissue, with a new title-page, of the first Cassell edition of 1886 (No. 125).

[1887]

129. The Fifth Cassell Reprint

CASSELL'S NATIONAL LIBRARY
THE COMPLETE ANGLER: . . . by Isaac Walton
Cassell & Company Limited 104 & 106 Fourth Avenue
New York [1887].

Copies examined: Harvard (2).

Size: Paper wrappers, $5\frac{3}{8}'' \times 3\frac{3}{4}''$; Cloth, $5\frac{7}{16}'' \times 3\frac{13}{16}''$.

Pagination summary: [1-3], 4-192, [16].

The title-page bears the publisher's circular device of La Belle Sauvage. The printer's imprint is lacking on page 192. The advertising at the end of the copy in paper wrappers consists of five pages devoted to such products as patent medicine, children's food and the department store of James McCreery & Co., plus 11 pages of Cassell publications where this reprint is listed as No. 4 in Cassell's National Library at 10 cents in paper wrappers and, in extra cloth, at 25 cents, and additional advertising on both sides of the back cover, and inside the front cover. The copy in cloth has 13 pages of Cassell advertising, and three pages for other products. Both copies have an advertisement for Colgate soap on the verso of the title-page.

The 10-cent version was issued in gray paper, imprinted in the center of the front cover with a large circular decoration in which appears, on a black background, "Cassell's National Library edited by Professor Henry Morley." Titling is above, and the publisher's address, "104 & 106 Fourth Ave., N. Y." below the decoration; "February 20, 1886" is imprinted on the upper right hand corner. The 25-cent version was issued in gray cloth, with the same decoration and titling on the undated front cover, where the publisher's address is imprinted as "739-741 Broadway, N. Y."

The 1886 date on the paper cover, and the address on the cloth cover, are both misleading as to the correct date for this issue. Since the title-page gives Cassell's address in New York as 104 & 106 Fourth Avenue which, according to *The Annual American Catalogue*, was the publisher's location in 1887, and until 1893, Cassell could not have issued this reprint in 1886, and must have bound it in paper and cloth covers remaining from the 1886 issue which were imprinted respectively with the original date and previous address. (See No. 127.)

A close approximation of the correct date for this issue may be determined from *The Annual American Catalogue* for publications of 1889, which states that Cassell is "now Cassell Pub. Co." and, since the two later Cassell editions issued from 104 & 106 Fourth Avenue are imprinted "Cassell Publishing Company" on the title-page, this fifth reprint must have been issued in 1887 or 1888.

Since Cassell's series of "Anglers" were very much in demand, the earlier date of 1887 has been assigned to this reprint. It is a reissue, with a new title-page of the first Cassell edition of 1886 (No. 125).

1887

130. The Fourth Nicolas Reprint

THE COMPLETE ANGLER . . . by Izaak Walton and . . .
Charles Cotton . . .
London Chatto and Windus, Piccadilly 1887

Copies examined: Harvard, Horne, Princeton, Yale. Others: CtHT, OO.

Size: 7½" × 5⅛".

Pagination summary: [i-v], vi-cxxxi, 132-135, [cxxxvi]-cci, 202-205, [3], [1]-320, [32].

On the title-page verso is "Ballantyne Press Ballantyne, Hanson and Co. Edinburgh and London" and, at the foot of page 320, "Printed by Ballantyne, Hanson and Co. Edinburgh and London."

The illustrations are the same, and in the same format, as the third Nicolas edition of 1875 (No. 94). The engraved title-page is undated and is at the front of the book — not at page one as indexed in the "List of Embellishments." The printed title-page, imprinted with a device of the publisher, calls this "A New Edition."

The 32 pages at the end consist of a list dated July, 1895, of Chatto & Windus publications. Oliver reported (his No. 122) examining a copy with the advertisements dated May 1901. This edition is described on page 25 of the list as having, "61 Illustrations, brown 8vo. cloth antique, 7s.6d."

This edition was issued in smooth antique brown cloth with chocolate-brown end papers. The cartouche enclosing the titling of the 1653 edition is gilt stamped within a ruled panel outlined in darker brown on the front cover. The back cover is plain. The spine is gilt ruled into five compartments with two gilt lines at the top and foot. The titling and publishers' names are in gilt on the spine; the former in the three central compartments, the latter between the two lines at the foot. The titling is in gilt. The leaf edges are untrimmed.

This is a reprint of the third Nicolas edition of 1875 (No. 94).

[135]

[1887]

131. The Third Baker and Taylor (6th Stock) Facsimile

THE COMPLETE ANGLER ; . . . by Izaak Walton.
New York: The Baker & Taylor Co., 9 Bond Street. [1887].

Copy examined: Yale.

Size: 5¾″ × 3¹³⁄₁₆″.

Pagination with Preface: [i-v], vi-x, [16], (1)-246.

This is a reissue of the Baker and Taylor facsimile of [1885] with the Preface
and the 36 typographical errors and irregularities of the first Stock facsimile
of 1876 (No. 98). See Appendix B.
    The publisher's binding seen is that of the *third* binding described for the
third Stock facsimile (No. 108) except that all edges are yellow.
    This facsimile is dated [1887] by Oliver (see his No. 123) and is followed herein.

[1887]

132. The Sixth Davies Reprint

"THE CHANDOS CLASSICS"
THE COMPLETE ANGLER by Izaac Walton and
Charles Cotton . . .
London: Frederick Warne & Co. [1887].

Copies examined: None seen.

Size reported: 12mo.

Pagination summary: [i]-xii, [1]-467.

According to information supplied by the publisher, this is a reprint, issued
in September 1887, of the second Davies edition of 1878 (No. 102) in the
"Chandos Classics" series. It had the device of the Wings and Horseshoe on
the title-page used by Warne after 1881. See note under the fourth Davies
reprint of 1884 (No. 117).
    This reprint is not listed in previous bibliographies of the *Angler*.

133. The Seventh Davies Reprint

"THE CHANDOS CLASSICS"
THE COMPLETE ANGLER by Izaac Walton and
Charles Cotton. . . .
London and New York: Frederick Warne and Co. 1888

Copies examined: Horne (2), Yale. Others: MH, NN.

Size: 7¼″×4⅞″.

Pagination summary: [i]-xii, [1]-467, [1].

"The Chandos Classics," and the Warne device, a horseshoe between two wings, with a spread of 1.8 cm. at the tips, appear on the title-page recto, and the printer's imprint on the verso reads: "Dalziel Bros., Camden Press, London, N. W." The page of advertising at the end is for Warne publications.

The illustrations and decorations are the same as the first Davies edition of 1878 (No. 101), lacking the frontispiece of Walton, the chapter heading decorations on page [ix], and the woodcut on page [374]. See the eighth Davies (No. 146) for additional details.

The *first* Horne binding is in very dark green cloth, pebbled on the sides, smooth and silk-like cloth on the spine, the latter having two leather lettering pieces impressed with the usual titling in gilt. The end papers are very dark brown and the top edges are gilt. The *second* binding is without gilt, in dark blue (faded to brown) cloth with a spine paper label where Walton's given name is spelled "Isaac," as contrasted with "Izaac" on the title-page (see the 13th Davies of 1899 (No. 185) for an "Izaak" spelling). The *third* binding (Yale) is in dark red cloth, rough to the smooth backing, slate gray end papers, top edges gilt, others untrimmed. The only decoration is a simulated lettering piece at the top of the spine, titled and framed in gilt, and "F. Warne & Co." in gilt within gilt rules at the foot.

There are four Warne-Davies *Anglers* with both New York and London on the title-page; this edition, the 10th of 1893, the 12th of 1895, and the 14th of 1930.

This is a reprint of the second Davies of 1878 (No. 102).

[1888]

134. The Seventh Bethune Reprint

THE COMPLETE ANGLER, . . . by Izaak Walton . . .
and . . . Charles Cotton. . . .
New York: Dodd, Mead & Company, Publishers. [1888].

Copies examined: Harvard, Horne. Others: CtY, OCl, OU.

Size: 8½" × 5¹¹⁄₁₆".

Pagination summary: Vol. I [2], [i]-xlvii, [xlviii], [1]-294; Vol. II [2], [i]-xxxii, [1]-215, i-xcii.

The title-page verso in both volumes is imprinted: "Press of J. J. Little & Co., Nos. 10 to 20, Astor Place, New York."
    The illustrations are the same as previous ordinary Bethune editions, plus a portrait of Bethune which serves as a frontispiece to the Bibliographical Note which in this reprint has been moved to the end of the second volume. It is still signed "G.B.D." [sic] as is the sixth Bethune and still erroneously states that the illustrations are from the 1808 Bagster edition, instead of from the fourth Major, 1844 (No. 55).
    The publisher's binding is in light green cloth with the title and a decorative group of fish, swimming in darker green waves, stamped in gilt on the front cover and spine.
    This edition is listed in *The Annual American Catalogue* as having been published in 1888 in "2 v. octavo cloth $3.50." It is a reissue with a new title-page, from the plates of the sixth Bethune edition of 1880 (No. 107).

[1888]
135. The Fourth Baker and Taylor (7th Stock) Facsimile

THE COMPLETE ANGLER; . . . By Izaak Walton. . . .
New York: The Baker & Taylor Company,
740 & 742 Broadway. [1888].

Copies examined: Harvard, Horne, Princeton. Others: CtY, MdBP, PU.

Size: 5⅞" × 4¹⁵⁄₁₆".

Pagination summary: [i-v], vi-x, [16], (1)-246.

This reissue of the Stock facsimile of 1876 (No. 98) is the same as the 1885 Baker and Taylor facsimile (No. 120), with the 1876 preface. It has the same six cuts of fish and two pages of music, the second of which, contrary to the explanation in the Preface that it should be upside down, is printed right side up. See Appendix B for listing of the 36 irregularities repeated from the first Stock of 1876.
    The publishers' binding of the Horne copy, in white and beige, is most unusual for an *Angler*. The white cloth used for the spine, extending to about two-thirds of each side, is stamped on the front cover with an oval decoration in gilt and blue resembling a hand mirror. The rest of each side is in

beige cloth, decorated with an overall embossed pattern in brown. The usual titling is in gilt within the front cover decoration and on the spine. The top edges are gilt, the others are untrimmed.

The Harvard copy is in cloth with an overall design tooled in blind, embossed to simulate natural leather. On the spine in a red leather lettering piece with gilt stamping reads, "The Compleat Angler 1653."

This facsimile reprint is not dated. Wood and Oliver agree on 1888, while the supplement to *Bibliotheca Piscatoria*, London, 1901, prefers 1889. The majority opinion has been followed herein.

1888

136. The Lea and Dove (1st Marston) Edition

THE COMPLEAT ANGLER . . . by Izaak Walton and
. . . Charles Cotton . . .
London: Sampson Low, Marston, Searle and Rivington Limited
St. Dunstan's House, Fetter Lane, E.C. 1888. [All rights reserved]

Copies examined: Harvard (2), Horne (2), Princeton, Virginia. Others: Royal quarto; CsMH, CtHT, CtY, NN, PPAN, ViW. Demy quarto; CSt, CtY, ICN, MH, MeB, MnU.

Size: Royal quarto: $12^{15}\!/_{16}'' \times 10''$, limited to 250 copies.
      Demy octavo: $10\frac{7}{8}'' \times 8^{11}\!/_{16}''$, limited to 500 copies.

Pagination summary: Vol. I, (roman numerals) [i]-c; (letters) [a]-t, [u]; Part I, [1]-118. Vol. II [2], 119-173; Part II, [174]-249, [250]; The Chronicle, [251]-330, 331-357, [358].

On the half-title verso in Volume I, the title-page verso in Volume II, and on page [358] is imprinted, "London: Printed by William Clowes and Sons, Limited, Stamford Street and Charing Cross." The "Chronicle" included in the pagination following Part II is a reprint of the 1883 edition of *The Chronicle of The Compleat Angler* by Westwood and Satchell, and is listed in Sources, Appendix A.

The illustrations, including a frontispiece of Walton in Volume I and of Cotton in Volume II, consist of 54 photogravures by R. H. Emerson; 103 woodcuts (the title-pages read "about 100" and the index lists 87), of which 91 are miniature scenes "interspersed in the text" engraved by F. Alphonse Stankoskie after drawings by F. Carless; music on two pages and three maps. The royal quarto illustrations are on India paper.

The title-pages, printed in red and black, described "The Chronicle" as "A Biographical (instead of Bibliographical) Record . . ."

In an advertisement at the end of R. B. Marston's *Walton and Some Earlier*

Writers on Fish and Fishing (London, 1894), an advertisement for this edition describes the "Large Paper Edition" as ". . . Royal Quarto, bound in full morocco, each copy numbered and signed £10 10s." and "The Demy Quarto edition [also signed by Marston], bound in half-morocco, gilt top, £5 5s." with very few copies of either remaining.

The royal quarto copy seen is in gray boards, white linen backed, printed paper labels on spine, all edges untrimmed; the demy octavo seen is in half green morocco and green cloth, four compartments on spine with angling tools, two with titling, all in gilt, end papers black, top edges gilt, others untrimmed.

Although the title-pages call this the "100th Edition," Marston felt he should justify the accuracy of this designation. In a note (vol. II, p. 329) in reference to the list of editions on pages [267] and 268, he wrote, ". . . the number chronicled by Messrs. Westwood and Satchell is ninety-seven, and to these (see p. 268) I have added five editions including the present, so that this edition is probably the one hundred and second; but inasmuch as two of those included were newspaper reprints, viz. in the *Fishing Gazette* and *Angler's Journal,* in each case extending over some months; I think I am still justified in calling this the one hundredth edition." It is listed herein as number 136.

This edition was edited by R. B. Marston, for many years editor of the *Fishing Gazette.* He also edited an edition of the *Angler* published in 1915 (reprinted in 1921) by the Oxford University Press and wrote the Preface which appears in some of the Thorpe reprints.

The text of this edition of the *Angler* is a reprint from the fifth edition of 1676 (No. 6).

1888

137. The Dodd, Mead, Lea & Dove (2nd Marston) Reprint

THE COMPLEAT ANGLER . . . by Izaak Walton and
. . . Charles Cotton . . .
New York: Dodd Mead & Co. 1888.

Copies examined: None seen.

Size reported: Royal and demy quarto.

Pagination summary: In two volumes, paged as in the Lea and Dove edition (No. 136).

This reprint is recorded in two publications edited by Marston, the supplement to Westwood and Satchell's *Bibliotheca Piscatoria,* 1901, and the "List of Editions," which follows his "Introductory Notes" in the 1915 Oxford University Press edition of the *Angler*. It is listed also in *The Annual American Cata-logue* for 1888 as "Lea & Dove ill. ed. N. Y. Dodd Mead & Co 1888. 2 v. ill. Quarto cloth $30; edition de luxe ill. Quarto cloth $60." Oliver, who did not see a copy and was skeptical of the existence of this reprint (his No. 125) cited its inclusion in *The Church Catalogue*, and *The American Catalogue* for 1891. Concerning the latter he observed "We suspect that this is a mistake for the Dodd, Mead, Bethune edition of the same year [1888] as that also is listed." Oliver referred also to Arnold Wood's note regarding this reprint which states that it was issued for the American market with the Dodd, Mead and Company imprint. Wood, however, in a list of errata at the end of his Bibliography, called this a misstatement.

It is most unlikely that Marston, a highly regarded and successful editor and publisher, would have allowed an incorrect statement about his own *Angler* to appear in two publications which he also edited. Moreover, Oliver might have been less skeptical had he been aware of the listing of this edition in the supplement to *Bibliotheca Piscatoria* and *The American Catalogue* for 1888, both of which are very clear in their descriptions of both the Lea and Dove, and Bethune editions, as two different publications. Wood gave no reason for changing his mind and, since his Bibliography was dated 1900, he could not have checked the yet unpublished supplement to *Bibliotheca Piscatoria*, although *The Annual American Catalogue* for 1888 was then available.

These two additional references to this Lea and Dove reprint of the *Angler* indicate a much more promising possibility of its publication by Dodd, Mead and Company than has been believed heretofore.

1888

138. The Second Nimmo (15th Major) Reprint

THE COMPLETE ANGLER . . . Of Izaak Walton and
Charles Cotton . . .
London John C. Nimmo 14, King William Street,
Strand, W.C. 1888.

Copies examined: None seen.

Size reported: 8vo.

Pagination reported: [i]-xv, [xvi], [1]-445.

Examination of four collections (CtHT, MH, NjP, Horne) of the *Angler* has failed to reveal this edition, and it is not in The National Union Catalog of the Library of Congress. It is included in the three previous lists cited below and a Nimmo edition is listed for 1888, followed by a question mark, in *The English Catalogue of Books*.

Westwood and Satchell's supplement to *Bibliotheca Piscatoria* (1901) describes it as follows: "Cr. 8 vo. 8s. 6d. [This is a reprint of the 1883 edition.] . . . (London) J. C. Nimmo, 88." The "List of Editions . . ." in the third Marston edition of 1915 (No. 255) reports it as "London, J. C. Nimmo, Major (1844)." Oliver, who did not see a copy, quoted the two previous references (see his No. 127), listed it as above, and presumed it to be a reprint with the same illustrations, of the Nimmo and Bain reprint of 1883 (No. 114). *The English Catalogue of Books* notice of this reprint reads, "1888? Nimmo-Major, Cr. 8vo. 8s. 6d."

It is hoped that this listing may be verified further at some future date. Pending description it is considered herein as a reprint.

1889

139. The Third Nimmo (16th Major) Reprint

THE COMPLETE ANGLER . . . of Izaak Walton and
Charles Cotton . . .
London John C. Nimmo 14, King William Street Strand 1889

Copies examined: Harvard, Horne.

Size: $6\frac{7}{8}'' \times 5\frac{1}{8}''$.

Pagination summary: [i]-xv, [xvi], [1]-445, [446], [2], [1]-16.

Both the title-page (with the vignette from the 1844 Major edition) and half-title are printed in red and black, the latter designating the addition at the end (John Jackson's, *The Practical Fly-fisher*, with a separate title-page and ten handcolored plates of flies), *A Treatise on Flies and Fly-Hooks*. On the half-title verso is imprinted, "Ballantyne Press, Ballantyne, Hanson and Co. Edinburgh and London," and, at the foot of the last page of *The Practical Fly-fisher*, "*Printed by* Ballantyne, Hanson & Co., *Edinburgh*."

The illustrations are described on the title-page as, "With Six Original Etchings, Two Portraits, and Seventy-four Wood Engravings." These are from the Nimmo and Bain reprint of 1883 (No. 114), with *The Practical Fly-fisher* added at the end.

1889

140. The Fourth Nimmo (17th Major) Reprint

THE COMPLETE ANGLER . . . of Izaak Walton and
Charles Cotton . . .
London John C. Nimmo 14, King William Street, Strand 1889

Copies examined: Horne (2), Virginia.

Size: $8\frac{3}{16}'' \times 5\frac{9}{16}''$.

Pagination summary: [i]-xv, [xvi], [1]-445.

On the title-page (with the vignette from the 1844 Major edition) verso is imprinted, "Printed by Ballantyne, Hanson & Co. At the Ballantyne Press, Edinburgh" and at the foot of page 445, "Printed by Ballantyne, Hanson & Co. Edinburgh & London." The title-page (with the vignette from the 1844 Major edition) is printed in red and black, where the illustrations are described as "With Eight Original Etchings and Seventy-four Wood Engravings."

This reprint was issued in dark green cloth. Titling and *"with eighty-two illustrations"* are in gilt on the spine. The front cover is decorated with three golden fish, with titling also in gilt. The top edges are gilt, others untrimmed.

This is a reprint of the third Nimmo reprint of 1889 (No. 139), with the same illustrations, although they are enumerated differently on the title-page. Jackson's *The Practical Fly-fisher* was not included at the end.

1889

141. The Putnam-Nimmo (18th Major) Reprint

THE COMPLETE ANGLER . . . of Izaak Walton and
Charles Cotton . . .
New York: G. P. Putnam's Sons. London: J. C. Nimmo 1889

Copies examined: Harvard, Horne, Princeton, Virginia, Yale. Others: CLSU, CoD, IaU, NN.

Size: $8'' \times 5\frac{1}{4}''$.

Pagination summary: [i]-xv, [xvi], [1]-445, [446], [2], [1]-16.

Both the title-page and half-title are printed in red and black, the latter designating the addition at the end (John Jackson's, *The Practical Fly-fisher*, with a separate title-page, and ten hand-colored plates of flies), *A Treatise on Flies and Fly-Hooks*. The half-title verso is imprinted, "Ballantyne Press,

[143]

Ballantyne, Hanson and Co. Edinburgh and London" and, at the foot of the last page of *The Practical Fly-fisher*, "Printed by Ballantyne, Hanson & Co., Edinburgh."

The illustrations are described on the title-page as follows: "With Six Original Etchings, Two Portraits, and Seventy-four Wood Engravings." These are from the Nimmo and Bain reprint of 1883 (No. 114).

The publisher's binding occurs in both light blue and green cloth, with black parallel lines at top and bottom of front and back covers in each version. The usual titling is in gilt on the spine, with "Putnam 1889" in gilt at the foot. This *Angler* is also decorated with three gilt fish, each of a different species, two on the spine and one on the front cover. The top edges are gilt, the others are untrimmed; the end papers are very dark blue.

This is a reprint of the Nimmo and Bain reprint of 1883 (No. 114), with *The Practical Fly-fisher* added at the end. It is described in *The Annual American Catalogue* as a quarto in cloth, published by G. P. Putnam's Sons in 1889, to sell for $3.00.

1889

142. The First Lowell Edition

THE COMPLETE ANGLER, . . . of Izaak Walton and
Charles Cotton. . . .
Boston: Little, Brown, and Company. 1889.

Copies examined: Harvard, Horne, N.Y. Public, Princeton, Virginia. Others: CSmH, CU, DLC, LU, MB, MiU, OCl, OClW, OU, PU, PWcT, ViW.

Size: regular "edition," $7\frac{13}{16}'' \times 5\frac{1}{16}''$, large paper state, $7\frac{7}{8}'' \times 5\frac{1}{8}''$.

Pagination summary: Vol. I, [i-v], vi-lxxvi, [1]-208; Vol. II, [i-v], vi, 209-465, [1].

The title-page of each volume is printed in red and black and, on the verso of each, is printed "*Copyright, 1889,* By Little, Brown, and Company," and "University Press: John Wilson and Son, Cambridge."

The plates, laid down in both issues, consist of six etchings by Harlow, of which four are full page, and two are title-page vignettes; in the large paper state the etchings are signed in pencil by Louis K. Harlow. In addition there are 11 engravings by Bone, H. Robinson, and J. T. Willmore after Absolon, Huysman, Inskipp and Lely. (In the "List of Embellishments," Absolon and Huysman are spelled Absalon and Housman.) The 74 woodcuts after paintings and drawings by J. W. Archer, A. Cooper, T. Creswick, Alex. Fussell, George Lance, F. R. Lee, K. Meadows, and W. Smith, are the same as the 4th Major of 1844 (No. 55), except that the cut of Sir Humphrey Davy's seal-ring is not in this edition. The 1653 title-page re-engraved on steel for the 1844 Major, is reproduced by woodcut in this first Lowell.

The two volumes of the regular "edition" were issued in smooth blue cloth, the ornate tan end papers printed with an overall vine-like Victorian pattern. The circular vignette of the Walton-Cotton cipher, on the title-page of Part II, is repeated in gilt on the front cover of each volume. The spines are titled in gilt, and are decorated with an emblematic design of fishing gear in gilt. All edges are untrimmed. The large paper state seen is rebound.

This is the first of the editions published with an Introduction by James Russell Lowell who, in addition, revised and eliminated some of the notes from the Major editions and added new notes of his own. According to *The Annual American Catalogue,* 500 copies with plates on India paper, were issued at $10.00, and 150 copies, with plates on Japan paper, were issued at $15.00.

This edition is a reissue of the Major text of 1844 (No. 55) which is from the fifth edition of 1676 (No. 6).

1889

143. The Second Lowell (Boston and London) Reprint

THE COMPLETE ANGLER . . . of Izaak Walton and
Charles Cotton. . . .
Boston: Little, Brown, and Company.
London: Macmillan and Co. 1889.

Copies examined: Horne, Princeton.

Size: 8¼″×5⅜″.

Pagination summary: Vol. I, [i-v], vi-lxxvi, [1]-208; Vol. II, [i-v], vi, 209-465, [1].

The title-page of each volume is printed in red and black and, on the verso of each, is imprinted, "University Press: John Wilson and Son, Cambridge, U.S.A.," and, in gothic black letter, "Only One Hundred and Fifty Copies of this Edition have been printed for America and England."

The illustrations are the same as the first Lowell (No. 142), except that only the four full-page etchings are signed in pencil by Louis K. Harlow. He did not sign the two title-page vignettes.

The two volumes were issued in smooth dark blue cloth with white end papers; all edges are untrimmed. There is no decoration and the titling is on a paper label faded to tan, on the spines.

This reprint, with a new title-page, is a reissue from the same plates of the first Lowell edition of 1889 (No. 142).

1889

144. The Seventh Jesse Reprint

THE COMPLETE ANGLER, . . . of Izaak Walton and
Charles Cotton. . . .
London: George Bell and Sons, York Street, Covent Garden. 1889.

Copy examined: Horne. Others: CtHT, CtY, ICN, MiU, PP, PPD, PSC.

Size: $6^{15}/_{16}'' \times 4\frac{1}{2}''$.

Pagination summary: [i]-xix, [xx], 1*l.*, [1]-496, [1]-24. Pages 23* and 24* at the
front are inserted after page 24.

The title-page verso is imprinted, "London: Printed by William Clowes and
Sons, Limited, Stanford Street and Charing Cross."
  The illustrations are the same 206 woodcuts and the 26 steel engravings
of the prior Jesse editions (for the first Jesse edition see No. 70). An attempt
was made to correct the listing errors of the engravings on wood, however,
only 203 of the 206 engravings are enumerated. In prior editions, figure six,
"Seal-ring, a bequest from Sir H. Davy . . . ," indexed as on page xli, but
never printed, has been eliminated from the list, and the "Engraved Dedication" page, not indexed in the prior editions, substituted as number two.
However, the engravings for the half-title and the two headpieces (pages
[i], [xv], and 484) are omitted as heretofore. The page indexed for the cut of
Madeley Manor has been corrected from xxi to xix, but the five plates of
"Angling Apparatus," which are on pages 334-338, continue to be indexed
as on pages 33-48. Walton's given name is spelled "Izaak" on the title-page,
and "Isaac" in the title of the biography, page [1].
  The 24 pages at the end comprise a *Catalogue of Bohn's Libraries* where this
reprint is listed on page 14, priced at 5s. The description includes reference
to "Where to Fish" by Henry G. Bohn (pp. [449]-483). These notes, reportedly
omitted in some cases (Oliver, his No. 136), are included in the copy examined.
  With the changes noted, this is a reprint of the first Jesse edition of 1856
(No. 70).

1889

145. The Sixth Cassell (Alden) Reprint

THE COMPLETE ANGLER. . . . by Isaac Walton.
New York John B. Alden, Publisher 1889

Copy examined: Oliver.

Size: $5\frac{5}{8}'' \times 3\frac{7}{8}''$.

Pagination summary: [1-3], 4-192.

The title-page bears the publisher's circular device of La Belle Sauvage. The printer's imprint is lacking on page 192.

The publisher's binding is in dark blue cloth, titled in gilt on front cover and spine.

This is a reissue with new title-page, of the first Cassell edition of 1886 (No. 125). It is not listed in the National Union Card Catalogue nor in any contemporary records examined by me.

1890

146. The Eighth Davies (1st Gibbings) Reprint

THE COMPLETE ANGLER by Izaac Walton and
Charles Cotton . . .
London W. W. Gibbings, 18, Bury Street, W. C.
Exeter: J. G. Commin 1890

Copies examined: Horne, Princeton, Publisher's. Others: MH, NN.

Size: $8\frac{5}{8}'' \times 5\frac{5}{8}''$.

Pagination summary: [i]-xii, [1]-467.

At the foot of page 467 is imprinted, "Dalziel Brothers, Camden Press, London. N. W." The title-page (lacking a Warne device) is printed in red and black.

The illustrations are the same as the seventh Davies reprint (No. 133) and consist of 65 woodcuts (including one repeat on pages v and 87) from the first Major edition of 1823; the headpiece on page 33 from the second Major edition of 1824; a facsimile of the title-page of the first edition of 1653; 22 additional woodcuts from previous Davies editions; 20 pages with illustrations of various kinds and types of fishing tackle; and 25 decorative chapter headings.

The Horne copy is bound in dark blue-green cloth with dark chocolate end papers, top edges gilt, others untrimmed; a copy owned by the publisher, and the Princeton copy, are in maroon cloth. The three copies examined are gilt stamped on the spine with the usual titling and, at the foot, with "Standard British Classics" gilt stamped on a pedestal bearing a lighted Aladdin's lamp.

According to Director R. A. V. Priddle of Warne, this edition was printed for W. W. Gibbings in June 1890, and consisted of about 500 copies for their series of *Standard British Classics*. *The English Catalogue of Books* lists it for August, 1890, priced at 7s. 6d.

It is a reprint of the seventh Davies edition of 1888 (No. 133).

[147]

147. The Ninth Davies Reprint

"THE CHANDOS CLASSICS."
THE COMPLETE ANGLER by Izaac Walton and
Charles Cotton . . .
London: Frederick Warne & Co., Bedford Street Strand [1890].

Copies examined: None seen.

Size reported: 12mo.

Pagination summary reported: [i]-xii, [1]-467.

According to information supplied by the publisher, this is a reprint of the second Davies edition of 1878, in the *Chandos Classics* series published in September 1890. It has the device of the Wings and Horseshoe on the title-page.
   This reprint is not listed in any previous bibliography of the *Angler*.

[1890]

148. The Seventh Cassell Reprint

THE COMPLETE ANGLER by Isaac Walton.
CASSELL'S NATIONAL LIBRARY Edited by Proffssor [sic]
Henry Morley 3D.
[Cassell & Company Limited: London, Paris, New York &
Melbourne. 1890]

Copy examined: Horne (in paper wrapper).

Size: $5\frac{9}{16}'' \times 3\frac{3}{4}''$.

Collation: [A^{16}(-A1)], B-F^{16}=95.

Contents: (wrapper title as above, title-page omitted) [1-2]; Morley's Introduction [3]-4; Text [5]-192; 2 leaves (pp. 1-4), Cassell publications.

Although with different marks, and lacking the title-page, the collation of the signatures and the pagination summary are the same as the first Cassell (No. 125), of which this is a reissue. At the foot of both page 192 and the outside back wrapper is imprinted, "Printed by Cassell & Company, Limited, La Belle Sauvage, London, E.C." The four pages of Cassell advertising at the end are the same as the first Cassell, including the listing of this reprint as the fifth title in Cassell's National Library, selling at 3d. in paper covers and 6d. in cloth.

This reprint, issued in gray-green paper, has the front wrapper imprinted in black with decoration and titling modified very slightly from that of the cloth bound first Cassell, except lacking the gilt and adding "3d." in large type in both of the lower corners. The back wrapper and the inside of both wrappers imprinted with advertisements, and the spine, titled lengthwise and numbered 5, are all the same as the first Cassell (No. 125).

The copy examined, with the title-page omitted (not missing), is believed to be a reissue, in paper wrappers, of the first Cassell (No. 125). While undated, such a reprint was listed but not described by Oliver (his No. 139) and by Wood, the latter also identifying it as number five in the series. It is also stated on the title-page verso of the eleventh Cassell reprint (No. 179) that such an *Angler* was reprinted in 1898.

This is a reissue of the first Cassell edition of 1886 (No. 125).

1891

149. The Eighth Cassell Reprint

CASSELL'S NATIONAL LIBRARY
THE COMPLETE ANGLER: . . . by Isaac Walton.
Cassell & Company. Limited: London, Paris & Melbourne. 1891.

Copies examined: Harvard, Horne.

Size: 5⁹⁄₁₆″ × 3¹¹⁄₁₆″.

Pagination summary: [1-3], 4-192, [4].

At the foot of page 192 is imprinted, "Printed by Cassell & Company, Limited, La Belle Sauvage, London, I.C." The circular device of Cassell & Company appears on the title-page.

This is a reissue of the first Cassell edition of 1886 (No. 125) with the same title-page except for the omission of "New York." At the end are four pages of advertising for Cassell's publications where this *Angler* is ninth of the volumes published in Cassell's National Library. The price was three pence in "Weekly Volumes," (paper) or six pence in cloth.

The cloth publisher's binding is dark blue. Titling is blind stamped on the front cover and, on the back, a Cassell cipher. The spine is gilt titled and, at the foot, is blind stamped with the numeral "5" identifying this as volume five in the Cassell National Library series. Four lines are ruled in blind at the top and foot of the covers and spine.

The English Catalogue of Books lists this reprint as published in March, 1891, to sell for six pence or three pence. It is also recorded on the title-page verso of the eleventh Cassell reprint (No. 179), that a reprint in this series was issued in 1891.

This is a reissue with a new title-page of the first Cassell edition of 1886 (No. 125).

[1891]

150. The Ninth Cassell Reprint

CASSELL'S NATIONAL LIBRARY
THE COMPLETE ANGLER : . . . by Isaac Walton.
New York Cassell Publishing Company,
104 & 106 Fourth Avenue [1891].

Copy examined : Princeton.

Size : 5½" × 3¹³⁄₁₆".

Pagination summary : [1]-192, [8].

The title-page bears the publisher's device of La Belle Sauvage, and on the verso is imprinted, "The Mershon Press, Rahway, N.J." This is the only Cassell issue recorded with the imprint of this press, and only this, and the tenth Cassell (No. 158), are imprinted "Cassell Publishing Company" on the title-page. The eight pages at the end advertise "Cassell's National Library," edited by Prof. Henry Morley, L.L.D. at ten cents per volume, where this *Angler* is listed as number 4. Inside the front and back paper covers are further listings in this series, with this reprint again shown as number 4 at ten cents, but also available in "Extra Cloth Binding at 25 cents per Volume." The outside of the covers is imprinted with Cassell advertising on the back, and the title on the front.

The date, "Feb. 20, 1886," on the upper right corner of the front cover is not that of this reprint, since the title-page gives Cassell's New York address as 104 & 106 Fourth Avenue which, according to *The American Catalogue,* was the publisher's address *after* 1886. Furthermore, Cassell did not use "Cassell Publishing Company" until 1889. So this reprint was apparently bound in the paper and cloth covers left over from the 1886 issue, as was done with the fifth Cassell reprint of 1887. (For additional data regarding dates and locations see the fifth Cassell notes, No. 129.)

Since Cassell's address and title-page style agree with *The Annual American Catalogue,* and since both Oliver and Wood list, although neither describes, an American Cassell reprint for 1891, this date has been assigned to the Ninth Cassell reprint.

This is a reissue with a new title-page of the first Cassell edition of 1886 (No. 125).

151. The Eighth Bethune Edition

THE COMPLETE ANGLER . . . By Izaak Walton, and . . .
by Charles Cotton. . . .
Ward, Lock and Co., London, New York, and Melbourne. 1891.

Copies examined: Boston Public, Harvard, Horne (2), Princeton, Yale (2).
Others: CtHT, NN, ViU.

Size: $8\frac{5}{16}'' \times 5\frac{15}{16}''$.

Pagination summary: Two vols. in one, [i]-xxxix, [xl], [1]-294; [i]-xxx, [1]-215, [216]; i-xcii.

There is no printer's imprint on the title-page verso.

The illustrations are those of the previous Bethune editions except that the cut from the *Treatyse of Fysshynge Wyth an Angle* is omitted. The "Bibliographical Note," now at the end, continues to be signed incorrectly "The American Editor, G.B.D." The error on the source of the illustrations in the first and second editions, corrected in the third, is on page lxxxix, as in the sixth Bethune edition (No. 107), and the seventh Bethune reprint (No. 134).

This edition was seen in three bindings issued by the publisher. The *first* is in very dark red cloth, smooth except for a rippled section next to the spine on each cover. Titling is printed in black on the front cover and in gilt on the spine, gilt stamped also at the top, "The Macaulay Library of Great Writers." The end papers are white. The *second* is in orange-tan cloth, the *third* is in pinkish-gray cloth, each with dark gray end papers, and titling the same as the first except for the addition of an Aladdin-type lamp within a three rule frame all in black in the lower right hand corner of the front cover.

This is a reissue from the plates of the sixth Bethune edition (No. 107), to which a two-page preface has been added, apparently by the London publisher, since it introduces Bethune and ". . . his edition of 'Walton's Angler' to British readers . . ." *The English Catalogue of Books* lists this edition as having been published in April, 1891, to sell for seven shillings, six pence. It is priced $1.50 in *The American Catalogue* as "8 vo. cloth $1.50."

152. The Third Lowell Reprint

THE COMPLETE ANGLER, . . . of Izaak Walton and
Charles Cotton. . . .
Boston: Little, Brown, and Company. 1891.

Copies examined: Harvard, Horne, Princeton, Yale.

Size: 7⅜"×5".

Pagination summary: Vol. I, [i-v], vi-lxxvi, [1]-208; Vol. II, [i-v], vi, [209]-465, [466].

The title-page of each volume is printed in red and black with the verso of each imprinted, "*Copyright, 1889,* By Little, Brown, and Company" and, "University Press: John Wilson and Son, Cambridge."
    The illustrations consist of four unsigned etchings by Louis K. Harlow, comprising a frontispiece and title-page vignette for each volume, plus 74 wood engravings, all from the first Lowell edition (No. 142).
    The Horne copy was issued in dark blue cloth, with the Walton-Cotton cipher from the title-page to Part II in gilt on the front cover of each volume, and titling in gilt on the spine. The top edges are gilt, the others untrimmed.
    This reprint of the first Lowell edition is listed in *The Annual American Catalogue* as having been published in 1891 in two volumes, priced $3.00 in cloth, $6.50 in half calf, and $7.50 in limp morocco extra.

153. The Fourth Lowell (Boston and London) Reprint

Walton (I.) — Compleat Angler. New ed. with Introduction by J. R. Lowell. Copyright 1889. 2 Vols. Illus. $3, half calf, $6.50. (Boston) Little, Brown & Co. (London) 9/-.

Copies examined: None seen.

The data in the entry above are from Westwood and Satchell's supplement to *Bibliotheca Piscatoria* (London, 1901). Such an edition is also listed in *The English Catalogue of Books* as having been published in October 1891, to sell at fifteen shillings.
    Just as the first Lowell edition was followed by a London imprint (No. 143), it seems very probable that this London imprint followed the third Lowell reprint (No. 152).

1892

154. The Fifth Lowell Reprint

THE COMPLETE ANGLER, . . . of Izaak Walton and
Charles Cotton. . . .
Boston: Little, Brown, and Company. 1892.

Copies examined: Harvard, Horne (2), Princeton, Yale. Others: CtHT, PPL.

Size: 7⅜″×5″.

Pagination summary: Vol. I, [i-v], vi-lxxvi, [1]-208; Vol. II, [i-v], vi, [209]-465, [466].

This is a reissue of the third Lowell reprint of 1891 (No. 152) with identical pagination, title-pages, illustrations, and publisher's binding, except that this reprint was seen in both dark blue and dark red cloth, the third Lowell only in dark blue.

[1892]

155. The Second Crowell (19th Major) Reprint

THE COMPLETE ANGLER; . . . of Izaak Walton and
Charles Cotton . . .
New York: Thomas Y. Crowell & Co.,
46 East Fourteenth Street. [1892]

Copies examined: Harvard, Horne, Princeton. Others: CtY, NN.

Size: 6⅝″×4⅜″.

Pagination summary: Vol. I, [i-iv], v-lx, 1-186; Vol. II, [2], 187-262; Part II, [263-264], 265-418.

The title-page of each volume is printed in red and black, and is decorated with the title-page cartouche (including its titling) from the 1653 edition, as a black vignette. Volume I only has an additional black and white title-page, without publisher's name, place, or date, but otherwise identical to the first Crowell title-page, including the quotation from Shakespeare on the verso. The three title-pages each state, "From the Fourth London Edition" (see notes to the first Crowell, 1884, No. 116).

The illustrations are those of the 1884 Crowell (No. 116), plus a frontispiece to volume I signed by Copeland ("copyright 1892 by T. Y. Crowell & Co."), and a photogravure frontispiece to volume II. The woodcut of Archbishop

Sheldon, indexed for page 203, is on page 202 as in the first Crowell.

The publisher's binding is in dark green cloth. The front covers of each volume are bordered by a single rule in gilt, with the cartouche from the 1653 title-page (framing only the words "The Compleat Angler") gilt stamped in the center. The back covers are plain. The usual titling appears in gilt on the spine. The top edges are gilt.

This reprint is listed in *The Annual American Catalogue* as published in 1892 in two volumes, 16mo, bound in cloth, with a selling price of $2.50. It is also assigned the same date, size, and price, by Westwood and Satchell's supplement to *Bibliotheca Piscatoria* (London, 1901).

This is a reissue of the first Crowell edition, 1884 (No. 116), which was from the Major edition of 1844 (No. 55).

1892

156. The Rendall Abridged Musical Edition

THE COMPLEAT ANGLER. An idyll in two days after
IZAAK WALTON set to Music . . .
by Edward Davy Rendall.
Laudy & Co., 139 Oxford Street, London W.
New York, Edward Schuberth & Co. Copyright 1892 . . .

Copy examined: Harvard.

Size: 10⅜″×6½″.

Pagination: 142 pages, engraved and printed at Leipzig by Oscar Brandstetter.

The excerpts from the *Angler* which make up this edition consist of introductory and connecting prose dialogues for each of the two days of the action, and 21 selections from verses, songs, and prose, all set to music.

An introductory note reads: "Although in most cases it will doubtless be found more convenient to have the connecting dialogue of this idyll recited by a separate reader, it was originally intended by the composer that it should be spoken by the singers with as much dramatic action as the conditions of the performance rendered possible. The words in all cases are actually taken from the 'Compleat Angler,' the text which is chiefly followed being that of the first edition."

However, since two of the songs, "I married a wife of late" and "While I listen to thy voice" first appeared in the fifth edition of 1676 (No. 6), it also must have been used. The song, "I in these flowing meads would be" had its first appearance in the third edition, 1661 (No. 3).

This musical adaptation was issued in a gray paper wrapper, with the title-page repeated on the cover. On the back cover is a list of "Laudy & Co.'s New Publications," with *The Compleat Angler* at the top of the page, priced at 3/-.

[1892]

157. The First Lovell, Coryell (20th Major) Edition

THE COMPLETE ANGLER . . . of Izaak Walton and
Charles Cotton . . .
New York: Lovell, Coryell & Company,
43, 45 and 47 East Tenth Street [1892].

Copies examined: Horne (2), Princeton, Yale. Other: NN.

Size: 7¼″ × 4¹³⁄₁₆″, both the Century and Universal Series.

Pagination summary: [1-5], 6-354, [4].

The illustrations consist of reproductions of the signatures of both Walton
and Cotton, two seal rings, Archer's headpiece of the Walton biographees,
19 woodcuts of fish, and one page of music, all from the 1844 Major edition
(No. 55).
    The four pages of advertising of Lovell publications at the end list this
edition in the "Century Series" in cloth at 75 cents per volume and, in the
"Universal Series" in "Fine half calf, gilt tops," boxed, at $2.50. per volume.
    The copy in the "Century Series" was issued in red cloth, rippled at the
outer corners and inner edges of the covers to simulate leather. Parallel gilt
lines separate the rippled and the smooth cloth on the front cover; these
lines are in blind on the back cover. Six compartments are stamped on the
spine, four with gilt decoration, and two with gilt titling. The "Universal
Series" copy was issued in tan calf, with tan marbled sides and end papers,
and the top edges gilt. A red lettering panel is at the top of the spine and a
blue one near the foot; the gilt beading and corner decorations of the center
panel frame a gilt flaming torch.
    This edition has been dated 1892, determined by Oliver from the publisher's
address for that date. It is reprinted from the Major edition of 1844 (No. 55).

[1892]

158. The Tenth Cassell Reprint

THE COMPLETE ANGLER . . . by Isaac Walton
New York: Cassell Publishing Company,
104 & 106 Fourth Avenue [1892].

Copy examined: Horne.

Size: 6½″ × 4⅜″.

Collation: A-F^{16}=96 leaves.

Pagination summary: [1-3], 4-192.

The numeral three is broken on page 63, as is the one on 156, and the second one on 181. The printer's imprint is lacking on page 192 and there are no illustrations or advertisements.

The title-page lacks a Cassell device, but this reprint, and the ninth Cassell (No. 150), are the only ones examined that have the title-page imprinted, "Cassell Publishing Company."

The publisher's binding is in gray cloth. The front cover is bordered by a design of brown quill-like twigs, and tiny brown shamrocks dot the front cover and spine. The gilt titling on the front cover is within a square near the top formed by an ornamental scroll-like band of gray on brown that is used also as strips above and below gilt titling on the spine. "Cassell's Selected Library" is gilt stamped within a brown laurel wreath near the foot of the front cover, and "Cassell Publishing Company" in gilt within a similar, smaller brown wreath at the foot of the spine.

This reprint is not listed in Wood or Oliver and neither makes reference to "Cassell's Selected Library."

In *The Annual American Catalogue* for 1892, on page 98, under "New Publications for 1892," Cassell listed and described *The Complete Angler* by Isaac Walton as "16 mo. cloth. 50 cents." The cloth binding, size, Cassell's New York location, and price describe this reprint which has not been listed previously by bibliographers. (For additional data regarding dates and locations see the fifth Cassell (No. 129) notes.)

This is a reissue, with a new title-page, of the first Cassell edition of 1886 (No. 125).

[1893]

159. The Third Crowell (21st Major) Reprint

THE COMPLETE ANGLER . . . of Izaak Walton and
Charles Cotton . . .
New York: Thomas Y. Crowell & Co.,
46 East Fourteenth Street. [1893].

Copies examined: None.

Size reported: 5⅛″ × 7⅛″.

Pagination: Not reported.

"The illustrations are a halftone frontispiece by Bone after Huysman and the seventy-four woodcuts of the earlier Fourth Major edition . . ."

The title-page data and quotation above are from Oliver's description (his No. 152) of his brother's copy. In addition, he was informed by the publisher that it was part of the "Standard Library," published to sell for $1.00.

Although a copy of this edition as listed and described by Oliver has not been seen, an undated $3\frac{1}{2}'' \times 5\frac{5}{8}''$ four-page folder listing some 145 volumes in "Crowell's Standard Library," including *The Complete Angler,* has been examined. The books are described as "cloth, gilt top, edges slightly trimmed, with ample margins. 12 mo. Price per volume, $1.00." A cut shows "Standard Library Edition" in the middle of the spine.

[1893]

160. The Tenth Ephemera Reprint

THE COMPLETE ANGLER By Izaak Walton & Charles Cotton . . . London: George Routledge and Sons, Limited Broadway, Ludgate Hill Manchester and New York [1893].

Copies examined: Congress, Horne, N.Y. Public.

Size: $7\frac{3}{16}'' \times 4\frac{3}{4}''$.

Pagination summary: [i]-xii, 13-313, [314], [6].

On page [314] is imprinted, "Printed by Ballantyne, Hanson and Co. London and Edinburgh." The title-page with a vignette of Walton, and the illustrations, are from previous Ephemera editions. The six pages at the end are advertisements for Routledge books, where the *Angler* is included as one of 70 volumes of "Books for the People," in "Crown 8 vo, Cloth 2/-each. Crown 8 vo, Paper Covers, 1/6 each."

Two copies examined were issued by the publisher in dark red cloth, with a single line ruled in blind on the edges of the front and back covers. Titling and *art nouveau* floral decorations are stamped in gilt on the spine. The end papers are white.

This is a reissue of the third Ephemera reprint, 1859 (No. 74) printed from the same plates. It is listed in *The English Catalogue of Books* as having been published in May, 1893, to sell for two shillings.

1893

161. The First McClurg Edition

THE COMPLETE ANGLER . . . of Izaak Walton . . .
Chicago: A. C. McClurg and Company, 1893.

Copies examined: Harvard, Horne (3), Princeton. Others: CU, CtHT, DLC, NN, PPD, PBm.

Size: Regular, 6⅜"×4⅛"; large paper, 9⅜"×6½".

Pagination summary: [i]-xxxiv, [35]-287, [288].

The title-page bears the acorn device of the publisher. The unsigned Preface, pages [v] and vi, explains that Cotton's part was omitted because, ". . . it falls far short of its prototype in literary worth. . . ." The editor, E. G. Johnson, provided a 17-page signed introduction dated October, 1892. The large paper state was limited to 500 copies, signed A. C. McClurg & Co. above the 1892 copyright date on the title-page verso.

The illustrations consist of an unsigned frontispiece portrait of Walton superimposed on an arrangement of fishing gear, below which is the title, place, MDCCCXCII (1893 on the title-page), and publisher. Each page of the text is set within a decorative border depicting American fishing scenes (some extend into the text) designed by Schmedtgen, printed in light green ink. These comprise 16 different border scenes repeated in the same sequence in successive 16-page "signatures."

The copy on large paper was issued bound in natural linen. The top edges are gilt, the others untrimmed. An elaborate rectangular decoration, with a green leafy border, extends lengthwise across the front cover; within this, among wavy green lines, four gilt fish swim between gilt titling. The leafy border design motif is repeated in green on the spine which is titled in gilt, and is gilt stamped at the foot with the publisher's acorn device. The large paper state was probably issued also to booksellers in sheets for hand binding since it has been seen in half polished morocco and natural linen (signed Adams Bindery), and in morocco backed marble paper covered boards (signed McNamee, Binder, Cambridge, Mass.). Both states appear to be a first binding of the sheets.

This edition, distinctive in its American flavor, may have been issued as a Waltonian souvenir of the World's Columbian Exposition of 1893 in Chicago, the place and date of this edition.

According to Westwood and Satchell's supplement to *Bibliotheca Piscatoria* (1901), the regular state in 16 mo. sold for $1.00; in half calf or half morocco, $2.50; in limp calf or morocco, $3.00; and in large paper, $4.00.

This is a new edition from Walton's Part I of the fifth edition of 1676 (No. 6).

1893

162. The Harting Edition

Tercentenary Edition
THE COMPLETE ANGLER ... by Izaak Walton and
Charles Cotton ...
London Samuel Bagster and Sons, Limited 1893

Copies examined: British Museum, Harvard, Horne (2), Princeton (2). Others: CtHT, CtY, CU, NN, RPB, ViW.

Size: $9\frac{13}{16}''\times7\frac{7}{16},''$ as issued; $9\frac{11}{16}''\times7\frac{3}{8}''$, rebound.

Collation: Vol. I: [a⁸], b², A-P⁸, Q³=133; Vol. II: [-²], A-P⁸, Q²=124. The Preface (b², Vol. I) and half-title ([-²], Vol. II) were probably printed in the same sheet, as probably Q³ (end of Vol. I) and Q² (end of Vol. II).

Pagination summary: Vol. I, [i]-[xx], [1]-[246]; Vol. II, [i-iv], [1]-[86], end of Part I. Part II, [87]-[244].

The title-page in each volume is printed in red and black, with the verso of each, and the last page of volume II (below an elaborate "finis"), is imprinted: "Printed by Ballantyne, Hanson & Co. At the Ballantyne Press, Edinburgh." The last page of volume I has the printer's device reading: "The Ballantyne Press 1796. Ballantyne & Hanson Edinburgh London." Decorative initials are in red.

One of the copies at Princeton is a publisher's dummy with sample pages (and blank leaves) and a title-page which reads in part, "With Fifty-eight Illustrations," instead of "With Fifty-three Illustrations," as finally published. However the title-pages of both are incorrect for there are actually 55 illustrations in both the dummy and the published volumes, together with a "List of Illustrations" which enumerates only 54 illustrations, the tailpiece on page 49, volume II, having been omitted. The result is a title-page calling for 53 illustrations, and a list of 54 illustrations, in an edition having 55 illustrations.

The plates are after Alexander, Thomas, Wale, Samuel, Linnell, Lely, and Huysman, by Audinet, Linnell, and Greig, with engravings after drawings of riverside animals and birds by G. E. Lodge.

The publisher's binding is in green cloth backed with vellum spines. The engraving of the heron by Lodge on page 97, volume I, is reproduced in gilt on the front cover of each volume, while on the spine in gilt is a trout rising to a May fly. Top edges are gilt, others are untrimmed. This two-volume set was limited to 350 copies, and was issued with jackets of the binding material for each volume.

This edition, as stated on the title-page, "Edited, with notes from a naturalist's point of view, by J. E. Harting, Librarian of the Linnean Society of

London," is from the fifth edition of 1676 (No. 6). *The English Catalogue of Books* lists its publication date as November, 1893, with a selling price of 126 shillings.

[1893]
163. The Tenth Davies Reprint

THE COMPLETE ANGLER. by Izaac Walton and Charles Cotton. London: Frederick Warne and Co. and New York. [1893].

Copies examined: Horne, Princeton, Publisher's Office.

Size: $7\frac{1}{4}'' \times 4\frac{7}{8}''$.

Pagination summary: [i-v], vi-vii, [viii-ix], xi-xii, 1-467.

On the verso of page 467 is imprinted, "Printed by Dalziel Brothers, Camdem Press, London, N.W."

The title-page bears the Warne device, a horseshoe between two wings, with a spread of 1.8 centimeters at the tips; "A New Illustrated Edition, with Notes," is in Old English (Gothic) type. It is one of four Warne-Davies *Anglers* with both New York and London on the title-page; the other three are the seventh of 1888, the twelfth of 1895, and the fourteenth of 1930.

The copy seen at the publisher's office is unbound, and contains manuscript notes for a new preface and alterations in the text which, although a reading of some 13 pages indicates obvious improvements, were never used.

This edition has been checked in two publisher's bindings. The first, at Princeton, is in dark red cloth, end papers black, top edges gilt; the second in smooth dark blue-green cloth, end papers very dark brown, leaves untrimmed; both with lettering pieces on the spine simulated by gilt rules.

According to information supplied by the publisher, this reprint, issued in July 1893, is a reissue of the second Davies edition of 1878 (No. 102) in the *Chandos Classics,* with a new title-page and the same illustrations.

[1894]
164. The First Burt (22nd Major) Reprint

Burt's Library of the World's Best Books. | — |
The | Complete Angler | Or, The | Contemplative Man's
Recreation | of | Izaak Walton And Charles Cotton, |
Edited by John Major. | Circular Publisher's Device |
New York: | A. L. Burt, Publisher. | [1894].

Copy examined: Trinity.

Size: 7 7/16″ × 5 1/16″.

Contents: pp. 1-354, and one plate, consisting of half-title, The Complete Angler p. [1]; blank p. [2]; title-page, as above, p. [3]; blank, p. [4]; "Contents," pp. [5]-7; blank, p. [8]; "Introductory Essay," pp. [9]-34; "The Epistle Dedicatory," pp. [35]-36; "To All Readers," etc., pp. [37]-39; blank, p. [40]; text, pp. [41]-233; blank p. [234]; title Part II, p. [235]; blank, p. [236]; text pp. [237]-305; "Linnaean Arrangement of the Fish . . .," pp. [306]-310; "Original and Selected Notes," pp. [311]-347; blank, p. [348]; "General Index," pp. [349]-354. At the end are five additional leaves advertising "Burt's Library of the World's Best Books." Although the *Angler* is not included among the 61 titles listed, it may be presumed to have been priced one dollar, since it is in the same format, "cloth, gilt top," and the preamble states that, ". . . the books will be . . . uniform in all respects with this volume . . ."

The publisher's circular device, reading on the perimeter, "Burt's Library of the World's Best Books," appears on the title-page just above the imprint. The title-page to Part II is imprinted with a circular Walton-Cotton cipher.

The illustrations consist of a full-page frontispiece of Walton, Archer's headpiece (to the "Introductory Essay") of Walton's biographees, small woodcuts of Sir Humphrey Davy's ring and Donne's seal, 19 woodcuts of fish, and one page of music.

The publisher's binding is in dark olive-green cloth, fancy cream-colored end papers with an overall pattern of bright green twigs. The publisher's device on the title-page is repeated in blind in the center of the front cover and in gilt at the foot of the spine, which is also titled in gilt at the head, between gilt rules. The top edges are gilt.

The following are present only in this issue of the Burt reprints examined: half-title page, frontispiece of Walton, five leaves of publisher's advertising at the end, and "of" instead of "by" Izaak Walton on the title-page.

A. L. Burt Co., which specialized in reprints, probably issued at least 15 reprints of the *Angler* between 1894 and 1934. Unfortunately none was dated. The copy listed here as Burt's first reprint apparently agrees with the brief description given by Wood, who stated that the plates used were supplied by the "Publisher's Plate Renting Co." Neither Oliver nor Wood cite any source for the publication date of 1894 which, pending further confirmation, has been followed here.

This is a reprint from the Major edition of 1844 (No. 55).

1895

165. The Eleventh Davies (Second Gibbings) Reprint

THE COMPLETE ANGLER by Izaac Walton and
Charles Cotton . . .
London: Gibbings and Company, Limited,
18 Bury Street, W. C. 1895

Copies examined: Harvard, Princeton, Yale.

Size: $8\frac{3}{8}'' \times 5\frac{5}{8}''$.

Pagination summary: [i]-xii, [1]-467.

The title-page, printed in red and black, has on its verso the printer's mark of two entwined pentagons enclosing a circular printing of "The Selwood Printing Works Frome & London" within which is another pentagon enclosing the initials "B & T" in cipher. At the foot of page 467 is imprinted "Butler & Tanner, The Selwood Printing Works, Frome and London."

This is a reissue, with the same illustrations, of the eighth Davies (1st Gibbings) edition of 1890 (No. 146). On page [ii] it is number 4 in a listing of 15 publications of the "Standard British Classics" series. A note at the foot of the page states that the volumes in the series were "kept in stock in half-calf gilt, or half-vellum extra gilt, top edge gilt."

The Harvard copy is in the publisher's binding of dark green cloth, gilt stamped on the spine with the title, names of the authors and, at the foot, the same "Standard British Classics" device used for the eighth Davies (1st Gibbings). The Yale copy is in dark red cloth with the same gilt stamping on the spine.

This is a reissue of the eighth Davies (1st Gibbings) reprint of 1890 (No. 146).

[1895]

166. The Twelfth Davies Reprint

THE COMPLETE ANGLER by Izaac Walton and
Charles Cotton . . .
London Frederick Warne & Co and New York [1895].

Copies examined: Horne (2).

Size (in red cloth): $7\frac{1}{16}'' \times 4\frac{11}{16}''$; (in blue-green cloth) $7\frac{5}{16}'' \times 5''$.

Pagination summary: [i]-xii, [1]-467.

The title-page verso is imprinted with the same printer's mark as the eleventh Davies (No. 165). At the foot of page 467 is imprinted, "Butler & Tanner, the Selwood Printing Works, Frome, and London." On page 348 the lower half of the numeral 3 is barely discernible. The Warne device of the Wings and Horseshoe on the title-page measures 1.8 centimeters between the tips of the wings; "A New Illustrated Edition, with Notes," is in small italic caps.

The pagination and illustrations are the same as the second and third Davies lacking the page of advertising at the end, the "Contents" heading, and the woodcut (p. [374]).

The publisher's binding of both copies is blind stamped in the lower right hand corner of the back cover with 58, the number of the *Angler* in Warne's *Chandos Classics* series. The end papers are identical, of cream-colored paper with an all-over arabesque decoration in white, featuring a wreath in the center encircling "The Chandos Classics." The spine of the red cloth copy is gilt stamped with titling and floral decorations; that of the dark blue-green cloth copy has the same simulated lettering pieces and titling as No. 163, but with top edges gilt, other untrimmed.

According to information supplied by the publisher, this reprint was issued by Warne about October 1895, and was printed by Butler and Tanner of Frome. Except as noted above, it is a reissue of the second Davies (No. 102), which was the first printing in the *Chandos Classics*.

[1895]

167. The Second Lovell, Coryell (23rd Major) Reprint

THE COMPLETE ANGLER . . . of Izaak Walton and
Charles Cotton
New York: Lovell, Coryell & Company,
310-318 Sixth Avenue [1895].

Copy examined: Oliver.

Size: $7\frac{1}{4}'' \times 4\frac{13}{16}''$.

Pagination summary: [1-5], 6-354.

This reissue of the first Lovell, Coryell (No. 157) is bound in red cloth. Cover edges are blind ruled. A lettering piece on the spine is gilt titled and gilt stamped with a blossom; at the foot, in gilt, a winged lion is above "Century edition." The top edges are gilt.

Oliver determined the date of publication through checking the publisher's address.

[1895]

168. The First Scott Edition

THE COMPLETE ANGLER of Walton and Cotton: . . .
London: Walter Scott, Ltd. Paternoster Square. [1895].

Copies examined: Horne (2), Princeton. Others: CLSU, CtY, CU, CU-A, DLC, FU, MH, NN.

Size: 6⅝″ × 4⅝″.

Pagination summary: [i-v], vi-xx, [1]-245, [246], [22].

At the foot of page 245 is the imprint, "The Walter Scott Press, Newcastle-on-Tyne." The half-title recto reads, "The Scott Library" and, beneath it, "The Complete Angler." On the half-title verso is imprinted, "For full list of the volumes in this series see catalogue [22 pages] at end of book," where this edition is listed as No. 98 of the Scott Library, selling at one shilling six pence. A second half-title, which follows the Introduction, is imprinted "The Complete Angler" on the recto; the verso is blank. There are no notes or illustrations.

The Princeton copy was issued in dark green cloth; the front cover is decorated with gilt ruling, and "The Scott Library" is gilt stamped in the top left hand corner. The back cover is plain; the usual titling appears in gilt on the spine. The first Horne copy is in dark red cloth, with the title and "Scott Library" in gilt on the spine, and a blind embossed publisher's device containing the letters "WSPC" on the front cover. The second Horne copy is in the same dark red cloth with the same titling in gilt on the spine, but the front cover is decorated with a blind stamped laurel wreath. It differs also in having only six pages of advertising at the end.

The 15-page introduction, dated 1895, is by Charles Hill Dick.

This is a reprint from the fifth edition of 1676 (No. 6), and is listed in *The English Catalogue of Books* as published in October, 1895, priced at 1 shilling 6 pence.

[1895]

169. The Second Scott Reprint

THE COMPLETE ANGLER of Walton and Cotton: . . .
London: Walter Scott, Ltd. Paternoster Square. [1895].

Copies examined: Horne, Princeton. Others: DLC, NcU, ViU.

Size: 6¼″ × 4⅝″.

Pagination summary: [i-v], vi-xx, [1]-245, [246], [22].

There is no half-title at the front, as in the first Scott reprint, but the second half-title following the Introduction, page [1], is present. At the foot of page 245 is the imprint, "The Walter Scott Press, Newcastle-on-Tyne." There are no illustrations.

The publisher's binding of the Horne copy is in dark gray cloth. The paper label on the spine has a red rule border, and is printed in black, with "Camelot Series" above the titling. An extra label is tipped on the last page of advertising. The Princeton copy in the same cloth, has no paper label on the spine, which is gilt stamped with the titling, "Camelot Series," and "112," probably its number in that series. The *Angler* listed as number 98 in the advertising at the end, in the Scott Library series of 1895, is the first Scott reprint (No. 168).

This is a reprint, in the Camelot Series, of the first Scott edition of 1895, with the same introduction by Charles Hill Dick.

The United States Catalog Supplement 1902-1905 lists a *Complete Angler* published by Simmons in a Camelot series, which was edited, and had an introduction, by C. Hill Dick. The selling price was 40 cents. Apparently it has not been seen or described by bibliographers, and is listed here for the record.

1896

170. The First Lang Edition

THE COMPLEAT ANGLER . . . by Izaak Walton . . .
London: *Published by J. M. Dent and Company*, at Aldine House. 1896.

Copies examined: Harvard, Horne, Princeton, Trinity. Others: CoD, CSmH, CtY, IaU, IU, MB, MiD, NBu, NcRS, NIC, NN, PP.

Size: $7\frac{7}{16}'' \times 5\frac{1}{8}''$.

Pagination summary: [i-vi], vii-xii, [xiii-xv], xvi-lviii, [1]-319.

At the foot of page [vi] is imprinted, "*Edinburgh:* T. & A. Constable, *Printers to Her Majesty.*"

The illustrations consist of a frontispiece and 88 woodcuts by E. J. Sullivan. The title-page, printed in red and black, is imprinted with a Dent device.

The binding in dark green cloth, is gilt stamped on the spine and front cover with an *art nouveau* piscatorial decoration designed by the illustrator. The title-page cartouche of the first edition (the center blank except for "Ex Libris" at the top) is printed on the front pastedown. The top edges are gilt, others untrimmed (see Figure 22).

Imprinted alone on page [xiv] is a "Note as to Text" which reads as follows,

The First Lang Edition (No. 170)

The Ninth Ephemera Reprint (No. 109)

The First Davies Edition (No. 101)

Figure 22   Publishers' Bindings

"The text here reprinted is, in the main, that of Sir Harris Nicolas, which was printed from Walton's Fifth Edition, 1676, the last that was revised by the author."

Andrew Lang, well-known author, editor, and critic of the late 19th century, wrote the introduction which, changed only by the inclusion of the "Note as to Text," appeared also in later Everyman *Anglers*.

1896

171. The Second Lang "Edition"

THE COMPLEAT ANGLER . . . by Izaak Walton . . .
New York: The Macmillan Company. 1896.

Copies examined: None.

Size reported: 12mo.

Pagination summary: 58+319 p.

This entry is from *The Annual American Catalogue*, for 1896, which calls it "New ed. edited with an intro. by Andrew Lang." The selling price was $2.00.

It is also listed in the appendix to the first Le Gallienne edition of 1897, and by Oliver (who did not see it), and who assumed it to be a reissue of the first Lang. *The American Catalogue* listing, not cited heretofore, affords some measure of increased evidence of its existence.

1896

172. The Eighth Jesse Reprint

THE COMPLETE ANGLER, . . . of Izaak Walton and
Charles Cotton. . . .
London George Bell and Sons, 1896

Copies examined: Princeton, Yale.

Size: 7" × 4⅜".

Pagination summary: [i]-xix, [xx], [2], [1]-496, [40].

The title-page verso is imprinted, "Reprinted from Stereotype plates." This is a reissue of the seventh Jesse edition of 1889 (No. 144), with the same 206 woodcuts, of which the index of engravings on wood continues to list only

203. Both copies examined contain the 26 extra cost steel plates found in some Jesse reprints.

At the end of the Princeton copy is a 40-page "Classified Catalogue" of the publications of George Bell & Sons, dated 1896. This reprint is listed under "Bohn's Libraries" priced at 5s.

1896

173. The Fifth Nimmo (24th Major) Reprint

THE COMPLETE ANGLER . . . of Izaak Walton and
Charles Cotton . . .
London John C. Nimmo 14 King William Street,
Strand MDCCCXCVI

Copy examined: Horne.

Size: 7¼" × 4¾".

Pagination summary: [i]-xv, [xvi], [1]-445.

The title-page verso is imprinted, "*Printed by* Ballantyne, Hanson & Co. *At the Ballantyne* Press" and at the foot of page 445 is, "*Printed by* Ballantyne, Hanson & Co. *Edinburgh and London.*" The title-page, with the vignette of the "View from Lea Bridge," is printed in red and black.

The illustrations are described on the title-page as "With Photogravure Portraits, Seven Full-Page Illustrations and Seventy-Four Wood Engravings," all of which are included in the "List of Embellishments." These are the same as in the 1883 Nimmo and Bain reprint (No. 114); the plates after the paintings by A. H. Tourrier, the woodcuts appeared originally in the Major edition of 1884 (No. 55). The photogravure frontispiece of Walton, imprinted "Swan Electric Engraving Company" was satisfactorily reproduced in a brown tone. The process and tinting labelled "Swantype," used for the rest of the plates, printed on coated paper, was not completely successful. The portrait of Cotton in the copy examined faces the title-page to Part II; in the sixth Nimmo reprint (No. 174) it follows the title-page to Part II, and faces the first page of text.

The copy examined was issued in maroon limp leather with very dark maroon end papers. The covers and spine are edged as a unit by a single gilt rule, and the spine is gilt titled. The leaf edges are gilt and rounded.

The English Catalogue of Books lists Nimmo *Anglers* for March and October 1896 priced at 6s. and 5s. respectively. This reprint in leather would probably sell at the higher price and has been assigned to March, and the following one (No. 174) to October. It is a reissue of the Nimmo and Bain reprint of 1883 (No. 114).

[168]

174. The Sixth Nimmo (25th Major) Reprint

THE COMPLETE ANGLER . . . of Izaak Walton and
Charles Cotton . . .
London John C. Nimmo, 14 King William Street,
Strand MDCCCXCVI

Copy examined: Horne.

Size: $7\frac{1}{4}'' \times 4\frac{3}{4}''$.

Pagination summary: [i]-xv, [xvi], [1]-445.

This reprint has the same title-page in red and black, printer's imprints, and illustrations as the fifth Nimmo (No. 173), although as noted thereunder, the plate of Cotton is inserted facing the first page of text rather than the title-page of Part II. There is no improvement in the plate impressions (for additional details in the plates see No. 173).

The publisher's binding is in dark red cloth with brick red end papers. The front cover is elaborately gilt decorated; at the top, Cotton's fishing house among trees on the bank of a river; in the center, titling in large capitals; and in the lower left hand corner, a device of the publisher within a square. The spine is titled and dated in gilt and in the middle, "With Eighty Two Illustrations" is stamped in gilt. The top edges are gilt, the others untrimmed.

As mentioned in the notes to the fifth Nimmo, this is believed to be the Nimmo issue published in October, 1896, in cloth, and to have sold for 5s.

This sixth Nimmo, like its predecessors, is a reissue of the Nimmo and Bain reprint of 1883 (No. 114).

175. The First Le Gallienne (8th Stock) Facsimile Edition

THE COMPLETE ANGLER; . . . By Isaak Walton. . . .
London: Elliot Stock, 62, Paternoster Row. 1896.

Copies examined: Harvard, Horne, Princeton. Others: CU, CtY, DLC, NcU, NN.

Size: $6\frac{3}{4}'' \times 4\frac{1}{8}''$.

Pagination summary: [i-v], vi-x, [16], (1)-246.

This is a facsimile reproduction of the 1st edition of 1653 with a preface by Richard Le Gallienne. There are six engravings of fish and two pages of music, the second of which (as in the original) is printed upside down.

The publisher's binding seen is in light tan cloth, with titling printed in dark brown. A reproduction of "The Breakfast," an engraving on copper by Ryland after Wale, which appeared initially in the first Hawkins edition of 1760 (No. 9), is also printed in dark brown on the front cover. This binding is the same as the first Stock facsimile of 1876 (No. 98).

This facsimile has the same 36 irregularities found in the first Stock facsimile, and is undoubtedly a reprint of that edition. However, the black marks on page 67, line 10, of the first Stock (No. 98), have been eliminated. (See Appendix B.)

The English Catalogue of Books lists this edition as published in November, 1896, priced at 2s 6d.

1897

176. The Second Le Gallienne (9th Stock) Facsimile

THE COMPLETE ANGLER; . . . By Isaak Walton. . . . London: Elliot Stock. New York: Dodd, Mead & Company. 1897.

Copies examined: Princeton, Yale (3). Others: CU, CtHT, TxU.

Size: 6⅞″ × 4″.

Pagination summary: [i-v], vi-x, [16], (1)-246.

This is a reissue of the first Stock Le Gallienne facsimile of 1896 (No. 175), with the same illustrations and irregularities, and the same preface by Richard Le Gallienne. (See Appendix B.)

It was issued by the publisher in at least two bindings. The *first* (at Princeton and Yale) is the same as No. 175; the *second* (at Yale) is in grayish-green cloth with the titling and "The Breakfast" in red on the front cover.

This facsimile was advertised by Dodd, Mead & Company in *The Annual American Catalogue*, 1897, as "A Facsimile Reprint of the First Edition, 12mo. $1.00."

1897

177. The First Le Gallienne Edition

THE COMPLEAT ANGLER by Izaak Walton and
Charles Cotton . . .
John Lane *The Bodley Head* London & New York MDCCCXCVII

Copies examined: Harvard, Horne (3), Princeton. Others: CLU-C, CSmH, CtHT, CtY, CU, ICN, ICRL, ICU, NIC, NN, NNC, PHC, TxU. In Parts, CtY and NN.

Size: Bound, 9¼"×7"; In parts, 9½"×7", measurements vary, leaves untrimmed.

Pagination summary: [i]-lxxxiv, [4], [1]-[428], [14], [2].

The 14 unnumbered pages at the end contain "The Anglers' Calendar," compiled by Hi Regan, which gives George Washington's birthday as January 11th. It was followed by two pages of the publisher's advertising. "Compleat Angler" and a vignette of Cotton's fishing house are in red on the title-page which is printed within a double rule. On the verso is "Printed by Ballantyne, Hanson & Co. at the Ballantyne Press." and, at the foot of the last page of *The Anglers' Calendar,* appears "Printed by Ballantyne, Hanson & Co., London & Edinburgh."

There are two photogravure plates, one of Walton and one of Cotton, 51 full-page illustrations and 190 smaller cuts, vignettes, and decorative initials engraved by E. H. New. The last are not included in "The List of Illustrations."

On page xxi there is an error in the "List," where the correct title for the illustration on page 98 is "Near Amwell," not "Amwell Magna Fishery . . ." which is on page 191.

This edition, edited by Richard Le Gallienne, English poet, novelist and critic, appeared originally in 13 monthly parts numbered and dated from April, 1896, through April, 1897, each uncut, in its own light green paper wrapper, priced one shilling net (Figure 23). The front of the wrappers is decorated with its own title-page designed by New for the parts. It is printed within a double rule, with the same vignette of Cotton's fishing house (in black) which is imprinted in red on the title-page of the book itself, with variant wording and format, and set in a different type font. *The Anglers' Calendar,* printed on the inside of the front cover of each part, was augmented, reprinted and included with Part XII. The publisher's advertising is on all the back covers. The inside of the back covers have Sampson Low, Marston & Co. advertising in numbers I-V; they are blank in VI-IX, and have "The New Walton" (publisher's note) in X-XIII. The half-title, general title-page, contents, list of illustrations and the introduction are in Part XIII.

"The New Walton" states in part, "A binding case, specially designed by Mr. E. H. New, in stamped buckram, will be supplied to subscribers at 2s.

Figure 23   The First Le Gallienne Edition (No. 177),
issued in 13 monthly parts

net." This case, in tan cloth, is decorated in dark green on the front cover and spine with stylized trees, Walton and Cotton cyphers and, on the back cover, with a die of Cotton's fishing house. It is the same as the binding in which the parts most frequently appear in book form, with top edges stained brown, others untrimmed.

With the same decorations in black, the cloth on one of the Horne copies is pea-green with top edges stained dark green, others untrimmed. The copy in this binding measures one quarter of an inch less in height and one sixteenth of an inch less in width than the measurements of the copies examined in brown cloth.

The English Catalogue of Books lists this edition as published in February, 1897, priced at fifteen shillings net. It is also listed in *The Annual American Catalogue* as "4to. cloth $6.00." It is a reprint from the fifth edition of 1676 (No. 6).

[1897]

178. The First Caldwell (26th Major) Reprint

Library of Famous Books by Famous Authors
COMPLETE ANGLER Walton and Cotton
H M Caldwell Company New York — Boston [1897].

Copy examined: Princeton.

Size: 7⅜″ × 4⅞″.

Pagination summary: [1-5], 6-354.

The *art nouveau* title-page, printed in red and brown, is imprinted with the publisher's device, a vertically raised arm holding a lighted torch above an open book. Wood states, "The plates from which this edition was printed were supplied by the 'Publishers' Plate Renting Co'."

The illustrations consist of a page of music, the headpiece of Walton's biographees, and 19 woodcuts of fish, all reproductions of the woodcuts in the Major editions (see No. 55).

This *Angler* was issued in dark red ribbed cloth, with the covers divided into four sections by a crossing of double lines ruled in blind, with the publisher's device in gilt on the front and in blind on the back. The spine is elaborately gilt with a pattern of vines and flowers, and another impression of the publisher's device.

This edition, a reissue of the Major edition of 1844 (No. 55), dated 1897 by Wood and by Oliver, is so dated herein.

1898

179. The Eleventh Cassell Reprint

CASSELL'S NATIONAL LIBRARY
THE COMPLETE ANGLER . . . by Isaac Walton
Cassell and Company, Limited London, Paris, New York &
Melbourne 1898

Copy examined: Princeton.

Size: 5½″×3¹¹⁄₁₆″.

Pagination summary: [1]-192, [4].

At the foot of page 192 is imprinted, "Printed by Cassell & Company, Limited,
La Belle Sauvage, London, E.C." The title-page, which bears the publisher's
circular device, has imprinted on the verso, "First printed in this series
January 1886. Reprinted February 1886, 1890, 1891, 1898." At the end are four
pages of advertising for Cassell publications, but the "Angler" is not included. There are no illustrations.

The date for this reissue, as for others of the Cassell reprints, is listed on
the title-page verso. It is recorded, but not described, by Wood, and by
Oliver (his No. 167) as a 24mo. volume.

This is another Cassell reissue, with the Morley introduction, but without
the author's dedication, of Walton's part of the fifth edition of 1676 (No. 6).

1898

180. The Twelfth Cassell Reprint

THE COMPLETE ANGLER . . . by Isaac Walton.
New York: Cassell & Company, 31 East 17th Street. 1898.

Copies examined: None seen.

Size reported: 24mo.

Pagination summary: [1]-192.

This reissue of the earlier Cassell reprints is listed as above by Oliver (his
No. 168). A reissue is also listed by Wood as volume 5 of "Cassell's National
Library," reprinted in 1898, but neither he nor Oliver (who did not see it)
provide a description.

This is presumably another Cassell reissue, with the Morley introduction,
but without the author's dedication, of Walton's part of the fifth edition
of 1676 (No. 6).

181. The Sixth Lowell Reprint

THE COMPLETE ANGLER, . . . of Izaak Walton and
Charles Cotton. . . .
Boston: Little, Brown, and Company. 1898.

Copies examined: Harvard, Horne, Princeton, Yale. Others: MiU, WaU.

Size: 7¼″ × 4⅞″.

Pagination summary: [i-v], vi-lxxvi, [1]-465.

The title-page, without vignette, is printed in red and black, and on the verso
is printed, "*Copyright, 1889,* By Little, Brown, and Company," and, "University
Press: John Wilson and Son, Cambridge."
 The illustrations, from the first Lowell edition (No. 142), consist of a
frontispiece of Louis K. Harlow's etching, *Ware on the Lea,* protected by two
tissue guards, the second having the title of the etching imprinted in red,
and 74 woodcuts.
 This one-volume reprint was issued in soft dull green cloth, with the spine
titled in gilt. The front cover and the spine are decorated in gilt from the
same dies used for the first Lowell edition. The top edges are gilt, others
untrimmed.
 This *Angler,* identified as a "New Edition" on the title-page, is listed in
The Annual American Catalogue as having been published by Little, Brown, and
Company in 1898, priced at $1.50 in cloth. It is a reissue of the first Lowell
edition of 1889 (No. 142).

[1898]

182. The Fourth Crowell (27th Major) Reprint

THE COMPLETE ANGLER; . . . of Izaak Walton and
Charles Cotton . . .
New York: Thomas Y Crowell & Co.
46 East Fourteenth Street. [1898].

Copies examined: Horne, Princeton.

Size: 6⅝″ × 4⅜″.

Pagination summary: [i]-lx, 1-418.

The title-page, in red and black, imprinted in black with the cartouche from
the 1653 edition, is followed by a second title-page in black and white, im-

printed with the vignette from the 1844 Major (No. 55). It reads at the foot, "New York: Thomas Y. Crowell & Co.," and has the quotation from Shakespeare on the verso. Neither title-page is dated, there are no dates in either copy examined, and both state, "From the Fourth London Edition."

The illustrations consist of a photogravure frontispiece by Copeland, and the 74 woodcuts from the second Crowell edition. The woodcut of Archbishop Sheldon, indexed for page 203, is on page 202.

The binding is in green cloth, with the usual titling in gilt, framed within a gilt stylized floral panel measuring $3^{15}/_{16} \times 1^{1}/_{2}$ inches stamped on the front cover, which is edged with three gilt rules. The spine has a similar gilt panel and is gilt titled. The top edges are gilt.

In an advertisement in *The Annual American Catalogue* for 1898, Crowell listed this reprint as a new volume in the "Faience Library" issued in cloth with gilt top to be sold at $1.00.

It is a reissue in one volume of the second Crowell reprint of 1892 (No. 155).

[1898]

183. The Fifth Crowell (28th Major) Reprint

THE COMPLETE ANGLER . . . of Izaak Walton and
Charles Cotton . . .
New York: Thomas Y. Crowell & Co.,
46 East Fourteenth Street. [1898].

Copies examined: None seen.

Size reported: $7^{3}/_{8}" \times 5"$.

The title-page is in two colors, and the illustrations consist of a photogravure frontispiece by Copeland and the 74 woodcuts of the earlier Crowell editions, of which this is a reissue. It is part of the "Waldorf Library," published to sell for seventy-five cents.

This listing is from Oliver (his No. 170) who did not see a copy, and stated that his information came from the publisher.

[1898]

184. The Sixth Crowell (29th Major) Reprint

THE COMPLETE ANGLER, . . . of Izaak Walton and
Charles Cotton. . . .
New York: Thomas Y. Crowell & Co., [1898].

Copies examined: Harvard, Princeton.

Size: 7⅛″×4¾″.

Pagination summary: [i-iv], v-lx, 1-418.

The illustrations consist of the 74 woodcuts from the fourth Crowell edition (No. 182) with the portrait of Archbishop Sheldon still listed for page 203, and appearing on page 202.

Both copies examined have been recased and lack the two-color title-page and frontispiece cited by Oliver, who, not having seen a copy, secured his information from the publisher, as well as the date, the selling price of sixty cents, and that it was issued as part of the "Astor Library" (see his number 171). The second title-page (as above) is present.

In *The Annual American Catalogue* for 1893 (p. 99), Crowell advertised "The Astor Library of Standard Literature" and described the volumes as "bound in half russia leather, cloth sides, gilt back and marbled edges. 12 mo. per vol. 75 cents."

The marbled edges of both copies, which do not occur in any other Crowell edition which has been examined, or others have described, may be used to identify them as the *Angler* which the publisher reported to Oliver. It was undoubtedly issued in cloth which could account for the lower price given Oliver.

Although the *Angler* was not mentioned in the 1893 advertisement, titles in such a series could certainly have been issued as late as 1898, the date furnished by the publisher for this edition.

It is a reissue of the earlier Crowell reprints.

1899

185. The Thirteenth Davies (Pearson) Reprint

THE COMPLETE ANGLER by Izaak Walton and
Charles Cotton . . .
London C. Arthur Pearson, Limited Henrietta Street 1899

Copy examined: Horne.

Size: 7⁵⁄₁₆″×4¹³⁄₁₆″.

Pagination summary: [i]-xii, [1]-467.

This is the only Davies *Angler* in which Walton's given name is spelled "Izaak" on the title-page; "Izaac" having been used for all the others. There is no Warne device on the title-page. At the foot of page 467 is imprinted, "Butler and Tanner, The Selwood Printing Works, Frome, and London."

The illustrations and decorations are the same as in the first Davies edition (No. 101), but lacking the frontispiece of Walton, the chapter heading decoration on page [ix], and the woodcut on page [374].

The publisher's binding examined in dark red cloth, is embossed on the front cover and spine, with an overall leaf and thistle pattern, featuring an heraldic shield. The usual titling in gilt is on the spine. The top edges are untrimmed.

This is a reissue of the first Davies edition of 1878 (No. 101).

[1899]
186. The Second Caldwell (30th Major) Reprint

Berkeley Library
COMPLETE ANGLER Walton and Cotton
H. M. Caldwell Co. Publishers New York — Boston [1899].

Copies examined: Horne, Princeton, Yale.

Size: 7½″×5″.

Pagination summary: [1-5], 6-354.

The *art nouveau* title-page, decorated with large flowers, which appear to be Oriental poppies, is printed in orange and black, and imprinted with the same lighted torch device used by the publisher for the first Caldwell reprint of 1897 (No. 178).

The illustrations consist of a photogravure of a river scene (lacking in the Horne copy), and the headpiece of Walton's biographees, 19 woodcuts of fish, and one page of music from the Major editions.

Three publisher's bindings of this reprint have been seen. The *first* (Princeton) in green cloth, has elaborate gilt decorations framing the title on the upper part of the front cover and, blind stamped on the lower part, "BL" (for Berkeley Library). Decorations and the publisher's device are gilt stamped on the spine. The *second* (Horne) in bright red cloth with white ribbon bookmark, has broad floral border blind stamped on the front cover forming a panel that reads "Complete Angler" at the top in large gilt capitals. A similar floral design is blind stamped on the spine, titled in gilt between gilt rules. The top edges are gilt. The *third* (Yale) is in light tan cloth having an overall dark brown floral pattern incorporating "Berkeley Library" and "H. M. Caldwell Co." printed in brown on the back cover. The upper part of the front cover and the top and foot of the spine are gilt titled. An elaborate ex libris is printed in tan on the front pastedown. The top edges are gilt, the others are untrimmed.

This reissue of the first Caldwell reprint of 1897, is likewise a reprint of the

Major edition of 1844 (No. 55). Oliver (without citing source) dates this edition 1899, which is followed herein.

1899

187. The First Dobson Edition

THE COMPLEAT ANGLER by Izaak Walton
MDCCCXCIX. Published by J. M. Dent and Co:
Aldine House, London W.C.

Copies examined: Harvard, Horne, Princeton. Others: CtY, NN.

Size: 5⅞" × 3¹³⁄₁₆".

Pagination summary: [i-v], 1-189, [190-191], 192-231, [232], 233-248.

At the foot of page 248 is the imprint "Turnbull and Spears, Printers, Edinburgh." On page [i] is a series title (the text in black, and a sundial vignette in red) which reads, "The Temple Classics Edited by Isreal Gollancz M.A." The title-page with an *art nouveau* decorative border, is also printed in red and black.

The illustrations consist of a full-page plate of the Huysman portrait of Walton, and two pages of music. On the front pastedown appears a printed memorial to Walton and the *Angler*, in the form of a headstone showing the years of Walton's birth and death, and the dates of the first and fifth editions of *The Compleat Angler*.

The blue cloth publisher's binding has the publisher's owl device stamped in blind on the front cover with gilt titling and decoration on the spine. The top edges are gilt, the others untrimmed. A red ribbon bookmark is included. *The English Catalogue of Books* states that it was also available in roan.

On page [232] appears the following, signed "I.G." and dated *August 4th*, 1899, "*This issue of Izaak Walton's* 'Complete Angler,' *based on the fifth edition of* 1676, *has been prepared for the press by* Mr. Austin Dobson, *who has revised the text, added the marginalia and contributed the accompanying notes.*" However this edition includes only Part I.

The English Catalogue of Books gives the publication date as 1899, priced at 1s 6d net, and 2s net in roan. The "List of Editions of the Compleat Angler" in the third Marston edition of 1915 (No. 255) and Westwood and Satchell's supplement to *Bibliotheca Piscatoria* (1901) list this edition as having been published in New York by The Macmillan Co., the supplement giving the selling price as "cloth, 50 cents; limp leather, 75 cents." No copy has been seen with the New York imprint.

188. The Seventh Crowell (31st Major) Reprint

THE COMPLETE ANGLER by Izaak Walton
New York and Boston: Thomas Y. Crowell and Company [1899].

Copy examined: Horne.

Size: 7¾6″ × 4¾″.

Pagination summary: [i]-lx, 1-418.

The title-page, in red and black, differs from all Crowell editions and reprints, except the eighth (No. 189), in not bearing Cotton's name on the title-page, and, from all other Crowell editions examined, in showing the publisher located in both New York and Boston. As in other Crowell reprints, there is a second title-page in black only which lacks publisher's name, place and date; it states "From the Fourth London Edition (No. 55)," and has the quotation from Shakespeare on the verso. (See notes to the first Crowell edition, 1884 (No. 116).)

The illustrations are those of the fourth Crowell reprint of 1898 (No. 182).

The publisher's binding seen is in green cloth with the usual titling, within a decorative panel (resembling a Chippendale mirror) 4¾″ high × 2⅛″ wide, stamped in gilt on the front cover. The spine is decorated and titled similarly. The top edges are gilt.

On the recto of the front end paper is the written signature of a former owner, and the date, "Oct. 1899," which, lacking other evidence, has tentatively been assigned to this reprint.

The undated seventh and eighth reprints differ in title-page particulars from all other Crowell *Anglers* which have been examined or have been seen in descriptive lists. They are listed with the hope that positive identification may be forthcoming.

189. The Eighth Crowell (32nd Major) Reprint

THE COMPLETE ANGLER by Izaak Walton
New York, Thomas Y. Crowell & Company, Publishers [1900].

Copy examined: Horne. Other: MH.

Size: 7¼″ × 4⅛″.

Pagination summary: [i]-lx, 1-418.

The title-page, in light orange and black, differs in this respect from other Crowell editions seen and, like the seventh Crowell, does not have Cotton's name on the title-page. As in other Crowell editions, there is a second title-page printed in black and white with the imprint "New York Thomas Y. Crowell & Co. Publishers'." It also is imprinted, "From the Fourth London Edition," but lacks the quotation from Shakespeare on the verso (see notes to the first Crowell reprint, 1884, No. 116).

The illustrations are those of the fifth Crowell reprint (No. 183).

The publisher's binding seen is in red cloth, with the usual titling within a decorative panel (resembling a Chippendale mirror) 3″ high ×1¾″ wide, stamped in gilt on the front cover. The spine is decorated and titled similarly. The top edges are gilt.

In view of the similarity of this and the preceding reissue, it has been assumed that they were published at about the same time, and this one has been tentatively dated 1900 (see the seventh Crowell reprint for additional comments).

[1900]

190. The Ninth Crowell (33rd Major) Reprint

THE COMPLETE ANGLER; . . . of Izaak Walton and
Charles Cotton . . .
New York: Thomas Y. Crowell & Co.
46 East Fourteenth Street. [1900].

Copy examined: Harvard.

Size: 6¾″×4⅜″.

Pagination summary: [i]-lx, 1-418.

The title-page, printed in red and black, has the cartouche from the 1653 edition printed in black as a vignette in the center of the page. This is followed by the Crowell title-page with the 1844 Major edition vignette, on which appears "From the Fourth London Edition," and, "New York Thomas Y. Crowell & Co Publishers." The quotation from Shakespeare is on the verso. See notes to the first Crowell edition of 1884 (No. 116).

The illustrations are those of the fourth Crowell reprint of 1898 (No. 182) with the woodcut of Archbishop Sheldon still listed on page 203 and appearing on page 202.

The publisher's binding is in soft dark red leatherette. The spine and the front cover are decorated with a small gilt design. On the end papers is a swirling *art nouveau* pattern in light green. The top edges are gilt, and it has a red ribbon bookmark.

This undated reprint is the only one seen with "Walton and Cotton" on the first title-page, and with "New York: Thomas Y. Crowell Co." on a second title-page which lacks the quotation from Shakespeare on its verso. It is not described in the published lists or annual catalogues reviewed and has been dated from the Harvard catalogue card.

1900

191. The Thirteenth Cassell Reprint

THE COMPLETE ANGLER . . . by Isaac Walton.
New York: Cassell & Company, 43 East Nineteenth Street. 1900.

Copies examined: None seen.

Size reported: 24mo.

Pagination summary: [1]-192.

This reissue of the earlier Cassell reprints is listed as above by Oliver (his No. 178). A Cassell reissue dated 1900 is also listed by Wood, "as a volume in the 'new series' of 'Cassell's National Library,' but without change," but neither he nor Oliver, who did not see it, provide a description.
   This reprint is also listed in *The Annual American Catalogue Cumulated 1900-1903* as having been published June 9, 1900, as volume 7, No. 359, of the National Library, New Series, 24mo, paper covers, priced at 10 cents. Although Cotton is mentioned as co-author, the details, as well as those furnished by Wood and Oliver, indicate that this, as the earlier reprints, did not include Cotton's part. It is presumably therefore, another reprint, with the Morley introduction, but without the author's dedication, of Walton's part of the fifth edition of 1676 (No. 6).

1900

192. The Third Lippincott (34th Major) Reprint

THE COMPLEAT ANGLER . . . by Izaak Walton and Charles Cotton.
Philadelphia: J. B. Lippincott Company. 1900.

Copies examined: None seen.

Size reported: 12mo.

This reprint, dated 1900 in Westwood and Satchell's supplement to *Bibliotheca Piscatoria* (1901), is listed as "... Illus. por. 12mo. $2, half-morocco, $4," and in Marston's "List ..." in his third edition of 1915. Through information secured from the publisher, Oliver treated this as a reprint of the Major edition of 1844 (No. 55), with the seven full-page plates and 74 wood engravings from the Nimmo and Bain reprint of 1883 (No. 114).

This is probably the reprint listed in *The Annual American Catalogue Cumulated 1900-1903*, as published on December 8, 1900, at the prices quoted above.

[1900]
193. The Second Burt (35th Major) Reprint

𝕭urts 𝕷ibrary of the 𝖂orld's 𝕭est 𝕭ooks.

THE COMPLETE ANGLER ... of Izaak Walton and
Charles Cotton. ...
New York: A. L. Burt, Publisher. [1900].

Copy examined: Princeton.

Size: 7⅝"×5".

Pagination summary: [1]-354, plus 5 leaves of publisher's advertising.

The title-page and text of this reprint are the same as the 1894 Burt (No. 164).

The illustrations are the same, lacking the full-page frontispiece of Walton; there is no internal evidence that there ever was one.

The publisher's binding is in dark red cloth with no decoration except the usual titling and "The Home Library" in gilt on the spine.

This is believed to be the first *Angler* issued in Burt's "Home Library" series and, as such, was published on January 25, 1900, and reprinted in 1905, 1909, 1913, 1915, 1919, 1922, 1924, 1926, and 1934 according to information furnished Oliver by the publisher (see his No. 180).

Burt's *Home Library* (no titles mentioned), was advertised in *The Publisher's Weekly* on June 16, 1900, which is the only contemporary reference found.

This is a reissue of the first Burt of 1894 (No. 164).

1900

194. The Second McClurg Reprint

THE COMPLETE ANGLER . . . of Izaak Walton . . .
Chicago A. C. McClurg & Co. 1900

Copies examined: Horne, Princeton, Yale.

Size: 6⅟₁₆″ × 4″.

Pagination summary: [i]-xxxiv, [35]-287, [1].

The title-page verso is imprinted, "Copyright By A. C. McClurg and Co. A.D. 1892." There are no illustrations. The page at the end advertises McClurg's "Laurel-Crowned Tales."

As in the first printing, the publisher's device on the title-page has the acorn as a motif, but in a different design for this reprint; on its perimeter is imprinted, "A.C. McC. & Co."

The binding is in dark blue cloth. In gilt on the front cover is a fish motif, *art nouveau* decoration, which includes the title and author's name. Gilt stamped on the spine is the usual titling, a flower, and a McClurg acorn. The top edges are gilt.

This is a reissue of the first McClurg edition of 1893 (No. 161).

[1900]

195. The Oxford-Thumb Miniature Edition

THE COMPLEAT ANGLER . . . by Izaak Walton
London: Henry Frowde Oxford University Press Warehouse
Amen Corner, E.C. [1900].

Copies examined: Harvard (2), Horne, Trinity. Others: CtY, DLC, NN, NjP.

Size: 2⅟₁₆″ × 1¹¹⁄₁₆″.

Contents: Preliminaries, [i-vi]; Epistle Dedicatory, viii-xii; To the Reader, xiii-xix, [xx], 1-2; Commendatory Verses, 3-24; Text, 25-[572]; Laws of Angling, 573-584; Contents, 585-[588].

Page 191 is unnumbered. On the title-page verso is imprinted, "Oxford: Horace Hart Printer to the University." This *Angler* is printed on India paper, and is the smallest ever produced.

The illustrations consist of two halftone full-page plates which depict a frontispiece of Walton opposite a plate of the cartouche from the first edition of 1653; ten cuts of fish in the text, and two pages of music, of which the second page is printed upside down.

Three different bindings occur in the copies examined; the *first* (Horne) in limp black morocco, with gilt titling on the front cover and spine, leaf edges gilt over red; the *second* (Harvard) in dark brown limp leather, cover edges ruled, the first edition cartouche blind stamped on the front cover, titling in blind on the spine, a white silk marker and all edges gilt; the *third* (Harvard) in parchment, the front cover hand decorated in pen and ink with a heraldic type shield in black enclosing the titling in red.

Although *The British Museum Catalogue* dates this edition [1899], it is dated 1900 in the Third Marston (Oxford) edition (1915) "List of Editions . . ." This is followed by Oliver and herein, since it would seem that Oxford, having printed both editions, would have made sure of the correct date.

This edition, as quoted on the verso of a2, is "From 'The Fifth Edition, much corrected and enlarged'." It has neither notes nor introduction.

1900

196. The Ninth Jesse Reprint

THE COMPLETE ANGLER . . . of Izaak Walton and
Charles Cotton. . . .
London George Bell and Sons 1900

Copies examined: Horne, Yale.

Size: 7$\frac{1}{16}$" × 4$\frac{5}{8}$".

Pagination summary: [i-vii], viii-xix, [3], [1]-496, [32]. Pages 23* and 24* are inserted after page 24.

On the title-page verso is imprinted "[Reprinted from Stereotype plates.]" On the half-title verso is imprinted, "George Bell & Sons London: York St., Covent Garden. New York: 66 Fifth Avenue, and Bombay: 53 Esplanade Road. Cambridge: Deighton Bell & Co."

The illustrations, errors in the list of engravings on wood, and the different spellings of Walton's given name are the same as in the seventh Jesse edition (No. 144).

The 32 pages of advertisements at the end are for both Bohn, and Bell publications. This reprint is listed on page 25 as part of Bohn's Libraries, priced at 5s.

The publisher's binding is in dark green cloth, with the edges of both covers bordered with a single rule in blind. The front cover is blind stamped with a circular device reading "Bohn's. G.B.&S. Libraries." On the spine in gilt is the usual titling and, at the foot, just above "Bohn's Libraries," is a gilt device composed of a bell and an anchor entwined with a dolphin. This mark also appears on the title-page of the Bell-Daldy and Low reprints of 1863 and 1864 as well as the Bell-Daldy reprint of 1864 where it also appeared in gilt on the front cover. The end papers are yellow. The leaves are untrimmed.

This reprint, apparently not listed in previous bibliographies, is a reissue of the seventh Jesse reprint of 1889 (No. 144).

[1901]

197. The Seventh Lowell Reprint

THE COMPLETE ANGLER . . . of Izaak Walton and
Charles Cotton . . .
Boston Little, Brown, & Company Publishers [1901].

Copy examined: Horne.

Size: 7½″ × 4¹⁵⁄₁₆″.

Pagination summary: [ii], [1]-414, [2].

On the verso of the title-page, which is printed in red and black within a decorative border, is imprinted, "*Copyright, 1889,* By Little, Brown, and Company. *All rights reserved,*" and, "University Press: John Wilson and Son, Cambridge, U.S.A."

The illustrations consist of the frontispiece of Walton by Bone after Huysman, and 64 of the 74 woodcuts from the first Lowell edition (No. 142).

This one-volume reprint was issued in dark green cloth with two stylized floral panels embossed in blind on the front cover and one on the spine. "Walton's Angler" is stamped in large gilt capitals between the panels on the cover. The usual titling, and a small square decoration (in the pattern of a front panel) are in gilt on the spine. The top edges are gilt.

This reprint apparently has not been described heretofore. Although the title-page reads, "With an Introduction by James Russell Lowell," the entire Introduction, the Dedication, and Walton's "To the Reader," at the beginning, as well as the Linnaean arrangement of the Fish, the Selected Notes, the Commendatory Verses, and the general Index at the end, were all omitted, leaving only the text. This printing has 127 fewer pages than any previous Lowell editions or reprints.

Oliver listed a two-volume Lowell edition (his No. 181) with the same woodcuts and pagination of the other Lowell editions, which he considered to be one of the "Readable Books." However, the unique points of this edition as compared to the other Lowells would hardly pass unnoticed, and Oliver's description could perhaps have been intended for the eighth Lowell (No. 225), one of the *Handy Volume Classics,* which he listed, but did not see (his No. 212).

The last leaf lists 201 titles in "The Readable Books" series, with *Walton's Angler* number 200. These are described as ". . . illustrated with frontispiece in photogravure and halftone, neatly and strongly bound in cloth, extra, gilt top, with gold lettering on back and sides, issued at the popular price of $1.00 per volume."

This edition is listed on page 472 of *The Annual American Catalogue Cumulated, 1900-1901*, as part of the "Readable Book Series, ea., 12°, cl. $1" and, since it did not appear in *The Annual American Catalogue*, 1900, it is dated 1901 herein.

It is a reissue of the text of the first Lowell edition of 1889 (No. 142).

1901

198. The First Macmillan Edition

THE COMPLETE ANGLER & The Lives of Donne, Wotton, Hooker, Herbert & Sanderson by Izaak Walton
London Macmillan and Co. Limited New York:
The Macmillan Company 1901

Copies examined: Harvard, Horne (2), Princeton, Trinity. Others: CLSU, CSmH, CtY, MiU, NN, OCl.

Size: $8\frac{11}{16}"$-$8\frac{13}{16}"\times5\frac{1}{2}"$-$5\frac{5}{8}"$, leaves untrimmed; $8\frac{1}{2}"\times5\frac{1}{4}"$, leaves trimmed.

Pagination summary: *Angler*, [i-v], vi-xi, [xii], [1]-180; *Lives*, [181]-497, [498], [2].

The half-title and the title-page are both printed in red and black. On the title-page verso and at the foot of page 497 is imprinted, "Glasgow: Printed at the University Press by Robert Maclehose and Co."

The only illustration is the music for the Angler's song.

Both Horne copies are in publisher's bindings. The *first* is in smooth red cloth. A narrow floral band is blind stamped at the top and foot of the front cover, and continued in gilt on both ends of the gilt titled spine. The back cover is plain. All leaves are untrimmed. The *second* is also in red cloth, but of a slightly abrasive texture. Two banding rules are stamped in blind at the top and foot of the covers and in the same position on the spine in gilt. A Macmillan device is blind stamped on the front cover, and the spine is titled in gilt. A large Macmillan Ex Libris is printed in tan on the front end paper. The top edges are gilt, the others are untrimmed.

The last leaf lists 13 authors, including Walton, represented in Macmillan's *Library of English Classics*, and edited by Alfred W. Pollard. The volumes are described as, "Demy 8 vo. Cloth Elegant. Price 3s. 6d. net per Volume." *The English Catalogue of Books* lists the publication date as February, 1901, and *The American Catalogue* as March 9th, 1901.

There is a short "Bibliographical Note" by Alfred W. Pollard, one time of the Department of Printed Books in the British Museum, and bibliographic author.
This edition is from Part I of the fifth edition of 1676 (No. 6).

1901

199. The First Buchan Edition

THE COMPLEAT ANGLER . . . By Izaak Walton and
Charles Cotton . . .
London Methuen & Co. 36 Essex Street W.C. MDCCCCI

Copies examined: Harvard, Yale (2).

Size: $5\frac{7}{8}'' \times 3\frac{3}{4}''$.

Pagination summary: [i-iv], v^r, (v^v repeat blank), vi, [vii], [viii omitted], ix-xl, [1-2], 3-223, [224-226], 227-310, [4].

At the foot of page 310 is imprinted, "Printed by Morrison and Gibb Limited, Edinburgh." The half-title is imprinted *Little Library*. The title-page is in red and black, within and divided into three sections by two black rules. The four pages at the end provide *A Prospectus of The Little Library* (last three words in red).

The frontispiece, Audinet's engraving of the Huysman portrait of Walton, is the only illustration (misspelled Housman on both the engraving and the title-page).

On page xxii of the introduction the editor, John Buchan, incorrectly cites 1678 as the date of the fifth edition of 1676.

The publisher's bindings examined are in red cloth with four heart-shaped impressions stamped in gilt on the front cover, four blind stamped on the back cover and one in gilt on the spine together with the title, authors' names, and publisher.

The English Catalogue of Books lists this edition as published in November, 1901, priced at 1s. 6d. net; leather 2s. 6d. net.

This edition is from Parts I and II of the fifth edition of 1676 (No. 6).

1901

200. The First Gay and Bird Edition

THE COMPLETE ANGLER by Izaak Walton
Gay and Bird 22 Bedford Street, Strand London 1901

Copies examined: Harvard, Horne (2), Virginia, Yale.

Size: 6⅟₁₆″ × 4¼″.

Pagination summary: [i-vi], vii-xi, [xii-xiv], xv-xvi, [1]-229.

The title-page verso is imprinted, "Edinburgh: T. and A. Constable, Printers to Her Majesty" and on the verso of page 229, "Printed by T. and A. Constable, Printers to Her Majesty at the Edinburgh University Press."

The woodcut illustrations and decorations by Herbert Cole consist of a frontispiece, three headpieces and three tailpieces repeated from five to eight times, vignettes for the half-title and title-page (that on the latter being a Gay and Bird device), and a woodcut border for the title-page.

On page 69, in the Milkmaids Song, verse one, line four, is the misprint, "sleepy" mountains instead of "steepy" mountains, which appears uncorrected in Gay and Bird reprints examined through that for 1963.

This edition, designated *The Sportsman's Classics* on the half-title, has a five-page introduction by "J.P.B." (*i.e.,* John Potter Briscoe), in which it is called a reprint of the fifth Hawkins edition (1791 or 1792). However, only Walton's Part I is present and this lacks the author's dedication, "To all Readers," and all but one of the laudatory verses (Jo. Florid's). The introduction incorrectly refers to Bagster's reprint of 1810 as a facsimile (see notes to No. 20).

This edition was issued in dark olive-green cloth with a green ribbon bookmark. It is blind stamped on each cover with a large sporting motif, with the center panel (2⅜ × 1⅝ inches) blind stamped "Walton's Complete Angler." Above the motif is blind stamped, "The Sportsman's Classics." The spine is gilt titled. The top edges are gilt, the others are uncut.

The English Catalogue lists this edition as having been published in March, 1901, priced at 1s 6d net.

1901

201. The Second Gay and Bird Reprint

THE COMPLETE ANGLER by Izaak Walton
Gay and Bird 22 Bedford Street, Strand London 1901

Copies examined: Horne, Yale.

Size: 6″ × 4⅛″.

Pagination summary: [i-vi], vii-xi, [xii-xiv], xv-xvi, [1]-229.

The title-page verso is imprinted, "Edinburgh: T. and A. Constable, Printers to Her Majesty at the Edinburgh University Press."
This is a reissue of the first Gay and Bird edition (No. 200), with the same

illustrations, half-title, misprint of "sleepy" for "steepy" on page 69, and introduction. The title-page lacks a publisher's device as in No. 200.

This reprint was issued in black polished limp morocco. The ribbon bookmark is light gray. The front cover is gilt decorated and titled with a smaller (center panel $1^{11}\!\!/_{16}''\times 1\!\!/_{16}''$) impression of the same sporting motif used in blind on the first Gay and Bird. The back cover is not decorated. Spine titling is in gilt. The top edges are gilt, the others untrimmed, which accounts for the slightly larger size of the first Gay and Bird reprint.

It is listed in *The English Catalogue* as having been published in May, 1901, priced as "leather 2s. net." Since the half-title identification of *Sportsman's Classics* was not mentioned in *The English Catalogue,* Oliver, who did not see a copy, erroneously concluded that it lacked the half-title, present in the copies examined.

1901

202. The Brentano (3rd Gay and Bird) Reprint

THE COMPLETE ANGLER by Izaak Walton
Brentano's New York: Chicago: Washington 1901

Copies examined: Horne, Princeton. Others: CtHT, CtY, MH, NN, PU.

Size: $6^{3}\!\!/_{16}''\times 4\frac{1}{4}''$.

Pagination summary: [i]-xvi, [1]-229.

The printer's imprint on the title-page verso has the misprint, "Edindurgh *[sic]*; T. and A. Constable Printers to her Majesty." On the verso of page 229 is the imprint, "Printed by T. and A. Constable, Printers to Her Majesty at the Edinburgh University Press."

This is a reissue of the first Gay and Bird edition (No. 200) with the frontispiece, title-page border and decorations by Herbert Cole. The misprint of "sleepy" for "steepy" mountains remains on page 69 and, in addition, the illustration on page 41 is printed upside down.

This reprint was issued in grayish-green cloth. The front cover has the same sporting decoration and titling in black which is blind stamped on both covers of the first Gay and Bird (No. 200). The back cover is without decoration and there is no bookmark. The spine is gilt-titled. The top edges are trimmed, the others untrimmed.

This is a reissue with a new title-page, of the first Gay and Bird edition of 1901 (No. 200).

1902

203. The Second Dobson Reprint

THE COMPLEAT ANGLER by Izaak Walton
MDCCCCII. Published by J. M. Dent and Co:
Aldine House London W. C.

Copies examined: N. Y. Public, Princeton, Yale. Others: MA, MH.

Size: 6″×3¹³⁄₁₆″.

Pagination summary: 1-248.

At the foot of the last page is imprinted, "Turnbull and Spears, Printers, Edinburgh." This reissue of the first Dobson edition (No. 187), with the title-page printed in red and black within the same *art nouveau* decorative border, and "The Temple Classics" half-title with the red sundial vignette, has imprinted on the verso of the latter, "First Edition, June 1899. Second Edition, February 1902."

The illustrations are the frontispiece portrait of Walton and two pages of music of the first Dobson. The front pastedown memorial is also present.

The publisher's bindings were seen in both blue cloth and purple leather with the publisher's owl device on the front cover, in blind on the former, in gilt on the latter. The spine of each is gilt titled and decorated, each has a red ribbon bookmark, and the top edges are gilt.

This is a reissue, with an updated title-page, of the first Dobson edition of 1899 (No. 187).

1902

204. The Winchester, Freemantle (1st Dewar) Edition

THE COMPLEAT ANGLER . . . by Mr Izaak Walton and . . .
by Charles Cotton, Esq. . . .
London: Published by Freemantle & Company in Piccadilly.
Anno Domini 1902.

Copies examined: Harvard, Horne, Princeton. Others: CtHT, CtY, DLC, MNS, NN, ViU.

Size: (Limited "edition") 10″×7¼″; (Regular "edition") 8¹³⁄₁₆″×6¹³⁄₁₆″.

Pagination summary: Vol. I, [i]-lxviii, [1]-169; Vol. II, [i]-ix, [x], [1-2], 3-232.

The half-title is printed in red, and the title-page in red and black. On the verso of page 169, Vol. I, and on page 232, Vol. II, is imprinted, "The Riverside Press Limited, Edinburgh."

The illustrations include ten full-page and 12 small etchings by William Strang, 19 full-page and 19 small etchings by D. Y. Cameron, a headpiece by R. L. Knowles, ten unsigned figures of fish, a facsimile of the 1653 title-page, and two pages of music.

In addition to the Introduction and "Walton in Hampshire" by the editor, George A[lbemarle] B[ertie] Dewar, there is a six-page essay by Sir Edward Grey headed "The Compleat Angler."

The publisher's binding is in light green cloth stamped in gilt. On the front cover of Volume I is the Device of Walton, impaling the Arms of his two wives, viz., Fludd and Ken; and on the front cover of Volume II, the Arms of Cotton, impaling the Arms of his two wives, viz., Hutchinson and Russell. These decorations were apparently taken from the headpiece to the Preface of the first Nicolas edition, 1836 (No. 43). On the spine in gilt is the usual titling with "Freemantle & Co" at the foot. The top edges are gilt, others untrimmed.

This edition was published simultaneously in two states: large paper in limited "edition" and one of regular size and "edition." The limited "edition" was of 150 copies and volume I was autographed by the artists, Cameron and Strang. The full-page etchings are in two states, and the smaller ones are on India paper laid down. It was issued bound in full vellum stained very dark reddish-brown.

Copy No. 63 of the large paper (i.e., limited) "edition" at Harvard (bound in four volumes) has a third set of the signed etchings, and the complete series of the original drawings by Cameron and by Strang for the smaller illustrations. This unique copy also has additional specially printed title-pages.

This edition is from Parts I and II of the fifth edition of 1676 (No. 6).

1902

205. The Winchester, Freemantle, 4th Lippincott (2nd Dewar) Reprint

THE COMPLEAT ANGLER . . . by Mr Izaak Walton and . . . by Charles Cotton, Esq.
London: Published by Freemantle & Company; and in America by J. B. Lippincott Company. Anno Domini 1902.

Copy examined: Horne.

Size: $8\frac{13}{16}'' \times 6\frac{13}{16}''$.

This is a two-volume reissue of the Winchester, Freemantle (1st Dewar) edition, with the same pagination, illustrations, and binding, but with "Lippincott," in place of "Freemantle & Co," at the foot of the spine.

1903

206. The Fifth Nicolas Reprint

THE COMPLETE ANGLER . . . by IZAAK WALTON and . . .
by CHARLES COTTON . . .
London Chatto & Windus 1903

Copies examined: Harvard, Horne (2), Princeton, Yale. Others: CtHT, DLC, MiU, PP.

Size: 6⁹⁄₁₆″ × 4⁵⁄₁₆″.

Pagination summary: [i-v], vi-cxxxi, 132-135, [cxxxvi]-cci, 202-[206]; [2]; [1]-320.

On the title-page verso is imprinted, "Printed by Ballantyne, Hanson & Co. At the Ballantyne Press" and, at the foot of page 320, "Printed by Ballantyne, Hanson & Co. Edinburgh & London." The title-page, printed in red and black, and imprinted with the publisher's device, designates this as "Fine-Paper Edition."

The only illustrations are of Byfield's wood engraving of the Walton-Cotton marital device drawn by Willement, as a headpiece to the Preface, and eight chapter headpieces engraved by Worthington after Stothard, originally in the Nicolas edition of 1836 (No. 43). Music is printed on pages 178 and 179.

It was seen in two publisher's bindings. The *first* is in purple cloth, with the front cover blind stamped with an overall design of repeated small curls interspersed with stylized blossoms, except for a smooth strip of blind stamped titling at the top. The spine is gilt titled and gilt stamped with the small curls of the cover design. The top edges are gilt. The *second*, also in purple cloth, is parallel ruled in blind at the top and foot of the front cover, with titling blind stamped beneath the top rules. The spine is parallel ruled top and foot and titled in gilt. The top edges are gilt. In cloth it was priced at two shillings. It was also available in leather, with all edges gilt, and a red bookmark, for three shillings.

This reprint of the 1887 Nicolas edition (No. 130) is one of the volumes in *The St. Martin's Library* series.

1903

207. The Tenth Jesse Reprint

THE COMPLETE ANGLER, . . . of Izaak Walton and
Charles Cotton. . . .
London George Bell and Sons 1903

Copies examined: Harvard, Horne.

Size: $7\frac{1}{16}'' \times 4\frac{9}{16}''$.

Pagination summary: [i-vii], viii-xix, [3], [1]-496, [32]. Pages identified as 23* and 24* are inserted after page 24.

The title-page verso is imprinted "[Reprinted from Stereotype plates.]" On the half-title verso is imprinted, "Cambridge: Deighton, Bell & Co. New York: The Macmillan Co. Bombay: A. H. Wheeler & Co."

The illustrations are the 206 wood engravings and 26 steel plates of the prior Jesse issues (see No. 144), with no corrections in the list of engravings on wood, or the spelling of Walton's given name as "Izaak" on the title-page, and "Isaac" in the title of the biography, page [1].

The 32 pages at the end are advertisements for both Bohn, and Bell publications, where this reprint is listed on page 24 as part of Bohn's Libraries, priced at 5s.

The publisher's binding is dark green cloth (also used for No. 196) with the edges of both covers bordered with a single rule in blind, and on the front cover blind stamped in a circular device is "Bohn's. G.B.&S. Libraries." On the spine in gilt is the usual titling and, just above "Bohn's Libraries" in gilt at the foot, a circular gilt device showing a bell in the center circled by a wheel on which appears, "Illustrated Library." The end papers are white. The leaves are untrimmed.

This is a reissue from the same plates of the ninth Jesse reprint of 1900 (No. 196).

1903

208. The Scott-Thaw Edition

THE COMPLETE ANGLER by Izaak Walton and Charles Cotton New York Scott-Thaw Co. MDCCCCIII

Copies examined: Harvard, Horne, Princeton. Others: CtY, NN, PU.

Size: $6\frac{1}{4}'' \times 4''$.

Pagination summary: [i-vii], viii-xvi, [1]-304. Page 281 is misnumbered 28.

The title-page, printed in red and black, is decorated with a Chiswick Press device, a heraldic lion rampant, combined with a dolphin entwining an anchor. On the title-page verso and at the foot of page 304, appears "Chiswick Press: Charles Whittingham and Co. Tooks Court, Chancery Lane, London."

The illustrations consist of a typeset 1653 title-page, lacking the cartouche, the Walton-Cotton cipher on the last page, and 13 unsigned engravings of fish.

The publisher's binding is in light green paper over boards. The spine is in darker green cloth, with a paper label at the top. The Chiswick Press device from the title-page is repeated in gilt on the front cover. The top edges are gilt, the others untrimmed.

This edition is listed in *The Publisher's Weekly* (February 28, 1903) as a part of the *Wayside Library,* 16mo. in cloth, priced at $1.25. It is from Parts I and II of the fifth edition of 1676 (No. 6), without notes or introduction.

1903

209. The First Methuen (36th Major) Edition

THE COMPLETE ANGLER of Izaak Walton and
Charles Cotton . . .
Methuen & Co. London 1903.

Copies examined: Horne, Princeton, Trinity (Dublin). Others: CtY, MH.

Size: 6½″ × 4⅛″.

Pagination summary: [i]-lviii, [1]-416.

At the foot of the last page is imprinted, "The Aberdeen University Press Limited." There are three titling pages: the half-title, at the top of which is printed, THE ILLUSTRATED POCKET LIBRARY OF PLAIN AND COLOURED BOOKS; the title-page, printed in red and black, which identifies it as, "A New Edition;" and a reprinted title-page of the second Major edition of 1824 (No. 24), on which this edition is founded.

The illustrations consists of reproductions of the 14 copperplates and reprints of the 77 woodcuts from the second Major edition (No. 24).

The earliest cataloguing of the titles in these pocket library books which has been checked, is at the end of *The Old English 'Squire* and *Real Life in London,* both issued as part of the Pocket Library series in 1905. Thirty-seven titles were listed, including this edition, which was priced 3s.6d.

The publisher's binding is in red cloth with a printed paper label on the spine. An extra label was tipped in at the end of some volumes in the series. The label for the London series, in addition to the usual titling, is imprinted at the top, "The Illustrated Pocket Library of Plain and Coloured Books" and, below the author's name, "Methuen and Co. London." This wording was omitted on the smaller label used for the New York Appleton edition (No. 215).

This edition is reprinted from the second Major edition of 1824 (No. 24).

[195]

[1903]

210. The Hurst (37th Major) Edition

THE COMPLETE ANGLER by Walton and Cotton
New York Hurst and Company Publishers [1903].

Copy examined: Harvard.

Size: 7¼″ × 4¾″.

Pagination summary: [1]-354. On page 85, the 8 of the folio number is broken, and on page 274, that of the 7 is broken.

The illustrations consist of Archer's headpiece of the Walton biographees, Sir Humphrey Davy's seal ring, Donne's seal ring, 19 woodcuts of fish, and one page of music. The Walton-Cotton cipher, enclosed in a wreath of flowers, is on the title-page to Part II.

The publisher's binding is in dark red cloth with blind stamped decoration in the form of a pommée cross having a shamrock in the center circle and a thistle in each of the four terminal circles on the front cover. The spine is blind stamped also with a shamrock within a smaller circle and "Hurst & Co," at the foot. At the top of the spine is "Complete Angler" between floral sprays and thistle, all stamped in gilt. The top edges are gilt.

Contemporary publishing records have not revealed a date for this edition. The Fearing Condensed Accession Book at Harvard, April 18, 1910 to June 7, 1912, lists this as number 1364 acquired May 10, 1911, from the Nassau Press, cost 60 cents. The publisher, replying to an inquiry from Harvard, stated in a letter dated July 1, 1919, that "Records in this office do not show the dates when we published this book and it must have been issued many years ago. . . ." Oliver (see his No. 190) states that he used Hurst's *Order List* ". . . which should show their complete list, does not mention *The Complete Angler* until 1903. . . .," as his basis for a publication date of 1903. This has been followed herein.

This edition is a reprint of the Major edition of 1844 (No. 55).

1903

211. The Second Le Gallienne Edition

THE COMPLEAT ANGLER by Izaak Walton & Charles Cotton . . .
John Lane: The Bodley Head London & New York. 1903.

Copies examined: None seen.

Size reported: 7⅞″ × 5″. Cr. 8vo.

Pagination: 546 pp.

This listing is from *The English Catalogue of Books,* which identifies it as part of the Crown Library (as is the third Le Gallienne reprint, 1904), and as published by Lane in September 1903, priced at 5s. net.

Oliver states (his No. 192) that it is a reprint of the first Le Gallienne edition of 1897 (No. 177), with the illustrations by E. H. New, and that it was listed in *The Annual American Catalogue* as "an illustrated 12 mo. published December 19th, 1903, for sale at $1.50." However, it is not a reprint of the first Le Gallienne, since the number of pages differs and it is not from the same plates or typesetting, and for this reason is treated herein as a new edition published for the Crown Library series.

In the sixth Le Gallienne (No. 278), on the title-page verso, this edition is listed as reprinted in 1903. It is from Parts I and II of the fifth edition of 1676 (No. 6).

1904

212. The Third Le Gallienne Reprint

THE COMPLEAT ANGLER by Izaak Walton & Charles Cotton . . . John Lane: The Bodley Head London & New York. MDCCCCIV.

Copies examined: Harvard, Horne, Princeton, Yale. Others: CtHT, DLC, N, NN, NcU, ICJ, ICRL, IU, OClW, OLak, OU, PBa.

Size: 7⅜″ × 5″.

Pagination summary: [i]-lxxxix, [5], [1]-454, [14], [12].

The imprint "William Clowes and Sons, Limited, London and Beccles" is on the title-page verso (within a double rule) with its Cotton fishing house vignette.

The illustrations consist of a photogravure frontispiece with small oval portraits of Walton and Cotton and 242 illustrations by E. H. New.

The decorative initials are included in the "List of Illustrations," and on page xxi the "Amwell Magna Fishery; . . .," is listed as on page 102 instead of on page 201. The correct title for the cut on page 102 is "Near Amwell." The "Angler's Calendar" miscites January 11th as George Washington's birthday.

On the fifth of the 12 pages of advertising at the end, this edition is identified as Volume II of the Crown Library, priced at 5s. net, postage 4d. or $1.50 net. On the half-title verso a special quarto edition de luxe is listed, priced at 15s. net or $6.00.

The publisher's binding is in light green cloth. The top edges are gilt, others untrimmed. A crown is stamped in gilt at the top of the spine above the gilt title.

This is a reprint, in the Crown Library series, of the second Le Gallienne edition of 1903 (No. 211).

213. The Pocket Library Routledge-Dutton Reprint

THE COMPLETE ANGLER by Izaak Walton and Charles Cotton
London: George Routledge & Sons, Ltd. New York:
E. P. Dutton & Co. [1904].

Copy examined: Harvard.

Size: 5¼″×3½″.

Pagination summary: [i]-xvi, [1]-304.

At the foot of the last page is imprinted, "Chiswick Press: Charles Whittingham and Co. Tooks Court, Chancery Lane, London." On the title-page is a
device of Routledge, the London publisher.

The illustrations consist of a typesetting of the 1653 edition title-page,
lacking the cartouche, 13 illustrations of fish, and, on the last page, the
Walton-Cotton cipher.

The publisher's binding is in light blue cloth with the usual titling and
a decoration in gilt on the spine, and on the front cover. Also in gilt in
the lower right hand corner of the front cover is "The Complete Angler –
Walton."

Pasted in the front of the Harvard copy is a clipping, apparently from a
bookseller's catalogue, identifying this as the "Pocket Library," priced at 1s.
On the following page, a handwritten note in ink reads "The Pocket Library.
Published May 1904."

This reprint, except for the plates of Walton and Cotton, is from the same
plates as the first Bell-Daldy and Low edition of 1863 (No. 81), with the same
pagination and woodcuts. Marston (1915) states that Routledge informed
him "that this Imperial 32 mo Pocket Library Edition was printed from
stereos purchased from George Bell & Sons." *The English Catalogue of Books*
lists May 1904 as the publication date, with the price 1s, leather 2s net.

This reprint of the first Bell-Daldy and Low edition (No. 81) is from Parts I
and II of the 1676 edition (No. 6).

1904

214. The Second Methuen (38th Major) Reprint

THE COMPLETE ANGLER of Izaak Walton and
Charles Cotton . . .
Methuen & Co. London 1904.

Copies examined: None seen.

Size reported: $6\frac{7}{8}'' \times 4\frac{1}{8}''$.

Pagination: 474 pp.

This listing, as was Oliver's (his No. 196), is from *The English Catalogue of Books,* which gives the publication date as January, 1904, the selling price as 3s. 6d., and designates it as "Illustrated Pocket Library."

The existence of this reprint, not yet seen or described by bibliographers, is undetermined. If it was published it will undoubtedly prove to be a reprint of the first Methuen edition of 1903 (No. 209).

1904

215. The Appleton (39th Major) Reprint

THE COMPLETE ANGLER of Izaak Walton and
Charles Cotton . . .
New York D. Appleton & Company. 1904

Copies examined: Horne, Princeton, Yale. Others: MA, OCIRC.

Size: $6\frac{11}{16}'' \times 4\frac{5}{16}''$.

Pagination summary: [i]-lviii, [1]-416.

At the foot of page 416 is imprinted, "The Aberdeen University Press Limited." This reprint of the 1903 Methuen edition (No. 209) lacks the half-title but repeats the title-page printed in red and black, with new imprint. This is followed by a reprinted title-page of the second Major edition of 1824 (No. 24), on which this edition is founded.

The illustrations and binding, except for the addition of gilt tops, are as described in the notes for the first Methuen edition of 1903, where the differences in the titling labels may be checked.

The United States Catalog Supplement, 1902-1905, records this as a "New Ed. (Popular editions of rare and famous books) 14 pls. 77 wdcts. $1.50 '04."

This is a reprint of the first Methuen edition of 1903 (No. 209).

1904

216. The Fourteenth Cassell Reprint

THE COMPLETE ANGLER . . . by Isaac Walton . . .
Cassell and Company, Limited London, Paris, New York and
Melbourne MCMIV

Copies examined: Harvard, Princeton, Virginia.

Size: $6\frac{1}{16}'' \times 4\frac{1}{16}''$.

Pagination summary: [1-3], 4-192. The o is broken on page 70.

At the foot of page 192 is imprinted, "Printed by Cassell & Company, Limited,
La Belle Sauvage, London E.C.," and at the foot of the half-title verso,
"Cassell & Company, Limited, London; Paris, New York & Melbourne."
Above this, in the list of "Cassell's National Library, New Series." This re-
issue is No. 45, the most recent publication issued.
    The only illustration is a photogravure frontispiece of Walton.
    The publisher's binding is in red cloth with a decorative pattern in yellow
at the throat of the front and back covers. Additional binding imprinting
in yellow includes "The Complete Angler" (in two lines), and "Cassell's
National Library" on the front cover, and "45" at the foot of the spine.
    The English Catalogue of Books lists this reprint as one of the "National Library"
published by Cassell in September, 1904, to sell for 6d.
    With a new title-page, this is a reprint from the same plates of the first
Cassell edition (No. 125) with the Morley introduction, but without Walton's
dedication, from Part I of the fifth edition of 1676 (No. 6).

1905

217. The Fifteenth Cassell Reprint

THE COMPLETE ANGLER . . . by Isaac Walton . . .
Cassell and Company Limited, London, Paris, New York and
Melbourne. MCMV.

Copies examined: None.

Size reported: 16mo.

Pagination reported: 1-192.

Oliver listed this reprint as above (his No. 201), but it may well be that his
reference to a Harvard copy, the only one he recorded, is in error, as
presently available records fail to show that Harvard ever possessed such
a copy.

It is not reported in contemporary records examined, or in the *National Union Catalog*, but it is listed in Bushell's *Private Angling Library* (1953), as above with the added comment that it was in "Limp leather binding."

It is treated as a reissue of the 14th Cassell (No. 216).

[1905]
218. The Third Burt (40th Major) Reprint

THE COMPLETE ANGLER ... By Izaak Walton and Charles Cotton ...
A. L. Burt Company, Publishers, New York [1905].

Copies examined: Horne, N.Y. Public.

Size: 7¾₁₆″ × 4⅞″.

Pagination summary: [1-4], including frontispiece, [5]-354. There is no half-title.

The publisher's circular device on the title-page reads, "Burt's Library of the World's Best Books" and, on the Part II title-page appears the Walton-Cotton cipher, within a circular wreath of flowers. The Gothic black-letter line on the title-pages of the first two Burt *Anglers* has been dropped.

The illustrations consist of a reproduction of H. Robinson's engraving of Inskipp's idealized frontispiece portrait of Walton (published by William Pickering in 1832), a reproduction of Archer's woodcut of the five Walton biographies as a heapiece to Major's Introductory Essay (from the 6th Major edition of 1844, No. 55), one page of music, and 19 figures of fish.

The copies examined were issued in red cloth with a single rule in blind on the edge of both covers. The usual titling and "The Home Library" are stamped in gilt on the spine. The top edges are gilt.

According to Oliver (his No. 180), who received his information from the publisher, this reprint in Burt's *Home Library* series was reissued in 1905 (see No. 193 herein).

[1905]
219. The Routledge (41st Major) Reprint

THE COMPLETE ANGLER by Izaak Walton and Charles Cotton. London: Routledge and Sons. [1905].

Copies examined: None seen.

Size reported: 8½″×5½″.

Pagination summary: [i]-xv, [xvi], 1-445.

> Note: The following descriptive information on this reprint is from Oliver (his No. 204).

The title-page verso reads, "Printed by Ballantyne, Hanson & Co. At the Ballantyne Press, Edinburgh," and at the foot of page 445, "Printed by Ballantyne, Hanson & Co, Edinburgh & London."

The illustrations are eight plates by Damman after Huysman, Lely, and Tourrier, and 74 wood engravings as in the Nimmo and Bain reprint of 1883.

Oliver's reference to a Harvard copy may well be in error, as presently available records there fail to show that Harvard ever possessed such a copy. He states further that "This edition is printed from stereos of one of the Nimmo-Major editions," and that the Nimmo copyrights were acquired by Routledge in 1902, "which accounts for this edition." Marston (1915) lists a 1905 Routledge edition reporting that it was published by Routledge and in a note, "printed from stereos of one of the editions published by Mr. Nimmo, edited by Major." *The English Catalogue of Books* gives May, 1905, as the date of such an edition, published by Routledge, priced at six shillings. The *Private Angling Library* (Bushell, 1953), in direct reference to Oliver's entry (his No. 204), reports the imprint as "London, Routledge, 1905. This copy, New York, E. P. Dutton and Co., 1905." While directly referring to Oliver's number 204, it conceivably could be a reference to number 220 herein with a New York imprint only or to number 221 herein, which has both a London and a New York imprint.

Based on Oliver's descriptive details, a comparison of the use of ampersands in the publisher's imprints (and their placement), and the enumeration of the illustrations, this is considered to be a reissue, from the same plates, of the fourth Nimmo reprint of 1889 (No. 140).

[1905]

220. The Dutton (42nd Major) Reprint

THE COMPLETE ANGLER by Izaak Walton and Charles Cotton. New York: E. P. Dutton & Co. [1905].

Copies examined: None seen.

Size reported: 8vo.

Pagination reported: 445 pp.

The illustrations are eight original etchings by Dammon after Huysman, Lely and Tourrier, and the 74 wood engravings of the Nimmo reprint of 1883.

The descriptive information above is from Oliver (his No. 205). He stated that "This is a reprint of the fourth Major edition [his No. 53] of 1844. It is listed in *The Annual American Catalogue* as having been published in June, and sold at $2.50. It is made from the plates of the earlier Nimmo editions, which had been acquired by Routledge in 1902, ..." No information is given as to printer. However Oliver's reference to a Harvard copy may well be in error (as in his No. 204), as presently available records there fail to show that Harvard ever possessed such a copy.

The United States Catalog Supplement lists this as "J. Major 8 orig. etchings, 74 wd. engravings Octavo 445p. $2.50 June 1905. Dutton." The listing in *The Annual American Catalogue* (Publisher's Weekly 1906) (cited in brief by Oliver), reads in full as follows, "Walton, I:, *and* Cotton, C: The complete angler; or, the contemplative man's recreation; ed. by J: Major; with 8 original etchings and 74 wood engravings. N.Y. Dutton, 1905. [Je.] 445 p. 8°, cl. $2.50."

Based on Oliver's descriptive details, and the catalogue references cited, this is considered to be an American reissue, from the same plates, of the fourth Nimmo reprint of 1889 (No. 140). However, since Dutton's trade practice (see No. 220) apparently was to use both Routledge (omitted here) and Dutton, there may possibly have been an error in transcription, and this may be the same as the Routledge-Dutton reprint (No. 220), which was not reported by Oliver.

[1905]

221. The Routledge-Dutton (42nd Major) Reprint

THE COMPLETE ANGLER . . . of Izaak Walton and Charles Cotton . . .
London George Routledge & Sons, Limited
New York: E. P. Dutton and Co. [1905]

Copies examined: Harvard, Horne, Princeton, Yale.

Size: 8⅛″×5½″.

Signatures: [-⁸], A-U⁸, X-Z⁸, 2A-2D⁸, 2E⁸ (-E8)=231. J appears to be marked F.

Pagination summary: [i]-xv, [xvi], 1-445.

On the verso of the title-page, which is printed in red and black, and has the vignette, "View from Lea Bridge," from the 1844 Major edition, is imprinted, "Printed by Ballantyne, Hanson & Co. At the Ballantyne Press" and at the foot of page 445, "Printed by Ballantyne, Hanson & Co. Edinburgh

& London." Under the vignette on the title-page is imprinted, "With Eight Original Etchings and Seventy-four Wood Engravings." These are from the Nimmo and Bain reprint of 1883 (No. 114), and the etchings, as noted, are probably better described as new interpretations.

This reprint was issued in both dark red and dark green cloth. Titling and *"with eighty-two illustrations"* are in gilt on the spine which is gilt stamped at the foot "Routledge." The front cover is decorated with three golden fish, with titling also in gilt. Top edges gilt, others uncut. The fourth Nimmo reprint (No. 140) binding is identical in the dark green cloth, except at the foot of the spine it is gilt stamped "John C. Nimmo London."

This reprint is a British-American issue of the two preceding *Anglers* (Nos. 219 and 220) with both the London and New York publishers' imprints on the title-page. The use of the two names, Routledge and Dutton, apparently was the Dutton trade practice at the time, followed also for the Pocket Library Reprint of 1904 (No. 213). In view of this trade practice, and the availability of this Routledge-Dutton reprint at Harvard (but not reported by Oliver), it seems possible that there may have been a transcription error in omitting the Routledge name in listing Oliver's so-called Dutton edition (No. 219 herein) and that this is the entry listed in the *U. S. Catalog* and *The American Catalog* as published by Dutton in June, 1905, priced at $2.50, even though the Routledge name is omitted.

This issue, not described heretofore as a Routledge-Dutton imprint, is a reissue of the fourth Nimmo reprint of 1889 (No. 140).

1905

222. The Third Dobson Reprint

THE COMPLEAT ANGLER by Izaak Walton MDCCCCV. Published by J. M. Dent and Co: Aldine House London W.C.

Copies examined: Princeton, Yale. Other: NN.

Size: 6″×3¹³⁄₁₆″.

Pagination summary: 1-248.

At the foot of the last page is imprinted, "Turnbull and Spears, Printers, Edinburgh." This is a reissue, with half-title verso and title-page updated, identical in all other respects (including the cloth binding) with the second Dobson reprint of 1902 (No. 203).

On the half-title verso is imprinted, "First Edition, June 1899, Second Edition, February 1902, Third Edition, April 1905."

1905

223. The Caradoc Edition

THE COMPLETE ANGLER...
The Caradoc Press Bedford Park Chiswick MDCCCCV

Copies examined: Harvard, Horne, Princeton. Others: CSt, CtHT, CtY, CU, DLC, NN, NNC, OrU.

Size: Paper, 8⅝"×5⅞"; Vellum, 8¾"×6".

Pagination summary: [10], [1]-155, [156].

The colophon at the end, printed in red, states that this is "Reprinted from: the first edition . . . MDCLIII . . . the ornaments initials and etchings designed and engraved by H G Webb and the whole printed and bound & published at the Caradoc Press Bedford Park Chiswick London Finished on the twenty-sixth day of August in the year of our Lord MDCCCCV." The edition was of 350 copies on paper, and 14 on vellum, which are slightly larger, and were examined at Harvard and at Princeton. The title-page is printed in red and black, and bears a red Caradoc device. The running heads, chapter titles, song titles, and margin notes are all in red.

The illustrations consist of a frontispiece portrait of Walton, the cartouche from the title-page of the first edition (1653, No. 1), a river scene, and six small engravings of fish. There are also two pages of music, the second of which is printed upside down (as in the 1653 edition).

The Horne copy, on paper, was issued in brown Persian calf. Embossed in blind in the center of the front cover is a small circle, enclosing three entwined fish. The usual titling, and the Caradoc device from the title-page, are gilt stamped on the spine. All edges are untrimmed, and a green silk marker is included. The copies on vellum were issued in full cream vellum with ties, and gilt titling on the spine.

The English Catalogue of Books lists this reprint as published in December, 1905, priced at twenty-one shillings. *The Monthly Cumulative Book Index* printed a listing in connection with this publication, which has given the impression that a Lippincott edition of the *Angler* was published in 1906. The *Index* record reads "Compleat Angler O[ctavo] 170p. Persian calf $6 net; half levant $12 net; full levant $20 net; '06 Lippincott." Even though the "Caradoc" identity was omitted, the number of pages (170) clearly identifies it with this edition, and could not apply to the 445-page nonexistent Nimmo reprint to which Oliver assumed it referred (see his No. 208).

Clarification is provided by *The American Catalog, 1905-1907* entry, which includes "Caradoc Press" in its description, as does *The Publishers Weekly*, for November 24, 1906 (page 122), under Holiday Gift-Books, as ". . . 'The Compleat Angler' by Izaak Walton, reprinted from the first edition published in London in 1653, and decorated with woodcut ornaments and etchings by H. C. Webb; . . ." and on February 23, 1907, as "Caradoc Press ed. Phil. Lippincott 1906, [1907] 170 p." This indicates clearly that Lippincott was acting as the American distributor for this Caradoc reprint and that *The Monthly Cumulative Book Index* did not refer to a Lippincott edition.

The Caradoc Press *Angler* is an unedited reprint from the first edition of 1653 (No. 1). The Press was operated by the artist and typographer, H. G. Webb and his wife.

1906

224. The Tenth Crowell (43rd Major) Reprint

THE COMPLETE ANGLER by Izaak Walton and Charles Cotton. New York: T. Y. Crowell & Co., 426-428 West Broadway. 1906.

Copies examined: None seen.

Size reported: 16mo.

Pagination reported: [i]-lx, [1]-418.

There is a two-color title-page.

The illustrations are those of the fourth Crowell reprint (No. 182). The descriptive information is from Oliver (his No. 210).

The *Publishers Trade List Annual* reports it as one of the *Caslon Classics*, priced at $1.00 boxed.

[1906]

225. The Eighth Lowell Reprint

THE COMPLETE ANGLER, . . . of Izaak Walton and Charles Cotton. . . .
Boston: Little, Brown, and Company. [1906].

Copy examined: Horne.

Size: $6\frac{15}{16}'' \times 4\frac{5}{16}''$.

Pagination summary: Vol. I, [i-v], vi-lxxvi, [1]-208; Vol. II, [i-v], vi, [209]-465, [466].

The title-page of each volume is printed in red and black and, on the verso of each appears, "*Copyright, 1889,* By Little, Brown, and Company," and, "The University Press, Cambridge, Mass., U.S.A."

The illustrations consist of four unsigned etchings by Louis K. Harlow, comprising a frontispiece and title-page vignette for each volume, plus 74 woodcuts from the first Lowell edition (No. 142).

The two volumes were issued in dark red cloth without decoration except for the gilt titling on the spine.

This reprint is listed in *The American Catalog, 1905-1907,* as published September 15, 1906, in two volumes, illustrated, 16mo. It was issued in the *Handy Volume Classics* series priced at $1.00 per volume, $2.00 per set.

In smaller size, this is a reissue, from the same plates, of the third Lowell reprint of 1891 (No. 152).

1906

226. The Second Macmillan Reprint

THE COMPLETE ANGLER & The Lives of Donne, Wotton, Hooker, Herbert & Sanderson by Izaak Walton London Macmillan and Co. Limited New York: The Macmillan Company 1906.

Copy examined: Horne. Others: CtHT, CtY, OClND, NIC, NN, TxU.

Size: 8¾″ × 5⅝″.

Pagination summary: *Angler:* [i-v], vi-xi, [xii], [1]-180; *Lives:* 181-497, [498], [2].

On the title-page verso is imprinted, "First Printed in Library of English Classics 1901. Reprinted 1906," plus "Glasgow: Printed at the University Press by Robert Maclehose and Co. Ltd," the latter imprint being repeated at the foot of page 497. The half-title and title-page are printed in red and black. The only illustration is the music for the Angler's song.

This reissue of the first Macmillan edition (No. 198) was published in smooth very dark blue cloth. A parallel rule in blind at the top and foot of the covers is continued in gilt on the spine, where in gilt are the title and publisher's name. All edges are uncut.

The end leaf lists 17 authors, including Walton, in Macmillan's *Library of English Classics,* as compared to 13 in 1901, when the volumes were offered in cloth only at 3s. 6d. net. While these were still available in 1906 at the same price, there was "Also a Roxburgh Binding. Specially suitable for Presentation. Green Morocco Backs, Cloth Sides, and Gilt Tops. Price 5s. net per volume."

This reprint of the first Macmillan edition of 1901 (No. 198) with Pollard's "Bibliographical Note," is from Part I of the fifth edition of 1676 (No. 6).

[207]

1906

227. The First Rouse Abridged Edition

Blackies' English School Texts Edited by W. H. D. Rouse, Litt.D.
Izaak Walton THE COMPLETE ANGLER
Blackie & Son Limited 50 Old Bailey London E.C. Glasgow
and Dublin 1906

Copies examined: Harvard, Yale.

Size: $6\frac{1}{2}'' \times 4\frac{1}{4}''$.

Pagination summary: [1-4], 5-120.

This edition, a volume of *Blackie's English School Texts* series, was edited by
W. H. D. Rouse, when he was Head-master of the Perse School, Cambridge,
England. He also wrote a one-page introduction, of which the final paragraph reads as follows, "*The Present Edition* contains about half the original
work. Parts of the more lengthy disquisitions have been omitted, together
with the more technical chapters vi. to xv. and xvii. to xx." There are no
illustrations.

The publisher's binding is in light blue limp cloth. On the front cover in
black is a large decorative design of a plant, together with all the title-page
text except the publisher's imprint. "Walton's Complete Angler" is printed
in black on the spine.

The title-page verso has a list of 39 titles in this series, priced at sixpence
each in cloth covers.

[1906]

228. The First Everyman (3rd Lang) Edition

THE COMPLEAT ANGLER by Izaak Walton
London: Published by J. M. Dent & Co. and in New York by
E. P. Dutton & Co. [1906].

Copies examined: Cambridge (England), Horne, Princeton, Trinity (Dublin),
Yale. Others: DLC, KyU, MU, MeB, OCl, OClND, OOxM, PP, PPGi, PPT,
PRosC, TU.

Size: $6\frac{3}{4}'' \times 4\frac{1}{4}''$.

Pagination summary: [i-vii], viii-xliv, [2], [1]-215, [216].

At the foot of page 215 is imprinted, "The Aberdeen University Press Limited."

With its title-page in the Kelmscott Press style, this is the first edition in the *Everyman's Library* series. Andrew Lang's introduction is followed by a list of Walton's works. There are no illustrations.

The half-title verso is imprinted (*inter alia*), "In two styles of binding, cloth, flat back, coloured top, and leather, round corners, gilt top." Both binding styles have been examined. The *first* (Yale copy) is in red leather, as described, with gilt decorations on the front cover and spine (also titled in gilt). The ribbon bookmarker is light blue. The *second* (Horne copy) is in terra-cotta cloth, the front cover having a single line blind ruled on the edges and a Dent device also in blind, top edges stained grayish-green. The end papers of both bindings are decorated in an overall rococo design printed in light green.

The date of this edition is from the title-page verso of the third Everyman of April 1908 (No. 234), which states, "First Edition March 1906. Reprinted July 1906; April 1908." Apparently it is the Everyman *Angler* listed in *The English Catalogue of Books* as having been published by Dent in April, 1906, priced 1s. net, and, in leather 2s. net.

This is a reprint of the first Lang edition of 1896 (No. 170), with the two and one-third pages of notes at the end omitted. The Preface states (p. vii), "The text here reprinted is, in the main, that of Sir Harris Nicolas, which was reprinted from Walton's Fifth Edition, 1676, the last that was revised by the author."

[1906]

229. The Second Everyman (4th Lang) Reprint

THE COMPLEAT ANGLER by Izaak Walton
London: Published by J. M. Dent & Co. and in New York by
E. P. Dutton & Co. [1906].

Copy examined: Princeton.

Size: 6¾″×4¼″.

Pagination summary: [i-vii], viii-xliv, [2], [1]-3, [4-5], 6-215, [216].

This reissue is identical to the first Everyman, and was reported in the third (No. 234) as "Reprinted July 1906."

The publisher's binding is the same as the second binding described for the first Everyman edition (No. 228).

This is a reissue of the first Everyman edition of March, 1906 (No. 228).

1906

230. The Sixteenth Cassell Reprint

THE COMPLETE ANGLER . . . by Isaac Walton . . .
Cassell and Company, Limited. London, Paris, New York and
Melbourne MCMVI

Copy examined: Harvard. Others: ICU.

Size: $6\frac{1}{16}'' \times 4\frac{1}{16}''$.

Pagination summary: [1-3], 4-192.

On page 70, the o, broken in the 1904 (No. 216) reprint, has been replaced. At
the foot of page 192 is the imprint, "Printed by Cassell & Company, Limited,
La Belle Sauvage, London. E.C," and below this, "30, 106," and at the foot
of the half-title verso, "Cassell & Company, Limited, London; Paris, New
York & Melbourne." Above this, in the list of "Cassell's National Library,
New Series" this reprint is No. 45.
    The photogravure frontispiece of Walton is the same as in No. 216.
    The publisher's binding is in flexible red cloth, with the same decorations,
titling, and numbering in black that are imprinted on the 14th Cassell (No.
216) in yellow; and with "The Complete Angler" printed on the front cover
in three, instead of two, lines.
    This is a reissue, with an updated title-page, of the 14th Cassell reprint
of 1904 (No. 216).

1907

231. The Seventeenth Cassell Reprint

THE COMPLETE ANGLER . . . by Isaac Walton . . .
Cassell and Company, Limited London, Paris, New York,
and Melbourne MCMVII.

Copies examined: None seen.

Size reported: 16mo.

Pagination reported: [1]-192.

This listing is from Oliver (his No. 215), whose data came from the publisher.
It is not listed in contemporary records which have been examined, or in
the National Union Catalog.
    It is treated as a reissue of the 14th Cassell reprint (No. 216).

232. The Eighteenth (Brooklyn) Cassell Reprint

THE COMPLETE ANGLER by Isaac Walton
Brooklyn: A. Wessells Co. 203 Fulton St. [1907].

Copies examined: None seen.

The listing above is from *The Cumulative Book Index,* 1908, where it is further described as one of the *World's Great Classics* series, with an introduction by J. Morley, priced at 50 cents.

Although neither this *Angler* nor the *World's Great Classics* series has been seen, the description indicates that this is probably a reissue of one of the Cassell reprints, which have an introduction by Henry (not J.) Morley and were priced about 50 cents. It is also reported although not seen by Oliver (his No. 217).

1907

233. The Wellcome (10th Stock) Facsimile

THE COMPLEAT ANGLER 𝖇𝖞 𝕴𝖟𝖆𝖆𝖐 𝖂𝖆𝖑𝖙𝖔𝖓
𝕱𝖆𝖈𝖘𝖎𝖒𝖎𝖑𝖊 𝖗𝖊𝖕𝖗𝖎𝖓𝖙 𝖎𝖓 1907 𝖔𝖋 𝖙𝖍𝖊 𝖋𝖎𝖗𝖘𝖙 𝖊𝖉𝖎𝖙𝖎𝖔𝖓 𝖕𝖚𝖇𝖑𝖎𝖘𝖍𝖊𝖉 𝖎𝖓 1653
𝕰𝖒𝖇𝖊𝖑𝖑𝖎𝖘𝖍𝖊𝖉 𝖜𝖎𝖙𝖍 𝖗𝖊𝖕𝖗𝖔𝖉𝖚𝖈𝖙𝖎𝖔𝖓𝖘 𝖔𝖋 𝖙𝖍𝖊 𝖔𝖗𝖎𝖌𝖎𝖓𝖆𝖑 𝖊𝖓𝖌𝖗𝖆𝖛𝖎𝖓𝖌𝖘 𝖈𝖔𝖓𝖙𝖆𝖎𝖓𝖊𝖉
𝖎𝖓 𝖙𝖍𝖊 𝖘𝖊𝖈𝖔𝖓𝖉 𝖊𝖉𝖎𝖙𝖎𝖔𝖓 𝖕𝖚𝖇𝖑𝖎𝖘𝖍𝖊𝖉 𝖇𝖞 𝕵𝖔𝖍𝖓 𝕸𝖆𝖏𝖔𝖗 [London].

Copies examined: Horne (3), Library of Congress, Princeton, Yale. Other: ViW.

Size: 6¾″×4¼″.

Pagination summary: [2 ff], [16], (1)-246.

This is a privately printed reissue of the first Le Gallienne (8th Stock) facsimile of 1896 (No. 175).

The illustrations consist of the six cuts of fish and the music (the second page printed upside down), from the first Le Gallienne (8th Stock) facsimile. In addition, there are eight photogravure plates from the illustrations in the Methuen edition of 1903 (No. 209), which was based on the second Major edition of 1824 (No. 24). On the title-page verso appears in black letter, "Tradition states that Izaak Walton oft fished the streams of Kent, and was wont to cast his line in the River Darent, neath a shady tree at Dartford."

It is now established that this edition, heretofore identified as "Anonymous," was printed as a Christmas present or greeting. On the recto (verso blank) of the leaf preceding the title-page is printed:

From
Mr. and Mrs. Wellcome
with Best Wishes
for
Christmas and the New Year
Christmas, 1907

Although the greeting page is present in three copies examined, it is lacking in two Horne copies and, since there is no evidence of its removal in these copies some were probably made up without it, although it may have been excised in the Yale copy examined. The Wellcome greeting page must have been lacking in the copy examined by Oliver (his No. 216) prompting him to name it "The Anonymous (11th) Facsimile." The copy described by C. W. Bushell, Snr., (1953, p. 116) has the "Greeting" page and the binding of the copies examined.

The bindings of the four copies (as issued) are identical; tan sheepskin over wooden boards. Enclosed near the top of the front cover is "The Compleat Angler | Izaak Walton." A large fish (hooked and running) is blind stamped on the lower portion of the front cover. The spine and back cover are not decorated.

Telephone calls, and correspondence with the Wellcome Historical Medical Museum in London, verified the private printing of this edition in 1907 by Mr. and Mrs. Henry Sullivan Wellcome, who in 1932 became Sir Henry and Lady Syrie Wellcome.

[1908]

234. The Third Everyman (5th Lang) Reprint

THE COMPLEAT ANGLER by Izaak Walton
London: Published by J. M. Dent & Co and in New York by E. P. Dutton & Co. [1908].

Copies examined: Harvard, Horne, Princeton, Yale. Others: MiU, NN.

Size: $6^{13}/_{16}$″ × $4^{3}/_{16}$″.

Pagination summary: [i-vii], viii-xliv, [2], [1]-3, [4-5], 6-215, [216].

On page [216] is imprinted "LETCHWORTH THE TEMPLE PRESS PRINTERS." On the title-page verso of this reissue of the first Everyman of 1906 (No. 228) appears, "First Edition March 1906, Reprinted July 1906; April 1908."

The publisher's binding (terra-cotta cloth) is the same as the second binding described for the first Everyman edition of 1906 (No. 228).

[1908]

235. The Quiller-Couch Abridged Edition

IZAAK WALTON
Selections arranged by A. T. Quiller-Couch
Oxford at the Clarendon Press [1908].

Copies examined: Harvard (2).

Size: 6½″ × 4⅛″.

Pagination summary: [1]-32.

At the foot of page 32 is imprinted, "Oxford: Printed at the Clarendon Press by Horace Hart, M.A." There are no illustrations.

Sir Arthur Thomas Quiller-Couch, editor of this and others of the "Select English Classics," provided a two and one-half page introduction to the selections, which are from the *Lives* as well as the *Angler*, the latter appearing on pages 21-32.

It was issued in cloth at four pence and in paper at three pence.

The two Harvard copies are in dark blue, almost purple, paper. This edition, with 14 other titles, is listed on the inside of the back cover. Printed in black on the outside of the front cover, in addition to titling and price, is a large Q in the middle, and, at the top, a silhouette of part of the city of Oxford. A gothic tower within a small square is printed in black on the outside of the back cover.

The date adopted for this edition, 1908, is that cited for it by *The British Museum Catalogue*.

1908

236. The First Collins Edition

THE COMPLEAT ANGLER by Izaak Walton
and Charles Cotton
London and Glasgow Collins' Clear-Type Press [1908].

Copies examined: Harvard, Horne, Oliver, Princeton, Yale. Other: IaU.

Size: 6″ × 3¹⁵⁄₁₆″.

Pagination Summary: [4], [1]-280, [8].

At the foot of page 280 is imprinted, "Collins' Clear-Type Press, London and Glasgow." Two title-pages follow the half-title; the first in photogravure has oval portraits of Walton and Cotton, and the second, used to list this reprint, is typeset within and divided horizontally by a red rule. The eight pages at the end list Collins' publications, where this reprint is number 88 of the *Illustrated Pocket Classics*. It is described as by "Izaak Walton and Richard [sic] Cotton" with "8 Illustrations by John Eyre," which includes the frontispiece. There are also ten woodcuts of fish. The volumes in this series were priced, "Cloth, Gold Back, 1/net. Leather, Gold Edges, Gold Autograph, 2/net."

This edition opens with the dialogue of Chapter I, all of Walton's preliminaries having been omitted. There are a few short footnotes from the first Bell-Daldy and Low edition of 1863 (No. 81).

The publisher's bindings examined in red cloth have dark red end papers and a red ribbon bookmark, with a blind stamped rule on the cover edges. "Walton and Cotton" is gilt stamped in script on the front cover. A strip pattern of leaf decorations and the titling are in gilt on the spine. The Oliver copy was issued in a purple suede Yapp binding, titled in gilt on front cover within a vine-leaf bordered blind stamped panel; spine titled vertically in gilt.

This edition is listed in *The English Catalogue of Books* as published in July, 1908. It is a reprint from the fifth edition of 1676 (No. 6).

1909

237. The Nineteenth Cassell Edition

THE COMPLEAT ANGLER by Izaak Walton and C. Cotton Cassell and Company, Ltd. London New York Toronto & Melbourne MCMIX

Copies examined: Harvard, Horne (5), Princeton. Others: CoD, CtY, DLC, NN, OCl.

Size: 7⅛″ × 4⁷⁄₁₆″.

Collation: [π⁴], 100-A*¹², 100-B⁴+100-B*¹² to 100-J⁴+100-J*¹², 100-K⁸, 100-L², 100-L*²=172.

Pagination summary: [1-8], 9-245, [246-248], 249-335, [336-338], 339-344, [4].

At the foot of page 335 (the last page of text) is imprinted, *"Printed by Hazell, Watson & Viney, Ltd., London and Aylesbury."* At the foot of page 344 is imprinted, "Printed by Cassell & Company, Limited, La Belle Sauvage, London, E.C." At the end is a four-page catalogue listing of the first 100 volumes in Cassell's "Peoples Library" where this edition is number 100, titled "The Compleat Angler—Walton," although Cotton's part is included for the first time in a Cassell *Angler*. The circular La Belle Sauvage device is imprinted on the last page of the catalogue.

Both the title-page, with its unusual "C" instead of Charles Cotton, and the facing page, with the editor's brief unsigned note about Walton and

Cotton, have elaborate *art nouveau* borders. Marston (1915, p. xliv) identifies the editor as Henry Morley. The notes signed "H" are by Sir John Hawkins, and those signed "E" are by Ephemera (Edward Fitzgibbon), reprinted from the first Ephemera edition of 1853 (No. 68).

The illustrations consist of a title-page facsimile of the first edition, a woodcut of a salmon fly, 17 woodcuts illustrating 19 species of fish, and, in the appendix, three pages illustrating natural flies, their imitations, and fly-making. All these are from the first Ephemera edition (No. 68).

The five Horne copies (identified as *A-E*) are in different publisher's bindings; (*A*) in red leather with the spine gilt stamped with four compartments containing conventional gilt decorations, plus two for the titling in gilt. The top edges are gilt. A purplish-red ribbon bookmark is included. (*B*) is in dark green cloth, the spine decorated in gilt with two similar *art nouveau* designs and gilt titled. The lower right corner of the front cover is blind stamped with the circular device of La Belle Sauvage. (*C*) is in brown leather with the same decorations on the spine and front cover as (*B*), but all in gilt, and with top edges gilt. (*D*) is in pinkish-red cloth, the spine decorated with a single, smaller, modified version of the decorations used on copies (*B*) and (*C*), but with the publisher's circular device blind stamped on the front cover as in (*B*). (*E*) is in smooth plain black cloth with a paper spine label. The publisher's name does not appear on the spine of copies (*A*) or (*E*); is stamped "Cassell & Co." on (*A*) and (*C*); and "Cassell" on (*D*).

The English Catalogue of Books lists this edition as one of the "People's Library" published by Cassell in April 1909, priced at 8d. in cloth, and 1s. 6d. in leather.

This edition is from Parts I and II of the fifth edition of 1676 (No. 6).

[1909]

238. The Asprey Reprint

THE COMPLEAT ANGLER Izaac Walton
Asprey & Co., Ltd. *Booksellers and Publishers.*
New Bond Street, London. [1909].

Copy examined: Virginia.

Size: 7⅛″ × 4⁷⁄₁₆″.

Collation: Same as No. 237, lacking π^1.

Pagination summary: Same as No. 236, lacking [1-2] and [4] at the end.

At the foot of page 335 (the last text page) is imprinted, *"Printed by Hazell, Watson & Viney, Ltd., London and Aylesbury"* and at the foot of page 344 "Printed by Cassell and Company, Limited La Belle Sauvage, London, E.C." This

Angler, with the same collation, pagination and illustrations, is a reissue of the 19th Cassell Reprint of 1909 (No. 237), lacking the half-title and four terminal pages of Cassell's catalogue of the Peoples Library series.

This reissue of the 19th Cassell reprint, with its Asprey title-page, was published in a special leather binding appropriate for the prosperous "carriage trade" of the early 20th century. The Virginia copy is bound in very dark blue polished morocco, with gilt tooling on the borders of both the front and back covers, gilt beading on the edges, and the inside borders gilt. All leaf edges are gilt. The copy has been rebacked and it is not possible to describe the original spine which probably was divided into gilt tooled panels by raised bands.

Neither Asprey nor Cassell (whose records were destroyed in World War II) were able to provide any information on the publication date of this reprint. Unreported in any previous bibliography of the *Angler*, it is tentatively dated 1909, the same year as the 19th Cassell. This reissue, with a new title-page, of the 19th Cassell, is from Parts I and II of the fifth edition of 1676 (No. 6), although Cotton is omitted from the title-page.

[1909]

239. The Fourth Burt (45th Major) Reprint

THE COMPLETE ANGLER . . . By Izaak Walton and
Charles Cotton . . .
A. L. Burt Company, Publishers, New York [1909]

Copies examined: None seen.

Oliver (see his Nos. 180 and 220), who received his information from the publishers, reported that this reprint in Burt's *Home Library* series was published on January 28, 1909. See also notes herein for No. 193, of which this is a later issue.

1909

240. The Riverside Press (Bruce Rogers) Edition

THE COMPLEAT ANGLER . . .
The Riverside Press Edition [Cambridge, Mass.] 1909

Copies examined: Harvard, Horne, Princeton, Yale. Others: CSmH, DLC, ICN, NN, NcU, OClRC.

THE COMPLEAT
ANGLER
Or, The Contemplative Man's
Recreation

BEING
A DISCOURSE OF FISH AND FISHING
NOT UNWORTHY THE PERUSAL OF
MOST ANGLERS

The Riverside Press Edition

1909

Figure 24   The Riverside Press (Bruce Rogers)
Edition (No. 240). One of Rogers' favorites

Size: $6\frac{5}{16}'' \times 4\frac{1}{8}''$.

Pagination summary: [18], [1]-263, [264-265], 266-302, [2].

On the recto of the leaf following page 302 is imprinted, "Four hundred and forty copies printed at the Riverside Press, Cambridge, for Houghton Mifflin Company: Boston & New York."

The illustrations consist of a tailpiece, six engravings of fish and two pages of music, the second of which is printed upside down as in the first edition, 1653 (No. 1). It is printed in Riverside Caslon, remodelled from foundry Caslon by Bruce Rogers (see Figure 24).

This edition (as the later Goodspeed edition, 1928) has much of the flavor to be found in the first edition of 1653, such as reproduction of the same text illustrations, and many typographical curiosities of the original, as "Compleat," on the title-page, and "Complete" in the running heads. There is a peculiar use of the Roman N among italic capitals in "Angler" on the title-page, in "John" on the following leaf recto, in "Anglers" on the two pages of music [264-265], and in "Finis." Frederic Warde wrote of this edition, "Few sextodecimos are more *aimable* than this, one of Mr. Rogers' favorite books." (See his *Bruce Rogers, Designer of Books*, 1925, quoted in *Typophile Chap Book: XV, B. R. Marks & Remarks*, Newark, 1946, pages 49 and 50.) The Harvard copy was signed by Rogers.

The book had a protective plain semi-transparent paper dust jacket and was issued in a slip case. It was cased in brown mottled boards. The leaves are untrimmed. Tipped in at the end is an extra printed spine label.

The text of this edition is a reprint from the first edition of 1653 (No. 1).

[1911]

241. The Fourth Everyman (6th Lang) Reprint

THE COMPLEAT ANGLER by Izaak Walton
London: Published by J. M. Dent & Sons Ltd., and in
New York by E. P. Dutton & Co [1911].

Copies examined: Oliver, Yale. Other: PHC.

Size: $6\frac{13}{16}'' \times 4\frac{3}{16}''$.

Pagination summary: [i-vii], viii-xliv, [2], [1]-215, [216].

This is a reissue of the third Everyman (No. 234), is dated January, 1911, on its title-page verso, and is imprinted, "Letchworth The Temple Press Printers" on page [216].

The half-title verso is imprinted (*inter alia*) "In four styles of binding: cloth, flat-back, coloured top; leather, round corners, gilt top; library binding in cloth, & quarter pigskin." Two of these bindings, represented here, are described in detail in notes to the first Everyman edition (1906, No. 228); the Yale copy, in dark red leather, is the same as the *first* binding; the Oliver copy, in terra cotta cloth, is the same as the *second* binding, except that the top edges are stained tan color.

[1911]

242. The First Thorpe Edition

THE COMPLEAT ANGLER . . . by Izaak Walton. . . . Hodder & Stoughton London-New-York-Toronto [1911].

Copies examined: Harvard (2), Horne, Princeton, Trinity (Hartford) (2), and Trinity (Dublin). Other: CtY.

Size: Regular, 10⅜"×8"; Large paper (limited), 11"×9".

Pagination summary: [i]-xv, [xvi], [1]-166, [167].

At the foot of the last page, [167], is imprinted, "Printed by T. and A. Constable, Printers to His Majesty at the Edinburgh University Press."

The illustrations consist of 25 mounted color plates, a title-page vignette, and decorated end papers, all by James Thorpe. The descriptive letterpress on the plate tissue guards is printed in green, as are the fish in the lower right-hand corners. On the plate facing page 88, the surname of Oliver Henley, friend of Walton, is misspelled "Heny."

This edition was published in two states, differing only in imprint notation, paper size, and binding. The large paper state, limited to 250 copies (seen at Harvard and Trinity), was signed by Thorpe. At the foot of the last page, "Illustrations by Henry Stone and Sons, Ltd. Banbury," has been added to the printer's imprint.

The regular state was issued in ribbed dark green cloth. In addition to the usual gilt titling on the front cover and spine, the large drawing of the angler portrayed on the white end papers is repeated in gilt on the front cover.

The large paper state was issued in full polished brown-black morocco with brown end papers, decorated with the drawing of the angler in the same manner as the regular state.

With its hyphenated London-New-York-Toronto imprint, and preface dated 1911, this *Angler*, following verification by the publisher, has been designated the first Thorpe edition. This imprint is not reported by Oliver. However, he reported a copy, apparently identical to this one, as "The First Thorpe Reprint" (his No. 225) for which he cited the title-page imprint to be, "London and New York: Hodder & Stoughton, St. Paul's House, Warwick

Square, E.C. 1911." Such an imprint is not present in the angling collections examined or catalogues checked for this bibliography, and although Oliver may well have seen such a copy, it seems possible that there may have been an error in transcription. The large paper state apparently was not known to Oliver.

This edition, with a preface by R. B. Marston, editor of the Lea and Dove edition (No. 136), and for many years editor of the *Fishing Gazette*, and with Walton's "To all Readers . . .," is from the fifth edition of 1676 (No. 6). *The English Catalogue of Books* lists a Hodder and *Stoughton* edition as having been published in October, 1911, priced at 15 shillings. According to information received from the publisher, the large paper state was priced two pounds, two shillings.

[1911]

243. The Second Thorpe Reprint

THE COMPLEAT ANGLER . . . by Izaak Walton. . . .
Hodder & Stoughton New York & London [1911].

Copy examined: Horne.

Size: $10\frac{3}{8}'' \times 8''$.

Pagination summary: [i]-xv, [xvi], 1-166, [167].

At the foot of page [167] is imprinted, "Printed by T. and A. Constable, Printers to His Majesty at the Edinburgh University Press."

The binding is the same as the regular state of the first Thorpe.

This is a reissue of the first Thorpe, differing only in a modification of the title-page imprint. It does not correspond to any of the Thorpe reprints described by Oliver. It is probably the "Doran Reprint" (his No. 228) which, not having seen, he reported from an entry in the *Cumulative Book Index*, presuming it to have been published by Doran, whose advertising, however, indicates that the firm merely was acting as distributor for it. In the *Publisher's Weekly*, September 30, 1911, the George H. Doran Co., 35 West 32nd St., New York, N.Y., signing as "Publishers in America for Hodder & Stoughton," included in their Art Gift Books advertisement, "*The Compleat Angler* by Izaak Walton. 25 plates in color by J. H. Thorpe. Handsomely bound. Quarto Cloth Boxed. New $5.00." While an *Angler* with the Doran imprint may possibly have been published, it seems more likely that Oliver's so-called Doran reprint is this second Thorpe, distributed by Doran in the United States.

This is a reissue, with a new title-page, of the first Thorpe edition of 1911 (No. 242), which is from Part I of the fifth edition of 1676 (No. 6).

[1911]

244. The Third Thorpe Reprint

THE COMPLEAT ANGLER . . . by Izaak Walton. . . .
Toronto: The Musson Book Company Limited. [1911].

Copy examined: Oliver.

Size: 10⅜"×8".

Pagination summary: [i]-xv, [xvi], 1-166, [167].

At the foot of page [167] is "Printed by T. and A. Constable, Printers to His
Majesty at the Edinburgh University Press."
    The illustrations and binding are the same as those for the regular state
of the first Thorpe.
    This is a reissue, differing only in a modification of the title-page imprint,
of the first Thorpe edition (1911, No. 242), which is from Part I of the fifth
edition of 1676 (No. 6).

1912

245. The Ninth Lowell Reprint

THE COMPLETE ANGLER, . . . of Izaak Walton and
Charles Cotton. . . .
Boston: Little, Brown, and Company. 1912

Copy examined: Horne. Others: CtHT, CtY, NN.

Size: 7¼"×4⅞".

Pagination summary: [i-v], vi-lxxvi, [1]-465.

On the title-page verso is printed, "*Copyright, 1889, By Little, Brown, and
Company.*"
    The illustrations consists of the title-page vignette etching by Louis K.
Harlow, which was originally used in the title-page to Volume II of the first
Lowell and the 74 woodcuts, all from the first Lowell edition (No. 142).
    This one-volume reprint was issued in bright red cloth. The front and
back covers are not decorated, but a large stylized floral design, and titling
at the top and foot, are printed in black on the spine. The top edges are gilt.
    In *The United States Catalogue Supplement, Books Published 1912-1917,* this reprint
is listed as one of the *Beacon Classics,* published in 1912, priced at $1.50 and, in
half crushed morocco, at $3.50.
    Except for the change in the use of Harlow's vignette etching, this is a
reissue of the sixth Lowell reprint of 1898 (No. 181).

246. The Brewer Abridged Edition

THE DIVINE ART OF CONTENTMENT
Cedar Rapids Iowa Privately Printed for
Luther A. Brewer and his Friends
Christmas Nineteen Twelve

Copy examined: Cleveland Public.

Size: 7⅞″×5⅛″.

Pagination summary: [1-4] (including front wrapper), 5-6, [7-8], 9-31.

The Cleveland copy is printed throughout within parallel red rules. On the title-page verso is imprinted, "Only seventy copies printed. Illuminated letter by Elinore Taylor Brewer. The Torch Press Cedar Rapids Iowa."

The illustrations consists of a frontispiece portrait of Walton, a title-page vignette of the "Farewell" (both photogravures), the first letter of the text "W", illuminated in blue and red by Elinore Taylor Brewer, a woodcut of a group of Cupids fishing and one of a pike used for a tailpiece. Both the "Farewell" and the Cupids first appeared in the first Major edition of 1823 (No. 23).

The text, titled "The Divine Art of Contentment," is from Part I, Chapter XII of the *Angler* and begins, "Well Scholar, having now taught you how to paint your rod, . . ." It is on pages 9-31, following a two-page "Foreword" by Luther A. Brewer.

The volume was issued in self-wrappers (the same paper as the text) and with the same parallel red rules enclosing the word "Contentment" on the front. The leaves are untrimmed.

This *Angler* excerpt is from Part I of the fifth edition of 1676 (No. 6). It is unreported in previous bibliographies of the *Angler*.

247. The Brewer Abridged Reprint

THE DIVINE ART OF CONTENTMENT
Privately Printed Nineteen Thirteen

Copy examined: Yale.

Size: 7⅞″×5⅛″.

Pagination: [1-4] (including front wrapper), 5-6, [7-8], 9-31.

On the title-page verso is imprinted, "Only ten copies printed. Illuminated letter by Elinore Taylor Brewer."

This is a reprint, with a new title-page, of the Brewer abridged edition (No. 246), printed throughout within parallel red rules, and having the same illustrations, "Foreword," and self-wrappers.

[1913]

248. The Fifth Everyman (7th Lang) Reprint

THE COMPLEAT ANGLER by Izaak Walton
London : Published by J. M. Dent & Sons Ltd. and in New York by
E. P. Dutton & Co [1913].

Copies examined : Horne, Oliver, Yale. Others : CtHT, MH.

Size : $6\frac{3}{4}'' \times 4\frac{1}{4}''$.

Pagination summary : [i-vii], viii-xliv, [2], [1]-215, [216].

On page [216] is imprinted "LETCHWORTH THE TEMPLE PRESS PRINTERS." The date for this reissue of the fourth Everyman (No. 241), December, 1913, appears on the title-page verso, preceded by dates of the earlier editions in the Everyman's Library series.

The four available bindings described on the half-title verso and the bindings represented here, the Oliver copy in dark red leather, the others in terra cotta cloth, are the same as those of the fourth Everyman (No. 241).

[1913]

249. The Fifth Burt (46th Major) Reprint

THE COMPLETE ANGLER . . . By Izaak Walton and
Charles Cotton . . .
A. L. Burt Company, Publishers, New York [1913].

Copies examined : None.

According to Oliver (see his Nos. 180 and 230), who received his information from the publishers, this reprint in Burt's *Home Library* series was published on April 9, 1913. See also notes herein for No. 193, of which this is a later issue.

[1913]
250. The Fourth Thorpe Reprint

THE COMPLEAT ANGLER . . . by Izaak Walton. . . .
Hodder & Stoughton New York & London [1913]

Copies examined: Harvard, Horne. Other: NN.

Size: 9 11/16″ × 7 1/8″.

Pagination summary: [i]-viii, 1-166, [167-168].

On page [168] is imprinted, "Text printed by T. and A. Constable, Printers to His Majesty, Edinburgh. The Coloured Plates printed by Henry Stone and Son, Ltd., Banbury."

The illustrations consist of 16 mounted color plates and a vignette in black on the title-page from the first Thorpe (No. 242). On the plate opposite page 88, Henley is spelled "Heny."

The publisher's binding is in pea-green cloth with the entire front cover embossed with a silhouette showing an angler working under a tree and along the bank of a river, against a lighter green background of the water and the distant landscape of the far side. The usual titling in gilt is on the front cover and spine, the latter with two small fish printed in the background color beneath the author's name.

Doran (the American distributor for Hodder and Stoughton, see No. 241) advertised this *Angler* in *The Publisher's Weekly*, November 22, 1913, under "Art Gift Books in Color" as follows, "*The Compleat Angler* by Izaak Walton. With sixteen plates in color by J. H. Thorpe. Small Quarto. New $2.00." The advertisement states further, "The above are selected from a sixty-five page illustrated descriptive announcement, The New Books of 1913 . . ." The publisher stated (in a London interview) that an American reprint of 2,000 copies was produced in 1913, but no record of the imprint is available due to war damage.

This is a reissue, from the same plates, of the first Thorpe reprint (No. 242), but has 16 instead of 25 colored plates, and lacks Marston's preface and Walton's "To all Readers. . . ."

1913
251. The Second Rouse Abridged Reprint

THE COMPLETE ANGLER by Izaak Walton
London Blackie & Son Limited 50 Old Bailey E. C. Glasgow and Bombay 1913
A Library of English Prose

Copy examined: The British Museum.

Size: 6⅜″ × 4⁵⁄₁₆″.

Pagination summary: [1-4], 5-120.

This reprint is part of *A Library of English Prose*, edited by W. H. D. Rouse, Litt.D., who wrote a one-page introduction of which the final paragraph reads as follows, "*The Present Edition* contains about half the original work. Parts of the more lengthy disquisitions have been omitted, together with the more technical chapters vi. to xv. and xvii. to xx." There are no illustrations.

The binding is dark blue cloth boards gilt stamped, and the selling price was 10d.

This reprint is a reissue of the Rouse Abridged edition of 1906 (No. 227), published as one of a different series, and is unreported in previous bibliographies of the *Angler*.

1913

252. The First Hankey Edition

THE COMPLEAT ANGLER by Izaak Walton . . .
T. N. Foulis London & Edinburgh 1913

Copies examined: Harvard, Horne, Princeton, Yale. Others: CtHT, NN, PU.

Size: 8⅛″ × 5⅛″.

Pagination summary: [10], [1]-[232], [6].

On the title-page verso is imprinted, "Published November 1913" and "Turnbull & Spears, Printers, Edinburgh." On page 143, line seven, "shred" is misprinted "shed." The six pages at the end are advertisements for Foulis publications.

There are 13 plates in color by W. Lee Hankey and four unsigned woodcut chapter tailpieces, three of which appear three times each, and one four times.

The publisher's binding is dark green cloth with gilt titling on the spine (T. N. Foulis at the foot) and front cover, the latter titled in black on the Yale copy. The end papers are light gray. The top edges are gilt, others untrimmed.

The English Catalogue of Books gives November 1913 as the publication date and the price as 5s. net. This edition is from Part I of the fifth edition of 1676 (No. 6).

[1914]

253. The Second Hankey (Phillips) Reprint

THE COMPLEAT ANGLER by Izaak Walton . . .
Boston: Le Roy Phillips London & Edinburgh: T. N. Foulis [1914].

Copies examined: Harvard, Horne. Others: CtY, NN.

Size: 8⅛″ × 5⅛″.

Pagination summary: [10], [1]-232, [8].

On the title-page verso is imprinted, "Printed by Morrison & Gibb Limited, Edinburgh." The eight pages of Foulis advertisements at the end show Le Roy Phillips as publisher. The misprint "shed" for "shred" on page 143, line seven, has not been corrected.

The color plates and the binding are the same as the first Hankey, except that Le Roy Phillips appears at the foot of the spine and the cloth is a lighter shade of green.

The U. S. Catalog Supplement Books Published 1912-1917, reports this reissue to have been published in 1914 priced at $1.50. It is a reissue, with a new title-page, of the first Hankey edition of 1913 (No. 252).

[1915]

254. The Sixth Burt (47th Major) Reprint

THE COMPLETE ANGLER . . . By Izaak Walton and
Charles Cotton . . .
A. L. Burt Company, Publishers, New York [1915].

Copy examined: Oliver.

Size: 7⁵⁄₁₆″ × 4⅞″.

Pagination summary: [1-4] including frontispiece, [5]-354 (no half-title).

This reprint has the same pagination, title-page, illustrations, and binding of the earlier Burt *Home Library Anglers* (see No. 218).

The Oliver copy examined (his No. 237) is dated April 9, 1915 in pencil, which is the date the publisher reported to Oliver that the reprint was issued in the Burt *Home Library* series (see No. 193 herein).

1915

255. The Third Marston Edition

THE COMPLEAT ANGLER By Izaak Walton & Charles Cotton . . .
Humphrey Milford Oxford University Press
London Edinburgh Glasgow New York Toronto Melbourne
Bombay 1915

Copies examined: Harvard, Horne (2), Princeton. Others: CU, DLC, MiD, PBm.

Size: 7⅛″×4¾″ (ordinary and India paper).

Pagination summary: [i]-xliv, [1]-340.

At the foot of page 340 is imprinted, "Printed in Great Britain by Richard Clay & Sons, Limited, Brunswick St., Stamford St., S.E., and Bungay, Suffolk." The Oxford University Press's mark is on the title-page, and there are typeset facsimiles of the 1676 title-pages for Part I (the second title, on lower half of page) and for Part II.

The illustrations are 13 plates consisting of frontispieces of Walton and of Cotton; a facsimile of the title-page (including the cartouche) to Part I of the fifth edition of 1676; four illustrations from the 1760 Hawkins edition (No. 9); one from the 1750 Moses Browne edition (No. 7); the Waltham Cross; the Tottenham High Cross; and (on three plates) ten fish from the 1676 edition. There are also two printed pages of music. The engravers were Burgh, Ridley, and Ryland; the artists Huysman, Lely, S. Wale, Shirt, and T. Smith.

This edition was published in two states: one on ordinary paper, the other on thin India paper. That on ordinary paper has been seen in two publisher's bindings. The *first* (Horne copy) is in light red cloth, with the edges of both covers ruled in blind. An elaborate design with a lyre in the center is blind stamped within a triple blind ruled panel on the front cover, and the lyre motif is repeated in the gilt decoration on the spine, and on the back cover within a parallel ruled panel. The titling is in gilt on the front cover and spine. The *second* (Princeton copy) is in rough blue cloth, with parallel rules in blind on the edges of the covers. The spine is gilt titled.

The *Angler* on India paper (Horne copy) was issued in smooth dark red cloth. The only decoration is a single rule, in gilt on the edges of the front cover, and blind stamped on the edges of the back cover. Single gilt rules are at the top and foot of the spine. The titling on the front cover and spine is gilt. The leaf edges are gilt over red. A red ribbon bookmark is present.

The text of this edition is from Parts I and II of the fifth edition of 1676 (No. 6), with an introduction by R. B. Marston and list of ". . . about 160 editions or issues of *The Compleat Angler* . . ." updated from the list in the Lea and Dove edition, 1888 (No. 136). *The English Catalogue* reports this as one of the Oxford edition of Standard Authors, published in July, 1915, priced at 2s. on ordinary paper, and 4s on India paper.

1915

256. The Gough and Balston Edition

Walton and Cotton
THE COMPLEAT ANGLER
Oxford at the Clarendon Press 1915.

Copies examined: Harvard, Horne (2), Princeton, Yale. Others: CtHT, ICU, IU, MiU, OCU, PBm.

Size: 7½″ × 4⅞″.

Pagination summary: [i-v], vi-xx, [1]-398.

The text, pages [1]-340, was printed from the plates used for the third Marston edition (No. 255) and, at the foot of page 340, has the same imprint: "Printed in Great Britain by Richard Clay & Sons, Limited, Brunswick St., S.E., and Bungay, Suffolk." On the title-page verso is imprinted, "Oxford University Press London Edinburgh Glasgow New York Toronto Melbourne Bombay Humphrey Milford M. A. Publisher to the University" and, at the foot of page 398, "Oxford: Horace Hart Printer to the University." In the introduction by A. B. Gough, he writes (p. xiii), "The total number of editions is now about 140." T. Balston contributed 58 pages of notes at the end.

The only illustrations are two printed pages of music.

Four publisher's bindings were examined. The *first* (Horne copy) in dark blue cloth, with blind parallel rules on the edges of the covers, and white parallel rules at the top and foot of the spine, which is titled in white. The *second* (Princeton copy) in dark gray cloth, and the *third* (Horne copy) in dark olive-green cloth, each with a blind rule on the edges of its covers, and with the titling and Oxford seal in gilt on the spine, gilt ruled at top and foot. The *fourth* (Yale copy) is in light blue cloth. A decorative border band enclosing titling and the Oxford seal are printed in black on the front cover. The spine is titled and ruled top and foot in black.

The English Catalogue lists this edition as having been published in February, 1915, priced at 3s. The text is a reprint from Parts I and II of the fifth edition of 1676 (No. 6).

257. The Sixth Everyman (8th Lang) Reprint

THE COMPLEAT ANGLER by Izaak Walton
London Toronto & Paris: J. M. Dent & Sons Ltd.
New York E. P. Dutton and Co. [1916].

Copy examined: Horne.

Size: 6¾″×4¼″.

Pagination summary: [i]-xliv, [2], [1]-215, [216].

On the Kelmscott-style title-page verso is imprinted, "First issue of this Edition March 1906 Reprinted July 1906; April 1908; January 1911; December 1913; September 1916." The following is imprinted (*inter alia*) on the half-title verso, "In four styles of binding: cloth, flat back, coloured top; leather, round corners, gilt top; library binding in cloth, & quarter pigskin." On page [216], with a printer's mark apparently derived from the border of the title-page, is imprinted, "The Temple Press Letchworth England."
    The copy examined is in the publisher's binding used for the second binding of the first Everyman (No. 228), except the top edges are black.
    This is a reissue of the first Everyman edition of 1906 (No. 228).

258. The Seventh Burt (48th Major) Reprint

THE COMPLETE ANGLER . . . By Izaak Walton and
Charles Cotton . . .
A. L. Burt Company, Publishers, New York [1918].

Copies examined: Horne, Yale.

Size: 6¹¹⁄₁₆″×4¼″.

Pagination summary: [1-2] lacking; [3-4], title recto, verso blank; [5]-354, which is the same as the *Home Library* series (see No. 218) except for the half-title and frontispiece, which are lacking in this reprint.

This reprint is one of Burt's *Standard Library* series, printed from the plates of the *Home Library* series, lacking the frontispiece plate of Walton. It is smaller in size, and printed on cheaper paper.
    It was issued in dark red simulated leather material with dark red end papers and top edges gilt. The front cover is bordered by a gilt rule, and gilt stamped with a small circle enclosing a book held open by a flaming torch. The spine is titled in gilt.

Oliver (see his No. 239), who received his information from the publisher, reports such "a reprint of the Major edition of 1844" (No. 55) was published in 1918, and was reissued in 1923, 1925, and 1927, in Burt's *Standard Library* series.

[1919]
259. The Eighth Burt (49th Major) Reprint

THE COMPLETE ANGLER . . . By Izaak Walton and
Charles Cotton . . .
A. L. Burt Company, Publishers, New York [1919].

Copies examined: None seen.

According to Oliver (see his No. 240), who received his information from the publisher, this reprint in Burt's *Home Library* series was published on June 2, 1919. See also notes herein for No. 193, of which this is a later issue.

[1920]
260. The Seventh Everyman (9th Lang) Reprint

THE COMPLEAT ANGLER by Izaak Walton
London & Toronto Published by J. M. Dent & Sons Ltd. & in
New York by E. P. Dutton & Co [1920].

Copies examined: Princeton, Yale. Other: CU.

Size: 6¾″ × 4³⁄₁₆″.

Pagination summary: [i]-xliv, [2], [1]-215, [216].

On the title-page verso is imprinted, "First Issue of this Edition, March 1906; Reprinted, July 1906; April 1908; January 1911; December 1913; September 1916; February 1920." On page [216] is imprinted "The Temple Press Letchworth England."
   The publisher's binding examined at Princeton is in a greenish-gray cloth titled in dark green on the spine. The Yale copy is that of the second binding of the first Everyman (No. 228), except the top edges are black.
   This is a reissue of the first Everyman edition of 1906 (No. 228).

[1916]

1920

261. The Gay and Hancock Reprint

THE COMPLEAT ANGLER by Izaak Walton.
London: Gay & Hancock, Ltd., 34 Henrietta Street,
Covent Garden, W. C. 2. 1920.

Copies examined: None seen.

Size: 6¼″×4¾″.

Pagination reported: 246 pages.

This listing is from Oliver (his No. 241), who cites *The Reference Catalogue of Current Literature* as evidence of publication of this reprint. Oliver's date is from the publisher's catalogue.
    This reprint is not listed in the National Union Catalog, or in any contemporary records that have been examined.

[1920]

262. The Fifth Thorpe Reprint

THE COMPLEAT ANGLER . . . by Izaak Walton . . .
Stewart & Kidd Company Publishers Cincinnati [1920].

Copies examined: Boston Public Library, Yale. Other: NN.

Size: 9⁹⁄₁₆″×7¹⁄₁₆″.

Pagination summary: [i]-viii, 1-166, [167-168].

On page [168] is imprinted, "Text printed by T. and A. Constable, Printers to His Majesty, Edinburgh. The Coloured Plates printed by Henry Stone and Son, Ltd., Banbury."
    The illustrations are those of the fourth Thorpe (No. 250).
    The publisher's binding is in avocado-green cloth, with the entire front cover having a silhouette showing an angler walking under a tree and along the bank of a river, against a mustard yellow background of the water and the distant landscape of the far side. The usual titling, in black, is on the front cover and spine; the latter with two small fish printed in the background color beneath the author's name. This is the same as the fourth Thorpe except for color.
    The United States Catalog Supplement lists this as published in 1920 priced at $3.50 in cloth, and $15.00 in morocco.
    This is a reissue, with a new title-page, of the fourth Thorpe reprint of 1913 (No. 250).

263. The Fourth Marston Reprint

Oxford Edition
THE COMPLEAT ANGLER by Izaak Walton & Charles Cotton ...
Humphrey Milford Oxford University Press London Edinburgh
Glasgow Copenhagen New York Toronto Melbourne
Cape Town Bombay Calcutta Madras Shanghai Peking 1921

Copies examined: Harvard, Horne (2). Others: CLSU, IU, IaU, NN, OCU, OClCC.

Size: 7¾₆″ × 4⅞″.

Pagination summary: [i]-xliv, [1]-340.

The title-page verso is imprinted, "Printed by Hazell, Watson and Viney, Ltd., London and Aylesbury," which, since it ends with a comma, probably should have been followed by, "England" as in the repeat of this imprint at the foot of page 340. The Oxford mark is imprinted on the title-page within the outline of a shield.

The illustrations are the same as the third Marston (No. 255).

The "List of Editions" following the introduction was not updated from the third Marston of 1915.

This reprint was checked in two publisher's bindings. The *first* is in Oxford blue cloth, with a panel outlined on each cover by blind rules which cross and project at the corners to a blind rule on the edges of the covers. The Oxford mark is in gilt within a small decorated oval on the front cover. Three pairs of blind parallel rules divide the spine into four panels. Blind rules are at the foot and top of the gilt titled spine. The *second* is in brown cloth with the blind edging on the covers, the decorative design gilt stamped in the middle of the front cover, and the gilt edging at the foot and top of the spine all composed from type ornaments. The spine is titled in gilt.

This is a reprint with a new title-page, of the Third Marston edition of 1915 (No. 255).

[1922]

264. The Ninth Burt (50th Major) Reprint

THE COMPLETE ANGLER ... By Izaak Walton and
Charles Cotton ...
A. L. Burt Company, Publishers, New York [1922].

Copies examined: None seen.

According to Oliver (see his No. 245), who received his information from the publisher, this reprint in Burt's *Home Library* series was published on August 22, 1922. See also notes herein for No. 193, of which this is a later issue.

[1923]
265. The Tenth Burt (51st Major) Reprint

THE COMPLETE ANGLER . . . By Izaak Walton and
Charles Cotton . . .
A. L. Burt Company Publishers, New York [1923].

Copies examined: None seen.

According to Oliver (see his No. 239), who received his information from the publisher, this reprint in Burt's *Standard Library* series was published in 1923. See also notes herein for No. 258, of which this is a later issue.

[1923]
266. The Fourth Le Gallienne Reprint

THE COMPLEAT ANGLER by Izaak Walton and
Charles Cotton. . . .
John Lane The Bodley Head Limited London [1923].

Copies examined: Harvard, Horne, Yale. Other: NjP.

Size: $7\frac{3}{16}'' \times 4\frac{7}{8}''$.

Pagination summary: [i]-lxxxix, [5], [1]-454, [14], [12].

The imprint "Made and Printed in Great Britain by William Clowes and Sons, Limited, London and Beccles." is on the verso of the title-page (within a double rule) with its Cotton fishing house vignette. The 12 pages of advertising at the end are for John Lane publications.

The illustrations and errata are those cited for the third Le Gallienne reprint of 1904 (No. 212).

The publisher's binding is in gray cloth. The usual titling, and a Walton-Cotton cipher, within a double rule, are printed in very dark green on the spine. The front cover is stamped in the same color, with a parallel rule border, and an enlarged reproduction of the title-page vignette of Cotton's fishing house. The top edges are stained very dark green.

It is now established that there were two Le Gallienne *Anglers* published in 1923; this reprint, undated, with the title-page imprinted "London," and one with the title-page imprinted "New York," and dated 1923 (No. 267).

This London imprint of 1923 is the only Le Gallienne *Angler* seen that cannot be dated either from the title-page, or the imprint on the title-page verso. However, the 1926 and the 1931 Le Gallienne each list a reprinting for 1923. Moreover, *The English Catalogue of Books* lists a Le Gallienne *Angler* for April 1923 priced at 6s. that is accepted as this reprint.

This is a reissue from the same plates of the third Le Gallienne reprint of 1904 (No. 212), but was not published in the Crown Library series.

1923

267. The Fifth Le Gallienne Reprint

THE COMPLEAT ANGLER by Izaak Walton & Charles Cotton...
New York Dodd Mead and Company 1923

Copy examined: Princeton. Others: CtHT, ICarbS, NN, OClh.

Size: 7⁵⁄₁₆″ × 4⅝″.

Pagination summary: [i]-lxxix, [5], [1]-454, [14].

The imprint, "Made and Printed in Great Britain by William Clowes and Sons, Limited, London and Beccles." is on the verso of the title-page (within a double rule) with its Cotton fishing house vignette. The 12 pages of advertising in the fourth Le Gallienne, "London" edition (No. 266) are lacking.

With the title-page imprinted "New York," and dated 1923, this is the same as the "London" edition of the same date, and is a reissue of the Le Gallienne reprint of 1904 (No. 212). (For additional comments see preceding entry.)

[1924]

268. The Eleventh Burt (52nd Major) Reprint

THE COMPLETE ANGLER . . . By Izaak Walton and
Charles Cotton . . .
A. L. Burt Company, Publishers, New York [1924].

Copy examined: Yale.

Size: 7¼″ × 4¹⁵⁄₁₆″.

Pagination summary: [1-4] including frontispiece, [5]-354.

Except for a minute difference in size, the copy at Yale, which is dated 1924 in pencil, is in all other respects the same as the copy described as the third Burt edition, 1905 (No. 218).

According to Oliver, who received his information from the publisher (see his No. 247), such a reprint in Burt's *Home Library* series was published on January 24, 1924. See also notes herein for No. 193, of which this is a later issue.

[1925]
269. The Twelfth Burt (53rd Major) Reprint

THE COMPLETE ANGLER . . . By Izaak Walton and
Charles Cotton . . .
A. L. Burt Company, Publishers, New York [1925].

Copies examined: None.

According to Oliver (see his No. 250), who received his information from the publisher, this reprint in Burt's *Standard Library* series was published in May, 1925. See also notes herein for No. 258, of which this is a later issue.

1925
270. The Third Macmillan Reprint

THE COMPLETE ANGLER &
The Lives of Donne, Wotton Hooker, Herbert & Sanderson
By Izaak Walton
Macmillan and Co., Limited St. Martin's Street, London 1925

Copies examined: Harvard, Oliver, Princeton, Yale. Others: OCU, OClW.

Size: $8\frac{13}{16}'' \times 5\frac{5}{8}''$.

Pagination summary: [i]-xi, [xii], [1]-497, [498], [2]. The last leaf is Macmillan advertising.

The half-title and title-page are in red and black. The title-page verso is imprinted "Copyright. First printed in Library of English Classics, 1901. Reprinted 1906, 1925. Printed in Great Britain." At the foot of page 497 is imprinted "Printed in Great Britain by Robert Maclehose and Co. Ltd.

The University Press, Glasgow." Pollard's four-page Bibliographical Note is retained.

Other than music for the Anglers Song on pages 148 and 149, there are no illustrations.

The publisher's binding is in smooth blue cloth with a gilt titled spine. The leaf edges are untrimmed. The brown paper dust jacket is printed and decorated in blue with titling and the Macmillan cipher on front and spine ("7/6 net" also on spine). The back bears a list of 18 titles in the Macmillan "Library of English Classics" (including this reprint), edited by A. W. Pollard, and described as ". . . in Library Form 8vo. Cloth elegant . . ."

This is a reissue of the first Macmillan edition of 1901 (No. 198), in the "Library of English Classics."

[1925]
271. The Eighth Everyman (10th Lang) Reprint

THE COMPLEAT ANGLER by Izaak Walton
London & Toronto Published by J. M. Dent & Sons Ltd & in New York by E. P. Dutton & Co [1925].

Copies examined: Horne, Princeton, Yale. Other: MH.

Size: $6\frac{11}{16}'' \times 4\frac{1}{2}''$.

Pagination summary: [i]-xliv, [2], [1]-215, [216].

On the title-page verso is imprinted, "First Issue of this Edition 1906 Reprinted 1906, 1908, 1911, 1913, 1916, 1920, 1925." On page [216] is imprinted, "Made at the Temple Press Letchworth Great Britain."

The publisher's bindings examined are the same as that used for the second binding of the first Everyman (No. 228), except the top edges are black. The Horne copy is in a brown dust jacket, titled on the front cover and spine and with Dent advertising on the back cover and flaps. The half-title verso states that "There is also a Library edition in reinforced cloth."

This is a reissue of the first Everyman edition of 1906 (No. 228).

1925
272. The Sixth Thorpe Edition

THE COMPLETE ANGLER . . . by Izaak Walton . . .
T. N. Foulis Ltd. London & Edinburgh [1925]

Copies examined: Harvard, Horne, Princeton, Yale. Other: DLC.

Size: 9¼"×7".

Pagination summary: [i]-xvi, [1]-221.

On the title-page verso is imprinted, "Printed in Great Britain by T. and A. Constable Ltd. at the University Press Edinburgh."

The frontispiece is a full-color reproduction of the Huysman portrait of Walton, and there are 20 full-page color plates by James Thorpe (not mounted, as in earlier Thorpe issues). On the plate opposite page 120, Henly is still misspelled "Heny" (see No. 241). The publisher's binding is in marbled boards with a green cloth spine. The usual titling, and "T. N. Foulis" are gilt stamped on the spine. The top edges are stained a very dark green, the others are uncut. It was issued in a white paper dust jacket with the Thorpe color plate opposite page 52, ". . . get secretly behind the tree," on the front cover. The spine is titled at the top and "T. N. Foulis Ltd." is printed at the foot.

This edition is similar to the earlier Thorpe reprints except that Walton's "To all Readers . . .," omitted in some of the reprints, has been included. Marston's preface from the first Thorpe reprint was not reprinted.

The English Catalogue of Books lists this reprint as published in May, 1925, priced 12s. 6d. It may also be dated from the title-page verso imprinted, "New Edition 1925."

Oliver's report of the publication of a Thorpe reprint in 1927 (his No. 263) is now negated by evidence from the Princeton and Horne copies of this 1925 edition. On the spine of its dust jacket, described above, "Peter Davies" is imprinted just above "T. N. Foulis," which has been cancelled, indicating that, at some date after 1925, Peter Davies, Ltd., 30 Henrietta Street, London, took over the marketing of this edition. On the evidence of the *Davies Catalogue* description (1928), Oliver, who did not see a copy, assumed that a new edition had been issued, that Peter Davies was its publisher, and listed it as his number 263, dated 1927. No such edition was published.

1925

273. The Seventh Thorpe Reprint

THE COMPLETE ANGLER . . . by Izaak Walton
D Appleton and Company New York MCMXXV

Copies examined: Harvard, Princeton, Yale. Others: IU, NN, NcC.

Size: 9⁹⁄₁₆"×7".

Pagination summary: [i]-xvi, [1]-221.

On the title-page verso is imprinted, "New Edition 1925," and "Printed in Great Britain by T. and A. Constable Ltd. at the University Press Edinburgh." The title-page is imprinted with the publisher's device. The full-color frontispiece and 20 unmounted color plates are those of the Thorpe edition of 1925 (No. 272).

The publisher's binding is in marbled boards with a green cloth spine. The usual titling and "Appleton" are stamped in gilt on the spine. The top edges are stained green, the others are uncut.

This is a reissue, with a new title-page, of the sixth Thorpe edition (No. 272).

1925

274. The Navarre Society (54th Major) Reprint

THE COMPLETE ANGLER . . . of Izaak Walton and Charles Cotton . . .
London: Privately Printed for the Navarre Society Limited, 23 New Oxford Street, W.C. MCMXXV

Copies examined: Harvard, Horne, Princeton. Others: CtHT, CtY, DLC, NN, NcD.

Size: $8\frac{7}{8}'' \times 5\frac{3}{4}''$.

Pagination summary: [i-v], vi-[xvi], [1]-445.

The half-title is printed in red. On its half-title verso is imprinted, "This edition of *The Complete Angler,* edited by John Major, with eight etchings by Damman on Japon [sic] Vellum, is printed upon paper specially made for this edition and is strictly limited." The title-page is printed in red and black. On its verso appears, "Printed in Great Britain by the Riverside Press Limited Edinburgh."

In addition to the Damman etchings, which originally appeared in the Nimmo and Bain reprint of 1883 (No. 114), there are 74 wood engravings reproduced from the Major edition of 1844 (No. 55).

The publisher's binding is in bright green cloth. The front cover, bordered with a blind parallel rule, is gilt stamped with the title-page cartouche of the 1653 edition. The spine, gilt bordered top and foot with a parallel rule and blossoms, is gilt titled, and panelled with a single rule. "Navarre Society" is gilt stamped at the foot of the panel. The top edges are gilt, the others are untrimmed.

This is a reprint, with a new title-page and half-title, from the same plates of the first Little, Brown edition of 1866 (No. 87) which is from the Major edition of 1844 (No. 55).

[1925]

275. The First Nelson Edition

THE COMPLEAT ANGLER by Izaak Walton and Charles Cotton.
Thomas Nelson and Sons Ltd.
London Edinburgh New York Toronto and Paris [1925].

Copies examined: Harvard, Horne.

Size: 6⅛″ × 4¼″.

Collation: ([1]⁴, 1a¹²) — (8⁴, 8a¹²), 9³, 9a¹³.

Pagination summary: [i-iv], v-[viii], 9-283, [4].

The half-title and the title-page are printed in black only. At the foot of page 283 is imprinted, "Printed in Great Britain at the Press of the Publishers." The four last pages advertise the *Nelson Classics* where this edition is listed in cloth gilt, priced at 1s. 6d. net.

The only illustration is the music on pages 174 and 175.

The publisher's binding is in light tan cloth with the titling gilt stamped on the spine. The publisher advises that it was issued in wrappers.

The publisher has reported (1967) that the Nelson Cloth Classics edition (this *Angler*) was first published in 1925, the Winchester Classics (No. 306) in 1934, The Parkside Classics (No. 368) in 1961; that they all contain the same sheets, "reset some years ago," and that the binding and dust jacket of the Cloth Classics were changed from time to time.

This *Angler,* listed in *The English Catalogue* as having been published in July, 1925, is from the fifth edition of 1676 (No. 6), with "The Epistle to the Reader" from the first (1653) and second (1655) editions added.

1926

276. The Second Nelson Reprint

THE COMPLEAT ANGLER by Izaak Walton and Charles Cotton
Thomas Nelson and Sons New York 1926

Copies examined: Harvard, Horne. Other: NN.

Size: 6 1/16″ × 4 1/16″.

Pagination summary: [i-iv], v-[viii], 9-283.

The half-title and title-page are printed in red and black. The half-title reads, "New Century Library Izaak Walton and Charles Cotton The Compleat

Angler." On the title-page verso and at the foot of page 283 is imprinted "Printed in Great Britain at the Press of the Publishers."

The publisher's binding seen is in dark blue limp leather with green marbled end papers. The outer edges of the covers, and the top and foot of the spine, are bordered with a single blind rule. The title, with a small fish and a fly is gilt stamped on the front cover. Titling, and a columnar decoration featuring five vertical rules, are in gilt on the spine. The top edges are gilt, and an orange silk bookmark is included. It was issued boxed titled in white.

This reissue of the first Nelson edition, printed on India paper, except as noted above, is unchanged from the 1925 edition (No. 275).

[1926]
277. The Thirteenth Burt (55th Major) Reprint

THE COMPLETE ANGLER . . . by Izaak Walton and Charles Cotton . . .
A. L. Burt Company, Publishers, New York [1926].

Copies examined: Harvard, Yale.

Size: 7¾₁₆″ × 5″.

Pagination summary: [1-4] including frontispiece, [5]-354.

According to Oliver, who received his information from the publisher (see his No. 259), such a reprint in Burt's *Home Library* series was published on March 16, 1926.

Both copies are in the same red cloth binding, with top edges gilt, as the other copies checked in this series, and also like the others, have *Home Library* stamped in gilt on the spine.

The Harvard copy was received there on March 10, 1930; it and the Yale copy are tentatively dated 1926. This is the nearest year prior to 1930 for which Oliver reports a reissue to have appeared in the *Home Library* series.

[1926]
278. The Sixth Le Gallienne Reprint

THE COMPLEAT ANGLER by Izaak Walton & Charles Cotton . . .
John Lane The Brodley Head Limited London [1926].

Copies examined: Boston Public Library, Horne, Princeton. Others: CU, CtHT, OClW, PP, PU, RPB.

Size: $6\frac{7}{8}'' \times 4\frac{3}{4}''$.

Pagination summary: [i]-lxxxix, [5], [1]-454, [14], [12].

The title-page verso is imprinted, "Made and Printed in Great Britain by William Clowes and Sons, Limited, London and Beccles."
    This is a reprint with the same illustrations and errata as described for the third Le Gallienne edition of 1904 (No. 212).
    The publisher's binding is the same as for the fourth Le Gallienne (No. 266).
    This issue is dated from the title-page verso, imprinted, "First published in 1897, Reprinted in 1903, 1923, 1926." For the final issue, see No. 297.

1926

279. The First Japanese Edition

Kenkyusha English Classics

THE COMPLETE ANGLER, . . . by Izaak Walton.
Tokyo Kenkyusha 1926

Copies examined: Harvard Yale. Other: NN.

Size: $7\frac{3}{8}'' \times 4\frac{13}{16}''$.

Pagination summary: [16], [i]-xxvii, [1], xxviii, [1], i-vi, [1]-338, [2].

On the verso of the last leaf is an imprint in Japanese headed, "Kenkyusha English Classics." On page 129 the running head has the misprint "Atgler" for "Angler."
    The illustrations consists of a frontispiece of Walton after Huysman, a facsimile of the title-page to Part I of the fifth edition of 1676 (No. 6), and three full-page plates of fish cuts from the 1676 edition, two with three fish each and one with four fish. There are also two pages of music.
    The introduction in Japanese and the notes in English are by Y. Okakura who, with S. Ichikawa were the general editors of the Kenkyusha English Classics. There is a list of *Angler* editions from 1653-1900. Walton's text is in English, followed by notes in Japanese and some comments in English.
    The publisher's binding of both copies seen is in red cloth. The edges of the front cover are single ruled in gilt with a winged lion gilt stamped in the center; the back cover is plain except for a single rule blind stamped on the edges; titling and a decorative tree are in gilt on the spine.
    A letter, dated Tokyo, Aug. 23, 1926, to the Harvard Librarian, Mr. Lane, is attached to the front end paper of the copy given to Harvard by the editor.

In its postscript, Okakura reports, "I have so far failed to come across a Japanese translation of *The Compleat Angler*; I am rather glad that none of my compatriot [*sic*] has been bold enough to attempt one. The work does not easily lend itself to an appearance in a foreign clothing. . . ."

This edition is from Part I of the fifth edition of 1676 (No. 6).

[1927]

280. The Fourteenth Burt (56th Major) Reprint

THE COMPLETE ANGLER . . . by Izaak Walton and Charles Cotton . . .

A. L. Burt Company, Publishers, New York [1927].

Copy examined: Oliver.

Size: 6¾″ × 4⁵⁄₁₆″.

Pagination summary: [1-2 (lacking)]; [3-4], title recto, verso blank; [5]-354. Same as No. 258.

This reprint is one of Burt's *Standard Library* series, and is a reissue, with same title-page and illustrations, of the seventh Burt (1918, No. 258).

It was issued bound in light red imitation leather, with white end papers; top edges gilt. The front cover has a blind rule border, and is gilt stamped with the encircled book and torch device of No. 258. The spine is gilt titled. The dust jacket is light red printed in black with a floral border text and the publisher's device. Its back and flaps list 124 titles (including this one) in Burt's "Pocket Edition of Standard Classics," priced $1.00 per volume, ". . . to be had uniform with this volume."

The copy examined is that reported by Oliver (his No. 252) who, informed by the publisher that this reprint was published May 3, 1927, so dated his copy.

[1927]

281. The Second Collins Reprint

THE COMPLEAT ANGLER | or the Contemplative Man's | Recreation |

by Izaak Walton & Charles Cotton | Illustrated by J, Eyre RBA

Copy examined: Horne.

Size: $5\frac{15}{16}'' \times 3\frac{15}{16}''$.

Pagination summary: [1]-280, [6].

The only printer's imprint is at the foot of page 280, which reads, *"Manufactured in Great Britain."* The half-title and printed title-page of the first Collins are omitted. The above title-page data are from the photogravure title-page with the oval portraits of Walton and Cotton, but no publisher's name or imprint which is the same as that which preceded the printed title-page in the first Collins (No. 236). The six terminal pages list Collins' publications, where this reprint is number 88 of the *Illustrated Pocket Classics*. The volumes in this series are priced, "Cloth, 2/net. Leather, Gilt top, 4/net," which is double the 1908 price.

    The illustrations consist of a frontispiece titled "The little fishing-house," and six plates, all in photogravure, and ten woodcuts of fish, all from the first Collins.

    The red cloth used for the publisher's binding checked appears to be the same as the 1908 reprint. The blind rule on the edges of the covers and the dark red end papers are the same, but there is no bookmark. The spine is titled in gilt between small gilt decorations and, at the foot, "Collins" is stamped in gilt between gilt rules.

    This is a reissue of the first Collins edition of 1908 (No. 236), which is from Parts I and II of the fifth edition of 1676 (No. 6). The date is from Oliver, whose authority was a letter from the publisher.

[1927]

282. The First Haldeman-Julius Edition

Big Blue Book No. B-11 Edited by E. Haldeman-Julius
THE COMPLEAT ANGLER Izaak Walton
Haldeman-Julius Company Girard, Kansas [1927].

Copy examined: Harvard. Other: KPT.

Size: $8\frac{1}{2}'' \times 5\frac{1}{2}''$.

Pagination summary: [1-5], 6-123, [5].

The five pages of terminal advertising are Little Blue Books at five cents each. There are no illustrations, notes, or introduction, and the Walton's "The Epistle to the Reader" is omitted. This undated edition was issued in blue-gray wrappers with the title-page repeated on the front wrapper.

    Through the courtesy of Gene De Gruson, Curator of the Haldeman-Julius Room at the Porter Library, Kansas State College of Pittsburg,

Kansas, the publication date of this edition is established as August 10, 1927, and although the printing record is not available, a standard run of the classics in 1927 was one of 10,000 copies.

It is a reprint from Part I of the fifth edition of 1676 (No. 6).

1927

283. The Second Haldeman-Julius Reprint

THE COMPLEAT ANGLER Izaak Walton
Haldeman-Julius Company Girard, Kansas [1927].

Copies examined: None seen. Other: KPT.

Size reported: 21.5 cm.

Pagination reported: 128 pp. [last two lvs. blank].

This reissue of the First Haldeman-Julius edition differs only in change of title and author's name as reported above on the front wrapper, and with the Girard Typographical Union label imprinted on the lower right corner of the back wrapper.

Gene De Gruson (see No. 282) kindly supplied the following information: "This second issue was catalogued as Big Blue Book No. B-355 from December 12, 1927, when Joseph McCabe's *Life Among the Many Peoples of the Earth (Key to Anthropology and Philology)*, Key to Culture Series No. 11, replaced it as catalogue item 11. The last copies in print were advertised by Henry Haldeman after E. Haldeman-Julius' death in 1951 as number 5355. Printing records for this title were destroyed by Mr. Haldeman in 1951."

This reissue of the first Haldeman-Julius edition of August 10, 1927 (No. 282) is from Part I of the fifth edition of 1676 (No. 6).

[1927]

284. The First Daglish (57th Major) Edition

THE COMPLEAT ANGLER . . . by Izaak Walton &
Charles Cotton . . .
Thornton Butterworth Limited 15 Bedford Street,
London, W.C. [1927].

Copies examined: Harvard, Horne, Princeton. Others: CtHT, CtY, NNC, PBL, ViU.

Size: regular "edition," $9^{11}/_{16}'' \times 7^{9}/_{16}''$;
    large paper "edition de luxe," $11^{11}/_{16}'' \times 9^{1}/_{8}''$.

Pagination summary: [1-8], 9-367.

On the title-page verso (which identifies the large paper state as above) is imprinted, "Made and printed in Great Britain" and at the foot of page 367, "Printed in Great Britain by Butler & Tanner Ltd., Frome and London." The circular device of the publisher appears on the title-page of both the regular and large paper states.

The illustrations consist of 16 wood engravings by Eric Fitch Daglish enumerated in the "List of Illustrations" on page 11; plus Archer's headpiece of the Walton's biographees, the Donne seal ring, and two pages of music that are not listed. The large paper state has an extra plate, signed by the artist, mounted on the verso of a leaf tipped under the front lining paper, with descriptive letterpress on the recto.

The regular "edition" has two changes in the text captions of the "List of Illustrations," which, since the descriptions on the tissue guards were not changed to correspond with the "List," resulted in different readings. Opposite page 146 the tissue guards reads, "The Salmon-Leap;" in the "List of Illustrations" the caption reads, "This leap or summersault of the Salmon." Opposite page 174 the tissue guard reads, "The Bream: He is very broad, with a forked tail, and his scales set in excellent order." The "List" omits "The Bream."

The large paper "edition deluxe," limited to 100 copies, was issued in parchment-backed boards covered with modernistic brownish-black and white zigzag design paper. A small leaping fish, in addition to the usual titling, are stamped in brown on the spine. The leaf edges are untrimmed. The regular "edition" was bound in cream-colored smooth cloth covers, with the spine in a slightly ribbed cloth of a somewhat darker shade. A small leaping fish is stamped in black on the front cover and the spine. It was issued in a dust jacket.

As stated on the title-page verso, "This edition is reprinted from Major's edition of 1889 and is published in 1927." There were three reprints of the Major edition in 1889, the third Nimmo, fourth Nimmo, and first Putnam Nimmo. All of these were reprints from the same plates of the first Little, Brown edition of 1866 (No. 87), which is from the Major edition of 1844 (No. 55). *The English Catalogue of Books* reports November, 1927, as the publication date with the regular "edition" priced at 42s and the large paper state at 5 guineas.

285. The Second Daglish (58th Major) Reprint

THE COMPLEAT ANGLER . . . by Izaak Walton &
Charles Cotton . . .
New York E. P. Dutton & Company 681 Fifth Avenue [1927].

Copies examined: Harvard, Horne, Princeton. Others: CtY, MiU, PBL, Vi.

Size: $9\frac{7}{8}'' \times 7\frac{5}{8}''$.

Pagination summary: [1-8], 9-367.

On the title-page verso is imprinted, "Made and printed in Great Britain"
and at the foot of page 367, "Printed in Great Britain by Butler & Tanner Ltd.,
Frome and London."
   The illustrations are those of the first Daglish.
   The publisher's binding is salmon boards with a tan cloth spine, the latter
imprinted with a double rule top and foot and the usual titling in black.
Pasted on the upper right corner of the front cover is a restrike of "The
Salmon-Leap" engraving, used also on the dust wrapper. The top edges are
stained light brown and the end papers are pinkish-tan with an overall
pattern in black. It was issued in a slipcase.
   This is from the same plates of the first Daglish edition and was probably
printed simultaneously with its two states (see No. 284), differing from the
regular state of that edition only in the title-page with its American imprint
and distributor, and in the binding.

[1928]

286. The Ninth Everyman (11th Lang) Reprint

THE COMPLEAT ANGLER by Izaak Walton
London & Toronto Published by J. M. Dent & Sons Ltd & in
New York by E. P. Dutton & Co [1928].

Copies examined: Horne, Princeton, Yale.

Size: $6\frac{11}{16}'' \times 4\frac{3}{16}''$.

Pagination summary: [i]-xliv, [2], [1]-215, [216], [8].

At the foot of page 215 is imprinted, "Made at the Temple Press Letchworth
in Great Britain." There are eight terminal pages of advertising for *Everyman's
Library* where this edition is listed as number 70.
   The Yale and Horne copies are in the same binding as that used for the

second binding of the first Everyman (No. 228), except the top edges are stained very dark green. The front and spine of the light blue paper dust jacket (of the Horne copy) are imprinted in black with Everyman devices and titling of the *Angler*, but with "Izaac" instead of "Izaak" as on the title-page. Ninety-one of the 400 Everyman authors including Walton, are listed on the jacket's back, and the *Angler* is included among the Everyman titles listed on the flaps. The Princeton copy is in grayish-brown cloth, titled on the spine in gilt. The half-title verso states that "There is also a Library edition in reinforced cloth."

The date of this reprint is on the title-page verso, preceded by the dates of the earlier *Anglers* in this series. It is a reissue of the first Everyman edition of 1906 (No. 228).

1928

287. The First Black Facsimile

THE COMPLEAT ANGLER . . .
London, Printed by T. Maxey for Rich. Marriot . . . 1653. [1928].

Copies examined: Harvard, Horne (2), Virginia. Others: CU-A, CtY, ICN, IU, MiU, NBu, NjP, OCU.

Size: $5\frac{5}{8}'' \times 3\frac{9}{16}''$.

Pagination summary: [16], (1)-246.

On the title-page verso is imprinted, "This facsimile of the first edition of "The Compleat Angler" is reproduced from the copy in the Grenville Collection at the British Museum and published by A. & C. Black, Ltd., Soho Square, London. 1928."

The illustrations consist of the six cuts of fish and two facing pages of music, the second of which is printed upside down as in the first edition. The catchword "to" on page 123 is omitted and, on page 245, line 8, the last word, "loves" reads "lov" as if cut by the binder. This facsimile has 42 of the 48 irregularities listed in Appendix B.

This edition was issued in a slipcase with a beige-colored dust jacket. On the front cover is stated, *inter alia*, "Letterpress and illustrations have been reproduced with photographic accuracy . . . and in all details of binding, paper, plate marking, eccentric pagination, etc., the first edition has been closely followed. Bound, as was the first edition in full brown sheep." The publisher's binding is as described, with the edges speckled with minute red dots. There is no titling or decoration except a blind tooled rule on the edges of the front and back covers, and seven blind tooled rules on the spine creating six panels. The usual titling and "A facsimile of the first edition 1653" is on the spine of the dust jacket; on the back is the circular device of the publisher. The case for this facsimile has paper title labels on the front side and spine.

The English Catalogue of Books reports the publication date as June, 1928 and the selling price as 10s 6d (the latter so stated in the Prospectus).

It is related by Oliver (p. 252), that a copy of this facsimile, with simulated aging of leaves achieved by staining with coffee, appeared at an auction in London some years ago, the fraud being exposed at the last minute, when someone detected the odor of the coffee.

It is the best of the facsimiles of the first edition produced to date.

1928

288. The Goodspeed (Bliss Perry) Edition

THE COMPLETE ANGLER . . . by Izaak Walton . . .
Boston C. E. Goodspeed & Co. 1928

Copies examined: Harvard, Horne, Princeton. Others: CSmH, CtHT, CU, DLC, FU, InU, MB, NBU, NSyU, NjN, PSC, ViU, ViW.

Size: $6\frac{7}{8}'' \times 4\frac{5}{8}''$.

Pagination summary: [i-iv], v-[xxxii], [1]-[324], [2].

There are three half-titles: preceding the title-page, Walton's dedication, and the text. The title-page is printed in red and black. On its verso is imprinted, "Copyright, 1928, by C. E. Goodspeed & Co." The statement "Printed in the United States of America," at the foot of the same page, is reported by Oliver, on information from Mr. Goodspeed, to have been omitted in three copies. The colophon at the end states, "Of this Edition of The Complete Angler six hundred copies have been printed by D. B. Updike The Merry-mont Press, Boston in the Month of April 1928." The introduction is by Bliss Perry.

The illustrations consist of five chapter headpieces by W. A. Dwiggins.

The publisher, C. E. Goodspeed, wrote of this edition, "When I saw the final result . . . I felt that this book indeed approached perfection." (*Yankee Bookseller* Boston, 1937, page 161.)

This edition was issued in a cardboard slipcase. The covers of the publisher's binding are boards covered with gray paper decorated in a green pattern of squares enclosing alternate figures of a stylized tree and a fisherman sitting cross-legged. Five gilt bands divide the spine into four blank and one gilt titled panel at the top. The top edges of the leaves are stained dark green, the others are untrimmed. The edition was priced at $12.50.

This edition is from Part I of the fifth edition of 1676 (No. 6).

289. The Third Collins Reprint

THE COMPLETE ANGLER by Izaak Walton and
Charles Cotton . . .
London and Glasgow: Collins' Clear-Type Press [1929].

Copies examined: None seen.

Size reported: 12mo.

Pagination reported: 280 pages.

From information received from the publisher, Oliver reported that "this
is a reissue of the earlier Collins reprints of the fifth edition of 1676." (See
Nos. 236 and 281 herein.)

290. The Third Nelson Reprint

THE COMPLEAT ANGLER by Izaak Walton and Charles Cotton
T. Nelson & Sons, Ltd. [1929]

Copies examined: Harvard, Oliver.

Size: $6\frac{1}{8}'' \times 4\frac{1}{4}''$.

Collation: $[1]^{16} - 9^{16}$.

Pagination summary: [i-iv], v-[viii], 9-283, [5].

The title-page has a woodcut border. On its verso and at the foot of page 283
is imprinted, "Printed in Great Britain at the Press of the Publishers." The
change in collation from the first Nelson is the resetting without revision
reported by the publisher (see No. 275).

The five terminal pages advertise *Nelson's Classics* (this reprint unlisted) in
cloth at 1s. 6d. net. The foot of the last page reads, "T. Nelson & Sons, Ltd.,
London, Edinburgh, & New York."

The only illustration consists of music on pages 174 and 175.

The publisher's binding is in light red cloth with the spine gilt titled. Two
panels are blind ruled on front cover, the upper one containing a circular
band of thistles in blind. A blind stamped thistle is in each small square
formed at the corners of the projection of the panel rules to the blind ruled
edges. The spine, titled in gilt, has a blind stamped thistle at top and foot.

The date assigned this reprint is not verifiable from publisher's records
in London, since they were destroyed by bombings. However, the publisher
has no evidence that it is incorrect.

[1929]

291. The De La More Abridged Edition

SONGS FROM THE COMPLEAT ANGLER
London at the De La More Press [1929]

Copies examined: Harvard, Horne.

Size: 7½" × 5."

Pagination summary: [1-4], 5-20.

On the half-title recto above the publisher's device, is imprinted, "The Saint George Series Published by Alexander Moring Limited, The De La More Press, 2A Cork Street, Bond Street, London, W.I." The titling is within a small square portion of the full-page woodcut on the title-page. Its verso is imprinted, "Publishers' Note. This edition of selected songs from 'The Compleat Angler,' by Isaac Walton, is decorated with drawings [eleven] in black & white by Miss A. G. Holman, and was first printed in 1929."
    The publisher's binding is in light green paper over boards, with the title-page repeated on the front cover. The spine has no identification.
    With modernized spelling, the seven songs and short prose selection which make up this abridged edition, are from Part I of the fifth edition of 1676 (No. 6). *The English Catalogue of Books* lists it as published in December, 1929.

1929

292. The Nonesuch (First Keynes) Edition

Izaak Walton The Compleat Angler
The Lives of Donne Wotton Hooker Herbert & Sanderson
With Love and Truth & Miscellaneous Writings . . .
The Nonesuch Press 16 Great James Street Bloomsbury 1929

Copies examined: Harvard, Horne, Princeton. Others: CSt, CU-A, CU-S, CtHT, CtY, DFo, DLC, ICU, IU, InU, NN, NcU, OC, OCU, PU, ViU, WU.

Size: 8³⁄₁₆" × 5⅛".

Pagination summary: [i-iv], v-x, [1]-631.

On the verso of page 631 is imprinted, "Printed and made in England." On page v is imprinted, "This edition consists of 1100 copies for sale in England by the Nonesuch Press and 500 copies for sale in the United States by Random House Inc. The text has been printed by R. & R. Clark in Edinburgh, the copperplate engravings by A. Alexander and Son in London; the drawings have been colour-stencilled by the Curwen Press, London: all under the care of Francis Meynell." The Nonesuch device on the title-page is a variation of the design by Stephen Gooden.

The illustrations consist of ten drawings of fish by T. L. Poulton, stencil colored by the Curwen Press. The frontispiece of Walton, and the portraits of the five biographees in the *Lives*, are interpreted by C. Sigrist from 17th-century portraits and printed from copper engravings by A. Alexander. Poulton also drew John Donne's seals, which are printed in red. There are also two pages of music.

In the "Appraisal" section of *The Nonesuch Century*, London, The Nonesuch Press, 1936, A. J. A. Symons wrote (page 18), "The Compleat Walton, No. 61, on the other hand, is delightfully readable, and is in every way a satisfying book. It is the only complete Walton."

This edition was issued in a slipcase marbled to match the end papers, and was published August 13, 1929, priced at three guineas. It was bound in full niger rust-colored morocco with marbled end papers. In gilt on the front cover is "I. W." within a decorative oval of printer's flowers. The only wording on the six compartment spine is, *The Compleat Walton*. The top edges are rough gilt, the others untrimmed.

The text is from the fourth edition of 1668 (No. 5). It was edited, with a life of Walton and bibliographical notes, by Sir Geoffrey L. Keynes, noted bibliographer, editor, and surgeon.

[1930]

293. The Fourteenth Davies Reprint

THE COMPLETE ANGLER by Izaac Walton and
Charles Cotton . . .
Frederick Warne & Co., Limited London and New York [1930].

Copies examined: Harvard, Horne.

Size: 7″ × 4⅞″.

Pagination summary: [i]-xii, [1]-467.

The Warne device of the Wings and Horseshoe measuring 1.8 centimeters between the tips of the wings, is on the title-page, on the verso of which is, "Printed in Great Britain," and, at the foot of page 467 is imprinted, "Printed by Purnell and Sons Paulton (Somerset) and London." There is no advertising leaf at the end.

This is a reissue of the second Davies of 1878 (No. 102) which was the first printing in the *Chandos Classics*. On the decorative end papers, it is designated "The Chandos Classics." All the important illustrations from the earlier edition are repeated, but many of the decorative chapter headings, a few of the flower woodcuts, and three elaborate initials have been eliminated.

Two publisher's bindings have been examined. The *first* (the Harvard copy), is in red cloth with decorative end papers (see above) and the usual titling in gilt on the spine. "The Chandos Classics" under the Warne Wings and Horseshoe are both blind stamped on the front cover. The *second* (the Horne copy apparently as issued by the publisher), is in full dark brown morocco, with light brown end papers. The front cover is paneled by three gilt rules along the edges with a gilt decoration at each corner, used also somewhat reduced with the gilt titling of both the front cover and the spine. The top edges of the leaves are gilt and a brown ribbon bookmark is provided.

The publisher has advised that this reprint was published in 1930, and is the last *Angler* produced to date by Warne. *The English Catalogue of Books* reports May, 1930, as the publication date, 2s 6d as the price, and lists it as one of the *Chandos Classics*.

There are four Warne-Davies *Anglers* with both New York and London imprint on the title-page; this reprint, the seventh of 1888 (No. 133), the 10th of 1893 (No. 163), and the 12th of 1895 (No. 166).

1930

294. The Third Daglish (59th Major) Reprint

THE COMPLEAT ANGLER . . . by Izaak Walton &
Charles Cotton . . .
London: Thornton Butterworth, Ltd.
(15 Bedford Street, Strand W.C.2). 1930

Copies examined: None seen.

Size reported: 10¼" × 7¾".

Pagination reported: pp. 368. Illustrated by E. Fitch Daglish.

Oliver (his No. 274) reported the descriptive data above from the Andrew Oliver copy of this reprint of the first Daglish edition of 1927 (No. 284). *The English Catalogue of Books* reports November, 1930 as its publication date, priced at 21 shillings.

[1930]

295. The Mason Abridged Edition

TWO PROSE IDYLLS
Abridgements of "The Compleat Angler," by Izaak Walton and
"Our Village," by Mary Russell Mitford. . . .
Thomas Nelson and Sons, Ltd. London, Edinburgh, and
New York [1930].

Copy examined: British Museum.

Size: 6⅛″ × 4³⁄₁₆″.

Pagination summary: [i-iv], v-vi, [7]-[256].

On the title-page verso is imprinted, "First published June 1930."
   The illustrations for *The Compleat Angler* consist of eight halftone plates on glossy paper reproduced from the Bagster and Ephemera editions (see Nos. 17 and 68): "Presenting The Chub at the Trout Inn" and "The Meeting;" stream insects; artificial fly making; natural stream flies; artificial flies; and two plates each with three fish. There is also a woodcut of a salmon fly.
   The *Angler* ends on page 135. The abridgement of *Our Village* ends on page 241, followed by two pages of music for "The Anglers Song." Pages 244-249 are "Appendix A" containing a few notes about Walton and "Some suggestions for Further Study" raising questions about the "Angler" for classroom discussion; pages 250-255, "Appendix B," in the format of *Our Village*, and page [256], a final "Appendix C" with "Further Suggestions" for the two books together.
   This edition is number 163 in the Nelson's "Teaching of English" Series, for which Sir Henry Newbolt was General Editor.
   The binding is in blue buckram.
   This abridged edition has not been reported in previous bibliographies of the *Angler*.

1930

296. The Adams Edition

THE COMPLEAT ANGLER . . . by Izaak Walton . . .
MCMXXX Published by Eyre & Spottiswoode (Publishers)
Limited London
and in New York by Charles Scribner's Sons.

Copies examined: Harvard, Horne, Princeton. Others: CtHT, CtY, ICU, MB, NN, NNC, OC, OU.

Size: 13⁷⁄₁₆″×8⁹⁄₁₆″.

Pagination summary: [10], [1]-124.

The title-page is printed in red and black within parallel rules and its verso, signed by Adams, states "This Edition, numbered and signed by the Artist, is limited to 450 copies, of which 250 are for sale in the British Empire and 200 copies in the United States of America." Subscribers received a special bookplate, inscribed with their name and the number of their copy, ruled and printed in gilt and pasted on the cover of the black box in which this edition was issued.

The decorative illustrations, all by Frank Adams, consists of a frontispiece color plate of Walton after the Huysman portrait, and nine chapter headings in color, each framed with elaborate piscatorial pen work; and 14 reproductions of his pen and ink drawings that include four chapter headings and ten tailpieces. Adams also designed the initial letters for the chapter headings.

The publisher issued this edition in vellum backed marbled boards with the spine titled in gilt. The top edges are gilt, the others untrimmed. It is covered with a white paper wrapper. Its box of issue, black with a red lining, identified on the top as mentioned above, is titled on the edge with a paper label.

The English Catalogue reports the publication date as November, 1930, and the price 4 guineas. It is from the first edition of 1653 (No. 1).

[1931]
297. The Seventh Le Gallienne Reprint

THE COMPLEAT ANGLER By Izaak Walton & Charles Cotton ...
London: John Lane The Bodley Head Ltd.
New York: Dodd, Mead and Company [1931].

Copies examined: Horne (2), Princeton. Other: NN.

Size: 7¹⁄₆″×4⁷⁄₈″.

Pagination summary: [i]-lxxxix, [5], [1]-454, [14], [4].

The title-page verso is imprinted, "Made and Printed in Great Britain by William Clowes and Sons, Limited, London and Beccles."

This is a reprint, with the same illustrations and errata as described for the third Le Gallienne edition of 1904 (No. 212), except that there are only four pages of advertising at the end for John Lane publications.

The publisher's binding, in light tan cloth, is otherwise the same as the fourth Le Gallienne reprint of 1923 (No. 266).

This issue is dated from the title-page verso, imprinted, "First Published in 1897, Reprinted in 1903, 1923, 1926, 1931."

[1931]

298. The Fourth Collins Reprint

THE COMPLETE ANGLER by Izaak Walton and
Charles Cotton . . .
London and Glasgow: Collins' Clear-Type Press [1931].

Copies examined: None seen.

Size reported: 12mo.

Pagination reported: 280 pages.

According to information which Oliver received from the publisher, "this is a re-issue of the earlier Collins reprints of the fifth edition of 1676." (See Nos. 236 and 281 herein.)

1931

299. The First Rackham Edition

THE COMPLEAT ANGLER . . . by Izaak Walton . . .
London: George C. Harrap & Co. Ltd [1931]

Copies examined: Harvard, Horne, Princeton, Trinity. Others: CLSU, CtY, InU, MiU, NN, ViU.

Size: 10¼″ × 7⁹⁄₁₆″.

Pagination summary: [1-4], 5-223, [224].

On the title-page verso is imprinted, "Published 1931" and "Printed in Great Britain by the Riverside Press Limited Edinburgh." Here also the publishers "acknowledge the courtesy of Messrs John Lane the Bodley Head, Limited, in permitting the use of their edition edited by Richard Le Gallienne, first published in 1897 [No. 177]. The text is from the fifth edition of 1676 . . ." Only Walton's part, with the spelling modernized, is included in this reprint. The Le Gallienne editing, however, has been eliminated and a preface by Henry Williamson has been substituted.

The illustrations, all by Arthur Rackham, consist of 12 color plates, 13 tailpieces, nine headpieces, two text illustrations, the title-page vignette, and decorated end paper. The vignette and words "The Compleat Angler" on the title-page are printed in green. The plates are accompanied by guard sheets with descriptive letterpress.

This limited edition consisted of 775 copies signed by Rackham, of which the first 12, with an original water color drawing, were especially bound in green morocco gilt. The rest were issued in full vellum, with the end paper decorations printed in brown on cream paper. Three rules in gilt are on the edges of the front cover which is titled in gilt as is the spine, the latter decorated with a gilt fish, which is a repeat of the tailpiece to Chapter XII. 1931 is gilt stamped at the foot of the spine. The copies in vellum, with the top edges gilt, others untrimmed, were issued in a spine titled cardboard slipcase. The first 12 copies were priced £75- each, the vellum copies 63s.

The English Catalogue of Books reports August 31, 1931 as the date of publication.

[1931]

300. The Second Rackham Reprint

THE COMPLEAT ANGLER . . . by Izaak Walton . . . London: George C. Harrap & Co. Ltd. [1931].

Copies examined: Horne (2), Yale.

Size: 9¾" × 7⅟₁₆".

Pagination summary: [1-4], 5-223, [224].

On the title-page verso is imprinted, "This reprint first published in 1931" and "Printed in Great Britain by the Riverside Press Limited Edinburgh."

This is a reissue of the August, 1931 printing of the first Rackham edition (No. 299). The publisher advises that 5,000 copies were printed.

This reprint has been examined in two different bindings. The *first* is in very dark green full morocco, with end paper decorations printed in dark blue on grayish-green paper. The front cover, titled in gilt (as is the spine), has a parallel gilt rule along the edges. The fish stamped in gilt on the front cover and spine repeats the tailpiece to Chapter XII. The top edges are gilt. It was wrapped in glassine and issued in a cardboard box, covered with mottled brown paper with a paper label pasted on one end of the top. The *second* is in dark bluish-green cloth, with end paper decorations as above. The front cover and spine are titled in gilt, both decorated with a gilt fish; that of the front cover repeats the tailpiece (here with a background added) to Chapter III, the fish on the spine is the same as on the morocco binding.

The top edges are gilt. The dust jacket has the color plate opposite page 82 reproduced on the front cover, and titling and piscatorial decoration in red and black at the top; at the foot, next to his name, Rackham portrayed himself in the form of a medieval manuscript grotesque. The spine, titled in red and black, has a blue ship publisher's device above "Harrap" in red at the foot. Two Harrap publications are advertised on the inside of the front flap.

The English Catalogue of Books reports this reprint as published September 30, 1931, priced at 15s. and in leather at 25s.

[1931]

301. The Third Rackham (McKay) Reprint

THE COMPLEAT ANGLER . . . by Izaak Walton . . .
Philadelphia David McKay Co [1931].

Copies examined: Boston Public, Horne (2), Princeton. Others: CtHT, DLC, FU, ICU, NSyU, NcRS, OO, OCl, PPGL.

Size: 9⅞" × 7⅜".

Pagination summary: [1-4], 5-223, [224].

On the title-page verso (undated here) is imprinted, "Printed in Great Britain by the Riverside Press Limited Edinburgh."
   This is a reissue of the first Rackham edition (No. 299). The publisher advises that 5,000 copies were printed.
   The publisher's binding in light green cloth is otherwise the same as the second binding of the second Rackham, and the same color plate, titling, and decoration is reproduced on the front of the dust jacket, but with the blue publisher's device eliminated and "McKay" printed in red at the foot. There is no publisher's advertising on the flaps.
   This reprint is listed in the *Cumulative Book Index* as published by McKay in 1931 priced at $3.50. It is the third Rackham *Angler* issued in the same year.

[1932]

302. The Tenth Everyman (12th Lang) Reprint

THE COMPLEAT ANGLER by Izaak Walton
London & Toronto Published by J. M. Dent & Sons Ltd & in
New York by E. P. Dutton & Co [1932].

Copy examined: Princeton.

Size: 6¹¹⁄₁₆″ × 4½″.

Pagination summary: [i]-xliv, [2], [1]-215, [216], [8].

At the foot of page 215 is imprinted "Made at the Temple Press Letchworth in Great Britain." There are eight terminal pages of advertising for *Everyman's Library*, where this edition is listed as number 70.

The binding is light olive cloth. The spine is gilt stamped as the second binding of the first Everyman (No. 228). The top edges of the leaves are stained black.

The date of this reprint is on the title-page verso, preceded by the dates of the earlier *Anglers* in this series. It is a reissue of the first Everyman edition of 1906 (No. 228).

[1932]
303. Eleventh Everyman (13th Lang) Reprint

THE COMPLEAT ANGLER Izaak Walton
London: J. M. Dent & Sons Ltd.
New York: E. P. Dutton & Co. Inc. [1932].

Copy examined: Horne.

Size: 6¾″ × 4¼″.

Pagination summary: [i]-xliv, [2], [1]-215, [216], [8].

On the title-page verso is imprinted, "Made in Great Britain at the Temple Press Letchworth" and, at the foot of page 215, "Made at the Temple Press Letchworth in Great Britain." The title-page verso states also ". . . decorated by Eric Ravilious . . ." which accounts for the modernized title-page and end papers which have replaced the Kelmscott style decorations. There are eight terminal pages of advertising for *Everyman's Library*, where this edition is listed as number 70.

The binding is orange cloth with the spine undecorated except for gilt titling. The front cover is blind stamped with a decoration presumably by Ravilious. The orange end papers are decorated with an overall pattern of white cobwebbed circles and streamers. The top edges are stained dark brown.

The title-page verso is dated as the tenth Everyman (No. 302). It is a reissue of the first Everyman edition of 1906 (No. 228) with a new title-page and binding, which has not been listed in previous bibliographies of the *Angler*.

[1934]

304. The Fifteenth Burt (60th Major) Reprint

THE COMPLETE ANGLER . . . by Izaak Walton and
Charles Cotton . . .
A. L. Burt Company, Publishers, New York [1934].

Copy examined: Oliver.

Size: 7³⁄₁₆″ × 5″.

Pagination summary: [1-4] (including frontispiece), [5]-354. No half-title.

This reprint has the same pagination, title-page, illustrations, and binding
(gilt top edges lacking), of the earlier *Anglers* in Burt's *Home Library* series
(see No. 218).

The paper dust jacket (not seen for other *Home Library* reprints) has the
usual titling, between light blue parallel rules, at the top of the front cover
and spine, and publisher and series designation at the foot. Broad orange
rules on the front lead to Burt's circular title-page device (see No. 164),
enlarged and printed on blue; the inner edge is banded in light blue. Decorative rules on the spine (faded) probably were orange as on the front. The
back, flaps, and inside, advertise and list the volumes in Burt's *Home Library*
(including this reprint), priced $1.00.

According to Oliver (see his No. 281), who received his information from
the publisher, such a reprint in Burt's *Home Library* series was published on
May 24, 1954. The Oliver copy examined is probably the one which he purchased from the publisher in 1935, and identified with this reprint, although
it lacks his personal annotation as such.

[1934]

305. The Fifth Collins Reprint

THE COMPLEAT ANGLER Izaak Walton & Charles Cotton . . .
London & Glasgow Collins' Clear-Type Press [1934].

Copies examined: Horne, Oliver.

Size: 5¹⁵⁄₁₆″ × 3¹⁵⁄₁₆″.

Pagination summary: [1]-280, [6].

The printer's imprint at the foot of page 280 (end of text) *"Printed in Great
Britain,"* occurs only in the leather bound copy (Horne) which lacks the six
terminal pages of publisher's advertising where this reprint is listed as in the

second Collins reprint of 1927 (No. 281). The photogravure title-page, with a vignette of a man sitting reading before a fireplace, is different from those in the previous Collins reprints seen, and is signed by Malcolm Patterson.

The illustrations by John Eyre are the same as the first Collins (No. 236).

Two publisher's bindings have been examined. The *first* is in dark red leather, with end papers and ribbon bookmarker in a similar color. The gilt titling and decoration on the spine are the same as the second Collins (No. 281). The top edges are gilt. The *second* (Oliver), in dark red cloth, is otherwise the same as that of the second Collins. This copy was issued in a paper dust jacket, whose tan front and spine are printed in black with the usual titling and, in the middle of the front cover, with the illustration (reduced) opposite page 128. A multicolored advertisement for Waterman's Ideal Fountain Pen is on the back. The volumes in *Collins Illustrated Pocket Classics* are listed on the flaps and the inside.

Oliver (his No. 282), reported that "This, according to the publisher, is a reissue of the earlier Collins reprints . . ." and chose to identify as this reissue, the cloth copy here described, which he purchased in 1935. The leather copy, of the same series, is undoubtedly of the same period.

This is a reissue, with a new title-page, of the first Collins edition of 1908 (No. 236).

[1934]
306. The Fourth Nelson Reprint

THE COMPLEAT ANGLER by Izaak Walton and Charles Cotton. Thomas Nelson and Sons Ltd London [1934].

Copies examined: None seen.

Size reported: 18mo.

Pagination reported: 283 pp.

This listing, from *The English Catalogue of Books*, 1931-1935, where this reprint is identified as one of the *Winchester Classics*, published in September 1934, and priced at two shillings, six pence, bound in rexine.

The publisher has reported (see No. 275), that the Winchester Classics reprint was first published in 1934. It is a reissue, with a new title-page, from the plates of the third Nelson reprint (No. 290).

[1935]

307. The Second Buchan Edition

THE COMPLEAT ANGLER by Izaak Walton and
Charles Cotton . . .
Oxford University Press London: Humphrey Milford [1935].

Copies examined: Harvard, Princeton. Others: DLC, ICarbS, MiU, OU.

Size: 5⅞″×3⅝″.

Pagination summary: [i]-xxiv, [1]-322, [323], [1], [16].

On the title-page verso is imprinted, *inter alia*, "The two parts together were first published in 'The World's Classics' in 1935." On page [323] appears, "Printed in Great Britain at the University Press Oxford by John Johnson Printer to the University." There are 16 terminal pages of advertising.

The illustrations consist of facsimiles of the title-pages to Parts I and II of the edition of 1676 (No. 6), two pages of music, and ten cuts of fish.

Although the introduction is marked "Revised 1935," the fifth edition continues to be misdated 1678 instead of 1676 (page xiv), repeated also on the title-page verso.

The publisher's binding is in Oxford blue cloth with the covers paneled by lines ruled in blind. The Oxford seal is blind stamped on the front cover. The only gilt is the title on the spine.

This revision of the first Buchan edition (No. 199), is one of the Oxford *World's Classics* series. *The English Catalogue of Books* lists this edition as published in August, 1935, to sell for 2s.

[1936]

308. The Fourth Japanese Reprint

THE COMPLEAT ANGLER, . . . By Izaak Walton . . .
Tokyo Kenkyusha [1936].

Copy examined: Princeton.

Size: 6¹³⁄₁₆″×4⁹⁄₁₆″.

Pagination summary: [i]-[xii], [i]-[xxviii], [i]-vi, [1]-203, [204], [205]-324, [325]-338.

The text is in English, with the Introduction (including a list of *Anglers* from 1653-1900), the Notes, and the Index to the Notes, in both English and Japanese. Tipped in on the blank leaf following page 338 is an extra titling label printed in English and Japanese.

The illustrations are as described for the first Japanese edition of 1926 (No. 279).

This reprint was issued in black cloth with a dragon in a small circle blind stamped on the front cover, and repeated in gilt on the spine, which is also titled in gilt. It has two white rayon bookmarks. The cream-colored paper dust jacket, decorated with a dragon, and the titling, has a listing in English and Japanese of the Kenkyusha Classics, identifying this as number 17 in the Essays and Criticism section.

This is a reprint, in the same series, of the first Japanese edition of 1926 (No. 279) which is from Part I of the fifth edition of 1676 (No. 6). The Introduction and Notes were provided by Hoshisaburo Okakura, Professor of English, who advanced from "Higher Normal School" in 1926 to Rikkyo University in 1936.

This fourth Japanese reprint and its date were verified by a Japanese linguist at Princeton. A search for the second and third Japanese Kenkyusha editions which began in 1964, has not been successful.

Two other "Editions" in Japanese have been reported:
1. Tsurigyo Taizen (The Compleat Angler) translated by Hirata Shuboku, published by Kokumin Bunko, 1936.
2. Tsurigyo Taizen (The Complete Angler) translated by Tajijima Hiko-saburo, published by Shunju-sha, 1940.

Continuing search has not revealed these, and no record of them was found in the Oriental section of the British Museum. Copies of them and records about them may have been destroyed during the Second World War.

[1936]

309. The Heritage Nonesuch Edition

THE COMPLEAT ANGLER, . . . by Izaak Walton . . .
by Charles Cotton . . .
New York: The Heritage Press The Nonesuch Press:
London [1936].

Copies examined: Congress, Princeton. Others: CtHT, MB, MoU, NN, OClCS, OClh, ViU, ViW.

Size: $10\frac{7}{16}'' \times 8\frac{1}{8}''$.

Pagination summary: [i-v], vi-[xii], [1]-241, [3].

On the title-page verso is imprinted, "The special contents of this edition are copyright 1936 by the Heritage Press, Inc. Printed in the United States of America."

On the recto of the last page is a colophon "About the Making of this Book" which refers to the type, the paper, the illustrations, and the binding which, although described as "full green buckram," is, in the copies seen, in full blue buckram with a simulated red lettering piece titled in gilt on the spine. The front cover and spine are decorated in gilt with Ball's designs, and he provided the decorative end papers. His pencil drawings, beginning with the half-title page design taken from the title-page cartouche of the first edition of 1653, appear on 100 pages. It was issued in a slipcase. The colophon states further that "The type was set up by the Marchbanks Press," and "the book was printed and bound by the Haddon Craftsmen."

This edition, without notes or introduction, is from Parts I and II of the fifth edition of 1676 (No. 6).

[1936]

310. The Odhams Press Reprint

THE COMPLEAT ANGLER by Izaak Walton and C. Cotton Odhams Press Limited Long Acre, London W.C. 2 [1936].

Copies examined: Horne (2).

Size: 7¼″ × 4¹³⁄₁₆″.

Pagination summary: [1-8], 9-17, [18], 19-245, [246-248], 249-335, [336-338], 339-344.

The title-page, printed within a decorative border, is imprinted on the verso, "Printed and Bound in Great Britain by Greycaine Limited, Watford, Herts."

The illustrations consist of a frontispiece of Walton signed DEM [Charles de Mornay], a facsimile of the 1653 edition title-page, 17 cuts of fish, one of a moth, and, in the appendix, three pages reproduced from the Ephemera editions, showing natural flies, their imitations, and fly tying.

There is a two-page, unsigned introduction. The notes to the text are from the Hawkins edition of 1760 (No. 9) and the Ephemera edition of 1853 (No. 68).

Two publisher's bindings have been examined. The *first* in mottled dark brown rexine, with tan end papers. Both covers are blind stamped with two parallel rules on the edges and small decorations at the corners. The ship device, imprinted in the base of the title-page border, is blind stamped on the front cover and at the foot of the spine which, in addition, has three blind stamped decorations and gilt titling within the panels formed by six sets of blind rules. There are parallel gilt rules at top and foot. The top leaf edges are stained reddish-brown. The *second* is in red cloth in a wavy pattern on the sides, smooth on the corners and backing. The gilt titling on the spine is within a shield-like gilt decoration, and there are parallel gilt rules at top and foot. Blind decorations below the shield and above the gilt rules at the foot are joined by a blind rule on the vertical edges of the spine. The end papers are decorated in an overall design featuring a quotation from Bacon, "Good Books are True Friends." The top edges are stained light red.

The librarian of the book division of the Odhams Press in London provided the date and other data for this edition which, due to destruction of records during World War II, are approximate. It was probably originally produced for mail order selling as one of the *People's Home Library* or one of the *Privilege Price Book Club* publications.

It is a reprint of the nineteenth Cassell of 1909 (No. 237).

1937

311. The First Black (4th Gay & Bird) Reprint

THE COMPLETE ANGLER . . . By Izaak Walton . . .
Adam and Charles Black 4, 5 and 6 Soho Square London W. 1 1937

Copies examined: Horne, Princeton, Yale.

Size: 6⅛″ × 4⅛″.

Pagination summary: (i)-xvi, [1]-229, [230].

The title-page verso states "First Published 1901 New Edition 1937." On page [230] is imprinted, "Printed in Great Britain by T. and A. Constable Ltd. at the University Press, Edinburgh."

This is a reissue of the first Gay and Bird edition with frontispiece and decorations by Herbert Cole, but lacking *The Sportsman's Classics* decoration on the half-title and the publisher's title-page vignette and woodcut border. The errata have not been corrected (see Nos. 200 and 202).

The publisher's binding is in dark green cloth with the usual gilt titling at the top of the spine, between a double rule that is repeated at the foot just below the publisher's name.

The English Catalogue of Books lists this edition as having been published in August 1937, priced at 3s.6d. net. The *Cumulative Book Index* lists The Macmillan Co, Toronto, as an additional distributor, with the world-wide distributors listed on the title-page verso.

[1937]

312. The Grosset and Dunlap Edition

THE COMPLEAT ANGLER . . . by Izaak Walton
Grosset & Dunlap New York [1937].

Copies examined: Princeton, Yale.

Size: 8″×5⅝₁₆″.

Pagination summary: [i]-xviii, 1-237, [238].

The title-page, printed within border decorations, is imprinted on the verso, "Printed in the United States of America by J. J. Little and Ives Company, New York."

The illustrations, by Ernest Townsend, consist of the 1653 title-page cartouche as a half-title; a frontispiece facsimile of the 1653 title-page and the cartouche on the seven full-page plates, nine headpieces, and 11 tailpieces (of which seven are repeated).

There is a short unsigned Foreword which states (page ix): "While Part II was entirely approved by Izaak Walton . . . your editor has not included it in the *Cameo* edition simply because of the fact that Izaak Walton did not write it."

The publisher's binding is in reddish terra-cotta cloth with a white Cameo of Gutenberg embossed on the front cover which is also gilt stamped with the usual titling and "Cameo Classics" at the foot. The spine is decorated and titled in gilt. It was issued in a black slipcase with the cartouche from the 1653 edition on the front.

This edition is listed in the *Cumulative Book Index*, 1938, published in 1937. It is from Part I of the fifth edition of 1676 (No. 6).

[1937]

313. The Caxton Press Reprint

THE COMPLEAT ANGLER . . . By Izaak Walton
Privately Printed [1937].

Copies examined: Horne, Princeton.

Size: 9″×6″.

Pagination summary: [i]-xviii, 1-237, [238].

The title-page, decorated with blue pen work and the 1653 title-page cartouche, is printed in blue on the half-title page which reads: "This special edition has been privately printed by the Caxton Press for presentation to Friends of the House and their Friends." A Caxton Press device is imprinted in blue on the dated (1937) page of acknowledgments (p. [238]) which lists Grosset & Dunlap, Inc. as holder of the *"Publishing rights and texts."*

The bindings examined are in blue cloth with light blue end papers. Five widely spaced lines of gilt waves extend across the front cover and onto the spine; above all but the upper one, on both the front cover and spine, is a stylized jumping gilt fish. Spine titling is in gilt on a black simulated lettering piece above looped black lines between the gilt waves.

This is a reissue, with new half-title, title-page and terminal leaf, from the same plates used for the Grosset and Dunlap edition (No. 312), including the unsigned Foreword and the illustrations. It is from Part I of the fifth edition of 1676 (No. 6).

[1938]

314. The Heritage Club Reprint

THE COMPLEAT ANGLER, . . . by Izaak Walton . . .
by Charles Cotton . . .
New York: The Heritage Club [1938].

Copy examined: Horne. Others: GU, MB, MeB, NNC, NcU, NjR.

Size: 10⅞6″ × 8⅞″.

Pagination summary: [i-v], vi-[xii], [1]-241, [242], [1 leaf].

On the title-page verso is imprinted, "The special contents of this edition are copyright 1938 by the Heritage Club Printed in the United States of America." The colophon on the recto of the last leaf states that "This edition of 'The Compleat Angler' was illustrated for the Heritage Club with pencil drawings by Robert Ball. The edition was designed by Edward Alonzo Miller, and the pages were composed at the Marchbanks Press, New York."

The illustrations and end paper decorations by Robert Ball are the same as in the Heritage Nonesuch edition (No. 309).

The publisher's binding is in dull green buckram decorated with Robert Ball drawings. Twenty-one fish and the Walton-Cotton cipher are portrayed on the front cover. Seven sets of triple rules in green divide the spine into six panels: four contain Ball's piscatorial drawings; one the illustrator's name; one a simulated lettering piece with gilt titling and decoration. The top edges are stained green. It was issued in a green slipcase.

This is a reissue of the Heritage Nonesuch edition of 1936 (No. 309).

[1939]

315. The Twelfth Everyman (14th Lang) Reprint

THE COMPLEAT ANGLER Izaak Walton
London: J. M. Dent & Sons Ltd.
New York: E. P. Dutton & Co. Inc. [1939].

Copies examined: Horne, Princeton. Other: NcRS.

Size: 6¾" × 4½".

Pagination summary: [i]-xliv, [2], [1]-215, [216], [8].

On the title-page verso is imprinted, ". . . Made in Great Britain at The Temple Press Letchworth . . .," and, at the foot of page 215, "Made at the Temple Press Letchworth in Great Britain."

This is a reissue of the eleventh Everyman reprint of 1932 (No. 303), with the same title-page and binding. In the eight terminal pages of publisher's advertising this is number 70 in the Everyman's Library.

The Princeton copy is in a light blue dust jacket with decorations (presumably by Ravilious) in black and white on the front cover and spine. Publisher's advertising appears on the jacket back and flaps.

The data of this reprint is on the title-page verso, preceded by the dates of the earlier *Anglers* in this series. This reissue of the first Everyman edition of 1906 (No. 228), is from Part I of the fifth edition of 1676 (No. 6).

[1939]

316. The First Modern Library (2nd Keynes) Edition

THE COMPLEAT ANGLER by Izaak Walton . . .
The Modern Library New York [1939].

Copies examined: Horne, Princeton. Others: CU, DLC, MiHM, MiU, OCl, PPLaS, PPT.

Size: 6½" × 4¾₁₆".

Pagination summary: [i-iv], v-vi, [1-2], 3-13, [14], 15-23, [24], 24-295.

This is number 26 in *The Modern Library of the World's Best Books* and the publisher advises that it was published on April 4, 1939 (first printing, March 6, 1939), and reprinted 12 times in this series, the last being November 12, 1954. The title-page, with its racing torchbearer mark, is printed within a double rule and divided horizontally by three single rules. On its verso is imprinted, "First Modern Library Edition 1939."

The illustrations consist only of the music on pages 226 and 227.

The 10-page life of Walton is reprinted from the Keynes Nonesuch Edition of 1929 (No. 292) with the reference retained (p. 12, line 5), "the copper plate in the present work" [*i.e.*, the 1929 edition], an editorial lapse that obviously should have been corrected.

This *Angler* was issued in dark blue cloth with the racing torchbearer mark gilt stamped on the front cover. The tan end papers, designed by Rockwell Kent, and patterned with "ml" and an open book, feature this mark in the center. The spine is gilt titled and the top edges of the leaves are stained blue. An angling scene is on the front of the three-color dust jacket.

This edition is from the fourth edition of 1668 (No. 5).

[1939]

317. The First Penguin Edition

Izaak Walton
THE COMPLEAT ANGLER
Penguin Books Limited Harmondsworth Middlesex England [1939].

Copies examined: Horne, Library of Congress, Yale. Other: CU.

Size: $7\frac{1}{16}'' \times 4\frac{3}{8}''$.

Pagination summary: [1-7], 8-247, [9].

On the title-page verso of this paperback edition is imprinted, "Published in Penguin Books 1939," and "Printed in Great Britain by William Clowes and Sons, Limited, London and Beccles." The last nine pages publicize Penguin publications.

The illustrations, by Gertrude Hermes, are nine wood engravings to illustrate the text, a frontispiece, and a piscatorial design, the last printed on a white band on the front of both the cover and the dust jacket (Figure 26), which are in yellow paper with identical covers and spines, both titled in black. The front and back flaps of the dust jacket have notes on the *Angler* and Walton, with his portrait on the latter.

An identical imprint on the backs of both the cover and the dust jacket states that this edition, No. 238 in the Penguin list, was published in November, 1939. It is part of Penguin's miscellaneous series issued in yellow covers and is without notes or introduction.

This edition, from Part I of the fifth edition of 1676 (No. 6), is the first paperback *Angler* published.

[1940]

318. The Second Penguin Reprint

IZAAK WALTON THE COMPLEAT ANGLER
Penguin Books Limited Harmondsworth Middlesex England [1940].

Copies examined: None seen.

Size reported: $7\frac{1}{4}'' \times 4\frac{1}{2}''$.

Pagination reported: 247 pp.

This reprint is listed as described in *The English Catalogue of Books* January, 1940, as one of the Penguin Series priced at 6d net. It is presumed to be a reissue of the 1939 edition published in the previous November.

[1941]

319. The Second Modern Library (3rd Keynes) Reprint

THE COMPLEAT ANGLER by Izaak Walton
The Modern Library New York [1939].

Copy examined: Horne.

Size: $7'' \times 4\frac{5}{8}''$.

Pagination summary: [i-iv], v-vi, [1-2], 3-13, [14], 15-23, [24], 25-295.

The publisher advises that the *Angler* was reprinted in The Modern Library on January 9, 1941. An undated reprint in this compiler's collection is probably typical of the 12 reprints.

The page size is slightly larger than the first printing, $7'' \times 4\frac{5}{8}''$ as compared to $6\frac{1}{2}'' \times 4\frac{3}{16}''$. The title-page has the title and author's name bordered by a heavy single rule, with the torchbearer above and the imprint below and, other than the date, the same general information as to production appears on the verso. The pagination and music are identical. The life of Walton (page 12, line 5) still contains the misleading reference to the copperplate of Walton which was not included in these reprints.

The Horne copy was issued in green cloth with the gilt torchbearer mark and simulated light red lettering pieces on the spine and front cover, both gilt stamped with titling. The end papers (here gray) are otherwise those of the first Modern Library edition (No. 316). The top edges are tinted red. An angling scene is on the front of the three-color dust jacket, numbered 26 on the spine. Publisher's advertising is on the back, the flaps and the entire inside.

This is a reissue of the first Modern Library edition of 1939 (No. 316).

[1941]

320. The Third Modern Library (4th Keynes) Reprint

THE COMPLEAT ANGLER by Izaak Walton
The Modern Library New York [1941].

Copies examined: None seen.

Size: Not reported.

Pagination: Not reported.

The publisher reports this issue in the Modern Library to have been reprinted on March 13, 1941.
  See notes to numbers 316 and 319.

[1942]

321. The Fourth Modern Library (5th Keynes) Reprint

THE COMPLEAT ANGLER by Izaak Walton
The Modern Library New York [1942]

Copies examined: None seen.

Size: Not reported.

Pagination: Not reported.

The publisher reports this issue in The Modern Library to have been reprinted on April 22, 1942.
  See notes to numbers 316 and 319.

[1942]

322. The First French Abridged Edition

I. Walton
LE PARFAIT PÊCHEUR A LA LIGNE . . .
Les Livres de Nature Éditions Stock
Delamain et Boutelleau 6, rue Casimir Delavigne Paris [1942].

Copies examined: Horne, Library of Congress.

Size: $7\frac{1}{4}'' \times 4\frac{5}{8}''$.

Pagination summary: [1-5], 6-234, [1 leaf].

On the recto of the terminal leaf is imprinted, "Achevé d'imprimé le 15 Mai 1942 sur les Presses de l'imprimerie régionale 59, Rue Bayard-Toulouse" and, on the verso of the same leaf, "TW 5976-30 Avril 1942."

[270]

The two illustrations are on one leaf following the title-page: a portrait of Walton on the recto, and a facsimile of the 1653 title-page on the verso.

The cover of this paperback (Figure 26) was designed by Masereel and is decorated with woodcuts printed in light green on the upper and lower portions of the front, back, and spine. Titling is in black on the front and back, the latter also having imprinted in black "Stock/23 fr" and "59," which is the number of this edition in "Les Livres de Nature" series. This edition and 28 other titles of the series are listed on the outside of the cover. Thirty-one additional titles appear on the verso of the half-title.

The Library of Congress copy, which is imprinted, "6ᵉ édition" (6th issue), on the front of the paperback cover, has an additional outer, coated paper wrapper. The titling, printed in black on its front cover, is framed in an elaborate piscatorial border printed in light blue, which features fishing flies on three sides and, at the base, a still life of angling equipment and three fish. Eight "Éditions Stock" are listed on the back of the outer wrapper. The Horne copy, imprinted "4ᵉ édition" on the front, lacks the extra outer wrapper.

The translation, and the 24-page Preface, are by Charles Chassé, in which he points out that this is the first time that one of the most popular books in English literature has been translated into French. Chassé gives a very brief biography of Walton, comments on his literary activities, and refers to Cotton's part of the fifth edition, which is not included. Much of what some may consider to be "extraneous matter" and some of the songs were omitted from the text.

This edition is listed in the 1943 issue of *Biblio* as published in 1942 as one of *Les Livres de Nature*, a series published under the direction of Jacques Delamain. It was priced at 23 francs.

The text is an abridgment from Part I of the fifth edition of 1676 (No. 6).

1942

323. The Monastery Hill Press Abridged Edition

A SERMON ON CONTENT from the Compleat Angler by Izaak Walton Ernst Hertzberg and Sons Monastery Hill Bindery Christmas, 1942.

Copy examined: Princeton.

Size: 7″×5″.

Pagination summary: [4], 1-9, [1].

The title-page is printed in red and black within a border of printer's flowers. On the last page is imprinted, "Printed at the Monastery Hill Press, Chicago, Illinois."

The only illustration is a hand-colored woodcut used as a headpiece on page one.

The publisher's binding is in green sewn-paper covers with titling on the front within printer's flowers all printed in red.

This short abridgment is from the fifth day, chapter XXI, of Part I of the fifth edition of 1676 (No. 6), beginning, "We having still a mile to go," and ending, "a meek and thankful heart which Almighty God grant to me, and to my honest scholar."

This edition was issued as a Christmas greeting, with a Note at the front recommending *The Compleat Angler* as "escape" literature in time of stress.

[1943]

324. The Fifth Modern Library (6th Keynes) Reprint

THE COMPLEAT ANGLER by Izaak Walton
The Modern Library New York [1943].

Copies examined: None seen.

Size: Not reported.

Pagination: Not reported.

The publisher reports this issue in The Modern Library to have been reprinted on August 30, 1943.

See notes to numbers 316 and 319.

1943

325. The First Danish Edition

DEN FULDKOMNE FISKER—THE COMPLEAT ANGLER . . .
By Izaak Walton and Charles Cotton . . .
Martins Forlag [Copenhagen] 1943

Copy examined: Horne.

Size: 8¾" × 5⅜".

Pagination summary: [i]-xxxvii, [xxxviii], [1]-402, [1 leaf].

This is the first translation of the *Angler* into the Scandinavian (Figure 25).

The Inskipp portrait plates of Walton and of Cotton (first published in the first Nicolas edition, 1836, No. 43) precede Parts I and II as frontispieces. Addi-

UDGIVET AF LYSTFISKERIFORENINGEN I KØBENHAVN
I ANLEDNING AF IZAAK WALTONS 350 AARS FØDSELSDAG
DEN 9. AUGUST 1943

DEN FULDKOMNE FISKER

THE COMPLEAT ANGLER

OR

THE CONTEMPLATIVE MAN'S RECREATION

BY

IZAAK WALTON

AND

CHARLES COTTON

OVERSÆTTELSE VED JOHANNE KASTOR HANSEN
DIGTENE OVERSAT AF OTTO GELSTED
ILLUSTRERET AF IB ANDERSEN
FORORD VED POUL HAUTON

MARTINS FORLAG

1943

Figure 25   The First Danish Edition (No. 325). The
first translation of the *Angler* into the Scandinavian

tional illustrations by I. Anderson consist of a title-page vignette very similar to that on the title-page of the Hawkins edition of 1822 (No. 22), 37 headpieces, and 52 text figures, none of which is repeated.

The cream-colored hard paper cover and the dust jacket are identical in typography and illustration, each with titling in black. A figure of a fish is in full color on the front cover, and a kingfisher in full color on the back. Printed in black at the top of the spine is a small fish and in the center an angling motif of equipment and fish. The leaves are untrimmed. It was issued in a slipcase.

This first Danish edition, with a Foreword by Poul Hauton, translated by Johanne Kastor Hansen, and illustrated and edited by I. Anderson, was issued by the Sport Fishing Society of Copenhagen (Lystfiskeriforeningen København) to commemorate Izaak Walton's 350th birthday, August 9, 1943.

The colophon (on the recto of the terminal leaf) states that 2,500 copies were printed of which 1,000 were numbered.

It is a translation of Parts I and II of the fifth edition of 1676 (No. 6).

1943

326. The Second Danish Reprint

DEN FULDKOMNE FISKER—THE COMPLEAT ANGLER . . .
By Izaak Walton and Charles Cotton . . .
Martins Forlag [Copenhagen] 1943.

Copy examined: Horne.

Size: $8\frac{3}{4}'' \times 5\frac{3}{8}''$.

Pagination summary: [i]-xxxvii, [xxxviii], [1]-402, [1 leaf].

This is a reissue of the first Danish edition (No. 325) with the same illustrations, binding, and dust jacket, except that no numbered copies are recorded by the colophon which identifies this as the "andet" or second edition [i.e., second printing or reissue].

For notes see No. 325.

1943

327. The Third Danish Reprint

DEN FULDKOMNE FISKER—THE COMPLEAT ANGLER . . .
By Izaak Walton and Charles Cotton . . .
Martins Forlag [Copenhagen] 1943

Copies examined: None seen.

Size reported: 8¾″×5⅜″.

Pagination reported: Identical to No. 325.

The publisher advises that this is a reprint of the first Danish edition (No. 325) with the same date, illustrations, and format (except that no numbered copies were reported), and that the colophon identifies this as the "tredie" or third edition [*i.e.*, third printing or reissue].
For notes see No. 325.

[1944]

328. The Thirteenth Everyman (15th Lang) Reprint

THE COMPLEAT ANGLER Izaak Walton
London: J. M. Dent & Sons Ltd. New York: E. P. Dutton & Co. Inc. [1944].

Copy examined: Horne.

Size: 6⁹⁄₁₆″×4³⁄₁₆″.

Pagination summary: [i]-xliv, [2], [1]-215, [216], [8].

The title-page verso reads ". . . Made in Great Britain at the Temple Press Letchworth . . . Last Reprinted 1944 . . . Book Production War Economy Standard. The Paper and Binding of this Book conform to the Authorized Economy Standards."
This is a reissue of the twelfth Everyman (No. 315) with the binding of the eleventh and twelfth issues except the top edges of the copy examined (now very dust soiled) appear not to have been stained.

[1944]

329. The Sixth Modern Library (7th Keynes) Reprint

THE COMPLEAT ANGLER by Izaak Walton
The Modern Library New York [1944].

Copies examined: None seen.

Size: Not reported.

Pagination: Not reported.

The publisher reports this issue in The Modern Library to have been reprinted on May 16, 1944.
See notes to numbers 316 and 319.

[1944]

330. The Seventh Modern Library (8th Keynes) Reprint

THE COMPLEAT ANGLER by Izaak Walton
The Modern Library New York [1944].

Copies examined: None seen.

Size: Not reported.

Pagination: Not reported.

The publisher reports this issue in The Modern Library to have been reprinted on October 30, 1944.
  See notes to numbers 316 and 319.

[1944]

331. The Fourth Danish Reprint

DEN FULDKOMNE FISKER—THE COMPLEAT ANGLER . . .
By Izaak Walton and Charles Cotton . . .
Martins Forlag [Copenhagen 1944].

Copies examined: None seen.

Size reported: $8\frac{3}{4}'' \times 5\frac{3}{8}''$.

Pagination reported: Identical to No. 325.

The publisher advises that this is a reprint of the first Danish edition of 1943 (No. 325), with identical illustrations and format (except that no numbered copies were reported), and that the colophon identifies this as the "fjerde" or fourth edition [i.e., the fourth printing or reissue].
  Although confirming its issuance, the publisher was unable to furnish a date for this reprint. It is tentatively dated 1944 since there were three issues in 1943, and another, the fifth, remained to be issued in 1944.
  For notes see No. 325.

1944

332. The Fifth Danish Reprint

DEN FULDKOMNE FISKER—THE COMPLEAT ANGLER . . .
By Izaak Walton and Charles Cotton . . .
Martins Forlag [Copenhagen] 1944

Copies examined: None seen.

Size reported: 8¾″×5⅜″.

Pagination reported: Identical to No. 325.

The publisher advises that this is a reprint of the first Danish edition of 1943 (No. 325), with identical illustrations and format (except that no numbered copies were reported), and that the colophon identifies this as the "femte" or fifth edition [i.e., fifth printing or reissue].
  For notes see No. 325.

1945

333. The Sixth Danish Reprint

DEN FULDKOMNE FISKER—THE COMPLEAT ANGLER . . .
By Izaak Walton and Charles Cotton . . .
Martins Forlag [Copenhagen] 1945

Copies examined: Horne, Yale. Others: DLC, NN.

Size: 8¾″×5⅜″.

Pagination summary: [i]-xxxvii, [xxxviii], 1-402, [1 leaf].

This is a reprint of the first Danish edition of 1943 (No. 325), with identical illustrations and format, except that there are no numbered copies recorded by the colophon which identifies this as the "sjette" or sixth edition [i.e., the sixth printing or reissue]. It was issued in a slipcase.
  For notes see No. 325.

[1945]

334. The Seventh Danish Reprint

DEN FULDKOMNE FISKER—THE COMPLEAT ANGLER . . .
By Izaak Walton and Charles Cotton . . .
Martins Forlag [Copenhagen 1945].

Copies examined: None seen.

Size reported: 8¾″×5⅜″.

Pagination reported: Identical to No. 325.

The publisher advises that this is a reprint of the first Danish edition of 1943 (No. 325), with identical illustrations and format (except that no numbered copies were reported), and that the colophon identifies this as the "syvende" or seventh edition [i.e., the seventh printing or reissue].

Although confirming its issuance, the publisher was unable to furnish a date for this reprint. It is tentatively dated 1945 rather than 1946 since the dates of the ten known issues from 1943 through 1964, indicate a rapidly diminishing demand starting in 1946, which would probably not justify more than the one reprint which is known to have been issued in that year.

See notes to No. 325.

1945

335. The Second Black (5th Gay & Bird) Reprint

THE COMPLETE ANGLER . . . by Izaak Walton . . .
Adam and Charles Black 4, 5 and 6 Soho Square London W.I 1945.

Copy examined: Horne.

Size: 6" × 4".

Pagination summary: [i]-xvi, [1]-229, [230].

The title-page verso states. "First published 1901. New edition 1937. Reprinted 1945," and imprinted on page [230] is "Printed in Great Britain by T. and A. Constable Ltd. at the University Press, Edinburgh."

The misprint "sleepy" for "steepy" mountains still appears on page 69, and the cut on page 41 is printed upside down (see notes to Nos. 200 and 202).

The publisher's binding is in light green cloth with the gilt rules and titling of the first Black (No. 311). The dust jacket is of tan paper imprinted in dark red: the Cole frontispiece is repeated on the front; the publisher's mark on the back; titling is on the spine. There is a note about Walton and the *Angler* on the front flap and the publisher's advertising is on the entire inside of the dust jacket.

This is a reissue of the first Black reprint of 1937 (No. 311).

[1945]

336. The Eighth Modern Library (9th Keynes) Reprint

THE COMPLEAT ANGLER by Izaak Walton
The Modern Library New York [1945]

Copies examined: None seen.

Size: Not reported.

Pagination: Not reported.

The publisher reports this issue in The Modern Library to have been re-printed on May 25, 1945.
   See notes to numbers 316 and 319.

[1945]
337. The Ninth Modern Library (10th Keynes) Reprint

THE COMPLEAT ANGLER by Izaak Walton
The Modern Library New York [1945].

Copies examined: None seen.

Size: Not reported.

Pagination: Not reported.

The publisher reports this issue in The Modern Library to have been re-printed on November 8, 1945.
   See notes to numbers 316 and 319.

[1945]
338. The First Swedish Edition

DEN FULLÄNDADE FISKAREN   THE COMPLEAT ANGLER . . .
by Izaak Walton and Charles Cotton . . .
Wahlström & Widstrand | Stockholm [1945].

Copies examined: Horne (2), Yale. Others: DLC, NN.

Size: 8¼″ × 5⅜″.

Pagination summary: [1]-[413].

On the title-page verso is imprinted, "Victor Pettersons Bokindustriaktie-bolag [Book Printing Establishment] Stockholm 1945."
   The illustrations consist of the Inskipp portrait plates of Walton and Cotton (see No. 325), and 36 headpieces, 12 tailpieces, and 29 text figures by Stig Åsberg, none of which is repeated.
   The binding of the Horne copies is in cream-colored paper over boards backed with light blue-green cloth. A small figure of a man fishing from a rowboat is printed in gray-green on the front cover. A dark green simulated lettering piece on the spine is titled, and single and wave ruled in gilt. The tops of the leaves are tinted very light green. The stiff paper cream-colored inner front cover (following the flyleaf) is imprinted with titling in rusty-red

and black, and is decorated with a vignette of a seated angler printed in black between horizontal rules in rusty-red.

This edition, translated and with a Foreword by Olof Lagercrantz, is from Parts I and II of the edition of 1676 (No. 6).

[1945]

339. The Fourteenth Everyman (16th Lang) Zepher Reprint

THE COMPLEAT ANGLER By Izaak Walton
Zepher Books The Continental Book Company AB
Stockholm | London [1945].

Copy examined: Yale.

Size: $7\frac{1}{16}'' \times 4\frac{5}{8}''$.

Pagination summary: [i-vii], viii-xliv, [2], [1]-3, [4-5], 6-215, [216].

On the title-page verso and at the foot of the back cover is imprinted, "This edition must not be introduced into the British Empire or the U.S.A. Printed by ALB. Bonniers Boktryckeri [Printing Establishment], Stockholm." At the foot of page 215 is printed, "STHLM. ALB. BONNIERS BOKTR. 1945." This paperback is identified also as volume 48 in "A Library of British and American Authors."

The binding, in stiff cream paper with horizontal parallel rules in orange on the covers has the Zepher Books symbol (also on the title-page) at the top of the front cover.

This is a paperback in the Everyman series printed in Sweden.

[1946]

340. The Tenth Modern Library (11th Keynes) Reprint

THE COMPLEAT ANGLER by Izaak Walton
The Modern Library New York [1946].

Copies examined: None seen.

Size: Not reported.

Pagination: Not reported.

The publisher reports this issue in The Modern Library to have been reprinted on February 1, 1946.

See notes to numbers 316 and 319.

1946

341. The Eighth Danish Reprint

DEN FULDKOMNE FISKER—THE COMPLEAT ANGLER . . .
By Izaak Walton and Charles Cotton . . .
Martins Forlag [Copenhagen] 1946

Copy examined: Horne.

Size: $8\frac{3}{4}'' \times 5\frac{3}{8}''$.

Pagination summary: [i]-xxxvii, [xxxviii], 1-402, [1 leaf].

This is an exact reprint of the first Danish edition of 1943 (No. 325), with identical illustrations and format, except that there are no numbered copies recorded by the colophon which identifies this as the "ottende" or eighth edition [*i.e.*, the eighth printing or reissue].
For notes see No. 325.

[1946]

342. The Second Swedish Edition

DEN FULLANDADE FISKAREN   THE COMPLEAT ANGLER . . .
by Izaak Walton and Charles Cotton . . .
Wahlstrom & Widstrand / Stockholm [1946]

Copies examined: None seen.

Size reported: $9\frac{5}{16}'' \times 6\frac{1}{4}''$.

Pagination reported: 413, (1) pp.

The descriptive data are from the copy in the Royal Library (Kungliga Biblioteket), Stockholm, through the courtesy of Magdalena Hellquist, assistant librarian.
    The title-page phraseology is that of the first Swedish edition (see Fig. 26).
    The illustrations and cover decorations are by Stig Åsberg. Probably included are the 16 additional illustrations of the third Swedish reprint not in the first Swedish edition.
    It was issued in half calf, and it is assumed from the xerox figures received that there is an inner stiff paper cover (see the first and third Swedish issues, Nos. 338 and 343). The front of this cover is decorated with a small figure of an angler standing near a tree, and with DEN (as it was printed in the title on the front cover of other issues seen) here printed DEN which, with

FULLANDADE FISKAREN, is in relatively larger type than on other such covers seen. A large wet fly is printed on the back cover. Titling, with a wood-cut of a large tree on the bank of a stream and an angler in a rowboat, is on the spine.

This is apparently the second Swedish edition, on large paper and probably with the additional illustrations mentioned above, translated and with a Foreword by Olof Lagercrantz, and issued in a limited printing of 300 copies. The Svensk Bokforteckning and the Royal Library of Stockholm both date it 1946.

[1947]

343. The Third (called Second) Swedish Edition

DEN FULLANDADE FISKAREN   THE COMPLEAT ANGLER...
by Izaak Walton and Charles Cotton . . .
Wahlstrom & Widstrand / Stockholm [1947]

Copy examined: Horne.

Size: 8⅝" × 5⅜".

Pagination summary: [1]-[413].

The title-page appears to be the same as the xerox title examined of the second Swedish edition. On its verso is imprinted, "Andra upplagan" [Second Edition] and "Victor Petterson's Bokindustriaktiebolag [Book Print-ing Establishment] Stockholm 1947." A page by page comparison with the first Swedish edition shows pages 189-194, 241-242, 279-283, 297-301, and 381-382 were reset for this printing to accommodate changes in, and additions to, the illustrations.

In addition to the Inskipp portrait plates of Walton and Cotton (see No. 325), there are 36 headpieces, 26 tailpieces, and 31 text figures by Stig Åsberg. This is 16 more than in the first Swedish edition (No. 338).

The binding of the Horne copy is in gray paper over boards, backed with gray-green cloth. The front cover is decorated with the small figure of an angler from the stiff paper cover of the second Swedish edition (No. 342). The spine titling is in gilt on a black, simulated lettering piece, single and wave ruled in gilt. The tops of the leaves are stained gray-green. The stiff paper inner front cover is the same as for the first Swedish edition (No. 338) except the vignette is from the second Swedish edition.

While this is called the "second edition" on the title-page verso, it is in reality the third edition in Swedish, since it was preceded not only by the first (1945) but also by a limited edition of 300 copies.

[282]

[1947]

344. The First Finnish Reprint

DEN FULLANDADE FISKAREN   THE COMPLEAT ANGLER ...
by Izaak Walton and Charles Cotton . . .
Holger Schildt/Helsingfors [1947].

Copy examined: Horne.

Size: 8⅝″ × 5⁹⁄₁₆″.

Pagination summary: [1]-[413].

This is a reissue or second state, of the third Swedish edition (No. 343), with a Finnish publisher's imprint on the title-page recto, which is otherwise unchanged, as is the verso.

The front cover of the stiff paper binding is the same (with its seated angler) as that of the first Swedish edition (No. 338). The back cover and spine are those of the second Swedish edition (No. 342). All edges of the leaves are untrimmed. The dust jacket, in cream-colored paper, is decorated and titled as the cover.

In Swedish, with a Finnish imprint, this issue is from Parts I and II of the fifth edition of 1676 (No. 6).

[1947]

345. The Peter Pauper Press Edition

THE COMPLEAT ANGLER . . . By Izaak Walton
with the Second Part, by Charles Cotton . . .
The Peter Pauper Press. Mount Vernon [1947].

Copies examined: British Museum, Congress, Horne (2). Others: CU, DLC, FTaSU, IU, MWelC, MeB, NN, NNUN-W, NRU, NcC, NcGW, NcRS, NjP, TxU, ViU.

Size: 10¹⁄₁₆″ × 6¹⁄₁₆″.

Pagination summary: [1-2], 3-219, [220].

The colophon on page [220] consists of a woodcut of a boy and girl as strolling minstrels, printed in green, below which is imprinted, "The text of this edition has been set in the Janson types, and has been printed on specially-made Peter Pauper paper."

All the illustrations are printed in green. The Boyd Hanna woodcuts include 15 text illustrations; four chapter headings, each repeated once; the title-page vignette, repeated for "The Retirement;" and the Walton-Cotton cipher on the title-page to Part II. In addition there are 16 woodcuts of fish from the Major edition of 1844 (No. 55).

The publisher issued this edition in covers of green paper decorated with an all over pattern of repeated impressions of the jumping trout woodcut on page four. The spine is in a monk's cloth type fabric, tan with a tinge of green. Its vertical titling is in gilt on a black panel framed with three gilt rules. The top edges of the leaves are tinted dark green. The publisher's slipcase is covered in green paper and decorated on the front with a title-page printed within a green band, omitting Cotton's name, and having the chapter heading from the "First Day" (p. 11) as a green vignette.

The Peter Beilenson checklist in Typophile Chap Book XXXX, *Recalling Peter . . . and His Peter Pauper Press,* New York, 1964, includes the *Angler* as issued in 1947, which the publisher has confirmed as the first printing, and has stated further that there were no reprints.

The English Catalogue of Books, under date of October 17, 1955, reports "Izaac Walton The Compleat Angler Illus. 6½″ × 10¼″. p. 219. 35s. (De Luxe Artists' Ed) (Peter Pauper Press) Mayflower Publishing Co. and Vision Press (Distributor)." The publisher advises that this *Angler* is the same as the American edition, with Mayflower and Vision acting merely as distributors. The copy in the British Museum, and the American copies, are the same.

This edition, which was selected for AIGA "Fifty Books of the Year" 1947 exhibitions, is unedited and reprinted from Parts I and II of the fifth edition of 1676 (No. 6).

[1947]
346. The Fifteenth Everyman (17th Lang) Reprint

THE COMPLEAT ANGLER Izaak Walton
London: J. M. Dent & Sons, Ltd. New York: E. P. Dutton & Co. Inc [1947].

Copy examined: Horne.

Size: 6⅝″ × 4³⁄₁₆″.

Pagination summary: [i]-xliv, [2], [1]-215, [216], [8].

The title-page verso is imprinted, "All rights reserved. Printed in Great Britain by Garden City Press Ltd. Letchworth Herts. for J. M. Dent & Sons Ltd. Aldine House Bedford St. London. First published in the edition 1906. Last reprinted 1947." The usual printer's imprint at the foot of page 215 is lacking. In the eight pages of advertising at the end for *Everyman's Library* this reprint is listed as number 70.

The title-page, dust jacket, and binding are the same as the twelfth Everyman (No. 315) of which this is a reissue.

347. The Second Navarre Society (61st Major) Reprint

THE COMPLETE ANGLER . . . of Izaak Walton and
Charles Cotton . . .
London: Privately printed for the Navarre Society Limited,
12-13 Grafton Street, Bond Street MCMXLVIII

Copies examined: Horne, Princeton, Yale.

Size: 8½″ × 5⁷⁄₁₆″.

Pagination summary: [i]-xiv, [1]-445, [2].

The half-title, printed in red, has no reference to a limited printing on its verso (see No. 274). The title-page, printed in red and black, is printed on its verso, "Printed in Great Britain of the Riverside Press, Edinburg." The title-page vignette is here changed from that of the first Navarre (first used in the 1844 Major, No. 55), to a repeat of the tailpiece on page 177. There are two terminal pages of publisher's advertising.

The illustrations are the same as the first Navarre edition except that the eight Damman etchings and their index are omitted, thereby reducing the preliminaries by one leaf.

The publisher's binding is in cobalt blue cloth gilt ruled top and foot and gilt stamped on the spine with the title and "Navarre" and on the front cover with the cartouche of the 1653 edition. There is a colorful dust jacket (lacking at Yale) (blue, white, red and black) titled in red on the front and spine and embellished with an angling tackle and equipment motif on the front. Navarre Society "Classics" are advertised on the back cover. It is priced "12/6" on the dust jacket flap.

This is a reissue of the first Navarre edition of 1925 (No. 274), with the changes noted above.

348. The Limited Editions Club Edition

THE COMPLETE ANGLER; . . . by Izaak Walton; . . .
by Charles Cotton; . . .
New York The Limited Editions Club 1948

Copy examined: Horne. Others: CtHT, DLC, LU, MB, MH, NNc, NjP, ViU.

Size: 12⅞″ × 8¾″.

Pagination summary: [i-ix], x-xlii, [1]-316, [2].

On the title-page verso is imprinted: "The special contents of this edition are copyright, 1948, by The Limited Editions Club for the George Macy Companies, Inc."

The colophon of the Horne copy reads, "Of this edition of 'The Compleat Angler' fifteen hundred copies have been made for the members of The Limited Editions Club. The composition of the text has been done by the Monotype & Linotype Corporation; the paper has been especially made by the Worthy Paper Company; the printing of the letterpress has been done by the Aldus Printers, of the photogravures by the Duenewald Printing Corporation, and of the engravings by Andersen-Lamb with hand-pulls; the binding has been done by the Russell-Rutter Company. The illustrations and engravings were executed by Douglas W. Gorsline, who here signs Douglas W. Gorsline [sig.] this copy, which is number 356."

Although the subscriber's notice of this edition stipulates ". . . a dozen hand-prints from his [Gorsline's] engravings in copper, and forty wash-drawings reproduced through sheet-fed gravure," there are actually 11 engravings and 31 reproductions of wash drawings. The engravings, and some of the drawings, are signed.

The publisher's binding is in blue paper covered boards, with the spine in ivory-colored calf. Both covers are decorated in blue ink, and the spine in gilt, with designs created by Glenn Foss from the large initial letters repeated here from the Limited Editions Club's *Bacon's Essays*. The Walton-Cotton cipher is the focal point of the cover design. The titling is in gilt on the spine. The top edges are stained very dark blue, others untrimmed. The edition was issued in a molded slipcase covered with the blue paper of the binding, but without the binding design.

This edition was limited to 1,500 copies signed by the artist. It contains a reprint of the Lowell introduction to the first Lowell edition of 1889 (No. 142), and is from Parts I and II of the fifth edition of 1676 (No. 6).

[1948]

349. The Heritage Press Reprint

THE COMPLEAT ANGLER ; . . . by Izaak Walton ;
by Charles Cotton ; . . .
New York The Heritage Press [1948].

Copies examined: Horne (2). Others: CLSU, DAU, DLC, MiDW, NcU, ViU.

Size: 11⅜″ × 7⅝″.

Pagination summary: [i-ix], x-xlii, [1]-316.

On the title-page verso is imprinted, "The special contents of this edition are copyright 1948, by The George Macy Companies, Inc."

The illustrations were reproduced photographically in gravure from the Limited Editions Club edition (No. 348), and are the same, except that Gorsline's name, and "Ny 1947" are omitted under the engravings.

The publisher's binding (copy #1) is in boards covered with cream-colored paper, with the spine in light green rough linen. The decorations and titling, in green and gilt, are the same design as for The Limited Editions Club reprint (No. 348). The top edges are stained very dark green, the others are untrimmed. It was issued in a board slipcase. Copy #2 is in what appears to be a trial binding of red paper over boards, with no decorations except parallel gilt rules at the top and foot of the spine which is gilt titled "Compleat Angler."

This is a reissue of The Limited Editions Club edition (No. 348), with the same Lowell introduction.

[1948]

350. The Edwards Edition

Izaak Walton & Charles Cotton
THE COMPLEAT ANGLER
Walter Edwards London [1948].

Copies examined: British Museum, Horne.

Size: $7\frac{3}{16}'' \times 4\frac{11}{16}''$.

Pagination summary: [1-16], 17-233.

On the half-title verso is imprinted, "Printed and made in Gt. Britain by the C.W.S. Printing Works, Longsight (Manchester), and Reddish." The title-page is printed within a border of type ornaments. The two illustrations consist of facsimiles of the title-page of the first edition (No. 1), and of the title-page for Part II of the edition of 1676 (No. 6).

This edition has a six-page Introduction titled "Izaak Walton" dated 1947, and one of two and one-third pages titled "Charles Cotton" (preceding Part II), each signed "Alfred Jas. Alderson."

The publisher's binding is in gray cloth. The front cover is gilt titled within a shield-like gilt decoration. The spine has gilt scroll decorations head and foot and gilt titling. A small white scroll is repeated in an overall pattern on the dark gray end papers. Titling on the front of the light green paper dust jacket (where this edition is designated "A Walter Edwards Classic") is printed on white within the design from the front cover of the binding outlined in black; titling is in black on the spine; publisher's advertising is on the back, and the two flaps contain a note about the *Angler*.

The English Catalogue of Books lists this edition as published in May 1948. It is priced "6s.od." on the dust jacket flap.

351. The Vane Edition

Goldfinch Titles
THE COMPLEAT ANGLER . . .
by Izaak Walton & Charles Cotton Nicholas Vane *London* [1948].

Copies examined: British Museum, Horne.

Size: 7$\frac{1}{16}$" × 4$\frac{5}{8}$".

Pagination summary: [1-10], 11-244.

The title-page verso states that this edition was ". . . First published in 'Gold-finch Titles' in 1948 by Nicholas Vane, Publishers, Ltd. 1 Trebeck Street, London, W.I." and ". . . was printed in Great Britain at the St Ann's Press by John Sherratt and Son, Park Road, Timperley, Cheshire." The cartouche (enclosing its titling) from the 1653 edition is printed on the title-page. Walton's birth, death and burial place is reported within the outline of a tombstone on the half-title verso.

There are no text illustrations.

The binding is in black cloth with silver stamped titling and the Goldfinch bird device on the spine and front cover. A black and white photographic reproduction of George Moreland's (1763-1804) painting of A Party Angling covers both facing end papers at the front; that of the Angler's Repast covers both those at the back. The top edges of the leaves are stained black. A large reproduction of the 1653 cartouche (enclosing its titling) is on both the front and back of the dust jacket (Horne copy), which is also titled on the spine. Goldfinch titles are advertised on the flaps. A broad dark brown band, printed in white with Walton's name on front and spine, and the Goldfinch device on back and flaps, extends along the entire top edge of the dust jacket.

The English Catalogue of Books reports this edition as published in September 1948, priced at eight shillings six pence net. It is from Parts I and II of the fifth edition of 1676 (No. 6).

352. The Eleventh Modern Library (12th Keynes) Reprint

THE COMPLEAT ANGLER by Izaak Walton
The Modern Library New York [1949].

Copies examined: None seen.

Size: Not reported.

Pagination: Not reported.

The publisher reports this issue in The Modern Library to have been re-printed on February 28, 1949.
    See notes to numbers 316 and 319.

1949

353. The First Folio Society Edition

THE COMPLEAT ANGLER . . . by Izaak Walton and
Charles Cotton . . .
London The Folio Society MCMXLIX

Copies examined: Horne, Yale. Other: IaU.

Size: 8¾″×5⅝″.

Pagination summary: [i-vi], vii-xii, [2], 1-272.

The title-page verso is imprinted, "This book has been composed in 12 pt. Caslon Old Face type, printed, and bound, by W. & J. Mackay & Co. Ltd., Chatham." The title-page is printed within a decorative border of green fleurons. There is a one-page unsigned Foreword.
    The end paper decorations, frontispiece portrait of Walton (within a border matching that on the title-page), and 28 text illustrations are by Lynton Lamb.
    The publisher's binding is in rough, dull green canvas. The gray end papers are decorated with a leaping fish in white line. The front and back covers are edged with double rule in blind. The titling, and "F. S." on the spine are in gilt on simulated lettering pieces in gray with a gilt border. It was issued with a dust jacket (see *Folio 21*, p. 28) not present with copies examined.
    This edition is reported in *The English Catalogue of Books* as published in April, 1949. It is described on page 28 in *Folio 21* (1968).
    This edition is from Parts I and II of the fifth edition of 1676 (No. 6).

1950

354. The Redcoat Press Abridged Edition

A DISCOURSE ON CONTENT from
The Compleat Angler by Izaak Walton
The Redcoat Press Westport, Conn. 1950

Copy examined: N.Y. Public.

Size: 6¹⁄₁₆″×4″.

Pagination summary: [i-v], vi-[xii], [1-3], 4-20, [21], [1 leaf].

[289]

The initial letter "W" of the text is printed in red. The printer's imprint, with its figure of a redcoat soldier, on the recto of the last leaf states, "Of this book one hundred seventy-five copies have been printed at the Redcoat Press December 1950." An eight-page introduction signed by the "Printers" and headed "To the Reader," which refers briefly to some of the early editions, and praises the *Angler* as ". . . truly an exquisite book . . ."

There are two illustrations in black and white adapted from the Breakfast and the Farewell in the Major editions.

It was issued in boards covered with light red paper. The spine is in light tan cloth with the titling printed in red.

This abridged edition, from the end of the fifth day on the walk toward home, begins "Well Scholar, having still a mile to Tottenham High Cross, . . ." and ends with Venator saying ". . . and so, Master, here is a full glass to you of that liquor." It is from Part I of the fifth edition of 1676 (No. 6).

[1951]

355. The Third Buchan Reprint

THE COMPLEAT ANGLER by Izaak Walton and
Charles Cotton . . .
Geoffrey Cumberlege Oxford University Press
London New York Toronto [1951].

Copy examined: Princeton.

Size: $5\frac{13}{16}'' \times 3\frac{9}{16}''$.

Pagination summary: [i]-xxiv, [1]-322, [2].

The title-page which has a "World's Classics" vignette, is imprinted, *inter alia*, on the verso, "The two parts together were first published in 'The World's Classics' in 1935, and reprinted in 1951," and on the last leaf recto, "Set in Great Britain at the University Press Oxford and printed by Merritt and Hatcher Ltd. London, S.E. 10."

The illustrations are those of the second Buchan edition of 1935 (No. 307).

As in the 1935 Buchan, the date of the fifth edition (1676) continues to be misdated 1678 (page xiv of the Introduction), and on the title-page verso. The error is repeated on the front flap of the dust jacket.

The publisher's binding is that of the second Buchan edition and the green paper dust jacket is decorated with an angling scene in black and white by Lynton Lamb. Both titles are in white on the front cover, *The Arte* is omitted from the spine which is titled in black.

This is number 430 in the *World's Classics* series and is a reissue of the second Buchan edition of 1935 (No. 307) which is a reprint from Parts I and II of the fifth edition of 1676 (No. 6). It was priced six shillings in the United Kingdom.

356. The Twelfth Modern Library (13th Keynes) Reprint

THE COMPLEAT ANGLER by Izaak Walton
The Modern Library New York [1952].

Copies examined: None seen.

Size: Not reported.

Pagination: Not reported.

The publisher reports this issue in The Modern Library to have been re-printed on August 8, 1952.
See notes to numbers 316 and 319.

1952

357. The Classics Book Club Edition

THE COMPLEAT ANGLER by Izaak Walton . . .
Classics Book Club 121, Charing Cross Road, London,
W.C. 2 [1952].

Copy examined: Horne.

Size: $7\frac{1}{16}'' \times 4\frac{13}{16}''$.

Pagination summary: [1-4], 5-216.

The title-page verso is imprinted, "This edition 1952" and "Printed in Great Britain by Ebeneezer Baylis and Son, Ltd., The Trinity Press, Worcester, and London."
There are no illustrations.
The Horne copy is bound in plain smooth dark blue cloth with the titling in gilt near the top of the spine between gilt decorated bands and, at the foot, "Classics Book Club" is stamped in gilt.
This edition, without notes or introduction, is from Part I of the fifth edition of 1676 (No. 6).

[1953]

358. The Sixteenth Everyman (18th Lang) Reprint

Izaak Walton THE COMPLETE ANGLER . . .
London J. M. Dent & Sons Ltd
New York E. P. Dutton & Co Inc [1953].

Copy examined: Horne. Other: CLSU.

Size: 7⅛″ × 4⁹⁄₁₆″.

Pagination summary: [i-vii], viii-xliv, [2], [1]-215, [216], [8].

The title-page verso is imprinted, "All rights reserved by J. M. Dent & Sons Ltd Aldine House, Bedford Street, London Made in Great Britain at the Aldine Press, Letchworth, Herts First published in this edition 1906 Last reprinted 1953." There are eight terminal pages of advertising for Everyman's Library.

The half-title and title-page have been reset and the latter is here first imprinted with the device of a dolphin (head turned opposite to that of Manutius) and anchor combined with the letters E and L (*i.e.*, Everyman's Library).

Andrew Lang's introduction (the heading reset) has a list of Biography and Criticism added at the end.

There are no illustrations.

The publisher's binding is in red cloth. A cipher combining the letters E and L is gilt stamped at the foot of the spine, and printed in orange on the end papers in an overall pattern. Titling is in gilt at the head of the spine under a parallel gilt rule. The top edges of the leaves are stained light orange. The dust jacket for the copy examined is lacking.

This is a reissue from the plates of the fifteenth Everyman (No. 346) with the changes noted above. It is listed in *The English Catalogue of Books, 1952-1955* described as a reprint in *Everyman's Library*, number 70, priced at six shillings net, and published July 16, 1953.

[1953]

359. The Third Navarre Society (62nd Major) Reprint

THE COMPLETE ANGLER . . . of Izaak Walton and
Charles Cotton . . .
London: Privately Printed for the Navarre Society Limited,
12-13 Grafton Street, Bond Street [1953].

Copy examined: Horne.

Size: $8\frac{1}{2}'' \times 5\frac{7}{16}''$.

Pagination summary: [i]-xiv, [1]-445, [2].

On the title-page verso is imprinted, "Reprinted MCMLIII" and "Printed in
Great Britain by the Riverside Press, Edinburgh."
   This is a reissue of the 1948 Navarre reprint, with the same illustrations
and pagination except that the terminal leaf advertises other Navarre publications.
   The dust jacket and the binding (except that the cloth is red) are the same
as for the 1948 reprint (No. 347).

[1953]

360. The Ninth Danish Reprint

DEN FULDKOMNE FISKER—THE COMPLEAT ANGLER . . .
By Izaak Walton and Charles Cotton . . .
Martins Forlag [Copenhagen 1953]

Copies examined: None seen.

Size reported: $8\frac{3}{4}'' \times 5\frac{3}{8}''$.

Pagination reported: Identical to No. 325.

The publisher advises that this is a reprint of the first Danish edition of 1943
(No. 325), with identical illustrations and format (except that no numbered
copies were reported), and that the colophon identifies this as the
"niende" or ninth edition [i.e., the ninth printing or reissue].
   For notes see No. 325.

1953

361. The Burns Abridged and Revised Edition

THE COMPLEAT ANGLER Tricentennial Edition
by Izaak Walton *Supplement by* Charles Cotton . . .
The Izaak Walton League *Sponsor* . . .
The Stackpole Company Harrisburg, Pennsylvania [1953].

Copies examined: Horne (2), Yale. Others: CtHT, DLC, NjP, PP.

Size: 8¼" × 5½".

Contents: [2], Introduction, 1-14; text, 15-[118], [2], 119-177, [178]; Izaak Walton League, 179-192.

The title-page is printed within a frame of double lines, the outer straight ruled, the inner formed by type ornaments. On the title-page verso, the publisher's spruce tree device is imprinted in the center and at the foot, "Printed in the U.S.A. *By* The Telegraph Press *Established 1831* Harrisburg, Pennsylvania." On page 15 in the eighth line of text, "till" is printed "til" and, at the end of Part I, the bible reference is misquoted as from verse two instead of verse eleven.

The illustrations consist of nine reproductions of photographs which include a frontispiece of the bust of Walton by Spero Anargyros, Cotton's fishing house with an insert of the plaque by Anargyros, three of the river Dove, the title-page of the first edition, 1653, and, in Winchester Cathedral, a panel of the Walton window, Walton's Tombstone and Prior Silkstead's Chapel, which is misspelled "Silksides" in the caption. There is also one printed page of music.

Eugene Burns provided a 14-page Introduction explaining his textual revisions and his elimination of "the lifeless stretches." In the last 13 pages, Robert Beatty, Editor of *Outdoor America,* reviewed the objectives, principles, and accomplishments of the Izaak Walton League of America.

This edition was issued in two states: the trade "edition" and a "limited tricentennial edition." The regular "edition" (Horne copy) is bound in black cloth with light tan end papers and titling in gilt on the front cover and spine. The front cover calls this the "Tricentennial Edition," as does the title-page. The Yale copy has a rough, beige, canvas-like binding with light tan end papers, gilt titled only on the spine. The black dust jacket (Horne copy), which calls this the "Anniversary Edition," is titled with gilt-like printing on the spine and front cover, the latter, in addition, decorated with a reduced gilt-like reproduction of the frontispiece bust of Walton. The flaps provide a brief description of the book, and the back cover advertises eight Stackpole Press publications.

The limited "edition" (Horne copy) so identified on the recto of the front end paper, where the copy's number is handwritten in ink above a printed facsimile of Walton's autograph. There is no report of the number of copies. It was issued boxed and bound in brown leather with padded front and back covers, and light green end papers. The spine and the front cover are titled in gilt. All leaf edges are gilt.

This is an abridged and revised edition from Parts I and II of the fifth edition of 1676 (No. 6). The review slip (regular Horne copy) states that the publication date was July 15, 1953.

1954

362. The Fifth Nelson Reprint

THE COMPLEAT ANGLER by Izaak Walton & Charles Cotton, London: Thomas Nelson & Sons Ltd. 1954.

Copies examined: None seen.

Size reported: 6¼″×4¼″.

Pagination reported: 283 pp.

This listing is from *The English Catalogue of Books, 1952-1955*, which reports October 14, 1954, as the date of publication, the price four shillings, and describes this reprint as a "New Edition" of the Nelson Classics.

The publisher has verified the publication of this reprint which is a reissue, with a new title-page, from the plates of the third Nelson reprint (No. 290).

[1954]

363. The Thirteenth Modern Library (14th Keynes) Reprint

THE COMPLEAT ANGLER by Izaak Walton
The Modern Library New York [1954].

Copies examined: None seen.

Size: Not reported.

Pagination: Not reported.

The publisher reports this issue in The Modern Library to have been reprinted on November 12, 1954.

See notes to numbers 316 and 319.

[1958]

364. The Hamburg und Berlin (2nd German) Edition

Izaak Walton
DER VOLLKOMMENE ANGLER
Verlag Paul Parey [Hamburg und Berlin, 1958].

Copy examined: Princeton.

Size: 7³⁄₁₆″ × 4¼″.

Pagination summary: [1-6], 7-193, [194], [2].

The title-page is printed in red and black, and decorated at top and foot with printer's flowers. On the verso of the last leaf, *inter alia* is imprinted, "Verlag Paul Parey, Hamburg und Berlin, 1958. Printed in Germany by Offizen Paul Hartung . . ."

The illustrations consist of an angling scene frontispiece, a headpiece to Chapter I, and nine full-page plates from the Moses Browne edition of 1750.

The publisher's binding is in red cloth. Two fish are blind stamped on the front cover and a black lettering piece on the spine is titled in gilt. The gray paper dust jacket is titled in red and black and the title-page cartouche from the 1653 edition is imprinted on the front.

This edition, from the fourth edition of 1668 (No. 5), was translated and provided with an epilogue by Martin Grunefeld.

1958

365. The Weimar (3rd German) Edition

Izaak Walton DER VOLLKOMMENE ANGLER
1958 Gustav Kiepenheuer Verlag Weimar.

Copies examined: Horne, Library of Congress.

Size: 6⁹⁄₁₆″ × 4⁵⁄₁₆″.

Pagination summary: [1]-[228], [2].

This is volume 12 in the Gustav Kiepenheuer Library Series. On the title-page verso it is stated that the translation is by Gertrud Eppenstein, revised and edited by the Publishing House. There is an Epilogue by Friedrich Minckwitz.

The illustrations consist of three plates, each showing three fish in color.

The imprint on the last page states that the illustrations are from *Porte-Feuille des Enfans,* by Friedrich Justin Bertuch, Weimar 1802; that the binding is by Arthur Liebig, Weimar; and that the book was printed in Germany.

It was issued in ivory-colored cloth. An elaborate "I.W." is in gilt within gilt scrolls on the front cover. The spine is titled vertically in gilt, the top edges of the leaves are tinted light blue.

This edition is from Part I of the fifth edition of 1676 (No. 6).

1958

366. The Hanau/M (4th German) Edition

Izaak Walton DER VOLLKOMMENE ANGLER
1958 Verlag Weimar Dausien Hanau/M

Copies examined: Horne, Princeton.

Size: 6⁹⁄₁₆″ × 4⁵⁄₁₆″.

Pagination summary: [1]-[226], [2].

This edition differs from the Weimar edition published the same year, in Friedrich Minckwitz's Epilogue, now set in two less pages. The translator, Gertrud Eppenstein, is the same, except that for this edition, according to the title-page verso, the translation was revised and edited by Noa Kiepenheuer.

The Princeton copy has the same illustrations (lacking in the Horne copy) as in the Weimar edition.

The last page reports that the printing (in Germany) was done with the permission of the Publishing House of Gustav Kiepenheuer, Weimar, as it is assumed that the Weimar edition was printed (in the same year) prior to this Hanau/M edition.

The ivory cloth binding, decoration, titling, and tinted leaf edges are the same as for the Weimar edition (No. 365). The Princeton copy has a dust jacket printed in black on white, showing two fish rampant, and on which Walton's first name is spelled Izaac, as contrasted with Izaak on the title-page.

This edition is from Part I of the fifth edition of 1676 (No. 6).

[1960]

367. The Fourth Buchan Reprint

THE COMPLEAT ANGLER by Izaak Walton and
Charles Cotton . . .
and an Appendix . . . of *The Arte of Angling* . . .
London Oxford University Press New York Toronto [1960].

Copies examined: Horne (2).

Size: 5¾″ × 3⁹⁄₁₆″.

Pagination summary: [i]-xxiv, [1]-322; Appendix, [323-363], [364].

The title-page, which lacks the "World's Classics" vignette of the third Buchan (No. 355), is imprinted, on the verso, ". . . *The two parts together were first published in* The World's Classics *in 1935, and reprinted in 1951 and 1960. The appendix containing* . . . The Arte of Angling (1577) *was added to this volume in 1960,*" and, on page [364], "Printed in Great Britain at the University Press, Oxford by Vivian Ridler Printer To the University." The errata of No. 355 are uncorrected here.

The illustrations are the same as the third Buchan (No. 355).

The binding and the dust jacket, except for the addition of *The Arte of Angling* to the titling, are the same as for the third Buchan.

The short "Publisher's Note" beginning on page [324] which introduces *The Arte of Angling,* refers briefly to the one surviving copy of the 1577 edition now at Princeton, and ". . . its possible or probable influence on Izaak Walton. . . ." and concludes, "These are questions on which each reader must make up his mind for himself. . . ."

This *Angler,* still numbered 430 in the Oxford *World's Classics* series, is a reprint of Parts I and II of the fifth edition of 1676. It was priced seven shillings six pence in the United Kingdom and $1.85 in the United States.

1961

368. The Sixth Nelson Reprint

THE COMPLEAT ANGLER by Izaak Walton and Charles Cotton. London: Thomas Nelson and Sons, Ltd. 1961.

Copies examined: None seen.

Size: 6¼″ × 4¼″.

Pagination reported: 283 pp.

The publisher has reported that this reprint was first published in the "Parkside Classics" series in 1961, from the same sheets as are in the "Winchester" (No. 306) and "Cloth Classic" series, but in a different binding, and priced at seven shillings. (See notes to Nos. 275 and 381.)

1961

369. The Dolphin Edition

THE COMPLETE ANGLER . . . by Izaak Walton . . .
Dolphin Books Doubleday & Company, Inc. Garden City,
New York [1961].

Copies examined: Horne (2).

Size: $7\frac{1}{8}'' \times 4\frac{3}{16}''$.

Pagination summary: [1-6], 7-192, (5).

The title-page verso of this paperback is imprinted, "Printed in the United States of America." There are two half-title pages, one before and one after the title-page, each imprinted only "The Complete Angler." Five pages of Dolphin publications are advertised at the end, where this edition is listed as number C102 under Essays and Letters. It has neither introduction nor illustrations.

The cover was designed by George Giusti and drawn by Edward Shenton (Figure 26). The front, printed in black and brown on blue, portrays an angler playing a large fish below the titling, and a fish at each corner of the top where "A Dolphin Book" and "95¢" are imprinted. A short note on Walton and the *Angler* is on the back cover. The usual titling and C102 are printed in black on the spine.

This edition is listed in the *Cumulative Book Index* as published in 1961, priced at ninety-five cents.

It is from Part I of the fifth edition of 1676 (No. 6).

[1962]

370. The Seventeenth Everyman (1st Bottrall) Edition

Izaak Walton THE COMPLEAT ANGLER
London J. M. Dent & Sons Ltd New York E. P. Dutton & Co
Inc [1962].

Copies examined: Horne, Princeton.

Size: $7'' \times 4\frac{9}{16}''$.

Pagination summary: [i-iv], v-xvii, [3], [1]-3, [4-5], 6-215, [216], [4].

The title-page verso is imprinted, "All rights reserved Made in Great Britain at the Aldine Press, Letchworth, Herts for J. M. Dent & Sons Ltd. Aldine

The Dolphin Edition (No. 369)

The First French Abridged Edition, 4th issue (No. 322).

The First Penguin Edition (No. 317)

Figure 26   Paperback Covers

House, Bedford Street, London. First published in Everyman's Library 1906 Last reprinted 1962." The Bottrall replaces the Lang introduction. There are four terminal pages of advertising for Everyman's Library.

The title-page is that of the 1953 Everyman reprint (No. 358) except announcing the introduction by Margaret Bottrall, M.A., which is followed by an enlarged "Select Bibliography." The text is from the plates of the sixteenth Everyman (No. 358).

The one illustration is a reproduction of the title-page of the first edition of 1653 (No. 1).

The publisher's binding and its titling is the same as that for the sixteenth Everyman (No. 358). The dust jacket is pinkish-red, and is decorated on the front with an angling scene by B.S. Biro in black and white. Walton is included in the Everyman list of "A Few of 500 Authors" printed on the back.

This edition is from Part I of the fifth edition of 1676 (No. 6).

[1962]

371. The Second Folio Society Edition

THE COMPLETE ANGLER . . . by Izaak Walton and Charles Cotton . . .
London The Folio Society MCMXLIX [1962].

Copy examined: Horne.

Size: $8\frac{11}{16}'' \times 5\frac{1}{2}''$.

Pagination: [i-vi], vii-xii, [2], 1-5, [6], 7-201, [202-204], 205-272.

Although the title-page is dated MCMXLIX as shown above, the title-page verso is imprinted, "Second impression (reset) 1962 Printed in Great Britain Printed and bound by W. & J. MacKay & Co. Ltd., Chatham. Set in 'Monotype' Caslon Old Face 12 point," thus identifying it as a second edition, and not a reprint of the first (No. 353).

The illustrations and decorations by Lynton Lamb are the same as for the first Folio Society edition.

The publisher's binding is green canvas, with the same simulated lettering pieces and end papers as the first Folio Society edition of 1949, but there is no edge ruling on the covers. The top edges of the leaves are stained greenish-gray. It was issued cased, not curved to fit the spine as is the case for the third Folio reprint.

The Folio Society advises that the reset type of this edition was that used for their third and fourth reprint. This edition is from Parts I and II of the fifth edition of 1676 (No. 6).

[301]

1962

372. The Second French Abridged Edition

Walton, Izaac
Peche à la Ligne.
Adapt. de l'Anglais par Jean Lestrade.
Les Cahiers du Nouvel Humanisme. 1962.

Copies examined: None seen.

Size reported: $9\frac{1}{4}'' \times 7\frac{1}{16}''$.

Pagination reported: 130 pages, illustrated.

The listing of this edition is from *Biblio,* 1963.

[1962]

373. The Collier Edition

Izaak Walton
THE COMPLETE ANGLER . . . Collier Books New York N.Y. [1962].

Copies examined: Horne (2).

Size: $7\frac{1}{16}'' \times 4\frac{1}{8}''$.

Pagination summary: [1-4], 5-190, [1].

On page [4] is imprinted, *inter alia,* "First Collier Books Edition 1962" and "Printed in the United States of America." The copyright 1962 is by the Crowell-Collier Publishing Company. The title-page is double spread on pages [2-3]. On the first page is a brief note about Walton, and an introduction by John Thompson on pages 5-9. The last page, titled "Further Reading," lists four works by or containing information about Walton.

There are no illustrations, but the Angler's Song music is included.

The cover of this paperback is printed in blue, black, and red. Titling on the front is in red and black and a large blue fish is printed on a red background. Information about the *Angler* appears on both covers. Titling on the spine is in red and black and HS2 is printed at the foot; this and "65¢" are printed on the front (see Figure 27).

The English Catalogue of Books lists this paperback *Angler* as published July 7, 1962, priced at five shillings. It is from Part I of the fifth edition of 1676 (No. 6).

[1963]

374. The Third Black (6th Gay & Bird) Reprint

THE COMPLETE ANGLER . . . by Izaak Walton . . .
Adam & Charles Black London [1963].

Copies examined: Horne, Princeton.

Size: 6″×4⅛″.

Pagination summary: [i]-xvi, [1]-229, [230].

The title-page verso states, "First published 1901. New Edition 1937. Reprinted 1945 and 1963," and imprinted on page [230] is "Printed in Great Britain by T. and A. Constable Ltd., Hopetoun Street, Printers to the University of Edinburgh."

The misprint "sleepy" for "steepy" still appears on page 69, but the salmon fly cut, upside down on page 41 in the 1937 and 1945 reprints, is now right side up.

The publisher's binding, here in brown cloth, is otherwise the same as the 1945 reprint. The dust jacket, here in cream paper, has the repeat of the Cole frontispiece (as in 1945) on the front cover, but the titling is printed in blue. The double rules are omitted on the spine and the back has publisher's advertising in place of the publisher's device in 1945. The information about Walton is repeated on the front flap where it is priced 10s.6d. net.

This is a reissue of the first Black reprint of 1937 (No. 311).

[1964]

375. The Eighteenth Everyman (2nd Bottrall) Reprint

Izaak Walton THE COMPLEAT ANGLER . . .
Dent: London Everyman's Library Dutton: New York [1964].

Copies examined: Horne, Princeton. Other: CtHT.

Size: 7⅛″×4¼″.

Pagination summary: [i-iv], v-xvii, [3], [1]-3, [4-5], 6-215, [216], [4].

This is an Everyman paperback reprint number 1070, of the 1962 (1st Bottrall) edition (No. 370) with the same introduction and bibliography by Margaret Bottrall, and illustrated with a reproduction of the 1653 title-page. A new anchor and dolphin device very similar to that used by Aldus Manutius appears on a reset title-page, the verso of which states, *inter alia,* "Last reprinted 1964." At the end are four pages advertising Everyman's Library.

The white paperback cover is in light blue, black and tan (Figure 27). The angling scene on the front by B. S. Biro is the same as that on the 1962 Everyman dust jacket, but here the foreground is in tan and black with light blue background. Titling above the black band is in black on blue (left) and white (right). The spine, in yellow and white, is titled in black (and numbered 1070), and has the 1962 dolphin and anchor at the foot. A note about the *Angler* is on the back.

The English Catalogue lists this paperback as having been published on May 7, 1964, with a selling price of 5 s. net. It is a reissue of the 1962 Everyman (No. 370).

[1964]

376. The Third Folio Society Reprint

THE COMPLEAT ANGLER . . . By Izaak Walton and
Charles Cotton . . .
London The Folio Society MCMXLIX [1964]

Copy examined: Horne.

Size: $8\frac{11}{16}'' \times 5\frac{9}{16}''$.

Pagination: [i-vi], vii-xii, (2), 1-5, [6], 7-201, [202-204], 205-272.

Although the title-page is dated MCMXLIX as shown above, on the verso of the title-page is imprinted, "Third Impression 1964 . . . ." As reported in the notes for the second edition (No. 371), this is a reissue of that printing from the same typesetting and without change of title-page date. Bibliographically it is a second state of that edition.

The publisher's binding is that of the second Folio Society edition (No. 371). It was issued cased, curved at the top and foot of the opening to fit the spine.

It is a reprint from Parts I and II of the fifth edition of 1676 (No. 6).

[1964]

377. The Tenth Danish Reprint

DEN FULDKOMNE FISKER—THE COMPLEAT ANGLER . . .
By Izaak Walton and Charles Cotton . . .
Martins Forlag [Copenhagen 1964].

Copy examined: Horne.

Size: $7\frac{3}{8}'' \times 4\frac{1}{2}''$.

Pagination summary: [i]-xxxvii, [1]-402, [2].

In a smaller size, this is a photo-offset reissue of the first Danish edition of 1943 (No. 325) with updated title-page, discontinuance of numbered copies and colophon identification as the "tiende" [tenth] "edition."

With a slightly softer cover than that of previous issues, it was considered in Denmark to be a paperback, although issued boxed with the same illustrations in full color, and black, on the cover and dust jacket as for the preceding issues.

For descriptive details see the first Danish edition of 1943 (No. 325).

1964

378. The Fourth Swedish Edition

DEN FULLANDADE FISKAREN   THE COMPLEAT ANGLER...
By Izaak Walton and Charles Cotton . . .
Wahlstrom & Widstrand Stockholm 1964

Copies examined: Horne (2).

Size: $7\frac{1}{2}'' \times 4\frac{1}{2}''$.

Pagination summary: [1-4], 5-[266], [1 leaf].

The imprint in Swedish on the title-page verso may be translated as follows, "Original English title The Compleat Angler. Translation [and Foreword] by Olof Lagercrantz. The Compleat Angler appeared in 1653. The first Swedish edition published by Wahlstrom & Widstrand 1945. The following [this edition] appeared as number 54 in the W & W establishment's series, 1964. Titles and drawings by Stig Åsberg. Cover design by Vidar Forsberg. Printed by Victor Pettersons Publishers, Inc. Stockholm 1964." The leaf at the end lists 59 W & W serien publications of which Den fullandade fiskaren is number 54.

There are 89 illustrations, consisting of the Inskipp portraits of Walton and Cotton (the plates almost worn out), the 36 headpieces and 32 text drawings (one is repeated, see pages 240 & 245) from the 1945 first Swedish edition (No. 338), plus 18 new text drawings.

The front cover of this paperback (Figure 27), in blue, white, and black, depicts a man seated fishing from the bank of a stream, with a goat grazing nearby. Titling is in blue and white on the front cover and in black on the spine on which is also printed "W & W serien 54." Comments on Walton and the Angler are printed on the back cover.

This edition is from Parts I and II of the fifth edition of 1676 (No. 6).

The Fourth Swedish Reprint (No. 378)

The Eighteenth Everyman (2nd Bottrall) Reprint (No. 375).

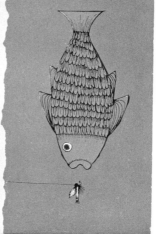

The Collier Edition (No. 373)

Figure 27   Paperback Covers

[1964]

379. The First French Unabridged Edition

Le parfit pêcheur à la ligne
ou le divertissement du contemplatif
Les Libraires Associés [1964]

Copies examined: Congress, Horne.

Size: 5″×7⅝″ oblong.

Pagination summary: [10], i-[vi], [1]-(240), [12].

On the title-page verso is imprinted "© *Les Libraire Associés* 1964." On the following page appears, "Prèmiere traduction intégrals française de *The Compleat Angler* d'Izaak Walton par Charles Chassé, présentée par Louis Bonnerot, avec le portrait au naturel des douze poissons cités par l'auter, suive d'une biographie." On the recto of the terminal page it is stated in part (in French) that ". . . the printing was finished the 10th of August 1964 . . . the edition comprising 3,000 copies reserved for members of the Book-sellers Club of France and 150 copies for the publishers, marked H. C. (Hors de Commerce [not for sale]). Printing in green is used on the rectos of all the preliminary pages and on the second half-title, which follows the Intro-duction; also, following the text, on page (217), "Izaak Walton et son oeuvre" (by Chassé); in full or in part on the last 12 pages (except blanks and the colophon page), and for author's names or initials appended to preliminary or terminal matter.

The illustrations consist of 12 small plates of fish, eight in color and four in black and white, after those in the *Natural History of Fish* (1785), by Marcus-Elieser Bloch. All are mounted on the recto of separate leaves titled in red on the verso. The one page of music has the words of the Angler's song in English.

The publisher's binding (Figure 28) of the regular state is in green cloth, with the full-color brown trout plate mounted on the front cover. Titling is in white on the front cover and spine. There is a green ribbon bookmarker and a transparent plastic dust jacket. The Library of Congress copy of the H. C. state of 150 copies, is bound in gray cloth printed with an overall decorative pattern of 11 figures of fish in different colors.

This edition is the Chassé unabridged translation of Part I of the fifth edition of 1676 (No. 6). It is listed in *Biblio* as published in 1964, priced at 26 francs.

Figure 28   The First French Unabridged Edition (No. 379).
The front cover and title-page

380. The Nineteenth Everyman (3rd Bottrall) Edition

Izaak Walton THE COMPLEAT ANGLER . . .
Dent: London Everyman's Library Dutton: New York [1965].

Copies examined: Horne (2).

Size: 7⅟₁₆" × 4⁹⁄₁₆".

Pagination summary: [i-iv], v-xvii, [3], [1]-3, [4-5], 6-215, [216], [217]-254, [2], 1-8, [2].

The title-page verso is imprinted, "All rights reserved Made in Great Britain at the Aldine Press, Letchworth, Herts for J. M. Dent & Sons Ltd Aldine House, Bedford Street, London First included in Everyman's Library 1906 Last reprinted 1965 No. 70." A reproduction of the title-page of the first edition (1653) precedes the text.

This edition, with the introduction by Margaret Bottrall and the same title-page as the paperback Everyman of 1964, is a reissue of the text of that edition, with a new typesetting (pp. [217]-254) of Andrew Lang's essay on Walton from previous Lang Everyman *Anglers*. Below the title for Lang's essay [page 217], it reads "An essay reprinted from his edition of *The Compleat Angler,* 1896." If this reference is to the first Lang edition of 1896, it is not wholly correct, since the sentence included in the essay at the foot of page [217] reads, "The text here reprinted is, in the main, that of Sir Harris Nicolas, which was printed from Walton's Fifth Edition, 1676, the last that was revised by the author." This is printed, in the first Lang edition, on a page by itself opposite the beginning of Lang's essay as a "Note as to Text."

Eight pages of advertising are at the end for Everyman's Library, where this edition is listed as number 70, followed by a two-page history of the Everyman Library.

Two colors of cloth binding have been examined, the *first* in black, the *second* in dark green. The gilt spine titling, end papers and top edges of the leaves, are the same as the seventeenth Everyman (1st Bottrall) edition (No. 370), as is the dust jacket, except that its color here is tan.

This edition is from Part I of the fifth edition of 1676 (No. 6).

381. The Seventh Nelson Reprint

THE COMPLEAT ANGLER . . . Izaak Walton and
Charles Cotton . . .
Thomas Nelson and Sons Ltd London Edinburgh Paris Melbourne
Johannesburg Toronto and New York [1965].

Copies examined: Horne, Princeton.

Size: 6⅛″ × 4¹⁄₁₆″.

Pagination: [i-iv], v-vii, [viii], 9-27, [28], 29, [30], 31-211, [212], 213, [214], 215-283.

On the verso of page 283 is imprinted, "Printed in Great Britain by Thomas Nelson and Sons Ltd, Edinburgh."

The only illustration is music for the Angler's Song on pages 174 and 175.

The publisher's binding is in tan cloth, gilt titled on the spine. The top edges of the leaves are stained gray. A dark brown paper dust jacket, issued with it, is decorated with an overall design in white, with the titling in white on green panels on the front cover and spine. The back of the dust jacket has a brief note on the development of the Nelson pocket editions. This reprint, with other titles, is listed on the front, and the inside of the back flap as one of the Nelson Classics.

British Books in Print (1965) reports the Nelson Classics series (as listed above) priced at six shillings; the Winchester Classics series at seven shillings; the Parkside Classics series at seven shillings; and the School Classics series at five shillings. The publisher advises that the same sheets were used for all the series mentioned above, and only the binding was different. In October, 1967, the only issue in print was in the Nelson Classics series, priced six shillings, six pence. Although no definite date was received from the publisher, it has been assumed that the copy described, a gift from the publisher, is the latest issue, and it has been assigned to 1965, as reported in *British Books in Print*.

All the issues referred to above are reissues of the third Nelson reprint (No. 290).

1965

382. The Fifth Swedish Reprint

DEN FULLANDADE FISKAREN
The Compleat Angler . . . by Izaak Walton and Charles Cotton . . .
Wahlstrom & Widstrand Stockholm 1965

Copy examined: Horne.

Size: 8⅜″ × 5¼″.

Pagination summary: [1-4], 5-[266], [1 leaf].

This is a reissue, on larger paper, of the fourth Swedish edition of 1964 (No. 378), but not in the "W & W serien." The imprint in Swedish on the title-page verso may be translated as follows, "Original English title The Complete Angler. Translation by Olof Lagercrantz. The Complete Angler appeared in 1653. The first Swedish edition published by Wahlstrom & Widstrand 1945. Titles and binding by Stig Åsberg. Printed by Victor Pettersons Publishers, Inc. Stockholm 1965."

The copy examined was issued in light blue cloth having a narrow band of white on the top and bottom edges. The headpiece from page 201 is repeated in black on the lower half of the front cover, which is gilt stamped near the top with "Izaak Walton/Charles Cotton" in large roman capitals, above *Den fullandade fiskaren* in italics. Vertical titling is in small gilt capitals on the spine. The top edges are stained light tan. It was issued in a clear plastic dust jacket.

With a half-title, instead of "W & W serien" on page [1], and a reset and updated title-page, this is a reissue of the fourth Swedish edition of 1964 (No. 378).

[1966]

383. The Fourth Folio Society Reprint

THE COMPLEAT ANGLER . . . by Izaak Walton and
Charles Cotton . . .
London The Folio Society MCMXLIX [1966].

Copies examined: None seen.

Size reported: $8\frac{3}{4}'' \times 5\frac{5}{8}''$.

Pagination reported: The same as for the 1964 Folio Society reprint (No. 376).

The above entry is from information received in London from the Folio Society, which advised further that the reset type of their second edition (No. 371) was that used for their third and fourth reprints issued in 1964 and 1968 respectively. Bibliographically it is a third state of the second edition.

For notes see Nos. 371 and 376.

1966

384. The Abercrombie & Fitch (2nd Black) Facsimile

THE COMPLEAT ANGLER . . . By Izaak Walton
Abercrombie & Fitch. New York
University Microfilms Inc. Ann Arbor . . . 1966

Copy examined: Horne. Other: DLC.

Size: $5\frac{1}{2}'' \times 3\frac{5}{8}''$.

Pagination summary: [xxiv], (1)-246.

On the title-page verso is stated, among other things, "Manufactured in the U.S.A. by the Arno Press Inc. New York." This is a reproduction with the same 42 irregularities found in the 1928 Black facsimile (No. 287), and was reprinted from a copy in the Library of the Racquet and Tennis Club. At the front is a two and one-half page, unsigned, Publisher's Note. (See Appendix B for list of the irregularities.)

The illustrations are six small plates of fish and two facing pages of music, the second of which is upside down as in the first edition, 1653.

The reddish-brown publisher's binding material has the usual titling in black on the spine in three sections formed by four parallel black rules. The front cover has a parallel rule black border on the edges, enclosing a black shield displaying three fish, below which is imprinted "Iz. Wa."

This facsimile, number 99-102 in The Abercrombie and Fitch Library, price $6.00, was produced by University Microfilms Inc., a subsidiary of Xerox Corporation.

[1967]

385. The Fifth Buchan Reprint

THE COMPLEAT ANGLER by Izaak Walton and
Charles Cotton . . .
and an Appendix . . . of *The Arte of Angling* . . .
London Oxford University Press New York Toronto [1967].

Copy examined: Horne.

Size: $5\frac{3}{4}'' \times 3\frac{9}{16}''$.

Pagination summary: [i]-xxiv, [1]-322; Appendix, [323]-363, [364].

This is a later issue of the fourth Buchan reprint (No. 367), with the 1967 date reported on the title-page verso, the revised publisher's address (now reading Ely House, W.1.) on the half-title verso, and the errata first cited herein for the first Buchan edition of 1901 (No. 199) here at last corrected.

The binding is the same as the third and fourth Buchan *Anglers* (Nos. 355 and 367). The green of the dust jacket is slightly lighter than for the two prior reprints but the front cover decoration and titling is the same with the phrase "with an Introduction by John Buchan" added. Spine titling is unchanged. A few revisions were made in the list of titles on the back cover.

This *Angler* is from Parts I and II of the fifth edition of 1676 (No. 6), and is numbered 430 in the Oxford *World's Classics* series. It was originally issued in the United Kingdom at 8s 6d, a price since increased to 9/6.

Appendix A

References Cited

The American catalogue . . . July 1, 1876-Dec. 31, 1910. New York, A. C. Armstrong & Sons, 1880-1911. Founded and edited by Frederick Leypoldt, compiled by Lynds E. Jones, later vols. edited by R. R. Bowker and published by the Publishers' Weekly. Reprinted 1941.

The annual American catalogue. [1st]-3rd year; 1869-1871. New York, Leypoldt & Holt . . ., 1870-72.

The annual American catalogue 1886 [-1900]; being the full titles, . . . of all books recorded in the Publishers' Weekly, 1886 [-1900] . . . New York, Publishers' Weekly, 1887-1901. 15 vols. Replaced by Annual American catalogue cumulated, 1900/1901-1909.

ANDREWS, WILLIAM LORING — *An English XIX century sportsman, bibliopole and binder of angling books.* New York, Dodd Mead & Co., 1906.—A facsimile reprint of Thomas Gosden's *Catalogue* (8 pp., 1825) is at the end.

BARTLETT, JOHN — *Catalogue of books on angling, including ichthyology, pisciculture, fisheries, and fishing laws. From the library of a practitioner of more than fifty years experience in the art of angling.* Cambridge, [Mass., J. Wilson & Son], 1882. *Supplement* . . . Cambridge, [Mass.], J. Wilson & Son, 1886.

[BENNETT, PAUL A. (ed.)] — *B. R. [Bruce Rogers] marks & remarks.* Typophile Chap Book no. 15. Newark, N.J., 1946. See pp. 49-50.

[————] — *Recalling Peter. The life and times of Peter Beilenson and his Peter Pauper Press.* The Typophiles Chap Book no. 40. New York, The Typophiles, 1964.

BETHUNE, GEORGE WASHINGTON — "A Waltonian library." In, Walton, Izaac & Cotton, Charles *The Compleat Angler.* New York & London, Wiley & Putnam, 1847. Pp. [151]-191. (The First Bethune edition, No. 60.)

"Biblio;" Catalogue des ouvrages parus en langue française dans le monde entier. Paris, n-p., 1935+. — This the annual title. Published monthly as: *"Biblio;" bulletin bibliographique mensuel des ouvrages parus* . . . Paris, 1933+.

Bibliotheca piscatoria. See: (1) Harrison, Wm., (2) Pickering, Wm., and (3) Westwood & Satchell.

BOTTRALL, MARGARET — *Izaak Walton.* New York & Toronto, Longmans, Green & Co. [for The British Council and the National Book League], [1955].

BRADLEY, VAN ALLEN — *The new gold in your attic.* New York, Fleet Press Corp., 1958.

BRITISH MUSEUM. *General catalogue of printed books.* London, Trustees of the British Museum, 1931+. (See vol. 252); *Ten-year Supplement, 1956-1965.* London, 1968 (see vol. 48).

BUSH, DOUGLAS — *English literature in the earlier seventeenth century, 1600-1660.* Oxford, The Clarendon Press, 1945.

BUSHELL, C. W., SR. (comp.) — *Catalogue of the private angling library of C. W. Bushell.* Haberfield [nr. Sydney], Australia, Bushell Publ. Co. Pty. Ltd., 1953.

Catalogue of books on angling. Ms., n.p., n.d. [English, ca. 1855]. — An anonymous manuscript from the Alfred Denison Collection, now in The Kienbusch Library on Fresh Water Angling in the Firestone Library, Princeton University.

CLUB OF ODD VOLUMES, *Boston — A Catalogue of an exhibition of Waltoniana . . . [April 23 to May 2, 1912].* Boston, The Club of Odd Volumes, [1912].

Contributions to a catalogue of the Lennox Library. No. VII, The Waltonian Collection. New York, Trustees of the Lennox Library, 1893.

COOPER, JOHN R. — *The art of The Compleat Angler.* Durham, N.C., Duke University Press, 1968.

The cumulative book index. New York, The H. W. Wilson Co., 1917+.

The English catalogue of books. London, S. Low, Marston & Co., 1864-1949. Reprinted for 1835-1967.

Field & Stream. Izaak Walton 300th anniversary issue. May, 1953. New York, J. P. Burkhard Publ. Co., 1953.

Folio 21. A bibliography of The Folio Society, 1947-1967. London, The Folio Press, 1968.

GOODSPEED, CHARLES ELIOT — *Yankee bookseller; being the reminiscences of . . .* Boston, Houghton Mifflin Co., 1937.

—— —— *Angling in America; its early history and literature.* Boston, Houghton Mifflin Co., 1939. — For: "Check-list of American angling publications relating to fresh-water angling . . . 1660-1900 arranged chronologically" see pp. 345-[365].

GROLIER CLUB, *New York — A catalogue of an exhibition of angling books . . . from December 7, 1911, to January 6, 1912.* New York, The Grolier Club, 1911.

—— —— *Catalogue of original and early editions of some of the poetical and prose works of English writers from Wither to Prior . . .* New York, The Grolier Club, 1905.

—— —— *Chronological hand-list of various editions of The Complete Angler by Izaak Walton and Charles Cotton; with a supplement embracing other writings of Walton and Cotton, etc. 1593-1893; exhibited at The Grolier Club, December 9-29, 1893.* [New York, The Grolier Club, 1893.]

HAMPTON, J. FITZGERALD — *Modern angling bibliography.* London, Herbert Jenkins Ltd., [1947].

HARRISON, J. CLEMENT — *Five hundred years of the printed Bible.* Pittsburgh, Pa., The Pittsburgh Bibliophiles, 1964.

HARRISON, WILLIAM — *Bibliotheca piscatoria, an analytical catalogue of books connected with angling.* Ms. of ca. 900 lvs., n.d. [ca. 1860]. In Kienbusch Library on Fresh Water Angling, Firestone Library, Princeton University.

HECKSCHER, JOHN GERARD — *Catalogue of the library of the late John Gerard Heckscher . . . To be sold . . . February 2nd-[March 4], 1909.* New York, Merwin-Calyton

[314]

Sales Co., [Albany, The Argus Co., 1909]. — See: lots 2009-2136 for *Angler* editions and reprints.

Henry E. Huntington Library — See: Wright, Lyle H. (comp.).

HILLS, JOHN WALLER — *A history of fly fishing for trout.* London, Philip Allan & Co., 1921.

Lennox Library — See: Contributions to a catalogue of . . . (1893).

LIBRARY OF CONGRESS (comp.) — *The national union catalog. Pre-1956 imprints.* London, Chicago; Mansell Information/Publishing Ltd., American Library Association, 1968. — Incompl., publ. cont'd., vols. 1-59 treat Aaa-Blad.

————— — *The national union catalog. A cumulative author list representing Library of Congress printed cards and titles reported by other American libraries.* New York, Rowman & Littlefield, Inc., 1963+. — For imprints of 1958-62, 50 vols.; [ser. 2] for imprints 1963-67, 67 vols.; [ser. 3] for imprints 1968+ in process.

MANLEY, JOHN JACKSON — *Literature of sea and river fishing.* London, William Clowes and Sons Ltd., 1883.

MARSTON, EDWARD — *Thomas Ken and Izaak Walton, a sketch of their lives and family connection.* London, et al., Longmans Green & Co., 1908.

MARSTON, ROBERT BRIGHT — *Walton and some earlier writers on fish and fishing.* London, Elliot Stock, 1894. — Reissued in 1903.

MARTIN, STAPLETON — *Izaak Walton and his friends.* London, Chapman & Hall, Ltd., 1903.

MASSAS, CHARLES DE — *Le pecheur à la mouche artificielle et la pecheur à toutes lignes.* Deuxieme édition revue et augmentée. Paris, Garnier Frères Libraires-Éditions, 1859.

The national union catalogue. See: Library of Congress.

The Nonesuch century. London, The Nonesuch Press, 1936.

NOVARR, DAVID — *The making of Walton's Lives.* Ithaca, N.Y., Cornell University Press, [1958].

OLIVER, PETER — *A new chronicle of The Compleat Angler.* New York, London; The Paisley Press, Inc., Williams & Norgate, Ltd., 1936.

Outdoor American. Izaak Walton anniversary issue, Sept./Oct. 1953. Madison, Wisc., Izaak Walton League of America, 1922+.

[PICKERING, WILLIAM] — *Bibliotheca piscatoria. A catalogue of books upon angling.* London, 1836. Published with: BOOSEY, THOMAS — *Piscatorial reminiscences.* London, William Pickering, 1835 [1836?]. — See also: Harrison, William for another work of same title (ca. 1860).

The Publishers' Weekly, the American book trade journal. New York, Office of the Publishers' Weekly, 1872+.

Quarto-Millenary; the first 250 publications . . . of the Limited Editions Club. New York, Limited Editions Club, 1959.

ROBB, JAMES — *Notable angling literature.* London, Herbert Jenkins Ltd., [ca. 1946].

SATCHELL, THOMAS — *The bibliography of Izaak Walton's Compleat Angler.* London, 1882. — An excerpt from WESTWOOD, THOMAS & SATCHELL, THOMAS — *Bibliotheca piscatoria,* reprinted "for presentation only."

SPARROW, WALTER SHAW — *Angling in British art through five centuries: prints, pictures, books, by* . . . London, John Lane, [1923].

The United States catalog; books in print, 1899. Edited by G. F. Danforth et al. Minneapolis, H. W. Wilson, [1900]. Ed. 2, 1902. Ed. 3, New York, H. W. Wilson Co., 1912. Supplements issued in 1918, 1921, 1924, 1928.

WESTWOOD, THOMAS — *Catalogue of a collection of angling books consisting of 788 volumes on the sport.* Brussels, 1869.

———— *The chronicle of the "Compleat Angler" of Izaak Walton and Charles Cotton; being a bibliographical record of its various editions and mutations.* London, Willis & Sotheran, 1864. — A "new edition" was edited by Thomas Satchell in 1883.

———— & SATCHELL, THOMAS — *Bibliotheca piscatoria: a catalogue of books on angling . . . the fisheries and fish-culture, with bibliographical notes and an appendix of citations . . . from old English authors.* London, W. Satchell, 1883.

———— & ———— *The chronicle of The Compleat Angler* . . . London, W. Satchell, 1883. — Reprinted in the first Marston edition of the *Angler* 1888 (No. 136).

———— & ———— *A list of books* . . . *to supplement the Bibliotheca piscatoria.* . . . London, Sampson Low, Marston & Co., 1901.

WETZEL, CHARLES McKINLEY — *American fishing books, a bibliography from the earliest times up to 1948, together with a history of angling and angling literature in America.* Newark, Del., Privately printed, 1950.

WOOD, ARNOLD — *A bibliography of "The Compleat Angler" of Izaak Walton and Charles Cotton; being a chronologically arranged list of the several editions and reprints . . . until the year MCM.* New York, Charles Scribner's Sons, 1900. — Limited edition of 128 copies.

WRIGHT, LYLE HENRY (comp.) — *Sporting books in the [Henry E.] Huntington Library.* Huntington Library List No. 2. San Marino, Calif., Henry E. Huntington Library, 1937.

Appendix B

Checklist of 48 misprints and variations noted in
copies of first edition of the *Angler*, and their occurrence in facsimiles*

Note: (—)=Present   (X)=Not present

	First Edition (1653)			Facsimile Editions			
	Morgan	Harvard (3 copies)	Horne	Stock 1876	Griggs 1882	Baker-Taylor 1885	Black 1928
Running head; C in Complete varies	—	—	—	X	—	X	—
Recto A3, line 13, Dilgence for Diligence	—	—	—	X	—	X	—
Verso A7, line 2, toread for to read	—	—	—	—	—	—	—
P. 37, line 14, tke for the	—	—	—	—	—	—	—
P. 39, line 9, o or too morrow for tomorrow	X	—	—	—	—	—	—
P. 44, line 18, Alehonse for Alehouse	—	—	—	X	X	X	—
P. 61, line 6, brothet for brother	—	—	—	—	—	—	—
P. 63, line 12, sighs for sights	—	—	—	—	—	—	—
P. 65, line 5, that repeated	—	—	—	—	—	—	—
P. 68, line 2, c ome for come	—	—	—	—	—	—	—
P. 70, misnumbered 80	—	—	—	—	—	—	—
P. 71, misnumbered 81	—	—	—	—	—	—	—
P. 73, misnumbered 37	—	—	—	—	—	—	—
P. 74, misnumbered 84	—	—	—	—	—	—	—
P. 75, misnumbered 85	—	—	—	—	—	—	—
P. 78, misnumbered 88	—	—	—	—	—	—	—
P. 79, misnumbered 89	—	—	—	—	—	—	—
P. 82, last line, vvill for will / tovvards for towards	—	—	—	—	—	—	—
P. 86, line 1, Fordig for Fordidg	—	—	—	—	—	—	—
P. 87, Signature G4, keyed F4	—	—	—	—	—	—	—
line 3, Fordig, for Fordidg	—	—	—	—	—	—	—
line 11, Fordig for Fordidg	—	—	—	—	—	—	—
P. 88, margin, Topſel of, for Topſel on	—	—	—	—	—	—	—
line 10, Fordig for Fordidg	—	—	X	X	—	X	X
P. 90, line 13, Snn for Sun	—	—	—	—	—	—	—
P. 101, line 24, cover d or coverd, for covered	—	—	—	—	—	—	—

	Morgan	Harvard (3 copies)	Horne	Stock 1876	Griggs 1882	Baker-Taylor 1885	Black 1928
P. 103, line 1, the "w" omitted in with	—	—	—	X	—	X	—
P. 113, last line, the "a" omitted before smoaking	X	1X 2—	X	X	—	X	X
P. 114, line 10, VVien for When	—	—	—	—	—	—	—
P. 116, line 23, whichis for which is	—	—	—	—	—	—	—
P. 123, line 4, yuo for you	X	X	X	—	X	—	X
P. 125, line 12, yon for you	—	—	—	—	—	—	—
P. 135, line 18, gro v, for grow	—	—	—	—	X	—	—
P. 136, line 16, the "i" omitted in swimm'd	X	X	X	X	X	X	—
P. 152, line 21, Padoc for Padock	X	X	X	X	X	X	X
P. 154, line 9, ynor for your	—	—	—	—	—	—	—
P. 163, line 8, the for they	—	—	—	—	—	—	—
P. 169, line 16, ate for late	—	—	—	—	—	—	—
P. 181, last line, sigh for sight	—	—	—	—	X	—	—
P. 186, line 15, Uſe for uſe	—	—	—	—	—	—	—
P. 194, line 21, E le for Eele	—	X	—	—	X	—	—
P. 197, line 9, Meker for Melter	X	X	X	X	—	X	X
P. 199, line 24, be o e for before	—	—	—	X	X	X	—
P. 225, line 3, in for it	—	—	—	—	—	—	—
P. 230, last line, the "d" in kinds broken	—	1X 2—	X	X	X	X	—
P. 245, line 17, contention for contentment	—	1— 2X	—	X	—	X	X

*Absence of the reported error from a facsimile edition suggests either (1) that it was not present in the selected copy of the 1653 edition, or (2) that it was "corrected" in the alleged facsimile, in which case it would be somewhat less than a true facsimile. Of the four facsimile editions, the Black facsimile (1928, No. 287) most closely agrees with leaves of any copies seen by Mr. Horne of the 1653 printing. (ED.)

Appendix C

List of 28 misprints and irregularities in the fifth edition (No. 6).

Retained from previous editions

carere for career (2nd ed., p. 9, line 2) 5th ed. Part I, p. 9, line 2
forraign for foreign (2nd ed., p. 11, line 21) 5th ed. Part I, p. 11, line 21
Topſel of for Topſel on (2nd ed., p. 69, 5th ed. Part I, p. 72, 2nd indention
   2nd indention)
Uſe for uſe (2nd ed., p. 187, line 13) 5th ed. Part I, p. 196, line 9
them for him (2nd ed., on Contents 5th ed. Part I (same locations)
   p. and heading Chapt. VI)
of for off (4th ed., p. 194, line 4) 5th ed. Part I, p. 203, line 5
at repeated before ſet (4th ed., p. 195, 5th ed. Part I, p. 204, line 29
   line 18) (both words "at" omitted)

New in the fifth edition

In Part I

[A7] verso, line 20, Wiil for Will
P. 44, line 29, mony for money
P. 49, line 25, own for one
P. 119, line 19, ſwells for ſmells
P. 144, line 20, Hee for He
P. 159, line 16, Simber-ſalts for
   Summer-ſaults
P. 223, line 16, livse for lives
P. 238, line 23, peices for pieces
P. 252, line 14, month for mouth
P. 264, lines 14 & 15, of repeated

In Part II

P. 5, line 25, and for any
P. 29, line 19, *Viat.* omitted
P. 56, line 4, Fiſhers for Flies
   line 5, North for month
P. 63, line 18, the redundant
P. 100, line 30, nnfit for unfit

In Part III

P. 10, line 12, Flie for File
P. 25, line 26, Fie for Flie
P. 34, lines 1, 16 & elsewhere, Menow for Minnow
P. 68, line 3, Roaeh for Roach
P. 73, line 3, Derwen for Derwent

Appendix D

Chronological checklist of ten translations of
the Bible published prior to the first edition of
The Compleat Angler, 1653, showing
variations in the translation of John 21.3

1. Wycliffe Bible, late 14th century
   "Symount Petre seith to hem, I go for to fysche.
   Thei seyn to him, And we comen with thee."

2. Tyndale's New Testament (1525)
   "Simon Peter sayde unto them: I go a fysshynge.
   They sayde unto him: we also will go with the."

3. Coverdale's Bible (1535)
   "Symon Peter sayde unto thē: I go a fyshinge.
   They sayde unto hē: We also wil go w̄ the."

4. Matthew's Bible (1537)
   "Simon Peter sayde unto thē: I go a fysthynge.
   They sayde unto him: we also will go with ẙ."

5. Taverner's Bible (1539)
   "Simon Peter sayeth unto them: I go a fysshynge.
   They sayde unto him: We also will go with the."

6. Great Bible (1539)
   "Simon Peter sayeth unto them: I wyll go a fisshinge.
   They saye unto him: we also wyll go with the."

7. Geneva Bible (1560)
   "Simon Peter sayd unto them, I go a fishyng.
   They sayd unto hym, We also will go wyth thee."

8. The Bishop's Bible (1568)
   "Simon Peter sayeth unto them, I goe a fishing.
   They say unto him, Wee also goe with thee."

9. Rheims New Testament (1582)
   "Simon Peter saith to them, I goe to fish.
   They say to him, We also come with thee."

10. King James (1611)
    "Simon Peter saith unto them: I go a fishing.
    They say unto him, We also go with thee."

The Compleat Angler (1653)
   "Simon Peter ſaid, I go a fiſhing:
   and they ſaid, We alſo wil go with thee."

[320]

Appendix E

Identification Symbols of Library Sources
from
Library of Congress, *National Union Catalog*

A
AU	University of Alabama, University, Ala.

C
CLSU	University of Southern California, Los Angeles, Calif.
CLU-C	William Andrews Clark Memorial Library, Los Angeles, Calif.
CSmH	Henry E. Huntington Library, San Marino, Calif.
CSt	Stanford University Libraries, Stanford, Calif.
CU	University of California, Berkeley, Calif.
CU-A	University of California, Davis, Calif.
CU-I	University of California, Irvine, Calif.
CU-S	University of California, San Diego, Calif.
CoD	Denver Public Library, Denver, Colo.
CtHT	Trinity College, Harford, Conn.
CtY	Yale University, New Haven, Conn.

D
DAU	American University Library, Washington, D. C.
DFo	Folger Shakespeare Library, Washington, D. C.
DI	U. S. Department of Interior Library, Washington, D. C.
DLC	Library of Congress, Washington, D. C.

F
FTaSU	Florida State University, Tallahassee, Fla.
FU	University of Florida, Gainesville, Fla.

G
GEU	Emory University, Atlanta, Ga.
GU	University of Georgia, Athens, Ga.

I
ICJ	John Crerar Library, Chicago, Ill.
ICN	Newberry Library, Chicago, Ill.
ICRL	Center for Research Libraries, Chicago, Ill.
ICU	University of Chicago, Chicago, Ill.
IU	University of Illinois, Urbana, Ill.
ICarbS	Southern Illinois University, Carbondale, Ill.
IaU	University of Iowa, Iowa City, Iowa.
InU	Indiana University, Bloomington, Ind.

KAS	St. Benedict's College, Atchison, Kans.
KPT	Kansas State College of Pittsburg, Pittsburg, Kans.
KU	University of Kansas, Lawrence, Kans.
KyBgW	Western Kentucky State College, Bowling Green, Ky.
KyU	University of Kentucky, Lexington, Ky.

L

LU	Louisiana State University, Baton Rouge, La.

M

MA	Amherst College, Amherst, Mass.
MB	Boston Public Library, Boston, Mass.
MH	Harvard University, Cambridge, Mass.
MU	University of Massachusetts, Amherst, Mass.
MWelC	Wellesley College, Wellesley, Mass.
MWiW-C	Chapin Library, Williams College, Williamstown, Mass.
MdBJ	Johns Hopkins University, Baltimore, Md.
MdBP	Peabody Institute, Baltimore, Md.
MeB	Bowdoin College, Brunswick, Maine.
MiD	Detroit Public Library, Detroit, Mich.
MiDW	Wayne State University, Detroit, Mich.
MiHM	Michigan College of Mining & Technology, Houghton, Mich.
MiU	University of Michigan, Ann Arbor, Mich.
MnU	University of Minnesota, Minneapolis, Minn.
MoU	University of Missouri, Columbia, Mo.

N

N	New York State Library, Albany, N. Y.
NBu	Buffalo & Erie County Public Library, Buffalo, N. Y.
NIC	Cornell University, Ithaca, N. Y.
NN	New York Public Library, New York, N. Y.
NNC	Columbia University, New York, N. Y.
NNU	New York University Libraries, New York, N. Y.
NNUN-W	United Nations Woodrow Wilson Memorial Library, New York, N. Y.
NRU	University of Rochester, Rochester, N. Y.
NSyU	Syracuse University, Syracuse, N. Y.
NcC	Public Library of Charlotte & Mecklenburg County, Charlotte, N. C.
NcD	Duke University, Durham, N. C.
NcGW	University of North Carolina at Greensboro, N. C.
NcRS	North Carolina State College of Agriculture & Engineering, Raleigh, N. C.
NcU	University of North Carolina, Chapel Hill, N. C.

NjN	Newark Public Library, Newark, N. J.
NjNbS	Gardner A. Sage Library, Theological Seminary, New Brunswick, N. J.
NjP	Princeton University, Princeton, N. J.
NjR	Rutgers—The State University, New Brunswick, N. J.

O

OC	Public Library of Cincinnati & Hamilton County, Cincinnati, Ohio.
OCU	University of Cincinnati, Cincinnati, Ohio.
OCl	Cleveland Public Library, Cleveland, Ohio.
OClCC	Cleveland College Library, Cleveland, Ohio.
OClCS	Case Institute of Technology, Cleveland, Ohio.
OClND	Notre Dame College, Cleveland, Ohio.
OClRC	Rowfant Club, Cleveland, Ohio.
OClW	Western Reserve University, Cleveland, Ohio.
OClh	Cleveland Heights Public Library, Cleveland, Ohio.
ODW	Ohio Wesleyan University, Delaware, Ohio.
OLak	Lakewood Public Library, Lakewood, Ohio.
OO	Oberlin College, Oberlin, Ohio.
OOxM	Miami University, Oxford, Ohio.
OrU	University of Oregon, Eugene, Ore.

P

PBL	Lehigh University, Bethlehem, Pa.
PBa	Academy of the New Church, Bryn Athyn, Pa.
PBm	Bryn Mawr College, Bryn Mawr, Pa.
PHC	Haverford College, Haverford, Pa.
PP	Free Library of Philadelphia, Philadelphia, Pa.
PPA	Athenaeum of Philadelphia, Philadelphia, Pa.
PPAN	Academy of Natural Sciences, Philadelphia, Pa.
PPD	Drexel Institute of Technology, Philadelphia, Pa.
PPFr	Friends Free Library of Germantown, Philadelphia, Pa.
PPGi	Girard College, Philadelphia, Pa.
PPL	Library Company of Philadelphia, Philadelphia, Pa.
PPLas	LaSalle College, Philadelphia, Pa.
PPT	Temple University, Philadelphia, Pa.
PPWI	Wistar Institute of Anatomy & Biology, Philadelphia, Pa.
PPiCI	Carnegie-Mellon University (Carnegie Institute of Technology), Pittsburgh, Pa.
PRosC	Rosemont College, Rosemont, Pa.
PSC	Swarthmore College, Swarthmore, Pa.
PU	University of Pennsylvania, Philadelphia, Pa.
PV	Villanova College, Villanova, Pa.
PWcT	West Chester State College, West Chester, Pa.

R

RPB   Brown University, Providence, R. I.

T

TU   University of Tennessee, Knoxville, Tenn.
TxU   University of Texas, Austin, Texas.

V

Vi   Virginia State Library, Richmond, Va.
ViU   University of Virginia, Charlottesville, Va.
ViW   College of William and Mary, Williamsburg, Va.

W

WU   University of Wisconsin, Madison, Wisc.
WaU   University of Washington, Seattle, Wash.

Appendix F

Chronological Checklist of *Angler* editions and reprints

Date	Number	Edition, Reprint, or Facsimile
1653	1	First Edition
1655	2	Second Edition
1661	3	Third Edition of 1661
1664	4	Third Edition of 1664
1668	5	Fourth Edition
1676	6	Fifth Edition
1750	7	First Moses Browne Edition
1759	8	Second Moses Browne Edition
1760	9	First Hawkins Edition
1766	10	Second Hawkins Reprint
1772	11	Third Moses Browne Edition
1775	12	Third Hawkins Reprint
1784	13	Fourth Hawkins Edition
1791	14	Fifth Hawkins Reprint
1792	15	Sixth (titled Fifth) Hawkins Reprint
1797	16	Seventh (titled Sixth) Hawkins Reprint
1808	17	First Bagster Edition (octavo, printed by C. Mercier & Co.)
1808	18	First Bagster (octavo, printed by Mercier & Chervet)
1808	19	First Bagster (quarto, printed by C. Mercier & Co.)
1810	20	Bagster's Reprint
1815	21	Second Bagster (ninth, half-titled eighth; Hawkins) Edition
1822	22	Tenth (called ninth) Hawkins Edition
1823	23	First Major Edition
1824	24	Second Major Edition
1824	25	First Tegg (11th Hawkins) Edition
[1824]	26	Maunder Edition
1825	27	Gosden (12th Hawkins) Edition
1825	28	Dove (13th Hawkins) Edition
1825	29	First Pickering Edition
1826	30	Second Pickering Edition
1826	31	Prowett (3rd Pickering) Reprint
1826	32	Second Tegg (14th Hawkins) Edition
1827	33	Fourth Pickering Reprint
1828	34	Cole Reprint
1833	35	First Rennie Edition
1834	36	Second Rennie Reprint
1834	37	Third Rennie Reprint
1834	38	Fourth Rennie Reprint
1834	39	Fifth Rennie Reprint

Date	Number	Edition, Reprint or Facsimile
1834	40	Sixth Rennie Reprint
1835	41	Seventh Rennie Reprint
1835	42	Third Major Reprint
1836	43	First Nicolas Edition
1836	44	Eighth Rennie Reprint
1836	45	Ninth Rennie Reprint
1836	46	Tenth Rennie Reprint
1837	47	Tilt (5th Pickering) Edition
1839	48	Lewis (4th Major) Edition
1841	49	Chidley Reprint
1842	50	Washbourne (5th Major) Reprint
1844	51	Sherwood and Bowyer Edition
[1844]	52	Lockwood Reprint
[1844]	53	Piper Reprint
[1844]	54	First Lippincott Reprint
1844	55	Sixth (titled 4th) Major Edition
1844	56	Eleventh Rennie Reprint
1846	57	Twelfth Rennie Reprint
1847	58	Thirteenth Rennie Reprint
1847	59	Fourteenth Rennie Reprint
1847	60	First Bethune Edition
1848	61	Second Bethune Reprint
1848	62	Fifteenth Rennie Reprint
1849	63	Sixteenth Rennie Reprint
[1849]	64	Seventeenth Rennie Reprint
1851	65	Eighteenth Rennie Reprint
1851	66	Causton (4th Moses Browne) Edition
1852	67	Third Bethune Edition
1853	68	First Ephemera Edition
1854	69	Second Ephemera Reprint
1856	70	First Jesse Edition
[1857]	71	Nineteenth Rennie Reprint
1857	72	Twentieth Rennie Reprint
1858	73	Groombridge (6th Pickering) Edition
1859	74	Third Ephemera Reprint
1859	75	First German (4th Ephemera) Edition
1859	76	Fourth Bethune Reprint
1860	77	Second Nicolas Reprint
1861	78	Second Jesse Reprint
[1862]	79	Fifth Ephemera Reprint
[1862]	80	Sixth Ephemera Reprint
1863	81	First Bell-Daldy & Low Edition
1864	82	Bell-Daldy Reprint
1865	83	Second Bell-Daldy & Low Reprint

Date	Number	Edition, Reprint, or Facsimile
1866	84	First Ticknor & Fields Reprint
1866	85	Second Ticknor & Fields Reprint
1866	86	Fifth Bethune Reprint
1866	87	First Little, Brown (7th Major) Edition
1867	88	Second Little, Brown (8th Major) Edition
1869	89	First Murray Edition
1870	90	Third Jesse Reprint
1870	91	Third Little, Brown (9th Major) Reprint
1872	92	Second Murray Reprint
[1872]	93	Anonymous Murray Reprint
1875	94	Third Nicolas Edition
1875	95	First George Bell Reprint
[1876]	96	Seventh Ephemera Reprint
1876	97	Fourth Jesse Reprint
1876	98	First Stock Facsimile
1877	99	Second Stock Facsimile
[1878]	100	Eighth Ephemera Reprint
[1878]	101	First Davies Edition
[1878]	102	Second Davies Reprint
[1878]	103	Ward Lock Reprint
1879	104	Second George Bell Reprint
[1879]	105	Third Davies (1st Scribner & Welford) Reprint
1879	106	Fishing Gazette Edition
1880	107	Sixth Bethune Edition
[1880]	108	Third Stock Facsimile
1881	109	Ninth Ephemera Reprint
[1881]	110	Second Lippincott (10th Major) Reprint
[1881]	111	Strahan (11th Major) Reprint
1882	112	Fifth Jesse Reprint
[1882]	113	Griggs Facsimile
1883	114	Nimmo and Bain (12th Major) Reprint
1884	115	Sixth Jesse Reprint
[1884]	116	First Crowell (13th Major) Edition
1884	117	Fourth Davies Reprint
[1884-1886]	118	Angler's Journal Edition
[1885]	119	Fifth Davies (2nd Scribner & Welford) Edition
[1885]	120	First Baker & Taylor (4th Stock) Facsimile
[1885]	121	Second Baker & Taylor (5th Stock) Facsimile
1885	122	Crawhall Abridged Edition
1885	123	First Nimmo (14th Major) Reprint
1885	124	Alfred Edition
1886	125	First Cassell Edition
1886	126	Second Cassell Reprint

Date	Number	Edition, Reprint or Facsimile
[1886]	127	Third Cassell Reprint
[1886]	128	Fourth Cassell (Leipzig) Reprint
[1887]	129	Fifth Cassell Reprint
1887	130	Fourth Nicolas Reprint
[1887]	131	Third Baker & Taylor (6th Stock) Facsimile
[1887]	132	Sixth Davies Reprint
1888	133	Seventh Davies Reprint
[1888]	134	Seventh Bethune Reprint
[1888]	135	Fourth Baker & Taylor (7th Stock) Facsimile
1888	136	Lea & Dove (1st Marston) Edition
1888	137	Dodd, Mead, Lea & Dove (2nd Marston) Reprint
1888	138	Second Nimmo (15th Major) Reprint
1889	139	Third Nimmo (16th Major) Reprint
1889	140	Fourth Nimmo (17th Major) Reprint
1889	141	Putnam-Nimmo (18th Major) Reprint
1889	142	First Lowell Edition
1889	143	Second Lowell (Boston & London) Reprint
1889	144	Seventh Jesse Reprint
1889	145	Sixth Cassell (Alden) Reprint
1890	146	Eighth Davies (1st Gibbings) Reprint
[1890]	147	Ninth Davies Reprint
[1890]	148	Seventh Cassell Reprint
1891	149	Eighth Cassell Reprint
[1891]	150	Ninth Cassell Reprint
1891	151	Eighth Bethune Edition
1891	152	Third Lowell Reprint
1891	153	Fourth Lowell (Boston & London) Reprint
1892	154	Fifth Lowell Reprint
[1892]	155	Second Crowell (19th Major) Reprint
1892	156	Rendall Abridged Musical Edition
[1892]	157	First Lovell, Coryell (20th Major) Edition
[1892]	158	Tenth Cassell Reprint
[1893]	159	Third Crowell (21st Major) Reprint
[1893]	160	Tenth Ephemera Reprint
1893	161	First McClurg Edition
1893	162	Harting Edition
[1893]	163	Tenth Davies Reprint
[1894]	164	First Burt (22nd Major) Reprint
1895	165	Eleventh Davies (2nd Gibbings) Reprint
[1895]	166	Twelfth Davies Reprint
[1895]	167	Second Lovell, Coryell (23rd Major) Reprint
[1895]	168	First Scott Edition
[1895]	169	Second Scott Reprint
1896	170	First Lang Edition

Date	Number	Edition, Reprint or Facsimile
1896	171	Second Lang "Edition"
1896	172	Eighth Jesse Reprint
1896	173	Fifth Nimmo (24th Major) Reprint
1896	174	Sixth Nimmo (25th Major) Reprint
1896	175	First Le Gallienne (8th Stock) Facsimile Edition
1897	176	Second Le Gallienne (9th Stock) Facsimile
1897	177	First Le Gallienne Edition
[1897]	178	First Caldwell (26th Major) Reprint
1898	179	Eleventh Cassell Reprint
1898	180	Twelfth Cassell Reprint
1898	181	Sixth Lowell Reprint
[1898]	182	Fourth Crowell (27th Major) Reprint
[1898]	183	Fifth Crowell (28th Major) Reprint
[1898]	184	Sixth Crowell (29th Major) Reprint
1899	185	Thirteenth Davies (Pearson) Reprint
[1899]	186	Second Caldwell (30th Major) Reprint
1899	187	First Dobson Edition
[1899]	188	Seventh Crowell (31st Major) Reprint
[1900]	189	Eighth Crowell (32nd Major) Reprint
[1900]	190	Ninth Crowell (33rd Major) Reprint
1900	191	Thirteenth Cassell Reprint
1900	192	Third Lippincott (34th Major) Reprint
[1900]	193	Second Burt (35th Major) Reprint
1900	194	Second McClurg Reprint
[1900]	195	Oxford-Thumb Miniature Edition
1900	196	Ninth Jesse Reprint
[1901]	197	Seventh Lowell Reprint
1901	198	First Macmillan Edition
1901	199	First Buchan Edition
1901	200	First Gay & Bird Edition
1901	201	Second Gay & Bird Reprint
1901	202	Brentano (3rd Gay & Bird) Reprint
1902	203	Second Dobson Reprint
1902	204	Winchester, Freemantle (1st Dewar) Edition
1902	205	Winchester, Freemantle, 4th Lippincott (2nd Dewar) Reprint
1903	206	Fifth Nicolas Reprint
1903	207	Tenth Jesse Reprint
1903	208	Scott-Thaw Edition
1903	209	First Methuen (36th Major) Edition
[1903]	210	Hurst (37th Major) Edition
1903	211	Second Le Gallienne Edition
1904	212	Third Le Gallienne Reprint
[1904]	213	Pocket Library Routledge-Dutton Reprint

Date	Number	Edition, Reprint or Facsimile
1904	214	Second Methuen (38th Major) Reprint
1904	215	Appleton (39th Major) Reprint
1904	216	Fourteenth Cassell Reprint
1905	217	Fifteenth Cassell Reprint
[1905]	218	Third Burt (40th Major) Reprint
[1905]	219	Routledge (41st Major) Reprint
[1905]	220	Dutton (42nd Major) Reprint
[1905]	221	Routledge-Dutton (43rd Major) Reprint
1905	222	Third Dobson Reprint
1905	223	Caradoc Edition
1906	224	Tenth Crowell (44th Major) Reprint
[1906]	225	Eighth Lowell Reprint
1906	226	Second Macmillan Reprint
1906	227	First Rouse Abridged Edition
[1906]	228	First Everyman (3rd Lang) Edition
[1906]	229	Second Everyman (4th Lang) Reprint
1906	230	Sixteenth Cassell Reprint
1907	231	Seventeenth Cassell Reprint
[1907]	232	Eighteenth (Brooklyn) Cassell Reprint
1907	233	Wellcome (10th Stock) Facsimile
[1908]	234	Third Everyman (5th Lang) Reprint
[1908]	235	Quiller-Couch Abridged Edition
1908	236	First Collins Edition
1909	237	Nineteenth Cassell Edition
[1909]	238	The Asprey Reprint
[1909]	239	Fourth Burt (45th Major) Reprint
1909	240	Riverside Press (Bruce Rogers) Edition
[1911]	241	Fourth Everyman (6th Lang) Reprint
[1911]	242	First Thorpe Edition
[1911]	243	Second Thorpe Reprint
[1911]	244	Third Thorpe Reprint
1912	245	Ninth Lowell Reprint
1912	246	Brewer Abridged Edition
1913	247	Brewer Abridged Reprint
[1913]	248	Fifth Everyman (7th Lang) Reprint
[1913]	249	Fifth Burt (46th Major) Reprint
[1913]	250	Fourth Thorpe Reprint
1913	251	Second Rouse Abridged Reprint
1913	252	First Hankey Edition
[1914]	253	Second Hankey (Phillips) Reprint
[1915]	254	Sixth Burt (47th Major) Reprint
1915	255	Third Marston Edition
1915	256	Cough & Balston Edition
[1916]	257	Sixth Everyman (8th Lang) Reprint

Date	Number	Edition, Reprint, or Facsimile
[1918]	258	Seventh Burt (48th Major) Reprint
[1919]	259	Eighth Burt (49th Major) Reprint
[1920]	260	Seventh Everyman (9th Lang) Reprint
1920	261	Gay & Hancock Reprint
[1920]	262	Fifth Thorpe Reprint
1921	263	Fourth Marston Reprint
[1922]	264	Ninth Burt (50th Major) Reprint
[1923]	265	Tenth Burt (51st Major) Reprint
[1923]	266	Fourth Le Gallienne Reprint
1923	267	Fifth Le Gallienne Reprint
[1924]	268	Eleventh Burt (52nd Major) Reprint
[1925]	269	Twelfth Burt (53rd Major) Reprint
1925	270	Third Macmillan Reprint
[1925]	271	Eighth Everyman (10th Lang) Reprint
1925	272	Sixth Thorpe Edition
1925	273	Seventh Thorpe Reprint
1925	274	Navarre Society (54th Major) Reprint
[1925]	275	First Nelson Edition
1926	276	Second Nelson Reprint
[1926]	277	Thirteenth Burt (55th Major) Reprint
[1926]	278	Sixth Le Gallienne Reprint
1926	279	First Japanese Edition
[1927]	280	Fourteenth Burt (56th Major) Reprint
[1927]	281	Second Collins Reprint
[1927]	282	First Haldeman-Julius Edition
1927	283	Second Haldeman-Julius Reprint
[1927]	284	First Daglish (57th Major) Edition
[1927]	285	Second Daglish (58th Major) Reprint
[1928]	286	Ninth Everyman (11th Lang) Reprint
1928	287	First Black Facsimile
1928	288	Goodspeed (Bliss Perry) Edition
[1929]	289	Third Collins Reprint
[1929]	290	Third Nelson Reprint
[1929]	291	De La More Abridged Edition
1929	292	Nonesuch (1st Keynes) Edition
[1930]	293	Fourteenth Davies Reprint
1930	294	Third Daglish (59th Major) Reprint
[1930]	295	Mason Abridged Edition
1930	296	Adams Edition
[1931]	297	Seventh Le Gallienne Reprint
[1931]	298	Fourth Collins Reprint
1931	299	First Rackham Edition
[1931]	300	Second Rackham Reprint
[1931]	301	Third Rackham (McKay) Reprint

Date	Number	Edition, Reprint or Facsimile
[1932]	302	Tenth Everyman (12th Lang) Reprint
[1932]	303	Eleventh Everyman (13th Lang) Reprint
[1934]	304	Fifteenth Burt (60th Major) Reprint
[1934]	305	Fifth Collins Reprint
[1934]	306	Fourth Nelson Reprint
[1935]	307	Second Buchan Edition
[1936]	308	Fourth Japanese Reprint
[1936]	309	Heritage Nonesuch Edition
[1936]	310	Odhams Press Reprint
1937	311	First Black (4th Gay & Bird) Reprint
[1937]	312	Grosset & Dunlap Edition
[1937]	313	Caxton Press Reprint
[1938]	314	Heritage Club Reprint
[1939]	315	Twelfth Everyman (14th Lang) Reprint
[1939]	316	First Modern Library (2nd Keynes) Edition
[1939]	317	First Penguin Edition
[1940]	318	Second Penguin Reprint
[1941]	319	Second Modern Library (3rd Keynes) Reprint
[1941]	320	Third Modern Library (4th Keynes) Reprint
[1942]	321	Fourth Modern Library (5th Keynes) Reprint
[1942]	322	First French Abridged Edition
1942	323	Monastery Hill Abridged Edition
[1943]	324	Fifth Modern Library (6th Keynes) Reprint
1943	325	First Danish Edition
1943	326	Second Danish Reprint
1943	327	Third Danish Reprint
[1944]	328	Thirteenth Everyman (15th Lang) Reprint
[1944]	329	Sixth Modern Library (7th Keynes) Reprint
[1944]	330	Seventh Modern Library (8th Keynes) Reprint
[1944]	331	Fourth Danish Reprint
1944	332	Fifth Danish Reprint
1945	333	Sixth Danish Reprint
[1945]	334	Seventh Danish Reprint
1945	335	Second Black (5th Gay & Bird) Reprint
[1945]	336	Eighth Modern Library (9th Keynes) Reprint
[1945]	337	Ninth Modern Library (10th Keynes) Reprint
[1945]	338	First Swedish Edition
[1945]	339	Fourteenth Everyman (16th Lang) Zepher Reprint
[1946]	340	Tenth Modern Library (11th Keynes) Reprint
1946	341	Eighth Danish Reprint
[1946]	342	Second Swedish Edition
[1947]	343	Third (called Second) Swedish Edition
[1947]	344	First Finnish Reprint
[1947]	345	Peter Pauper Press Edition

Date	Number	Edition, Reprint or Facsimile
[1947]	346	Fifteenth Everyman (17th Lang) Reprint
1948	347	Second Navarre Society (61st Major) Reprint
1948	348	Limited Editions Club Edition
[1948]	349	Heritage Press Reprint
[1948]	350	Edwards Edition
[1948]	351	Vane Edition
[1949]	352	Eleventh Modern Library (12th Keynes) Reprint
1949	353	First Folio Society Edition
1950	354	Redcoat Press Abridged Edition
[1951]	355	Third Buchan Reprint
[1952]	356	Twelfth Modern Library (13th Keynes) Reprint
1952	357	Classics Book Club Edition
[1953]	358	Sixteenth Everyman (18th Lang) Reprint
[1953]	359	Third Navarre Society (62nd Major) Reprint
[1953]	360	Ninth Danish Reprint
1953	361	Burns Abridged and Revised Edition
1954	362	Fifth Nelson Reprint
[1954]	363	Thirteenth Modern Library (14th Keynes) Reprint
[1958]	364	Hamburg und Berlin (2nd German) Edition
1958	365	Weimar (3rd German) Edition
1958	366	Hanau/M (4th German) Edition
[1960]	367	Fourth Buchan Reprint
1961	368	Sixth Nelson Reprint
1961	369	Dolphin Edition
[1962]	370	Seventeenth Everyman (1st Bottrall) Edition
[1962]	371	Second Folio Society Edition
1962	372	Second French Abridged Edition
[1962]	373	Collier Edition
[1963]	374	Third Black (6th Gay & Bird) Reprint
[1964]	375	Eighteenth Everyman (2nd Bottrall) Reprint
[1964]	376	Third Folio Society Reprint
[1964]	377	Tenth Danish Reprint
1964	378	Fourth Swedish Edition
[1964]	379	First French Unabridged Edition
[1965]	380	Ninteenth Everyman (3rd Bottrall) Edition
[1965]	381	Seventh Nelson Reprint
1965	382	Fifth Swedish Reprint
[1966]	383	Fourth Folio Society Reprint
1966	384	Abercrombie & Fitch (2nd Black) Facsimile
[1967]	385	Fifth Buchan Reprint

Index

Entries on individual artists, booksellers, designers, editors, engravers, places of imprint, printers, publishers, and translators are given under those headings

Dodd, Mead, Lea & Dove reprint (of 1st Marston No. 136) (1888) No. 137
Dolphin Books series No. 369
Dolphin edition (1961) No. 369
Donne, Dr. John – gift to Walton of his seal p. 59; life of No. 292
Donne's seal ring No. 210
Doran, George H. Co., see Nos 243, 250
Doran reprint, see Nos. 243, 250
Douce, Francis – proof set of 1st Major woodcuts p. 39
Dutton reprint (of 6th Major ed. No. 55) [1905] No. 220
Dwiggins, W. A. – headpieces by No. 288

E=Ephemera, *pseud.* for Edward Fitzgibbon No. 237
Éditions Stock No. 322
Editors – Alfred, H. Jervis No. 124; Anderson, I. No. 325; Bagster, Samuel No. 17; Bethune, George B.: See Nos. 60, 61, 67, 76, 86, 107, 134, 151; Briscoe, John Potter No. 200; Browne, Moses Nos. 8, 11; Buchan, John No. 199; Causton, Henry Kent No. 66; Chassé, Charles No. 322; Davies, G. C. Nos. 101, 102, 105, 117, 119, 132, 146, 147, 163, 165, 166; Delamain, Jacques No. 322; Dewar, George Albermarle Bertie Nos. 204, 205; Dick, Charles Hill Nos. 168, 169; Dobson, Austin Nos. 187, 203, 222; Ellis, Henry No. 21; Fitzgibbon, Edward (as Ephemera, *pseud.*) No. 68; Gollancz, Israel No. 187; Gough, A. B. No. 256; Griggs, William No. 113; Haldeman-Julius, E. Nos. 282, 283; Harper, Charles No. 5; Harting, J. E. No. 162; Hawkins, John Nos. 9, 13; Ichikawa, S. No. 279; Jesse, Edward Nos. 70, 78, 90, 97, 112, 115, 144, 172, 196, 207; Johnson, E. G. No. 161; Keynes, Sir Geoffrey L. No. 292; Lang, Andrew Nos. 170, 171, 228, 234; Le Gallienne, Richard Nos. 175, 176, 177, 211, 212, 299; Lowell, James Russell: See Nos. 142, 143, 152, 153, 154, 181, 197; Major, John Nos. 23, 164, 274; Marston, R. B. Nos. 106, 136, 137, 256; Morley, Henry Nos. 125, 127, 129, 147, 150, 179, 180, 191, 216, 232, 237; Newboldt, Henry No. 295; Nicolas, Sir Harry Nos. 43, 170, 228; Okakura, Hoshiaburo No. 308; Okakura, Y. No. 279; Pollard, Alfred W. No. 198; Quiller-Couch, Sir Arthur Thomas No. 235; Rennie, James Nos. 35-41; Rouse, W. H. D. Nos. 227, 251; Thompson, Richard No. 23
Editors of, the Angler, commentary on p. *xii*

Edwards edition [1948] No. 350
Ellis, Sir Henry, editor of 2nd Bagster p. 37
Elzivir Series Nos. 82, 83, 95, 97, 119
Engravers – Adcock, J. Nos. 43, 123; Alexander, A. No. 292; Alfred, W. H. Jr. No. 124; Archer, J. W. Nos. 23, 42, 48, 55, 70, 87, 101, 110, 111, 157, 210, 218; Armytage, J. G. Nos. 43, 123; Ashby, R. Nos. 23, 42, 48, 101; Audinet, Philip Nos. 17, 18, 19, 20, 21; Audinet, ——— No. 162; Bentley, C. Nos. 110, 111; Berryman, ——— No. 17; Bewick, Thomas No. 70; Bone, C. R. Nos. 55, 87, 97, 142, 159; Branston, R. Nos. 23, 42, 48, 101; Burgh, H. Nos. 8, 255; Byfield, ——— Nos. 43, 206; Cameron, D. Y. Nos. 204, 205; Clennel, ——— Nos. 19, 21; Cole, Herbert Nos. 200, 201, 202; Cook, H. Nos. 23, 42, 48, 66, 101; Cooke, W. J. Nos. 43, 123; Cooper, A. Nos. 55, 87, 110, 111; Copeland, ——— No. 155; Crawhall, Joseph No. 122; Creswick, T. Nos. 55, 87, 110, 111; Damman, Ben Nos. 114, 274, 347; Davis, S. T. Nos. 110, 111; Derby, ——— No. 123; Elmer, Stephen Nos. 22, 27; Eyre, John No. 236; Fox, Augustus Nos. 29, 43, 123; Freebairn, ——— Nos. 43, 123; Fussell, Alexander Nos. 55, 87; Gibbon, B. No. 24; Giller, ——— No. 27; Godden, J. Nos. 110, 111; Gompertz, ——— Nos. 55, 87; Gorsline, Douglas W. Nos. 348, 349; Greig, George M. Nos. 21, 27, 162; Harlow, Louis K. Nos. 142, 143, 152, 181, 225; Harvey, ——— No. 32; Hayteer, Charles No. 21; Henshall, W. Nos. 110, 111; Hove, F. H. van No. 6; Hughes, W. Nos. 23, 42, 48, 101; Humphrys, W. Nos. 43, 123; Jackson, John Nos. 55, 87; Jackson, Mason Nos. 55, 87; Kernot, ——— No. 27; Knowled, R. L. Nos. 204, 205; Lance, George Nos. 55, 87; Landells, Ebenezer Nos. 73, 79; Lee, ——— Nos. 55, 87; Leitch, ——— Nos. 55, 87; Linnell, ——— No. 162; Linton, W. Nos. 110, 111; Lizars, W. H. Nos. 35, 44, 45, 46, 55-59, 63, 64, 65, 70; Lombart, Peter (Pierre) No. 1; Lowry, Wilson Nos. 22, 27; Maile, George Nos. 22, 27; Meadows, K. Nos. 55, 87; Mitchell, ——— Nos. 33, 81, 84; Mosses, T. Nos. 23, 42, 48, 101; Nash, ——— No. 66; Nasmyth, Patrick Nos. 22, 27; New, E. H. Nos. 177, 211, 212; Orr, J. W. Nos. 60, 67; Pearson, Cornelius Nos. 68, 96, 109; Pye, Charles Nos. 23, 42, 48, 66, 101; Raddon, W. No. 24; Richardson, J. Nos. 43, 123; Ridley, ——— No. 256; Roberts, ——— No. 43; Roberts, H. Nos. 16, 123; Robinson, Henry Nos. 43, 55, 87, 123, 142, 218; Robin-

Illustrated Pocket Library series Nos. 209, 214, 236
Illustrations *Angler* ed. 1 p. 3; ed. 2 p. 7; ed. 3 (1661) p. 9; ed. 3 (1664) p. 12; ed. 4, p. 14; ed. 5 pp. 16, 17, 18; Alfred ed. (No. 124), in parts, p. 129; First Bagster (quarto) ed. (No. 19) p. 34; First Bethune ed. (No. 60), publisher's binding, p. 63, title-page, p. 74; Collier ed. (No. 373), publisher's binding, p. 306; First Danish ed. (No. 325), title-page, p. 273; First Davies ed. (No. 101), title-page, p. 107, publisher's binding, p. 166; Dolphin ed. (No. 369), publisher's binding, p. 300; Ninth Ephemera reprint (No. 109), publisher's binding, p. 166; Eighteenth Everyman reprint (No. 375), publisher's binding, p. 306; First French Abridged ed. (No. 322), publisher's binding, p. 300; First French Unabridged ed. (No. 374), binding and title-page, p. 308; Gosden ed. (No. 25), binding and title-page, p. 44; First Hawkins ed. (No. 9) p. 25; First Le Gallienne ed. (No. 177), in parts, p. 172; First Lang ed. (No. 170), publisher's binding, p. 166; Lewis ed. (No. 48), publisher's binding, p. 63; First Moses Browne ed. (No. 7) p. 22; First Nicolas ed. (No. 43), in parts, p. 58; First Penguin ed. (No. 317), publisher's binding, p. 300; Prowett ed. (No. 31) p. 49; Riverside Press ed. (No. 240), title-page, p. 217; Fourth Swedish ed. (No. 378), publisher's binding, p. 306; Tilt ed. (No. 47), publisher's binding, p. 63.
Illustrators of, commentary on p. *xiii*
Izaak Walton League of America No. 361

J. P. B.=John Potter Briscoe No. 200
Jackson, John – *The Practical Flyfisher* cited Nos. 139, 141; *Treatise on Flies and Fly-Hooks* Nos. 123, 139, 141
Japanese editions and reprints: 1st (1926) No. 279; 4th [1936] No. 308
Jesse, Edward – editor p. 83
Jesse editions and reprints: 1st (1856) No. 70; 2nd (1861) No. 78; 3rd (1870) No. 90; 4th (1876) No. 97; 5th (1882) No. 112; 6th (1884) No. 115; 7th (1889) No. 144; 8th (1896) No. 172; 9th (1900) No. 196; 10th (1903) No. 207
Johnson, Samuel – suggests the *Piscatorial Eclogues* p. 21
Journal of the Lake Piseco Trout Club, extracts of No. 60

Ken and Chalkhill, pedigrees cited p. 87

Kenkyusha English Classics series No. 279
Kent, Henry – printer p. 79
Keynes, Sir Geoffrey L. – biobibliographical notes by No. 292; editor of Nos. 292, 316
Keynes editions and reprints: 1st ed. (1929) No. 292; 2nd ed. [1939] No. 316; 3rd reprint [1941] No. 319; 4th reprint [1941] No. 320; 5th reprint [1942] No. 321; 6th reprint [1943] No. 324; 7th reprint [1944] No. 329; 8th reprint [1944] No. 330; 9th reprint [1945] No. 336; 10th reprint [1945] No. 337; 11th reprint [1946] No. 340; 12th reprint [1949] No. 352; 13th reprint [1952] No. 356; 14th reprint [1954] No. 363
Kiepenheuer, Noa – translator No. 366

La Belle Sauvage yard, London No. 125
Lagercrantz, Olof – foreword by Nos. 338, 342, 343, 378, 382
Lake Piseco Trout Club, Journal extracted No. 60
Lambert, Samuel W. – copy of Gosden's edition, p. 45; ex libris of No. 126
Laneare, Nicholas – portrait cited No. 110
Lang, Andrew – biographical essay on Walton, No. 380; introduction by Nos. 170, 171, 228, 229, 358
Lang editions and reprints: 1st edition (1896) No. 170; 2nd "edition" (1896) No. 171; 3rd edition [1906] No. 228; 4th edition [1906] No. 229; 5th reprint [1908] No. 234; 6th reprint [1911] No. 241; 7th reprint [1913] No. 248; 8th reprint [1916] No. 257; 9th reprint [1920] No. 260; 10th reprint [1925] No. 271; 11th reprint [1928] No. 286; 12th reprint [1932] No. 302; 13th reprint [1932] No. 303; 14th reprint [1939] No. 315; 15th reprint [1944] No. 328; 16th reprint [1945] No. 339; 17th reprint [1947] No. 346; 18th reprint [1953] No. 358
Lathy, Thomas P. – *The Angler* (1819), cited pp. 43, 45
Lawes, Henry – songs by No. 1, p. 1
"Lawes of Angling," added, in 3rd ed. pp. 8, 11
Laudatory verses, dates of in 1st ed. pp. 4-5
Lea & Dove edition (1888) No. 136 (see also No. 137)
Lea & Dove reprint: see No. 137
Lea bridge, view from – 1st in No. 55; see also p. 115, Nos. 70, 114, 173, 221
Leadenhall Press No. 122
Le Gallienne, Richard – preface by Nos. 175, 176, 177

Le Gallienne editions and reprints: 1st edition (1897) No. 177; 2nd edition (1903) No. 211; 3rd reprint (1904) No. 212; 4th reprint [1923] No. 266; 5th reprint (1923) No. 267; 6th reprint [1926] No. 278; 7th reprint [1931] No. 297, reissued No. 299

Le Gallienne facsimiles: 1st (1896) No. 175; 2nd (1897) No. 176, reissued No. 233

Leighton, Son and Hodge – bookbinders p. 121

Leipzig reprint: see No. 128

Lestrade, Jean – translator No. 372

Letchworth, The Temple Press Printers Nos. 241, 248

Lewis edition (1839, a reissue of 3rd Major ed.) No. 48

Library of British and American Authors Nos. 198, 339

Library of Choice Reading series p. 75

Library of English Classics series No. 226, 270

Library of English Prose series No. 251

Limited Editions Club edition (1948) No. 348, reprinted as Heritage Press edition No. 349

Linnaean arrangement of the fish Nos. 164, 197

Linnean Society librarian, editor No. 162

Lippincott reprint [1844] No. 54

Little, Brown 1866 edition reprinted Nos. 274, 284

Little Library series No. 199

Livres de Nature, Les series No. 322

Lockwood reprint [1844] No. 52

Lombart, Peter (or Pierre) – engraving of in 1st ed., pp. 1, 2

Lovell's Century series No. 157

Lowell, James Russell – introduction by Nos. 348, 349

Lowell editions and reprints: 1st edition (1889) No. 142; 2nd reprint (1889) No. 143; 3rd reprint (1891) No. 152; 4th reprint (1891) No. 153; 5th reprint (1892) No. 154; 6th reprint (1898) No. 181; 7th reprint (1901) No. 197; 8th reprint [1906] No. 225; 9th reprint (1912) No. 245

Lowndes, H. L. – sale catalogue of, cited No. 89

Lystfiskeriforeningen København No. 325

Macaulay Library of Great Writers p. 151

Macmillan edition and reprints: 1st edition (1901) No. 198; 2nd reprint (1906) No. 226; 3rd reprint (1925) No. 270

Macy, George Companies, Inc. Nos. 348, 349

Madeley Manor, figure of cited p. 83; illustration No. 144

Major, John – introduction to 1st Major ed p. 40; introductory essay by No. 218; poem by p. 41

Major editions and reprints (named for John Major): 1st (1823) No. 23; 2nd (1824) No. 24; 3rd (1835) No. 42; 4th (1839) No. 48; 5th (1842) No. 50; 6th (titled 4th) (1844) No. 55; 7th (1866) No. 87; 8th (1867) No. 88; 9th (1870) No. 91; 10th (1881) No. 110; 11th [1881] No. 111; 12th (1883) No. 114; 13th [1884] No. 116; 14th (1885) No. 123; 15th (1888) No. 138; 16th (1889) No. 139; 17th (1889) No. 140; 18th (1889) No. 141; 19th [1892] No. 155; 20th [1892] No. 157; 21st [1893] No. 159; 22nd [1894] No. 164; 23rd [1895] No. 167; 24th (1896) No. 173; 25th (1846) No. 174; 26th [1897] No. 178; 27th [1898] No. 182; 28th [1898] No. 183; 29th [1898] No. 184; 30th (1899) No. 186; 31st [1899] No. 188; 32nd [1900] No. 189; 33rd [1900] No. 190; 34th (1900) No. 192; 35th [1900] No. 193; 36th (1903) No. 209; 37th [1903] No. 210; 38th (1904) No. 214; 39th (1904) No. 215; 40th [1905] No. 218; 41st [1905] No. 219; 42nd [1908] No. 220; 43rd [1905] No. 221; 44th (1906) No. 224; 45th (1909) No. 239; 46th (1913) No. 249; 47th (1915) No. 254; 48th [1918] No. 258; 49th [1919] No. 259; 50th [1922] No. 264; 51st [1923] No. 265; 52nd [1924] No. 268; 53rd [1925] No. 269; 54th (1925) No. 274; 55th [1956] No. 277; 56th [1927] No. 280; 57th [1927] No. 284; 58th [1927] No. 285; 59th (1930) No. 294; 60th [1934] No. 304; 61st (1948) No. 347; 62nd [1953] No. 359

Major's Illustrated edition p. 70

Marchbanks Press – typesetters Nos. 309, 314

Margrave, John – advertiser in 5th ed. p. 19

Marston, Robert B. – "Bibliography of Walton's Compleat Angler" p. 113; introduction by No. 255; editions of the Angler to 1915, No. 255; List of Editions of the Compleat Angler (1915), cited p. 128; on dating of 1st ed. pp. 4-5; preface to 1st Thorpe No. 24; preface to 1st Thorpe No. 24

Marston editions and reprints: 1st edition (1888) No. 136; 2nd reprint (1888) No. 137; 3rd edition (1915) No. 255; 4th reprint (1921) No. 263

Mason abridged edition [1930] No. 295

Massas, Charles de – La Pecheur à la Mouche Artificielle . . . (ed. 2, 1859) p. 113

Maunder (Samuel) edition No. 26

McClurg edition and reprint: 1st edition (1893) No. 161; 2nd reprint (1900) No. 194

McClurg's Laurel-Crowned Tales series No. 194

Perry, Bliss – introduction by No. 288
Peter Pauper Press edition [1947] No. 345
Phillips reprint [1914] No. 253 (of 1st Hankey ed. No. 252)
Pickering editions and reprints: 1st edition (1825) No. 29; 2nd edition (1826) No. 30; 3rd reprint (1826) No. 31; 4th reprint (1827) No. 33; 5th edition (1837) No. 47; 6th edition (1858) No. 73
Pickering's Diamond Classics series Nos. 28, 29
Piper reprint [1844] No. 53
Pisces Waltoniana at Oxford p. 40
Places of imprint (nos. in [ ]s lack city name on t-p) – Ann Arbor, Mich.: No. 384; Berlin, Germany: No. 364; Bombay: Nos. 251, 255; Boston: Nos. 84, 85, 87, 88, 90, 142, 143, 153, 154, 181, 186, 188, 197, 225, 245, 253, 288; Brooklyn, N.Y.: No. 232; Cambridge, Mass.: No. 240; Cedar Rapids, Iowa: Nos. [246], [247]; Chicago, Ill.: Nos. 161, 194, 202, [323]; Chiswick, Engl.: Nos. 25, 32, 223; Cincinnati, Ohio: No. 262; Copenhagen: Nos. [325], [326], [327], [331], [332], [333], [334], [341], [360], [377]; Dublin, Eire: Nos. 35, 40, 41, 58, 227; Edinburgh: Nos. 35, 40, 46, 47, 252, 253, 255, 272, 275, 295, 381; Exeter, Engl.: No. 146; Garden City, N. Y.: No. 369; Girard, Kansas: Nos. 282, 283; Glasgow: Nos. 32, 41, 227, 236, 251, 255, 284, 298, 305; Halifax, N.S.: No. 72; Hamburg: Nos. 75, 364; Hammondsworth, Engl.: Nos. 317, 318; Hanau, Germany: Nos. [365], 366; Harrisburg, Pa.: No. 361; Helsingfors, Finland: No. 344; Johannesburg: No. 381; Leipzig: No. 128; Liverpool, Engl.: Nos. 56, 62; London: Nos. 1-24, 26(?), 27-31, 33-53, 55, 60, 61, 63, 66, 68-70, 73, 74, 77-83, 89, 90, 92-104, 106, 109, 111-115, 117, 118, 122-126, 130, 132, 133, 136, 138-141, 143, 144, 146-149, 153, 156, 160, 162, 163, 165, 168-170, 172-177, 179, 185, 187, 195, 196, 198-201, 203-207, 209, 211-214, 216, 219, 221, 226-231, [233], 234, 236, 238, 241, 242, 243, 248, 250-253, 255, 257, 260, 261, 263, 266, 270-272, 274, 275, 278, 284, 286, 287, 289, 290-300, 302, 305, 307, 311, 315, 328, 335, 339, 346, 347, 350, 351, 353, 355, 357-359, 367, 368, 370, 371, 374-376, 380, 381, 385; Manchester, Engl.: Nos. 56, 57, 59, 63-65, 71, 96, 110; Melbourne: Nos. 125, 126, 148, 149, 151, 179, 216, 217, 230, 231, 237, 255, 381; Mt. Vernon, N.Y.: No. 345; New York: Nos. 60, 61, 67, 74, 76, 78-80, 86, 96, 100, 105, 107, 109, 116, 119-121, 125-127, 129, 131, 133, 134, 135, 137, 141, 145, 148, 150, 151, 155-160, 164, 171, 176-180, 182-184, 186, 188-191, 193, 198, 202, 208, 210-213, 215-218, 220, 221, 224, 226, 228-231, 234, 237, 238, 239, 241-243, 248-250, 254, 257-260, 264, 265, 267-269, 271, 273, 275-277, 285, 286, 293, 295-297, 302-304, 312-316, 319-321, 324, 328-330, 336, 346, 348, 349, 352, 355, 356, 358, 367, 370, 373, 380, 381, 383, 385; Oxford, Engl.: Nos. 235, 256; Paris: Nos. 125, 126, 148, 149, 151, 179, 216, 217, 230, 231, 275, 322, 355, [372]; Philadelphia, Pa.: Nos. 47, 54, 110, 192, [205], 301; Stockholm: Nos. 338, 342, 343, 378, 382; Tokyo: Nos. 279, 308; Toronto: Nos. 237, 242, 244, 255, 260, 271, 275, 286, 302, 367, 385; Washington, D. C.: No. 202; Weimar, Germany: No. 365; Westport, Conn.: No. 354
Pocket Edition of Standard Classics series No. 279
Pocket Library series No. 213
Pollard, Alfred W. – bibliographical note by No. 198
Porter Library, Kansas State College of Pittsburg, Kans. p. 282
Powel, Rev. Edward – verses by in 1st ed. p. 5
Priddle, R. A. V. p. 108; cited p. 146; quoted No. 117
Printers – Aberdeen University Press Ltd. Nos. 209, 215, 228; Aldine Press Nos. 370, 380; Aldus Printers No. 348; Alexander, A. & Son No. 292; Arno Press, Inc. No. 384; Ballantyne & Co. No. 94; Ballantyne, Hanson & Co. Nos. 96, 109, 114, 123, 130, 139, 140, 141, 160, 162, 173, 206, 219, 221; Baylis, Ebenezer & Son, Ltd. No. 357; Billing, —— (Guilford) No. 89; Black, A. & C., Ltd. No. 287; Bonniers Boktryckeri No. 339; Bradbury, Agnew & Co. No. 103; Bradbury & Evans Nos. 47, 70, 78; Bradbury Evans & Co. No. 92; Butler & Tanner, Selwood Printing Works, Nos. 165, 166, 185; Butler & Tanner Ltd. Nos. 284, 285; Camden Press No. 101; Caradoc Press No. 223; Cassell & Co. Nos. 125, 126, 127, 128, 148, 179, 180, 216, 217, 230, 231, 232, 237, 238; Causton, Henry Kent No. 66; Causton, Richard & Henry No. 11; Caxton Press No. 313; Chiswick Press Nos. 81, 82, 83, 84, 85, 95, 104, 208, 213; Clark, R. & R. No. 292; Clay, Richard & Sons, Ltd. Nos. 255, 256; Clowes, William & Son Nos. 90, 97, 112, 115, 136, 144, 212, 266, 267, 278, 297, 317, 318; Collins' Clear-Type Press No. 236; Constable, T. & A. Nos. 170, 200, 201, 202, 242, 243, 244, 250, 262, 272, 273, 311, 335, 374; Craighead, Robert Nos. 60, 67; Curwen Press, Ltd. No. 292; C. W. S. Printing Works No. 350; Dalziel Brothers Nos. 101,

This book is printed in an edition of 500 copies on Curtis rag paper of which 300 have been bound. Twenty-five additional copies are printed on mould made Rives paper. Types used are Hunt Roman and Monotype Spectrum. Composition and letterpress printing is by Davis & Warde, Inc., Pittsburgh, under the supervision of Thomas C. Pears III. Four-color process frontispiece and jacket, and text illustrations, are printed by Meriden Gravure Company, Meriden, Connecticut, under the direction of John Peckham. Binding is by Russell-Rutter Company, Inc., New York.

Bernard Shea Horne, author of this bibliography, was born 6 September 1905, in Keswick, Virginia, and died 4 January 1970, in Hyannis Port, Massachusetts.

No. **446**

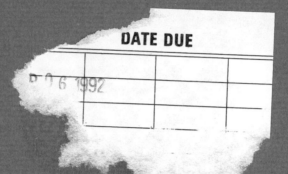